KINGS AND LORDS IN CONQUEST ENGLAND

ROBIN FLEMING

Assistant Professor of History, Boston College

CAMBRIDGE
UNIVERSITY PRESS

PUBLISHED BY THE PRESS SYNDICATE OF THE UNIVERSITY OF CAMBRIDGE
The Pitt Building, Trumpington Street, Cambridge, United Kingdom

CAMBRIDGE UNIVERSITY PRESS
The Edinburgh Building, Cambridge CB2 2RU, UK
40 West 20th Street, New York NY 10011–4211, USA
477 Williamstown Road, Port Melbourne, VIC 3207, Australia
Ruiz de Alarcón 13, 28014 Madrid, Spain
Dock House, The Waterfront, Cape Town 8001, South Africa

http://www.cambridge.org

First published 1991
Reprinted 1995
First paperback edition 2004

A catalogue record for this book is available from the British Library

Library of Congress Cataloguing in Publication data
Fleming, Robin.
Kings and Lords in Conquest England / Robin Fleming.
p.   cm. – (Cambridge studies in medieval life and thought;
fourth series, 15)
Includes bibliographical references.
ISBN 0 521 39309 4
1. Great Britain – History – William I, 1066–1087.   2. Great
Britain – History – Canute. 1017–1035.   3. Great Britain – Kings and
rulers.   4. Land tenure – England – History.   5. England – Nobility –
History.   I. Title.   II. Series: Cambridge studies in medieval
life and thought: 4th series, 15.
DA197.F57   1991
942.02′1–dc20   90-1565   CIP

ISBN 0 521 39309 4 hardback
ISBN 0 521 52694 9 paperback

Cambridge studies in medieval life and thought

KINGS AND LORDS IN CONQUEST ENGLAND

Cambridge studies in medieval life and thought
Fourth series

General Editor:

D. E. LUSCOMBE

Professor of Medieval History, University of Sheffield

Advisory Editors:

R. B. DOBSON

Professor of Medieval History, University of Cambridge, and Fellow of Christ's College

ROSAMOND MCKITTERICK

Reader in Early Medieval European History, University of Cambridge,
and Fellow of Newnham College

The series Cambridge Studies in Medieval Life and Thought was inaugurated by G. G. Coulton in 1920. Professor D. E. Luscombe now acts as General Editor of the Fourth Series, with Professor R. B. Dobson and Dr Rosamond McKitterick as Advisory Editors. The series brings together outstanding work by medieval scholars over a wide range of human endeavour extending from political economy to the history of ideas.

Titles in the series

★ Also published as a paperback

For my parents

I will send the sword against you, and your enemies will slay you and then will brutally waste your land. And your cities will be broken and despoiled. Then will I send cowardice into your hearts so that no one among you can withstand your enemies.

Ælfric
De Oratione Moysi

CONTENTS

ix

FIGURES

List of figures

TABLES

PREFACE

The great lay lords of the late tenth and eleventh centuries were at once co-operative and predatory.[1] The Anglo-Scandinavian and Norman aristocrats who fought for the king, represented him in the hundred and shire courts, and witnessed his solemn diplomas were also fully capable of practising an extravagant and self-interested hooliganism to improve their own standing in the world. Many, like the damned crowd, the *familia Herlechini*, encountered by Orderic Vitalis's priest of Bonneval, not only fought for the king, but at one time or another carried 'across their necks and shoulders animals and clothes, and every kind of furnishing and household goods that raiders usually seize as plunder'.[2] They did serve the king, but when given the opportunity they grasped what they could for themselves. When the desires of these enterprising bully boys, their kinsmen, and their hangers-on were the same as those of the king (sometimes a kinsman and a bully himself), the results, institutionally and politically, could be impressive. Such co-operation produced many of the glories of Edgar the Peaceable's reign and William the Conqueror's rule. But the mix of king and powerful aristocrats with a localized administration was a volatile one. When the interests of the *Rex Anglorum* and his greatest aristocrats were no longer in harmony, or if the wealth of important men began to eclipse that of the king, there could be a rapid dissolution of royal power.

Many of the wonders of tenth- and eleventh-century England have been credited to its kings. Yet the kingdom's growing prosperity and its institutional precocity were not simply the handiwork of unwavering royal will, but the product of this complex relationship between English kings and the men who

[1] D. C. Douglas, *William the Conqueror* (Berkeley, 1966); David Bates, *Normandy before 1066* (London, 1982); Eleanor Searle, *Predatory Kinship and the Creation of Norman Power 840–1066* (Berkeley, 1988).   [2] OV, iv, pp. 236–50.

opposed or supported them. The growth of English institutions, therefore, was neither steady nor assured, and their evolution cannot be gauged simply by examining the reigns of individual kings or by charting changes in diplomatic style. Such exercises allow us to plot the fluctuating power and prestige of the monarchy, distinguish able kings from less effective ones, and view the growth of royal prerogatives. But the king remains an isolated figure, judged only in the company of other kings and measured against the waxing or waning of royal institutions. It is difficult to assess him in relation to his aristocratic contemporaries, whom the chroniclers mention only infrequently. A comparison of landed wealth and aristocratic alliances, however, enables us to examine the geographical and economic balance between monarchy and aristocracy throughout the period and see how this relationship helped to shape the kingdom of England.

Certainly, for contemporaries, institutions were less important than the private arrangements that so often bolstered them. It was well understood that the ties which bound great men to one another, to the king and to their dependants, also influenced political behaviour. This is reflected very clearly in the writings of Bishop Wulfstan. As Archbishop of York and a chief counsellor both to Æthelred and Cnut, his mark on English institutions is evident, especially in the realm of law.[3] In Wulfstan's vision of a properly ordered polity, the role which kinsmen and lords played in governing their associates and maintaining the peace lay at the heart of royal authority. It was the private arrangement, the personal relationship that insured the settlement of disputes and guaranteed the maintenance of peace. The personal and the political, therefore, were inseparable.[4] Wulfstan's so-called 'Institutes of Polity' survives as one of the few contemporary articulations of what suited a man to high office.[5] In his section concerning earls, he lists no particular qualifications of literacy, legal learning, or administrative expertise. Instead, Wulfstan concerns himself with two things: the character of great men and the company they keep. Wulfstan knew what modern historians so often forget, that in traditional societies like his own, personal

---

[3] Dorothy Whitelock, 'Wulfstan and the laws of Cnut', *EHR*, 59 (1954), pp. 72–85.
[4] II Cnut 20.1, 23.1, 25.1, 30.1, 31.7, 57, 70.1.
[5] *Die 'Institutes of Polity, Civil and Ecclesiastical'*, *ein Werk Erzbischof Wulfstans von York*, ed. Karl Jost (Bern, 1959).

associations and private values often had a greater effect on the practical workings of a kingdom than did the machinery of government. In his *Sermo Lupi ad Anglos*, he laments that God's wrath, in the form of political disintegration, was loosed upon the kingdom, not because of inadequate administration or weakening institutions, but because of the breakdown of traditional associations and mores.[6]

Another of the underlying assumptions of Old English politics was the fundamental importance of the rights exercised by powerful lords, including the king, over land. Gifts of land cemented many relationships and even helped to secure salvation. It served as the ultimate reward for good service and the great guarantee for faithful action. As the greatest source of wealth, land was almost exclusively the avenue to secular power. The importance of many estates, moreover, was determined not only by the income they produced, but by their location. The proximity of estates to major land and water routes and their relationships to areas vulnerable to Viking armies or Welsh marauders had a profound effect on the role great landholders played in the defence or disruption of the kingdom. Wulfstan's contemporary Ælfric the Homilist recognized the centrality of land to politics. When the 'master' in his dialogue for schoolboys asks the 'wiseman' which of all secular occupations is most important, he answers without hesitation, the ploughman 'because he feeds us all... because the ploughman gives us bread and drink';[7] and in his use of the *topos* of the three-tiered social hierarchy composed of those who fight, those who pray, and those who cultivate the land, Ælfric emphasized the dependence of the two former classes on the latter.[8] The social ideal he helped to fashion was more than pious rhetoric. It mirrored his own world with its limited resources and powerful landlords. So immediate was the vocabulary of landholding that it could be evoked to explain more foreign things. When King Alfred wished to illustrate how he had come to choose certain of St Augustine's passages over others, he explained his choices through

---

[6] Wulfstan, *Sermo Lupi ad Anglos*, ed. Dorothy Whitelock (London, 1963).

[7] *Ælfric's Colloquy*, ed. G. N. Garmonsway (London, 1947).

[8] *The Old English Version of the Heptateuch, Ælfric's Treatise on the Old and New Testament and his Preface to Genesis*, ed. S. J. Crawford, *Early English Text Society*, 160 (1922), p. 71.

the metaphors of the building of halls, the exploitation of land, and the granting of estates in perpetuity.[9]

Landholding and alliance are, therefore, the two chief concerns of this book. The period it covers – c. 950 to 1086 – is one in which lay lords and their families rose fast and fell hard. It is also an epoch of dizzying tenurial change. These things make the period interesting. What makes it possible to study is the survival of sufficient evidence to identify many of the kingdom's chief men and their kinsmen and allies. One can also, thanks primarily to Domesday Book, reconstruct an important portion of these men's estates and sometimes determine how they got possession of them. A study of the ebb and flow of the period's landed wealth and alliances enables us to view the geographic and economic balance between kings and aristocrats throughout the period, and see how this relationship helped to shape the kingdom of England, its monarchy, and its institutions. Such a study casts light on a number of central historical issues – the impact of Cnut's conquest on England, the quality of Edward the Confessor's kingship, the means by which the Norman settlement was carried out and the effect of William's conquest on England.

This book was written over the course of a number of years, and during that time I have incurred a mountain of debts. Many of the ideas and much of the research for the first three chapters of this book were developed while I was a graduate student at the University of California at Santa Barbara. To my adviser C. Warren Hollister and to the UCSB Department of History, which provided me with fellowships and research money, I owe much. The writing of the whole book and the research for the second half was done in the three years that I was a Junior Fellow at the Harvard Society of Fellows. The Society's support and my colleagues' keen insights, interest, and good company have made the completion of this book possible. The National Endowment for the Humanities, which funded the project to computerize Domesday Book, provided me with the time and resources to examine the document in depth. Milton Funds, generously granted by the Harvard Medical School, have further supported my research. A number of friends have also contributed to this work. Warren Hollister, of course, has read the whole. Simon

[9] *King Alfred's Old English Version of Saint Augustine's Soliloquies*, ed. H. L. Hargrove, *Yale Studies in English*, 13 (New York, 1902).

Keynes and Katie Mack Roberts have read various versions of this manuscript, offering good advice, interesting insights, and careful criticism. Seth Schwartz and Martin Claussen have also read and helped with portions of this book. Finally, the encouragement and the close reading of J. C. Holt, who has generously volunteered to act as general editor for this book in the first busy year of his 'retirement', has improved it immeasurably. I am grateful to them all. Sung Rhee, my Research Assistant while at Harvard, fetched hundreds of books from the Widener Library, xeroxed articles, and proofed the bibliography. Trudi Tate, of Cambridge University Press, has helped in the preparation of this manuscript, and Bridgette Sheridan has laboured over the proofs and index. Jonathan Smolen, who has written dozens of computer programs for me, washed the dishes, and twice moved to accommodate my career, deserves more thanks than I can give. This book would be dedicated to him, had I not a debt of longer standing.

ABBREVIATIONS

Anglo-Norman Studies	*Proceedings of the Battle Conference on Anglo-Norman Studies*, ed. R. Allen Brown, 1–4 (1979–82), continued from 1983 as *Anglo-Norman Studies*
ASC	Anglo-Saxon Chronicle [References are to J. Earle and C. Plummer, *Two of the Saxon Chronicles Parallel* (2 vols., 1892, 1899), or to the translation in D. Whitelock, D. C. Douglas, and S. I. Tucker (eds.) *The Anglo-Saxon Chronicle: A Revised Translation* (1961)]
ASE	*Anglo-Saxon England*
BL	British Library
Cal. Doc. Fra.	*Calendar of Documents Preserved in France*, ed. J. H. Round (HMSO, 1899)
Cart. Rams.	*Cartularium Monasterii de Rameseia*, ed. W. H. Hart and P. A. Lyons, RS, 3 vols. (London, 1884–93)
Chron. Ab.	*Chronicon Monasterii de Abingdon*, ed. Joseph Stevenson, RS, 2 vols., (London, 1858)
Chron. Ev.	*Chronicon Abbatiae de Evesham*, ed. W. D. Macray, RS (London, 1863)
Chron. Rams.	*Chronicon Abbatiae Ramesiensis*, ed. W. D. Macray, RS (London, 1886)
DB	Domesday Book [References are to *Domesday Book seu liber Censualis Wilhelmi Primi Regis Angliae*, ed. A. Farley, 2 vols. (1783); vols. iii, iv, ed. H. Ellis (1816), or to *Domesday Book, Facsimile Edition* (London, 1986–)]

De Ant. Glast.	John Scott, *The Early History of Glastonbury. An Edition, Translation and Study of William of Malmesbury's De Antiquitate Glastonie Ecclesie* (Woodbridge, Suffolk, 1981)
DOD	*De Obsessione Dunelmi*, in *Symeonis Monachi Opera Omnia*, ed. Thomas Arnold, RS (London, 1882), i, pp. 215–20
Dom. Mon.	*The Domesday Monachorum of Christ Church, Canterbury*, ed. D. C. Douglas (Royal Historical Society, 1944)
ECNM	Cyril Hart, *Early Charters of Northern England and the North Midlands* (Leicester, 1975)
EHD	*English Historical Documents*, ed. D. C. Douglas [vol. i, c. 500–1042, ed. D. Whitelock, 2nd edn, 1979; vol. ii, 2nd edn, D. C. Douglas and G. W. Greenaway (1981)]
EHR	*English Historical Review*
EYC	*Early Yorkshire Charters*, 13 vols., i–iii, ed. William Farrer, iv–xii, ed. C. T. Clay (Yorkshire Archaeological Society, Record Ser., Extra Ser., 1914–65)
FE	J. H. Round, *Feudal England* (London, 1895)
Fl. Wig.	Florence of Worcester (a.k.a. John of Worcester), *Chronicon ex Chronicis*, ed. B. Thorpe, 2 vols. (English Historical Society, 1848–49)
Freeman, *NC*	E. A. Freeman, *The History of the Norman Conquest of England* (i, ii, 2nd edn. 1870; iii–v, 1st edn 1869–75)
GP	*Willelmi Malmesbiriensis Monachi de Gestis Pontificum Anglorum Libri Quinque*, ed. N. E. S. A. Hamilton, RS (London, 1870)
GR	William of Malmesbury, *De Gestis Regum Anglorum Libri Quinque*, ed.

	W. Stubbs, RS, 2 vols. (London, 1887–89)
Harmer, *Writs*	F. E. Harmer, *Anglo-Saxon Writs* (Manchester, 1952)
Hemming	*Hemming: Chartularium Ecclesiae Wigorniensis,* ed. T. Hearne (Oxford, 1727)
ICC	*Inquisitio Comitatus Cantabrigiensis, Subjicitur Inquisitio Eliensis,* ed. N. E. S. A. Hamilton (1876)
IE	*Inquisitio Comitatus Cantabrigiensis, Subjicitur Inquisitio Eliensis,* ed. N. E. S. A. Hamilton (1876)
LE	*Liber Eliensis,* ed. E. O. Blake, Royal Historical Society, Camden Third Series, 92 (London, 1962)
Mon. Ang.	W. Dugdale, *Monasticon Anglicanum,* revised edn, J. Caley, H. Ellis and B. Bandinel, 6 vols. in 8 parts (London, 1817–30)
OV	Ordericus Vitalis, *The Ecclesiastical History,* ed. M. M. Chibnall, 6 vols. (Oxford, 1969–80)
Regesta	*Regesta Regum Anglo-Normannorum,* 4 vols., ed. H. W. C. Davis and others (Oxford, 1913–69)
Robertson, *Charters*	*Anglo-Saxon Charters,* ed. and trans. A. J. Robertson (Cambridge, 1939)
RS	Rolls Series
S	*Anglo-Saxon Charters: an Annotated List and Bibliography,* ed. Peter Sawyer (Royal Historical Society, 1968)
Sim. Dur., *Opera Omnia*	Simeon of Durham, *Symeonis Monachi Opera Omnia* ed. T. Arnold, RS, 2 vols. (London, 1882–85)
TRE	*Tempore regis Eadwardi*
TRHS	*Transactions of the Royal Historical Society*
TRW	*Tempore regis Willelmi*
VCH	*Victoria County History,* 1900–

VER	*Vita Ædwardi Regis*, ed. and trans. Frank Barlow, (London, 1962)
Wills	D. Whitelock, *Anglo-Saxon Wills* (Cambridge, 1930)
YAJ	*Yorkshire Archaeological Journal*
Winchester Studies, I	Frank Barlow, Martin Biddle, Olof van Feilitzen and D. J. Keene, *Winchester in the Early Middle Ages. An Edition and Discussion of the Winton Domesday*, *Winchester Studies*, I (Oxford, 1976)

1 CNUT'S CONQUEST

.

Chapter 1

LANDHOLDING AND ALLIANCE
IN LATE SAXON ENGLAND

The *Anglo-Saxon Chronicle* records, in exhausting and imaginative detail, the descent of King Alfred's father through Woden, Noah, Enoch and Adam.[1] The genealogy, stretching back some forty generations, preserves the paternal descent of West Saxon kings from the age of Germanic settlement in England to 855. Like other royal genealogies of the period, however, the list is wanting in a number of ways. Old English kings' descent through Germanic gods, equine brothers and Hebrew patriarchs is hardly credible. The names of these rulers' mortal ancestors in the epoch before the Anglo-Saxon invasions are based on fancy rather than fact, and the inclusion of some of their descendants in the historic period were determined by political ideology and convention rather than blood.[2] And because royal genealogies interest themselves only in that neat succession of one king to the next, they do not preserve the names of maternal kindred nor do they record non-ruling siblings and offspring. As haphazard and as difficult as the material in this and other royal genealogies may be, it provides more information about the West Saxon kings' factual and fictive kin that exists *in toto* for any of the great Anglo-Saxon aristocrats from Hengest and Horsa to Harold Godwineson. Evidence for the complex collateral kindreds of the Saxon Age is extremely fragmentary and must be pieced together from the occasional family relationship noted in the attestation lists of royal charters or mentioned in the bequests and obits of pre-Conquest

[1] *ASC*, s.a. 855.
[2] Kenneth Sisam, 'Anglo-Saxon royal genealogies', *Proceedings of the British Academy*, 39 (1953), pp. 287–346; David N. Dumville, 'Kingship, genealogies, and regnal lists', in *Early Medieval Kingship*, ed. P. H. Sawyer and I. N. Wood (Leeds, 1979), pp. 72–104; 'The Anglian collection of royal genealogies and regnal lists', *ASE*, 5 (1976), pp. 23–50. These three articles aptly show what Pierre Bourdieu has seen in other cultures, that genealogy can be official rather than historical, and that its twin functions are to order the social world and to legitimize that order. (Pierre Bourdieu, *Outline of a Theory of Practice*, trans. Richard Nice (Cambridge, 1977), p. 34.)

England. The chronicle-cartularies of a number of England's monastic houses also from time to time preserve information on the families of their house's lay benefactors and despoilers: hence the *Ramsey Chronicle* preserves information on the family of Æthelwine 'Friend of God'; the *Liber Eliensis* on Bryhtnoth, his friends and relations; and Hemming's cartulary on Earl Leofric's descendants. An anonymous monk of Durham, describing the patrimony of Saint Cuthbert, incidentally preserved a rich if somewhat confusing catalogue of Earl Siward's in-laws, including three daughters of Ealdorman Uhtræd who shared the name Ælflæd, a complication which reflects accurately the confounding nature of the period's genealogical material.[3] Finally, the *Vita Eadwardi Regis*, in presentation a royal biography but in fact a piece of special pleading for Queen Edith and her relatives, tells something of Earl Godwine's family. Other than a few genealogical asides in the *Anglo-Saxon Chronicle*, 'Florence of Worcester', and William of Malmesbury, little else survives to connect one pre-Conquest aristocrat with another. Sparse though the evidence is, it is sufficient to flesh out important connections between many of the dominant lords of the tenth and eleventh centuries and between Old English kings and the aristocrats who were both their allies and their competitors.[4]

Despite the paucity of information on the specific links between the aristocrats whose names are commemorated in the *Chronicle* or preserved in the witnesses lists of surviving diplomas, there is an abundance of legal and literary testimony which sets forth the obligations and duties entailed by these relationships. The clans and vast cousinages that formed the families of Europe's Germanic settlers in Victorian historiography have long been in retreat, and it is now clear that although Englishmen cultivated and kept track of a wide circle of kinsmen, their most intimate kin had a special place in customs revolving around property, salvation, and honour.[5] The *healsfang*, or first instalment of the wergeld, for example, was paid exclusively to the children,

---

[3] *DOD*, pp. 215–20.   [4] See below, chapters 2 and 3.

[5] For a history of the theories of Germanic kinship structure see Alexander C. Murray, *Germanic Kinship Structure: Studies in Law and Society in Antiquity and the Early Middle Ages* (Toronto, 1983), pp. 11–32. For the characterization of Anglo-Saxon kinship as both cognatic and especially concerned with the closest of relations, see Lorraine Lancaster, 'Kinship in Anglo-Saxon society', *British Journal of Sociology*, 9 (1957), pp. 230–50, 359–77 and H. R. Loyn, 'Kinship in Anglo-Saxon England', *ASE*, 3 (1974), pp. 197–209.

brothers and paternal uncles of the victim,[6] and the property of a man who died intestate was divided only among his wife, children and near-kinsmen (*neahmæg*).[7] Similarly, the morning gift of a woman who remarried within the first year of widowhood reverted to her former husband's closest relatives (*nidfreond, neahfreond*).[8] Pious donations made to monasteries for the sake of relatives' souls appear to have been offered primarily for this same small circle of kin. Parents and grandparents, spouses and children benefited from the gifts their relatives bequeathed to religious communities, but the spiritual welfare of nephews, cousins and more distant kinsmen was not generally provided for, nor did the individuals whose wills survive leave gifts especially marked for the salvation of members of the larger and less specific *parentela*.[9] A man's honour could be damaged by the infidelity of his closest kinswomen, and he was allowed to wreak vengeance, without fear of the feud, on any man caught behind closed doors or 'under the same blanket' as his mother, wife, sister or daughter. By the same token, only the behaviour of his close kinswomen could damage his reputation.[10] Similarly, bishops and priests were allowed to receive no women guests except for their mothers, sisters, and maternal or paternal aunts.[11] The threat to pride and good name and the safety of chastity resided not in a great crowd of female relatives, but only in the closest of kinswomen.

Below this most intimate level of kindred there existed a vast

---

[6] Wer. In the *Leges Henrici Primi* it is the fathers, sons, and brothers who are paid the *healsfang*. (*Leges Henrici Primi*, ed. L. J. Downer (Oxford, 1972), c. 76.) For a discussion of the importance of these two conflicting texts, see T. M. Charles-Edwards, 'Kinship, status, and the origin of the hide', *Past and Present*, 56 (1972), pp. 22–3.

[7] II Cnut 70.1. [8] II Cnut 73a.

[9] For bequests made to the church for the souls of parents, grand-parents, and ancestors see S 1526, 1483, 1485, 1511, 1494, 1486, 1501, 1536, 1503, 1538, 1489, 1521, 1530, 1519, 1533, 1514, Thorpe, *Diplomatarium Anglicum Ævi Saxonici* (London, 1865), pp. 585–9; for spouses see S 1188, 1483, 1493, 1496, 1485, 1498, 1487, 1486, 1501, 1498, 1537, 1530, 1531, 1535, 1519, 1520, 1525, 1510, 1513, 1533, 1514, Thorpe, *Diplomatarium* pp. 585–9; for children see S 1188, 1483, 1510, 1528, 1535, Thorpe, *Diplomatarium* pp. 585–9; for brothers and sisters see S 1485, 1486, 1536, 1516; for nephews see S 1516. In western France in the eleventh and twelfth centuries donations were most commonly made for this same group of kinsmen, but they were also made for sons-, fathers-, and sisters-in-law, former husbands, and the like. (Stephen D. White, *Custom, Kinship, and Gifts to the Saints: The Laudatio Parentum in Western France 1050–1150* (Chapel Hill, 1988), pp. 109–14). [10] Alfred 42§7.

[11] Ælfric, 'Pastoral Letter for Wulfsige III', *Councils and Synods with other Documents Relating to the English Church*, ed. D. Whitelock, M. Brett and C. N. L. Brooke (Oxford, 1981), i, p. 198; Ælfric, 'First Old English Letter for Wulfstan', *ibid*, p. 278.

and etymologically undifferentiated group of relations.[12] *Nefa* was used to express nephew, grandson, stepson, or cousin of any degree; *nefene* meant equally niece or granddaughter.[13] *Mæg*, the most common term for kinsman, was used not only for distant collateral relations, but for sons and brothers as well.[14] This absence of a distinctive collateral terminology, which is exemplified by such roundabout phrases as *his modar his broðar dohtar* for maternal grandnephew, makes it unlikely that each degree of kinship had its own specific duties.[15] Distant cousins, like more immediate kinsmen, were nonetheless necessary to guarantee an individual's personal safety, witness his legal transactions, and provide support in difficult times. These assorted and generally undifferentiated kinsmen can be seen acting as compurgators, as collectors or payers of wergeld, and as the protectors of their kinsmen both in and out of court.[16] They supplied relatives with food when they were in prison and lent them aid in their bid for profferment. They defended them when attacked, took care of them in ill health and madness, and avenged their deaths.[17] Kinsmen were also obliged to guarantee the good behaviour of less trustworthy members of their families, to vouch for relatives' good character, to act as sureties in marriage agreements,[18] and to

---

[12] Lancaster, 'Kinship', pp. 237–8.

[13] Joseph Bosworth, *An Anglo-Saxon Dictionary, Based on the Manuscript Collections of the late Joseph Bosworth*, ed. and enl. T. Northcote Toller (Oxford, 1954), *sub verbo*. For words used as 'cousin' see *genefa*. [14] Bosworth and Toller, *Dictionary, sub verbo*.

[15] Literally 'A's mother [is] B's brother's daughter'. (S 1200.)

[16] For kinsmen as protectors, see Alfred 1§2, 42§1, 42§6, II Æthelstan 11, II Æthelred 6; II Cnut 56. For kinsmen as the payers of wergeld, see Ine 74§1, II Æthelstan 1§4, 6§1; VI Æthelstan 1§4; VIII Æthelred 23; Cnut 5§2b. For kinsmen as collectors of wergeld, see Ine 23, II Edmund 4, 7, 7§1; I Cnut 2§5, II Cnut 39; *Mircna laga*, 4. For kinsmen as compurgators see Ine 21§1; *Be Wifmannes Beweddung* 1, 6; II Æthelstan 1§3, 6§1, VI Æthelstan 6§1, *Northumbrian Priests' Law*, 51; Robertson, *Charters*, n. 40. In court kinsmen tried to jolly up the judges. For an example of this, see *Firthegodi Monachi Breuiloquium Vitae Beati Wulfredi et Wilfstani Cantoris Narratio Metrica de Sancto Swithuno*, ed. Alistair Campbell (Zurich, 1950), p. 152.

[17] For the obligation of kinsmen towards their imprisoned relatives, see Alfred 1§2; II Æthelstan 6§1. Kinsmen are also to be notified when a relative is in the custody of his enemies (Alfred 5§3). For kinsmen as the bearers of the feud, see II Æthelred 6, II Edmund 1§3, II Cnut 56, VIII Æthelred 23, *DOD*, pp. 218–220, and (for Welshmen) DB, i, 179r. For kinsmen giving aid to mad relatives see *Vita Wulfstani*, pp. 27, 29. For the help they offered to ill relatives, see Ælfric 'Saint Swithun', *Lives of the Saints*, i, pp. 455, 461; *Vita Wulfstani*, p. 7. They also procured leases for relatives (S 1242).

[18] For kinsmen's responsibility for the good behaviour of family members see II Æthelstan 1§3, 1§4, 2, 2§1, 6§1, 8; VI Æthelstan 1; II Edmund 7§1. For kinsmen's obligations in marriage agreements see Ine 31, *Be Wifmannes Beweddung*, 1, 5, 6. For kinsmen's responsibilities as character witnesses see *Vita Wulfstani*, p. 7.

6

protect their property rights.[19] They were also entrusted with the welfare of the souls of those kinsmen who died before them, fasting after their deaths,[20] and they were buried alongside one another, so they could wait out the Second Coming together.[21] These ties of mutual dependence in this world and the next created strong personal bonds. Indeed, *freond* could mean 'friend' or 'relative' and *freondleas* 'friendless' or 'orphan',[22] and often a man's kith and kin – his *cognati atque amici* – were one and the same.

Within this amorphous kin-group, Anglo-Saxons emphasized agnatic connections. Paternal kinsmen were favoured when property was bequeathed in wills,[23] and there was a rich paternal vocabulary – *fædera* (father's brother), *faðu* (father's sister), *fæderencyn*, *fæderenmæg* (paternal kinsman) – used to denote the relationship between a man and his paternal kinsmen.[24] Cus-

---

[19] E.g., in *LE*, ii, c. 25 two nephews claimed some of Ely's land for their uncle, and took the monks to court over it. In a writ of Edward the Confessor to the Abbot of Bury St Edmunds, the king promised to protect the Abbot's land 'as if he were my brother'. (S 1083.)

[20] *Die Canones Theodori Cantuariensis und ihre Überlieferungsformen*, ed. Paul Willelm Finsterwalder (Weimar, 1929), pp. 318, 319. In the will of Æthelgifu various friends and kinsmen were left property, but in return were to give 'swine at Martinmass', food rents or a 'barrel full of ale' to various monasteries for her soul and the soul of her dead kindred. (*The Will of Æthelgifu*, trans., ed. and commentary Dorothy Whitelock, Neil Ker and Lord Rennell, The Roxburghe Club (Oxford, 1968).) King Æthelstan's drowned brother Edwin was buried at St Bertin by Count Adelolf of Flanders because 'he was his kinsman'. (*Folcwini diaconi gesta abbatum S Bertini Sithensium*, in *MGH Scriptores*, 13 (1881), ed. O. Holder-Egger, c. 107, trans. in *EHD*, i, 26.)

[21] For examples of kinsmen choosing burial places together see below, chapter 2. Monastic brothers, no less kin than worldly brothers, were buried together for just this reason. (Donald Bullough, 'Burial, community and belief in the early medieval West', in *Ideal and Reality in Frankish and Anglo-Saxon Society*, ed. Patrick Wormald with Donald Bullough and Roger Collins (Oxford, 1983), pp. 177–8.) If a man had been denied burial in consecrated ground because he had been executed for theft, his kinsmen could undergo the ordeal to clear his name and thereby reclaim the man's right to a proper burial (Æthelred 7§1).

[22] Bosworth and Toller, *Dictionary, sub verbo*. Other cultures have this same confusion of terms. See, for example, J. K. Campbell, *Honour, Family, and Patronage* (Oxford, 1964), p. 38.

[23] E.g., in the will of Ealdorman Alfred (871 × 889), the ealdorman declared that if his daughter had no heir 'then the next of kin descends from her direct paternal ancestry'. (S 1508.) See also S 1482, 1507. Royal genealogies trace descent through the male line, and patronymics were fairly common in pre-Conquest England, while metronymics were rare. Gosta Tengvik, *Old English Bynames* (Uppsala, 1938). For metronymics, see pp. 228–32. For patronymics, see pp. 146–227.

[24] Bosworth and Toller, *Dictionary, sub verbo*; Lancaster, 'Kinship', p. 237.

tomary law, too, stressed the rights and obligations of agnatic relations. An unborn child's wergeld was set by the status of its *fæderencnosl* or paternal kin.[25] Paternal relatives also play a greater role in the collection and payment of their kinsmen's wergeld[26] and were more often used as oath keepers.[27] Nonetheless, the kinship system of pre-Conquest England was not exclusively paternal. There was some vocabulary, like *modrige* (maternal aunt) and *eam* (mother's brother), that specified maternal links.[28] English aristocrats with more illustrious maternal kin, like their Ottonian contemporaries, at times traced their descent through their mothers,[29] and the right of women to inherit and bequeath property encouraged a lively interest in maternal relations. The tract *De Obsessione Dunelmi*, for example, traces a Northumbrian aristocrat's claim to former Durham lands through his mother, grandmother and great-great-grandmother.[30] The legal obligations of maternal kinsmen to aid family members in the payment of wergeld and the vouching of warranty indicate that close affiliations with maternal as well as paternal relations were of fundamental importance.[31] Husbands were known to take on the feuds of their fathers-in-law,[32] a widow's kinsmen fought from time to time for her rights in court,[33] and maternal kinsmen got . a portion of their relatives' wergeld.[34] In the tract *Be Wifmannes Beweddunge*, we are told that if a woman, after her marriage, moved to another district, her kinsmen nonetheless continued to act as her compurgators and to contribute to any fines she might incur.[35]

Despite the obligations imposed by kinship, men could legally dissociate themselves from incorrigible relations who were penally

---

[25] Alfred 9; *Leges Henrici Primi*, 68§3b; 75§7.   [26] Wer.   [27] II Æthelstan 11.

[28] Bosworth and Toller, *Dictionary*, *sub verbo*.

[29] E.g., Ælfwine son of Ælfric, who evokes the name of his maternal grandfather Ealhhelm at the Battle of Maldon (*Battle of Maldon*, line 218); Edward the Confessor's staller Robert, who is commonly identified by the metronymic 'fitz Wimarc' (Tengvik, *Old English Bynames*, *sub nomine*); and Wulfric Spot, who is described as the 'son of Wulfrun' (S 886). Karl Leyser 'Maternal kin in early medieval Germany', *Past and Present*, 49 (1970), pp. 126–7.   [30] *DOD*, pp. 215–20.

[31] A third of the wergeld went to maternal kinsmen, two-thirds to the paternal kinsmen (II Æthelstan 11; *Leges Henrici Primi*, 74§1a, 75§8, 75§9). Similarly, a third of those who stood surety were from the maternal kinsmen, and two-thirds from the paternal (Alfred 30; Wer 3; II Æthelstan 11; II Edmund 7§2; *Leges Henrici Primi*, 76§1a).

[32] Ealdorman Uhtræd promised, as part of the bargaining that went into the formation of one of his marriage agreements, to kill his future father-in-law's enemy (*DOD*, p. 218).   [33] Robertson, *Charters*, n. 59.   [34] Alfred 8§3, and above n. 26.

[35] *Be Wifmannes Beweddunge*, 7.

enslaved or who had involved themselves in unwelcome feuds.[36] At the same time custom and Christian practice allowed the inclusion of those who shared no ties of blood into the charmed circle of the family. Relationships formed by marriage and other Christian rituals created strong familial bonds between individuals with no common ancestor, and were formed by free will and probably a good deal of forethought. Affinal bonds came with their own set of legal responsibilities. The laws of Hlothhere and Eadric suggest that the relationship between a woman and her husband's family was continued after her spouse's death. While the widow was to maintain custody of her children, one of her deceased husband's kinsmen was to serve as their guardian until they reached the age of ten. This suggests that the widow and her husband's family remained in close contact, possibly for many years after the legislated twelve months of mourning.[37] Old English, moreover, had a rich affinal vocabulary. Special words existed for a husband's brother (*tacor*), sister's husband or son-in-law (*aðum*), daughter-in-law (*snoru*), mother-in-law (*sweger*), and father-in-law (*sweor*).[38] This is hardly surprising, since parents' in-laws would be their children's blood relations, forming the maternal and paternal kindreds of the next generation. As such, families linked by marriage would share many of the same legal responsibilities. The life-long bonds of affection and obligation formed by such ties are attested by the frequent bequests of thegns and ealdormen to sons-, sisters-, and brothers-in-law, and to step-children.[39] The Anglo-Saxon dooms indicate that bonds of ritual kinship could also be as strong as consanguineal ties.[40] Godfathers, like other kinsmen, were entitled to a portion of their charges' wergeld and so probably shared in the responsibility of their protection and good behaviour.[41] Certainly godfathers at times acted as compurgators for troubled godchildren and pleaded for them in court.[42] The status of the godfather, like that of the natural father, could affect the wergeld of the child: the godsons of kings

---

[36] Ine 74§2; II Edward 6; II Edmund 1§1; II Æthelstan 1§4.

[37] Hlothhere and Eadric 6. See also Ine 38; *Be Wifmannes Bewuddunge*, 6.

[38] Bosworth and Toller, *Dictionary, sub verbo. Sweor* could also be used as another word for cousin. [39] S 1483, 1484, 1494, 1519, 1521.

[40] For godparenthood in the early Middle Ages, see Joseph H. Lynch, *Godparents and Kinship in Early Medieval Europe* (Princeton, 1986).

[41] The godfather received compensation for slain godchildren (Ine 76). See also *ASC*, s.a. 755.

[42] E.g., in the late ninth century the thief Helmstan 'begged [his godfather] to be his advocate because [he] had stood sponsor to him before he committed that crime [*ic his*

and bishops had higher wergelds than did the godsons of other men.[43] Indeed, the relationship between sponsor and child was perceived, by the late Saxon period, as so intimate that marriage between them was forbidden on the grounds of incest.[44] It is not surprising, then, that kings from the Age of Bede through the Viking invasions sat sponsor to defeated warlords and potential allies.[45] Co-sponsors and godchildren were remembered in the wills of their ritual kinsmen,[46] and Old English had a word, *gefæðeran*, to describe the relationship between co-sponsoring god-parents.[47] Another set of pseudo-kin were guild-brethren. The language the guilds adopted when drawing up their statutes was that of kinship.[48] Like born-family, guild members acted as compurgators, collectors and payers of compensation, and as the avengers of slain brethren. They helped their fellows in illness and with burial, and they remembered them in their prayers.[49] Indeed, a bidding prayer, dating from the first half of the eleventh century, underscores the strength of such ritual ties. In it special prayers were offered for sponsors, godfathers, and guild-brothers and sisters.[50]

Thus collateral and lineal ties, along with relationships formed by marriage and ritual, were powerful forces in Anglo-Saxon

hæfde ær onfongen æt biscopes honda]. Then I pleaded and interceded for him with King Alfred' (S 1445).   [43] Ine 76, 76§1, 76§3.

[44] VI Æthelred 12§1; I Cnut 7§1; Northumbrian Priests' Law 61.1. In earlier days, however, such marriages did not trouble English churchmen. See Boniface, *Die Briefe des Heiligen Bonifatius und Lullus*, ed. M. Tangl, MGH, *Epistolae Selectae*, vol. 1 (Berlin, 1916), pp. 57–8.

[45] Olaf Tryggvason became godson of King Æthelred. In 920 King Edward the Elder was made the Norseman Ragnald's 'father and lord.' (*ASC*, s.a. 878, 995 (C, D, E).) Earlier alliances were similarly formed. Oswald was the godfather of Cynegisl and then married his daughter (Bede, *Hist. Ecc.*, iii, c. 7). When King Æthelstan became the godfather of the Breton Alan Crooked Beard, having 'lifted him from the holy font, this King had great trust in him because of... the alliance of his baptism' (*EHD*, i, n. 25).   [46] S 1485, 1536; *The Will of Æthelgifu*, p. 14.   [47] *Wills*, p. 123.

[48] The Exeter statutes, for example, legislate for masses for a dead *frynd* and psalms for a *brothur* (*Councils and Synods*, p. 59).

[49] The texts of the surviving guild regulations are printed in Benjamin Thorpe, *Diplomatarium Anglicum Ævi Saxonici* (London, 1865), pp. 605–17. They are found in translation in *EHD*, i, n. 136–9. For guild brethren as the payers of wergeld and avengers in feud see the Cambridgeshire regulations; for guild brethren's duties to pray for living and dead brethren see the regulations for Exeter, Bedwyn, and Abbotsbury. For their obligation to give aid when disaster hits, see the regulations for Exeter and Bedwyn.

[50] W. H. Stevenson 'Yorkshire surveys and other eleventh-century documents in the York Gospels', *EHR*, 27 (1912), pp. 1–25; Simon Keynes, 'The additions in Old English', in *The York Gospels*, ed. Nicholas Barker, The Roxburghe Club (London, 1986), p. 97.

society. They worked alongside lordship to help guarantee the safety of individuals and maintain the peace. These relationships, moreover, involved everyone. Even the kinless men of Saxon society – monks and strangers – were drawn into the system of kinship by a legislative fiction that made them kinsmen of the king.[51] Peasants, ceorls, and earls were equally governed by this family structure. It is unwise, therefore, to ignore the fact that the lives of great English aristocrats and the king, like the lives of lesser men, were shaped by these same bonds, obligations and rights; and it is important to remember that the system of kinship current in pre-Conquest society affected their lives as strongly as it did those of lesser men. An understanding of these relationships is vital for an understanding of the period's political organization and action.

As we have seen, although there is little evidence by which to link the aristocrats of tenth- and eleventh-century England, much has survived to indicate the obligations such ties entailed. With respect to landholding, however, the opposite is true. There is a vast amount of evidence on individual holdings, but few contemporary utterances which describe the effects such holdings had on the politics and history of the period. A vast quantity of information on landholding is preserved in Domesday Book, which records the comprehensive inquest of English lands undertaken in 1086 on the orders of William the Conqueror. Its entries, which provide relatively standardized, detailed, and quantified information for nearly every farm and village in eleventh-century England south of the Tees, constitute the most complete body of statistical, tenurial and geographical information on English land in the Middle Ages. The amount of information in Domesday Book, however, is staggering. It provides us with detailed information on some 45,000 landholdings across the kingdom. The document preserves information on peasant population, agricultural productivity, tax assessment, and land values – recording among other things thousands of mills, pastures, woodlands, iron works and slave women. Of equal importance, Domesday Book records names. Generally the document tells us who held the manors and

[51] II Cnut 40. That monks left the obligations of kinship behind when they entered a monastery is made clear in VIII Æthelred 25, where it is stated that they were not obliged to provide compensation nor were they entitled to a portion of their kinsmen's wergeld.

farmsteads recorded in England both in January 1066 – immediately before the Conquest – and in 1086 – the year of the Domesday inquest. The survey also records the names of the subtenants, retainers and allies of great Saxon and Norman lords. It notes the tenures by which Englishmen and Normans held their land and periodically preserves the legal disputes into which they entered and the land transferences they made. This vast array of tenurial and manorial information is organized geographically, and we are able to identify the great bulk of Domesday places – some 14,000 in all – and thus locate lordships, swine pastures, waste land, or areas of highest land value in eleventh-century England. Finally, Domesday Book bridges the Norman Conquest, describing tenurial conditions as they existed both in 1066 and again in 1086. Hence, it discloses the wealth, power and political structure of two distinct cultures and societies, and illuminates the revolutionary transformation in landholding that the Conquest brought about. Although occasionally ambiguous, inaccurate or incomplete, Domesday Book is singularly reliable by the standards of pre-scientific societies. It has rightly been called 'the most remarkable statistical document in the history of Europe'.[52] Indeed, no land survey until the nineteenth century approached it in comprehensiveness or detail.

Existing alongside Domesday Book are a number of satellite surveys, which provide additional information on eleventh-century landholdings for the counties of Cambridgeshire,[53] Somerset, Devonshire, Dorset, Cornwall and Wiltshire,[54] and for the lands of Ely,[55] Christchurch, Evesham,[56] and St Augustine's Canterbury.[57] Monastic histories of Abingdon, Ely, Worcester, Evesham, Peterborough, Ramsey and Durham also preserve

---

[52] H. C. Darby, 'Domesday England', *A New Historical Geography of England*, ed. H. C. Darby (Cambridge, 1973), p. 39. See also J. McDonald and G. D. Snooks, *Domesday Economy: A New Approach to Anglo-Norman History* (Oxford, 1986), pp. 32–6.

[53] *Inquisitio Comitatus Cantabrigiensis...subjicitur Inquisitio Eliensis*, ed. N. E. S. A. Hamilton (London, 1876). For an excellent overview of these texts, see Elizabeth M. Hallam, *Domesday Book through Nine Centuries* (London, 1986), pp. 17–31.

[54] The Exon Domesday is printed in *DB*, vol 4. Not all the Liber Exoniensis survives. Somerset and Cornwall are complete and Devonshire is shy of only six fiefs, but Dorset and Wiltshire are only poorly represented. (H. C. Harby, *Domesday Geography of South-West England*, pp. 393–428; F. H. Baring, 'The Exeter Domesday', *EHR*, 27 (1912), pp. 309–18; R. Weldon Finn, 'The immediate sources of the Exchequer Domesday', *Bulletin of the John Rylands Library*, 41 (1959), pp. 360–87.)

[55] See above, n. 53.   [56] *Dom. Mon*; BL Cotton MS Vespasian B xxiv.

[57] *An Eleventh-Century Inquisition of St Augustine's Canterbury*, ed. Adolphus Ballard, in *Records of the Social and Economic History of England and Wales*, iv, pt 2 (London, 1920).

valuable information on the lands given to these foundations by pious benefactors, stolen by greedy aristocrats, or restored through the mysterious powers of God. Toponymics, too, give indications of early landholding patterns. The Kingstons, Coninsboroughs and Aldermastons of England bear silent testimony to their early Saxon lords. Happily, a great deal of work has been done on English place-names and is available through the publications of the English Place-Name Society.[58] This evidence is further supplemented by some 1,700 pre-Conquest charters, writs, wills and memoranda of varying shades of authenticity, which record the transference, maintenance or loss of about 3,500 different pieces of land. There are also approximately two hundred post-Conquest charters and writs dating from William I's reign, along with a handful of memoranda dealing with some of the important pleas held to adjudicate disputes over land in the first years after the Conquest.

The landscape itself is invaluable in interpreting the meaning of landholding patterns. Extensive analyses of England's topography and river morphology are available,[59] along with detailed information on Roman and medieval road systems,[60] Iron and Dark Age earthworks, Scandinavian settlement patterns and the paths taken by conquering Norman armies.[61] Administrative districts, too, can be reconstructed, as can the bounds of a number of estates.[62] Once geographical information is plotted, infor-

---

[58] English Place-Name Society, general editors A. Mawer and Sir Frank Stenton (vols. 1–19), Bruce Dickins (vols. 20–2), A. H. Smith (vols. 23–43), and K. Cameron (vols. 44–) (Cambridge, 1924–).

[59] *British Rivers*, ed. John Lewin (London, 1981); T. S. Willan, *River Navigation in England (1600–1750)* (London, 1964); Francis John Monkhouse, *Landscape from the Air: A Physical Geography in Oblique Air Photographs*, 2nd edn (Cambridge, 1971).

[60] Ivan D. Margary, *Roman Roads in Britain*, 3rd edn (London, 1973); Christopher Taylor, *Roads and Tracks of Britain* (London, 1979).

[61] J. Ford-Johnston, *Hillforts of the Iron Age in England and Wales: A Survey of the Surface Evidence* (London, 1976); B. W. Cunliffe, *Iron Age Communities in Britain* (London, 1974); Leslie A. Alcock, 'Hillforts in Wales and the Marches', *Antiquity*, 39 (1965), pp. 184–95; D. W. Harding, *The Iron Age in the Upper Thames Basin* (Oxford, 1974); Ian Burrow, *Hillfort and Hill-Top Settlement in Somerset in the First to Eighth Centuries A.D.*, BAR (Oxford, 1981); Cyril Fox, *Offa's Dyke* (London, 1955); C. A. R. Radford, 'The later pre-Conquest boroughs and their defences', *Medieval Archaeology*, 14 (1970), pp. 83–103. For a convenient and fairly current bibliography of articles dealing with archaeology of Anglo-Saxon earthworks see *The Archaeology of Anglo-Saxon England*, ed. David M. Wilson (Cambridge, 1976), pp. 463–511.

[62] O. S. Anderson, *The English Hundred-Names* (Lund, 1934); *The English Hundred-Names: The South-Western Counties* (Lund, 1939); *The English Hundred-Names: The South Eastern Counties* (Lund, 1939).

mation from the chronicles can be superimposed. Such a political and geographical reconstruction of English history can then be overlain with the tenurial information provided by charters, monastic chronicles and Domesday Book. Thus, evidence which is geographical in nature but arising from a variety of sources can aid in determining the origin, function and effect of landholding configurations preserved in the record sources.

Although evidence on landholding is abundant, it presents a difficult set of problems. The shortcomings of Domesday Book have been chronicled over the course of a century of close scholarship. As detailed and comprehensive as the document initially appears, its information, as its critics have pointed out, is not always exact and must be used cautiously. The geld assessments and values of many estates in Domesday are divisable by five or by four – favourite numbers of account in eleventh-century England – so are doubtless approximations. There are also a number of scribal errors and lacunae. More serious than Domesday's minor inaccuracies is the information which the survey fails to record. Neither London nor Winchester was included in the Survey, nor were the counties of Durham and Northumberland. Anglo-Scandinavian personal names have been conflated by the Domesday commissioners, who were sloppy in their recordings of Alwigs and Æthelwigs, Ælfrics and Alrics, and in several counties the names of the majority of Anglo-Saxon tenants have been omitted.[63] Furthermore, the Saxon tenures recorded in the survey present a host of problems. Over two hundred phrases are used to describe the tenurial arrangements of pre-Conquest England, but it is difficult to match this confusion of terms with the commendation, bookland, loanland, and folkland known from other sources.

Since the inquest was carried out in different circuits, and since customs changed from region to region, there are also important variations in Domesday's terminology and information. In most of England south of Watling Street land was assessed in hides and organized by hundreds; in the north taxes were levied on the carucate, and shires were divided into wapentakes. Some circuits witness the careful recording of pre-Conquest tenures and overlords, while other circuits rarely bothered; and in some circuits hundreds or wapentakes are conscientiously rubricated,

---

[63] E.g. Oxfordshire and Leicestershire (DB, i, 154r–162r; 230r–237r).

but elsewhere in the survey there is little effort made to keep these districts straight. Estates in Domesday were also valued very differently. The value of some were given at twenty pence to the ora. Others rendered pounds by tale, and still others money that had been weighed or blanched. Although most estates were given annual values in pounds, to a number were appended a series of arcane customary renders. Scattered in the survey's folios we find land rendering foodstuff such as cheese,[64] wine,[65] bread,[66] flour,[67] honey,[68] wheat, barley and oats,[69] bacon-pigs[70] and porpoise;[71] livestock such as cows,[72] sheep,[73] hawks and dogs;[74] raw material such as timber,[75] boxwood[76] and iron;[77] manufactured goods such as salt,[78] spurs[79] and ploughshares;[80] and labour services such as riding, sowing, ploughing and harrowing.[81] Clearly, no absolute value can be assigned to estates that rendered these customary dues in addition to money. To further complicate matters, such details are normally suppressed in Domesday, although it is quite clear that nearly every tenant was encumbered with similar kinds of dues, and that all great lords received thousands of hours of grudging labour each year along with a mountain of produce and squealing livestock. But the inclusion of these dues in Domesday Book is too haphazard and idiosyncratic for us to quantify them in any way. Some royal and comital estates are given no value at all, but rendered night's farm, an ancient customary food rent. It is difficult to compare these often enormously valuable but unvalued estates with estates valued in pounds, shillings and pence.[82] None of these problems, however, is insurmountable, and most are the exception rather than the rule. The vast majority of estates have been identified, are assigned TRE and TRW tenants, and are given values and assessments which can, at least roughly, be compared. Domesday evidence enables us to plot the bulk of great men's landholdings and to calculate their relative wealth. As Sally Harvey has aptly noted,

Rightly...the deficiencies of the Domesday text have been minutely researched by commentators in the last two decades or so; but there is

[64] DB, i, 59v. [65] DB, i, 43r. [66] DB, i, 162v. [67] DB, i, 12r.
[68] DB, i, 173r. [69] DB, i, 172v; 179v. [70] DB, i, 97r. [71] DB, i, 5v.
[72] DB, i, 162v. [73] DB, i, 179v. [74] DB, i, 187r. [75] DB, i, 173r.
[76] DB, i, 252v. [77] DB, i, 87v. [78] DB, i, 281v. [79] DB, i, 276v.
[80] DB, i, 39v. [81] DB, i, 163r; 174v; 179v.
[82] For a further discussion of night's farm, see *FE*, p. 114; Paul Vinogradoff, *English Society in the Eleventh Century* (Oxford, 1908), pp. 142, 327; Carl Stephenson, 'The "firma noctis" and the customs of the hundred', *EHR*, 39 (1924), pp. 161–74.

a danger of their being over stressed. The preliminary caveats are now so numerous that the undergraduate approaches a question on D[omesday] B[ook] with the air of one requested to defuse an explosive device.[83]

Approached cautiously, and with the realization that its figures represent approximations rather than exact numbers, Domesday information on landholding provides our best evidence for the political history of eleventh-century England.

Historians using Domesday find themselves on the shoulders of giants. The studies of F. W. Maitland, Frederic Seebohm, H. Munroe Chadwick, Paul Vinogradoff, and John Horace Round laid the foundation for all subsequent Domesday scholarship. More recently fundamental research on Domesday Book has been produced by Sir Frank Stenton, Reginald Lennard, R. Weldon Finn, Sally Harvey, V. H. Galbraith, H. C. Darby, and John MacDonald and Graem Snooks. Their commentaries on the pitfalls of Domesday and their efforts to solve many of its puzzles are of fundamental value. Most of these scholars, however, have limited their investigations to one side of the Norman Conquest, to a particular region, to a single person, family or ecclesiastical house, or to one specific aspect of Domesday's manorial or institutional information. My study is an attempt to combine systematically the survey's prosopographical, manorial and geographical evidence, and to discuss the implications of this evidence on the political events of late Saxon and early Norman England.

Anglo-Saxon wills, charters, writs and memoranda present a different set of problems. First, it is difficult to correlate known aristocrats with known lands because the beneficiaries of royal diplomas and private grants cannot always be identified. Saxon naming practices, which discouraged toponymics, patronymics or cognonyms, impede the reconstruction of blood relationships among donors and grantees.[84] Similarly, the relationships between the beneficiaries of late Saxon grants and those who possessed their lands by 1066 are often impossible to determine, since we possess so little genealogical information for the late Saxon period. The physical condition of the charters themselves also creates difficulties. The bulk have come down to us in post-Conquest monastic cartularies, and many have been poorly

---

[83] Sally P. J. Harvey, 'Recent Domesday studies', *EHR*, 94 (1979), p. 130.
[84] Tengvik, *Old English Bynames*, pp. 28–138, 146–233.

copied, subtly altered, or highly abbreviated. Few have survived in manuscripts dating from the Saxon period and fewer still are original instruments. Furthermore, the preservation of Saxon charters has generally been determined by their continued utility after the Conquest. Since charters in favour of secular grantees had little value under the Norman regime, those held in private hands have not been preserved. Consequently, ecclesiastical lands are over-represented in the corpus of surviving Anglo-Saxon charters, and secular holdings can usually be traced only through documents which benefited the Church.[85] Only 10 per cent of the places preserved in surviving royal charters dating from the reign of Alfred to the Conquest were granted to lay people. But even this figure is misleading. While some documents drafted in favour of lay beneficiaries were placed in monasteries for safekeeping, most were maintained in monastic archives because they benefited the community in some way. More often than not, grants which appear to have created secular bookright were no more than an intermediate stage in a granting process which required that land already in a secular lord's possession be booked to him in order to alienate it permanently from his kindred. Such land could then be bequeathed with the rights of perpetual inheritance to a monastery or cathedral chapter. It is not surprising, then, that charters which appear to benefit laymen are commonly preserved in cartularies associated with ecclesiastical institutions which possessed the lands recorded in them by 1066. For example, of the twenty-three places granted to laymen in Hampshire between 871 and 1066, 70 per cent were in the hands of either Old or New Minster by the Conquest.[86] Records of all but two of these ecclesiastical estates are preserved in the twelfth-century Old Minster cartulary. The remaining two are found in documents associated with St Peter's, Winchester.[87] The two surviving grants of land in Middlesex to laymen from this same period both involve estates held by Westminster in 1066 and both are found in documents associated

---

[85] Simon Keynes, *The Diplomas of King Æthelred 'The Unready' 978–1016* (Cambridge, 1980), pp. 1–13; Nicholas P. Brooks, 'Anglo-Saxon charters: the work of the last twenty years', *ASE*, 3 (1974), pp. 211–31.

[86] The following Hampshire charters have secular grantees: S 589, 532, 874, 598, 600, 446, 604, 463, 754, 800, 430, 680, 840, 417, 811, 619, 754, 857, 636, 418, 613, 687, 488, 511. Of these the Hampshire lands disposed of in S 589, 532, 600, 446, 463, 430, 680, 840, 417, 811, 619, 754, 636, 488, 511, and 874 are held by Old Minster in Domesday Book (DB, i, 40r–41v).

[87] BL Add. 15350. Only S 418 and 687 are preserved elsewhere (BL Cotton Domit. xiv, fos. 115–16; BL Cotton Aug. ii, 40; BL Cotton Claud. B vi, fo. 71rv).

with that house.[88] In Somerset, of the twenty-two places granted to laymen in the same period, twelve were in the hands of the Church in 1066. Those in Glastonbury's hands are found in a Glastonbury manuscript;[89] those belonging to Winchester in Old Minster's cartulary;[90] those belonging to Bath in a Bath manuscript;[91] those belonging to Athelney in the Athelney Register.[92] It is clear, then, that many ostensibly secular charters benefited the Church in some way, and can therefore tell us little about the descent of lay landholding in the late Saxon period. Nevertheless, since cartularies do not simply maintain records of the lands their houses have accumulated, but also record the names of secular benefactors, they provide some indication of pre-Domesday aristocratic holdings.

More serious than the problem of preservation is the fact that many of the surviving documents are spurious. A great number of charters have been improved upon or are the concoctions of pious forgers who attempted to compensate for lost charters or to provide a stronger claim to land for which there was a tradition of title, but no written record. Still, traditions of landholding can be as interesting as proven title, and much can be learned from the forgeries.

An analysis of the chronological and geographical distribution of all reputedly Saxon charters quickly reveals the strong regional and temporal bias of this material. Land is granted, confirmed or exchanged in the surviving documents 5,036 times, but the apportionment of these place-names is divided unevenly throughout the realm. Kent is the best documented county, with estates appearing in charters 487 times. Worcester estates, with 378 appearances, and Somerset estates, with 342, are the next best documented counties. In total, seventeen shires have place-names appearing in more than one hundred instances. Out of the remaining eighteen counties, charter information is especially poor for Durham, Lancashire, Bedfordshire, Cheshire and

---

[88] S 805, 702. The manuscript in which the first of these charters was preserved is lost, but in 1702 Madox published it from a manuscript houses in Westminster Abbey (Thomas Madox, *Formulare Anglicanum* (London, 1702), p. 174). The second is Westminster Abbey, WAM X.

[89] S 462, 431, 481, 509 are all found in Marquess of Bath Longleat, 39.

[90] S 606, 440, 475, 441, 571 are all found in BL Add. 15350.

[91] S 593, 476, 627, 711 and 508 are all found in Cambridge, Corpus Christi College, 111.

[92] S 652 is found in an eighteenth-century transcript made by David Rogers, (Oxford, Bodleian Library) pp. 89–91.

Herefordshire. Thus, charter information varies significantly by region, and this fact must be taken into account before stressing any local peculiarities. A number of apparent regional differences may well be the product of uneven evidence rather than political reality. Evidence is also unevenly allocated between the various types of charters. The bulk of information on individual landholdings is found in the royal charters, which also provide over half the places mentioned in twenty-six shires. 88 per cent of all charter information dealing with Northamptonshire, for example, is preserved in royal charters, 85 per cent for Lincolnshire, and 80 per cent for Huntingdonshire. Royal charters disclose much less information on lands in Bedfordshire, Essex, Gloucestershire, Herefordshire, Norfolk, Nottinghamshire, Suffolk and Yorkshire. At least 50 per cent of all land mentioned in these counties comes from non-royal documents. Thus any landholding analysis in this second group of counties rests more heavily on ecclesiastical grants, on wills, or on other miscellaneous documents. Wills play an especially important role in the reconstruction of landholding patterns in East Anglia and its neighbouring counties, where they provide over half of our information. In the eastern counties, therefore, we have relatively little knowledge of the king's role in granting land to his great nobles, but information on the lands of ealdormanly families – of which the wills are a remarkably rich storehouse – is greater there than elsewhere in the kingdom. The distribution of charter information over time presents further problems. When the number of places recorded in the charters is broken down by reign, evidence is uneven. The reigns of Edgar, Æthelred, and Edward the Confessor each have preserved the disposition of over 200 pieces of land, the reigns of Æthelstan through Eadwig between 110 and 180. But estate histories during the reigns of Alfred, Edward the Elder, Edward the Martyr, Edmund Ironside, and Cnut and his sons are much more difficult to reconstruct.

Thus a great diversity exists in the charter evidence by century, by instrument, and by reign, region and shire. An investigation of the charters from one particular county, reign or century can provide examples which may or may not indicate general trends. However, the use of all of these documents over the large span of the Anglo-Saxon and Anglo-Norman periods and across all of England tends to smooth the holes and discrepancies in the data. A broad overview of the charters and Domesday evidence lessens the peculiarities of specific regions or individual reigns. Over time and over a broad expanse of territory these sources enable us to trace the general movement of landed wealth from one group of landholders to another, to identify periods in which landholding was in a state of flux, and to compare the landed wealth of English kings and their great aristocrats, thereby casting new light on the aristocratic environment in which the *Rex Anglorum* lived and ruled, freeing him from his customary isolation.

Chapter 2

CNUT'S CONQUEST AND THE DESTRUCTION OF THE ROYAL KINDRED

Ecclesiastical writers, commenting on the years following Cnut's coronation, portrayed the king as Edmund's legal heir and the preserver of Edgar's laws[1] and praised him as a devoted protector of the English Church and its faith.[2] Cnut's surviving charters support this contemporary view, demonstrating that English thegns and sheriffs continued, as custom dictated, to aid in the governance of the realm, and establishing that the new king's diplomatic practices were firmly rooted in those of his predecessors.[3] The only administrative innovation that both the Dane's contemporaries and later historians have noted is Cnut's introduction of a new secular official, the earl, paired with the gradual extinction of the office of ealdorman during his reign.[4]

---

[1] See especially Cnut's law code of 1018 (printed in A. G. Kennedy, 'Cnut's law code of 1018', *ASE*, 11 (1982), pp. 72–81); Letter of 1020 and 1027; Fl. Wig., i, p. 182.

[2] The laws formulated for the new king by Archbishop Wulfstan emphasize Cnut's position as defender of the Christian faith (see especially Cnut 1018 and I Cnut.) For Wulfstan's authorship see Dorothy Whitelock, 'Wulfstan and the laws of Cnut', *EHR*, 63 (1948), pp. 433–52; 'Wulfstan's authorship of Cnut's laws', *EHR*, 70 (1970), pp. 72–85), but others wrote in the same vein. The author of the *Encomium Emmae* describes Cnut as 'a friend and intimate of ecclesiastics, so much so that he seemed to bishops to be a co-bishop because of his display of perfect religion, to monks not a secular but a monk because of his striving for the humblest devotion...He built and honoured churches, he loaded priests and clergy with dignities...' (*Encomium Emmae Reginae*, ed. A. Campbell, Camden Third Series, 72 (London, 1949), pp. 34–6). Cnut was remembered as a great protector of both Glastonbury and Christchurch privileges, and as a patron of Ely. (*De Ant. Glast.*, c. 65. S 985; Nicholas Brooks, *The Early History of the Church of Canterbury* (Leicester, 1984), pp. 288–9; *LE*, ii, c. 82, 84, and especially 85). Recently Pamela Nightingale has expressed the sensible opinion that Cnut's ecclesiastical patronage may have been 'designed to stifle opposition' (Pamela Nightingale, 'The origin of the Court of Husting and Danish influence on London's development into a capital city', *EHR*, 102 (1987), p. 567). Propaganda or not, the press Cnut received from churchmen for his ecclesiastical policies was favourable.

[3] *The Crawford Collection of Early Charters and Documents*, ed. A. S. Napier and W. H. Stevenson (Oxford, 1895), p. 137; Florence E. Harmer, *Anglo-Saxon Writs* (Manchester, 1952), pp. 13–18; *Facsimiles of English Royal Writs to A.D. 1100*, ed. T. A. M. Bishop and P. Chaplais (Oxford, 1957), pp. xi–xii; Keynes, *Æthelred*, pp. 140–5.

[4] *ASC*, s.a. 1017 (C, D, E); Fl. Wig., i, p. 181. Modern scholars have also noted Cnut's use of stallers and housecarls, but the king's own contemporaries never felt it necessary

Even this reform, however, is thought to have had only slight effect. The powers with which Cnut's earls were endowed and the regions with which they were entrusted, mirrored those pertaining to the ealdormen of his predecessor's day.[5] What few modifications to the office there were – the increasing emphasis on large regions of responsibility and a greater delegation of authority[6] – are generally attributed to the military demands of Cnut's northern empire rather than the political circumstances in which England found itself after the Viking conquest.[7] The transformation from ealdorman to earl, therefore, is seen as one of title rather than responsibility. Yet it is difficult to gauge administrative change without determining the effects such change had on the men who traditionally held high office, since upheavals within the office-holding aristocracy could more radically affect a kingdom than institutional change. Indeed, an examination of the tenth- and eleventh-century aristocracy reveals that the men who were ealdormen differed fundamentally from the men who were earls, and that the move from ealdorman to earl was symptomatic of more profound changes within the administrative aristocracy.

A careful investigation of the ealdormen of the second half of the

to comment on these innovations. For historians' views of stallers see T. J. Oleson, *The Witenagemot in the Reign of Edward the Confessor* (Toronto, 1955), pp. 56–9; William A. Morris, *The Medieval English Sheriff to 1300* (Manchester, 1927), pp. 37–8, and most recently Katharin Mack, 'The stallers: administrative innovation in the reign of Edward the Confessor', *Journal of Medieval History*, 12 (1986), pp. 123–34. For housecarls see Nicholas Hooper, 'The housecarls in England in the eleventh century', *Anglo-Normal Studies*, 7 (1984), pp. 161–76; and James Campbell, 'Some agents and agencies of the late Anglo-Saxon state', *Domesday Studies*, ed. J. C. Holt (Woodbridge, Suffolk, 1987), pp. 201–18.

[5] L. M. Larson, Cnut's biographer, noted long ago that 'the first recorded act of the new sovereign was the division of the kingdom into four great earldoms. Much has been made of this act in the past: the importance of the measure has been overrated ... what Cnut did at this time was merely to recognize the status quo' (Larson, 'The political policies of Cnut as king of England', *American Historical Review*, 15 (1910), pp. 724–5). Pauline Stafford, too, has argued that the consolidation of administrative districts, ascribed to the introduction of the earldom, occurred under Cnut's predecessor Æthelred. (Pauline Stafford, 'The reign of Æthelred II: a study in limitations of royal policy and action', *Ethelred the Unready: Papers from the Millenary Conference*, ed. David Hill, *BAR British Series*, 58 (1978), pp. 15–46). For the most complete institutional study of ealdormen see H. M. Chadwick, *Studies on Anglo-Saxon Institutions* (Cambridge, 1905), pp. 161–97.

[6] H. R. Loyn, *The Governance of Anglo-Saxon England 500–1087* (Stanford, 1984), p. 179.

[7] Stenton, *Anglo-Saxon England*, pp. 398, 414; Larson, 'The political policies of Cnut as king of England', pp. 724–5, and *Cnut the Great* (London, 1912), pp. 114–15.

tenth century – those men living and thriving before the Viking invasions had begun to take their toll – reveals that the most powerful among them were part of a tightly knit aristocracy bound to one another and to the king through ties of kinship, marriage, lordship and close association. (See figure 2.1.) Ealdorman Ælfhere, for example, whose attacks on the Mercian monasteries gained him notoriety among ecclesiastical chroniclers, was the brother of another ealdorman, Ælfheah.[8] His father was ealdorman of Mercia[9] as was his brother-in-law.[10] Another member of Ælfhere's family, his nephew Ælfwine, was a kinsman of Ealdorman Bryhtnoth, making Ælfhere a relative either by blood or by marriage to the English leader at Maldon.[11] Bryhtnoth himself was tied to other leading families. He was married to the daughter of Ealdorman Ælfgar of Essex, and was the brother-in-law of Ealdorman Æthelstan 'Rota',[12] who was himself probably the son of his predecessor and namesake.[13] Bryhtnoth was also acknowledged as a kinsman by Æthelmær the Fat, the ealdorman of western Wessex.[14] Æthelmær, in his turn,

---

[8] S 1485, 582. For the best treatment of Ælfhere's family see Ann Williams, '*Princeps Merciorum Gentis*: the family, career, and connections of Ælfhere, Ealdorman of Mercia 956–983', *ASE*, 10 (1981), pp. 143–72; and *The Crawford Collection*, p. 84.

[9] There are two pieces of evidence for this assertion. First, Ælfhere took land from Evesham during the 'anti-monastic reaction'. His predecessor Ealhhelm, according to evidence in the late Evesham chronicle, got lands from the defunct monastery there. It looks, therefore, as if Ælfhere's move against the monastery was an attempt to recover family property. (*Chron. Ev.*, p. 77; Williams, 'Ælfhere', pp. 145–6). Secondly, Ælfhere's nephew calls himself the grandson of Ealhhelm *The Battle of Maldon*, which makes Ælfhere at the very least an in-law of Ealhhelm's (*Battle of Maldon*, ed. E. V. Gordon (London, 1937), lines 217–18). The Evesham connection, however, makes it more likely that Ælfhere was the ealdorman's son.

[10] Ælfhere's brother-in-law may have been ealdorman Ælfric Cild. An Ælfric was married to the 'Æthelflæd Ealhhelm's daughter', remembered in Wynflæd's will. (S 1539; Gordon, *Battle of Maldon*, p. 83. See also Cyril Hart, *ECNM*, p. 260.)

[11] Ælfwine is described as Ælfhere's sister's son in S 1485. The poet of the *Battle of Maldon* has Ælfwine call himself the grandson of Ealhhelm (lines 217–18), and kinsman of Bryhtnoth (line 224).

[12] Ealdorman Ælfgar's will is S 1483. His daughters were Æthelflæd and Ælfflæd. The former was the wife of Æthelstan 'Rota' (*LE*, c. 64; her will is S 1494), and the latter was the wife of Bryhtnoth (*LE*, appendix D, pp. 422–3). Her will is S 1486. For the best treatment of Ealdorman Bryhtnoth and his family see *LE*, appendix D, pp. 422–3. For an imperfect description of Bryhtnoth's family connections, see E. D. Laborde, *Bryhtnoth and Maldon* (London, 1936), pp. 9–19, which is followed by Gordon, *Battle of Maldon*, pp. 15–21. [13] *ECNM*, p. 300.

[14] This relationship is likely asserted in the will of Ælfflæd (S 1486), although the MS is not absolutely clear on this point. The will reads 'Eðelmere mines...e'. The British Museum facsimile transcription has supplied 'Edelmere mines hlafordes mege' to fill the gap. (*Wills*, p. 145).

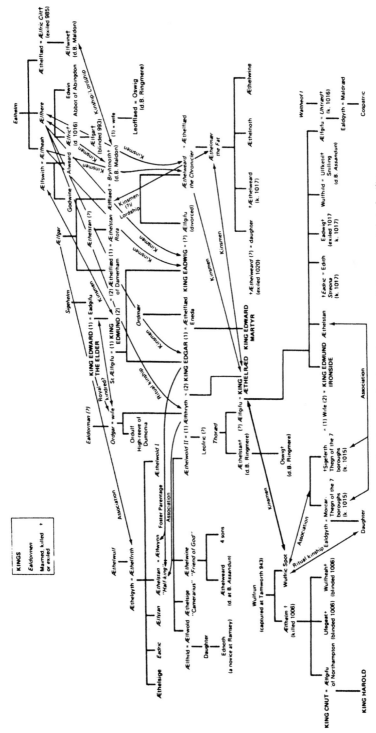

Figure 2.1 Genealogy of tenth- and early eleventh-century ealdorman and their families

may have been the father-in-law of the Ealdorman Æthelweard forced into exile by King Cnut in 1020.[15] Æthelmær's father, Æthelweard the Chronicler, was also an ealdorman in the west,[16] and claimed kinship with Ealdorman Ælfheah, the brother of Ælfhere of Mercia.[17] Æthelstan Half-King, Ealdorman of East Anglia, was the son of an ealdorman, the father of two others, Æthelwine 'Friend of God' and Æthelwold II,[18] and was the brother of three more – Eadric, Ælfstan, and Æthelwold I.[19]

A complex network of alliances woven through lordship, friendship and ritual kinship linked these men and their families even more tightly. Queen Ælfthryth, the mother of King Æthelred, was bound to Ealdorman Ælfheah by godparenthood: either the queen and the ealdorman shared the same godchild or one was godparent to the other's child.[20] Such an association, with its legal and canonical responsibilities, bespeaks a close relationship between the two, and suggests that deeper, hidden ties may have existed between Ælfheah's family and either the queen's father and brother, or the queen's first husband, all of whom were ealdormen.[21] Ælfheah was also the 'beloved friend' of Bishop Ælfsige of Winchester, who made the ealdorman the guardian of his kinsmen and his will, disclosing ties of lordship and patronage between the two men. Ælfsige left his friend an estate at Crondall for one life, perhaps in return for his advocacy.[22] A similar

---

[15] *The Crawford Collection of Early Charters and Documents*, p. 79; S 911; *ASC*, s.a. 1020 (C, D, E, F); Flower, *Exeter Book*, pp. 85–9.

[16] Æthelweard first attests as an ealdorman in 977 (S 831, a not altogether satisfactory charter). Another charter describes Æthelweard as 'Occidentalium Provinciarum dux'; (S 891; *Wills*, p. 145). For the best treatment of Ealdorman Æthelweard, see *The Chronicle of Æthelweard*, ed. Alistair Campbell (London, 1962), pp. xii–xviii.

[17] Ælfheah bequeathed an estate to his kinsman Æthelweard, probably Æthelweard the Chronicler. (S 1485; *Wills*, p. 124; Williams, 'Ælfhere', p. 150).

[18] *Cart. Rams.*, iii, p. 165; *LE*, ii, c. 7, 112. For the most complete study of Æthelstan Half-King see Cyril Hart, 'Athelstan 'Half-King' and his Family', *ASE*, 2 (1973), pp. 115–44.

[19] *Vita Oswaldi Archiepiscopi Eboracensis*, in *Historians of the Church of York*, ed. James Raine, RS (London, 1879), i, pp. 428–9; Hart, 'Half-King', pp. 118–20.

[20] S 1485; *Wills*, p. 123.

[21] Ælfthryth was the daughter of Ordgar (*ASC*, s.a. 965 (D, F); Fl. Wig., i, p. 142). Gaimar adds that Ordgar was the son of an ealdorman and that his wife was of royal birth, but this source is late and unreliable (*L'estorie des Engles*, ed. Alexander Bell, Anglo-Norman Text Society (Oxford, 1960), lines 3606–8, 3629–30). Ælfthryth's first husband was Ealdorman Æthelwold, son of Æthelstan Half-King (Fl. Wig., i, p. 140).

[22] S 1491. Ælfheah, in turn, was a patron of Old Minster, Winchester (S 1485) and a copy of his will was preserved in Old Minster's *Codex Wintoniensis*.

relationship was shared by Ealdorman Bryhtnoth's wife Ælfflæd and Æthelmær the Fat, to whom she bequeathed an estate with the stipulation that 'he be a true friend and advocate'. She left him another in return for his promise to support her will and those of her ancestors.[23] Thus, patronage and friendship bound a woman who was the wife, the daughter, and the sister-in-law of three ealdormen with an ealdorman from another powerful family. Lordship also subordinated Ælfwine, the nephew of Ealdorman Ælfhere, to Ealdorman Bryhtnoth. The speech placed in his mouth by the Maldon poet stresses the connection between Ælfwine and Bryhtnoth, not only as kinsman and kinsman, but as man and lord.[24]

The benefactions many of these men made to bishoprics and abbeys further suggest a shared community of interests among important aristocratic kindreds. Both the families of Ealdorman Ælfhere and Æthelstan Half-King forged intimate ties with St Dunstan. Ælfhere's father, Ealdorman Ealhhelm, bequeathed land to St Dunstan's brother, a man closely connected with Glastonbury Abbey,[25] and his brother Ælfheah consented to sell several estates to St Dunstan.[26] At the same time, Half-King was one of the saint's closest friends.[27] Members of each family were also patrons of Glastonbury.[28] Æthelstan Half-King, Ælfheah's

---

[23] S 1486.

[24] *Battle of Maldon*, line 224.

[25] *ECNM*, pp. 371–2; Williams, 'Ælfhere', pp. 154–5.

[26] S 1447.

[27] *Vita Sancti Dunstani, Auctore B*, in *Memorials of Saint Dunstan Archbishop of Canterbury*, ed. William Stubbs, RS (London, 1874), pp. 44–5.

[28] S 866, 1485; *De Ant. Glast.*, c. 62. A thirteenth-century list of the contents of Glastonbury's lost cartulary contains notices of a number of royal grants made in favour of these ealdormen, but preserved at Glastonbury, either because Glastonbury was given rights to them or because the monastery was safeguarding these ealdormen's charters. Included in this catalogue is a record of a grant to Ælfhere's for land at Buckland (S 1737), Westbury-on-Severn (S 1747, 1760), Orchardleigh (S 1759), and Cranmore (S 1746); King Eadred's grant to Ælfheah of Henstridge (S 1736) and Compton (S 1705), and King Edgar's grant of Merton; Ælfheah's wife of *Pendesclive* (S 1748), Nyland, Stratton (S 1761), and Winscombe from Kings Eadwig and Edgar (S 1762); Æthelwold I of Chelworth (S 1721); and Æthelwold II of Camerton (S 1738) and Hannington (S 1763; Cambridge, Trinity College, MS R 5.33, fo. 77rv). A list of pre-Conquest charters made in 1247 which contained a record of land still held by the Abbey lists Merton and Dulwich, Surrey, as land granted by King Edgar to Ælfheah. (Cambridge, Trinity College, MS R 5.33., fos. 102r–103v, printed in *Johannis ... Glastoniensis Chronica sive Historia de rebus Glastoniensibus*, ed. T. Hearne, 2 vols. (Oxford, 1726), ii, p. 405).

brother Ælfwine, and Ealdorman Æthelwine retired there,[29] and Ælfhere, Ælfheah, and Æthelstan chose Glastonbury as their final resting place.[30] In the *Liber Eliensis* we read of a thegn named Sigfert, who near death, chose Ely as his burial place because 'sui karissimi et fidelissimi amici ibi essent sepulti'.[31] Such reasoning could well lie behind similar decisions made by ealdormen. Ælfhere and his family were also patrons of Abingdon – granting it lands and witnessing its charters[32] – and one of his sons became abbot of that house.[33] Ælfhere's kinsman Bryhtnoth was also a patron of Abingdon,[34] as were Half-King's relatives.[35] Thus the two families, so often portrayed as antagonists,[36] shared important ecclesiastical friends and interests and were instrumental in rebuilding the same two ecclesiastical establishments. The sister of Ealdorman Æthelweard also left a bequest to Abingdon,[37] and Edwin, Ealdorman of Sussex, was buried there, so he too must have been a friend and benefactor of that house.[38] Ramsey was another centre of ealdormanly patronage. The house, founded at the urging of St Oswald by Æthelwine 'Friend of God', became the focus of benefactions for Æthelwine's family.[39] Impressive amounts of land were donated by Æthelwine, his mother,

---

[29] *Chron. Rams.*, p. 12; *De Ant. Glast.*, c. 53.

[30] *De Ant. Glast.*, c. 31; S 1485; John of Glastonbury, *Cronica sive Antiquitates Glastoniensis*, ed. James P. Carley (Woodbridge, Suffolk, 1985), i, p. 36. Ealdorman Æthelwine and Ealdorman Æthelnoth were also buried at Glastonbury (*De Ant. Glast.*, c. 31).

[31] *LE*, ii, c. 11. If 'amicus' is a translation of *freond* it carries the double meaning of 'friend' and 'kinsman'. Eadwig, brother of Edmund Ironside, was buried at Tavistock, the foundation of his maternal grandfather, and throughout the Middle Ages, on the anniversary of the Ætheling's death bells were rung, wine was given to the monks for dinner, and bread was distributed to the poor. (H. R. P. Finberg, *Tavistock Abbey* (Cambridge, 1951), p. 226).

[32] S 1216.

[33] See below, n. 91. On the legality of this election see S 876.

[34] Bryhtnoth was granted Tadmarton in 956 (S 617). Abingdon claimed that King Eadwig granted (or more likely confirmed) Bryhtnoth's gift to the abbey (S 584).

[35] S 1208, S 525. S 480 is a grant of land at Appleton and *Ærmundeslea* by King Edmund to Æthelstan Half-King, preserved in the Abingdon cartulary. (BL Cotton Claud. B vi, fos. 27–8). Abingdon claimed *Ærmundeslea* (which included Appleton) after the Conquest (S 239; F. M. Stenton, *The Early History of the Abbey of Abingdon* (Reading, 1913), p. 11).

[36] Hart, 'Athelstan 'Half-King', p. 135; D. J. V. Fisher, 'The anti-monastic reaction in the reign of Edward the Martyr', *The Cambridge Historical Journal*, 10 (1950–2), pp. 255, 268–9; Williams, ' Ælfhere', p. 165.

[37] S 1484.   [38] *ASC*, s.a. 982 (C).

[39] Eadmer, *Vita Sancti Oswaldi*, in *Historians of the Church of York and its Archbishops*, ii, p. 17; *Cart. Rams.*, iii, p. 170; *Chron. Rams.*, p. 35.

brothers, and three wives;[40] and Eadnoth Abbot of Ramsey fought and died along side Æthelwine's son, Æthelweard, at the Battle of *Assandun*.[41] Ealdorman Bryhtnoth, too, granted land to the monastery at its foundation,[42] and would have given more had not the Abbot of Ramsey refused the ealdormen and his men hospitality on one occasion.[43] Still, the anniversary of Bryhtnoth's death was remembered by Ramsey's monks.[44] Æthelweard the Chronicler's sister was also a benefactress of Ramsey.[45] New Minster's *Liber Vitae* records the names of benefactors who the monks of Winchester remembered in their prayers. Among those listed were Ealdormen Æthelwine, Bryhtnoth, and Ælfric,[46] and the sister of Ealdorman Æthelweard.[47] Æthelweard himself patronized the abbey and was buried there, as was Æthelmær ealdorman of Hampshire.[48] Burton Abbey, founded by Wulfric Spot and patronized by other members of his family, may also have received gifts from the family of Ælfhere and Ælfheah: among the Burton muniments was a charter of their father, given to him by King Alfred's daughter.[49] Bath was endowed by Ealdormen Ælfhere and Ælfheah[50] as well as the family of Æthelweard the Chronicler;[51] Old Minster was endowed by Ealdorman Ælfheah and his friends[52] and by the sister of Æthelweard the Chronicler,[53] who along with Ealdorman Æthelwold I, brother of Half-King, was buried there.[54]

As tenth-century ealdormen bound themselves to one another through kinship, lordship and benefaction, so too did West Saxon kings associate themselves with their greatest aristocratic families. King Edmund's second wife, Æthelflæd of Damerham,[55] was a daughter, a widow, a sister-in-law and probably a daughter-in-law of four different ealdormen; King Edmund's marriage to her thus strengthened his ties to a number of key aristocratic families. Evidence in the *Chronicle* suggests that King Eadwig's abortive marriage to a noble woman named Ælfgifu was an attempt to associate himself more closely with the family of the West Saxon

[40] *Cart. Rams.*, i, p. 268; *Chron. Rams.*, pp. 51–8, 62–4.   [41] *Cart. Rams.*, iii, p. 172.
[42] *Chron Rams.*, p. 56; *Cart. Rams.*, i. p. 280.   [43] *Chron. Rams.*, pp. 116–17.
[44] *Cart. Rams.*, iii, p. 162.   [45] S 1484.
[46] *Liber Vitae: Register and Martyrology of New Minster and Hyde Abbey, Winchester*, ed. Walter de Gray Birch, Hampshire Record Society (1892), p. 54.   [47] *Ibid.*, p. 57.
[48] S 1498; *ASC*, s.a. 982 (C); Fl. Wig., i, p. 147. In New Minster's *Liber Vitae*, Æthelmær is remembered as a benefactor (p. 21).   [49] S 224.   [50] S 1485.   [51] S 1484.
[52] S 1485, 1491.   [53] S 1484.   [54] S 1504.
[55] *ASC*, s.a. 946 (D); *LE*, ii, c. 64. Her will is S 1494.

ealdorman Æthelweard.[56] King Edgar's first wife was the daughter of Ealdorman Ordmær,[57] and his second wife was the daughter of Ordgar, a man soon made ealdorman, and the sister of Ordulf, 'high-reeve of Dumonia'.[58] She was also the widow of Ealdorman Æthelwold and thus the former sister-in-law of Ealdorman Æthelwine and the former daughter-in-law of Æthelstan Half-King.[59] King Æthelred, in his turn, wed the daughter of Ealdorman Thoræd[60] and married at least two of his own daughters to ealdormen.[61] Thus, during the course of half a century, these four kings' choice of spouses for themselves and their daughters drew their house into alliances with over a dozen ealdormen.[62]

Marriage was only one of several ways in which West Saxon kings were joined to ealdormen and their kin. Exact relationships are rarely explicit in the sources, but skeletal genealogies of West Saxon kings and their aristocrats leave no doubt that a great number of ealdormen were related to the king by blood. Ælfheah, Ealdorman of eastern Wessex, is styled 'kinsman' in the charters of Eadred, Eadwig, and Edgar.[63] His wife Ælfswith was

---

[56] *ASC*, s.a. 958 (D); *Wills*, pp. 118–19. Furthermore, the mother of Eadwig's wife is described as 'of noble birth' in *Vita S. Oswaldi*, c. 21.

[57] Fl. Wig., i, p. 140; Eadmer, *Vita Sancti Dunstani*, *Memorials of St Dunstan*, p. 210.

[58] *ASC*, s.a. 964 (D, F); Ordgar was granted an ealdordom in the same year his daughter married the King. (Ordgar first attests among the ealdormen in a charter of 964 (S 724)). A spurious charter of the same year purports to be a grant by King Edgar to his new queen. In this charter Ordgar still attests as a thegn (S 725). Ordgar signs at the bottom of the list of ealdormen in S 735 and 736, both dated 965. The relationships are described in William of Malmesbury, *GR*, ii, pp. 202–3. On Ordulf, see Fl. Wig., i, p. 153. The most thorough study of Ordgar and his family is found in H. P. R. Finberg, 'The house of Ordgar and the foundation of Tavistock Abbey', *EHR*, 58 (1943), pp. 190–201.   [59] Fl. Wig., i, p. 140.

[60] *EHD*, i, p. 48; Ailred of Rievaulx, Migne, *Patrologia Latina*, 195, col. 741.

[61] Ealdorman Uhtræd was married to one (*DOD*, p. 216) and Eadric Streona to another (Fl. Wig., i, p. 161).

[62] One could say that English kings had no choice but to marry their daughters into the families of English ealdormen. King Æthelstan, however, chose not to marry his sisters (and one imagines his daughters, if he had had any) to the local nobility, but instead found them husbands among Viking and Continental princes (Stenton, *Anglo-Saxon England*, pp. 339–40; R. L. Poole, *Studies in Chronology and History* (Oxford, 1934), pp. 115–22). Æthelred's second wife came from Normandy, and Cnut chose to marry Æthelred's widow rather than a member of the English aristocracy (although his handfast wife was a member of an important English kindred). Cnut married his daughter abroad as well (Hemming, i, p. 267). In the eleventh century some English aristocrats chose to marry their daughters to foreigners. Earl Ælfgar's daughter married Gruffydd ap Llewelyn (Freeman, *NC*, ii, pp. 444–5) and Godwine's son Tostig was married to the daughter of the Count of Flanders. (*VER*, pp. 24–5.)

[63] S 564, 585, 586, 702.

called *propinquus* by King Edmund, and 'kinsman' by King
Eadwig.[64] Ælfheah's brother Ealdorman Ælfhere, is called *regis
Anglorum Eadgari propinquus* in 'Florence' of Worcester's chronicle[65] and described as a kinsman in the witness lists of royal
charters.[66] Æthelweard, ealdorman of the western shires, wrote in
his own chronicle of his descent from King Æthelred I, Alfred the
Great's brother;[67] and his son, Ealdorman Æthelmær, is described
by King Æthelred as a man 'closely tied to me by kinship'.[68] One
also encounters allusions to the 'nobility of lineage' of Wulfric
Spot, the brother of Ealdorman Ælfhelm.[69] The *Chronicle's*
description of their mother's capture by the Danes at Tamworth
in 943 suggests that the two brothers were descendants of the
Mercian ruling house; if so, they shared a common Mercian
ancestor with King Æthelred.[70] Æthelstan Half-King's son is
described as distantly related to the West Saxon kings.[71]
Ealdorman Ordgar of Devon was King Æthelred's maternal
grandfather; his son Ordulf, the 'high-reeve' of Dumonia, was
the King's uncle;[72] and Ealdorman Ordmær was Edward the
Martyr's maternal grandfather.[73] Such alliances, buttressed by
blood and by marriage, reached back into the ninth century and
beyond. King Alfred, for example, was the brother-in-law of one
Mercian ealdorman, and he made his daughter the wife of
another.[74] Ealdorman Osferth, remembered generously by King
Alfred in his will, was described as a 'royal kinsman' in the

---

[64] Ælfheah's wife Ælfswith, to whom she was married by 940 (S 462), was described as
King Edmund's *propinquus* (S 462), and in the endorsement of a charter of Eadwig
she is styled 'kinswoman' (S 662).   [65] Fl. Wig., i, p. 147.
[66] S 555, 564, 582, 585, 586.   [67] *The Chronicle of Æthelweard*, p. 38.
[68] S 937. It is likely that Æthelmær's sister is the woman Ælfgifu whose will survives
(S 1484. Whitelock makes this identification in *Wills*, p. 119). Certainly, we know that
King Edgar had a kinswoman of this name (S 738, 737).   [69] S 906.
[70] *ASC*, s.a. 943 (D), and p. 71, n. 5. Wulfric is styled 'Wulfric Wulfrun's son' in S 886.
For the most complete study of Wulfric Spot and his family, see *Charters of Burton
Abbey*, ed. P. H. Sawyer (Oxford, 1979), pp. xxxviii–xlvii, especially p. xl. But see
Whitelock, *EHD*, i, p. 90.
[71] The *Vita S. Oswaldi* describes him as 'a descendant from the royal lineage', and the
Chron. Rams. suggests that he was a distant relation to the king (p. 11). Both are tracts
written at the family's foundation, and the authors of both had an abundance of
material on Æthelwine's family. Nonetheless, the language used to describe the
family's connection to the West Saxon kings is extremely vague. It is possible that their
claims are a genteel exaggeration of the descent of Ramsey's founder's family.
[72] So called in S 937 and 876.   [73] See n. 58.
[74] *The Chronicle of Æthelweard*, p. 32; *Asser's Life of King Alfred*, ed. W. H. Stevenson
(Oxford, 1904), c. 75.

charters of Edward the Elder.[75] King Æthelstan married his sister to Sihtric, the Viking ruler of York,[76] and Ealdorman Sighelm of Kent was the grandfather of Kings Edmund and Eadred, and the great-grandfather of Kings Eadwig and Edgar.[77]

When no blood was shared, no marriage possible, alliances were cultivated in other ways. King Edmund had his son Edgar the Peaceable fostered by Ælfwynn, the wife of Æthelstan Half-King. Thus, the ætheling was reared in the household of one of his father's closest allies and raised among Half-King's own brothers and sons, five of whom at one time or another were ealdormen. Since Half-King was an intimate of the reform circle, in particular with St Dunstan, Edgar came of age in an atmosphere dominated by the ideals of monastic reform.[78] Some of Edgar's affection for monks and his determination to revive Benedictine monasticism must have been acquired in this household of his youth.[79] Dunstan and other of his intimates were certainly drawn into the circle of the young king's foster family. The family of Ælfhere and Ælfheah, for instance, had the closest of dealings with Dunstan and could have gained access to the young king through their association with the saint.[80] Furthermore, bonds of godparenthood were shared by Ælfhere and King Edgar's wife Ælfthryth. Ælfthryth herself was deeply involved with the reform circle, and her brother Ordulf was the founder of one of England's new Benedictine monasteries.[81] Thus a number of links, not all of them links of kinship, connected King Edgar with Ealdorman Ælfhere and his family, with the family of Ordgar and Ordulf, and with Æthelstan Half-King, his children and his brothers.

That Anglo-Saxon kings were aware of the benefits of ruling with the aid of their cousins, uncles and in-laws is patently clear.

[75] S 1507, 1286, 378. For the nature of Osferth's relationship with Alfred, see Simon Keynes and Michael Lapidge, *Alfred the Great. Asser's Life of King Alfred and other Contemporary Sources* (Harmondsworth, 1983), p. 322, n. 79.

[76] William of Malmesbury, *GR*, i, c. 134; Roger of Wendover, *Flores Historiarum*, ed. H. O. Coxe (London, 1841–42), s.a. 925.

[77] A grant of land by Eadgifu, King Edmund's and King Eadred's mother includes the history of an estate held by her father Ealdorman Sighelm (S 1211). He died in battle against the Vikings in 903. (*ASC*, s.a. 903 (A, D, C, D).)

[78] *Chron. Rams.*, pp. 11, 53.   [79] Hart, 'Æthelstan Half-King', p. 124.

[80] See above, nn. 25, 27.

[81] At Tavistock (Finberg, 'Ordgar', pp. 191–2). The foundation charter is printed in Finberg, *Tavistock Abbey*, pp. 278–83. Ordulf also advised his nephew, King Æthelred, to give a number of estates to Abingdon, as compensation for others held by him, but granted to Abingdon by his father (S 937; translated in *EHD*, i, n. 123).

Tenth-century kings habitually elevated their close kinsmen to high office. Eadwig, for example, appointed two of his cousins to ealdordoms – Ælfhere and Ælfheah – during the three short years of his reign,[82] Edgar appointed his father-in-law Ordgar as ealdorman of Devon,[83] and Edward the Martyr gave an ealdordom to his kinsman Æthelweard.[84] Moreover, prominent new men were routinely absorbed into the royal kindred through marriage. Ulfketil Snilling, the leader of East Anglian resistance against the Vikings in the 1010s, was given one of Æthelred's daughters in marriage.[85] In much the same manner Uhtræd, who defended Northumbria against both the Scots and the Danes, was provided with another of Æthelred's daughters.[86] Eadric Streona, yet another rising star unconnected, so far as we can tell, to Æthelred or his *witan*, was married into the royal family soon after his first appearance as ealdorman.[87] Thus, the impulse of English kings to appoint their relatives to high office and to bind themselves affinally to secular officials formed one of the bases of their political practice.

This genealogical sketch only begins to describe the carefully crafted alliances of the tenth century. Because so much information has been lost or has gone unrecorded, it is often impossible to name great men's maternal kin, or the kin of their wives; and although there is every indication that ealdormen had more than one godparent, their sponsors are rarely identified.[88]

---

[82] Both these men attest as thegns in Eadred's authentic charters. Ælfhere must be Eadwig's earliest appointment as ealdorman. Eadwig made two grants to him in the first months of his reign, addressing him as 'ealdorman'. Ælfheah witnessed these grants as a thegn (S 587, 588), and Ælfhere attests as an ealdorman before his brother (S 581, 584). Ælfheah attests in the first year of Eadwig's reign as a *cyninges discthen* (S 597, 1292) and *minister* (S 610, 590, 594). From the end of 956 onwards, however, he also signs as an ealdorman (S 604, 619, 645, 639, 653).   [83] See above, n. 58.

[84] Æthelweard first attests as ealdorman in 973 (S 751).

[85] So reports the unreliable *Jomsvikinga Saga*, c. 51.   [86] *DOD*, p. 216.

[87] Fl. Wig., i, p. 161.

[88] The canons of Theodore and the laws of Ine suggest that most children had at least one sponsor at baptism, and one for confirmation (Canons of Theodore, Book 2, c. 4§8. *Die Canones Theodori Cantuariensis und ihre Überlieferungsformen. Untersuchungen zu den Bussüchern des 7., 8., und 9. Jahrhunderts*, ed. Paul Finsterwalder, vol. 1 (Weimar, 1929); Ine, 76§1, 76§3. Wulfstan suggests the same when he admonishes 'let us love God and follow God's laws, and very diligently practice what we promised when we received baptism – or those who were our sponsors at baptism'. Wulfstan, *Sermo Lupi ad Anglos*, ed. Dorothy Whitelock, 2nd edn (Exeter, 1976), lines 200–4. The earliest bidding prayer to survive, is preserved in an Old English gospel book. Included in its list of those who should receive prayers are godparents (*The York Gospel*, ed. Nicolas Barker (London, 1986), fol. 161v).

Little information, moreover, survives to link the bishops and abbots of the period to secular aristocratic families. It is clear, however, that great monastic kindreds, related in some way to the West Saxon royal house, guided the kingdom's monastic reform in its earliest stages. King Edgar's distant cousin St Dunstan, for example, as well as Dunstan's kinsmen Bishop Ælfheah the Bald and Cynesige Bishop of Lichfield were instrumental in yoking royal power to Benedictine monasticism – one of the most significant developments of the tenth century. Another cadre of monastic kinsmen, Oda Archbishop of Canterbury, his nephew Oswald Bishop of Worcester and later Archbishop of York, Oscytel Bishop of Dorchester, and Thorketil Abbot of Bedford were sponsors of the revival as well.[89] Although nothing survives to link these monks to any secular royal kinsmen, it is likely that such ties existed.[90] Many of the ecclesiastics whose family connections are known to us were members of England's dominant kindreds. Edwin, brother of Ealdorman Ælfric of Hampshire, was abbot of Abingdon.[91] Bishop Ælfwold of Crediton sprang from a prominent West Country family,[92] and Beorhtheah Bishop of Worcester was from a well-to-do Worcester family.[93] From surviving evidence, fragmentary though it is, one can only conclude that the majority of great tenth-century aristocrats, lay and ecclesiastical, were related to other ascendant families and to the king, and that ties of patronage, clientage and friendship enmeshed them all, creating a web of alliances.

Because England's greatest men built their alliances so carefully, it would be unwise for historians to reduce the politics of the tenth century to a simple pallet of kings against aristocrats, of monks against lords, or family against family. The relationships

---

[89] Vita S. Oswaldi, in *Historians of the Church of York*, i, p. 404; *ASC*, s.a. 971 (B, C).

[90] *Vita Sancti Dunstani, Auctore B*, pp. 11, 13, 32; and lxxv, n. 8. Furthermore, Bryhthelm Bishop of Winchester c. 958 was a kinsman of King Edgar (Brooks, *Early History of the Church of Canterbury*, p. 239). Wulfstan the Homilist was the uncle of Beorhtheah Bishop of Worcester (*LE*, ii, c. 87). Ælfric Archbishop of Canterbury was brother of Abbot Leofric of St Albans (S 1488). Ann Williams builds a tantalizing case which links Ælfwine, brother of Ealdormen Ælfhere and Ælfheah to Wulfric brother of St Dunstan, suggesting that Saint Dunstan's brother was perhaps Ælfwine's father-in-law (Williams, 'Ælfhere', pp. 154–5).

[91] S 876; Keynes, *Æthelred*, p. 177, n. 91; Williams, 'Ælfhere', 144 and n. 138.

[92] In his will, S 1492 (translated in *EHD*, i, n. 122), the Bishop leaves a large personal fortune to his well-to-do kinsmen. [93] Hemming, i, p. 266.

enveloping tenth-century kings and their administrative and monastic aristocracies were too compelling and complex. Many of the king's familiars would have been hard pressed to form a faction that excluded all their enemies' kinsmen, and most kings would have found it impossible to move unreasonably against a lord without endangering the position of that man's or his own powerful kindred. Furthermore, these relationships were built upon certain expectations of political behaviour and engendered certain moral obligations. Uhtræd, the earl of Northumbria, for example, was drawn more closely to King Æthelred through gifts of office and marriage. For an historian at Durham, writing in the late eleventh century, the twin bonds of lordship and kinship that Æthelred had forged between them, guaranteed the earl's loyalty absolutely. As the author of *De Obsessione Dunelmi* explains:

Cnut...upon arriving in England with a great multitude of men, sent for Earl Uhtræd and all who he was able to command against King Æthelred, swearing that he would have all honour and power should he agree. Uhtræd, however, had power enough, in as much as he had the earldoms of York and Northumbria, and he refused to do anything to harm his lord and kinsman. 'No reason could persuade me,' he said, 'to act as I ought not. I shall serve King Æthelred faithfully as long as he shall live. *He is my lord and also my father-in-law*, by whose gift I have riches and honor enough. I will never betray him.' And so Cnut had no help from Uhtræd.[94]

'Florence' of Worcester attributes a similar set of impulses to the loyalty of Æthelweard, the son of Æthelmær the Fat. Cnut, so the story goes, wished to procure the death of Ætheling Eadwig, so naturally he turned to the arch-villain Eadric Streona for advice. Eadric informed the king that

he knew another man, named Æthelweard, who would be able to betray [Eadwig] to death more easily then he himself could. He should have a talk with him and promise him a huge reward. Having learned the man's name, the king called [Æthelweard] to him, saying most astutely, 'Thus and thus has Ealdorman Eadric told me, saying that you can betray the Ætheling Eadwig so that he can be killed. Agree now to our counsel, and you will have all the honours and dignities of your ancestors. Bring me his head and you will be dearer to me than my own brother.' [Æthelweard] indeed said that he would seek [Eadwig] out so that he could be killed, if by any means he was able. Nonetheless, he did

[94] *DOD*, p. 215.

not wish to kill him, but promised this as a pretense, *for he was descended from the noblest English family.*[95]

In a period in which guarantees for the good behaviour and faithful service of great men were piteously weak, kinship and lordship created powerful bonds of loyalty,[96] and the intimacy between kings and their councilors, developed through the exploitation of traditional ties, helped to counterbalance regional particularism and poor communication.

This is not to say, however, that all cousins, uncles and lords loved one another and supported one another always. The landscape of high English politics was littered with the victims of familial intrigue. King Alfred and his heirs had periodic trouble with their paternal cousins,[97] and Eadwig and Edward the Martyr were ruined by factions surrounding their younger brothers.[98] Among the greatest magnates we have the Godwinesons, a family that well knew the advantages of familial solidarity, but even they were twice threatened by brotherly squabbles.[99] Among well-to-do thegns we have evidence of stepsons threatening their stepmothers,[100] mothers disinheriting their sons and cousins killing one another.[101] Kinship and lordship created no absolute guarantee of loyalty. That is one reason why, over the course of the last millenium, sophisticated institutions, national armies and political ideologies have been fostered by powerful elites. But in the tenth and eleventh centuries it can be argued that private associations formed the strongest warranties of correct behaviour and loyalty. Anglo-Saxon laws, heroic poetry, homiletic literature and historical events make it clear that these imperfect relation-

[95] Fl. Wig., i, p. 180. Æthelweard is identified by Whitelock as the son of Ealdorman Æthelmær, killed in 1017. (*EHD*, i, 285, n. 1.)

[96] This deliberate advancement of kinsmen coupled with the marriage of high administrative officials is overlooked by Pauline Stafford in her interpretation of Æthelræd's ealdormen not as his allies, but as his opponents. She states that 'separatism is an expression of local noble feeling that their best interests are not necessarily served by absolute loyalty to Wessex'. For Stafford, the leaders of this sentiment are the ealdormen (Stafford, 'The reign of Æthelræd II', pp. 18, 21).

[97] E.g., S. 1507. David N. Dumville provides a catalogue of purges of royal kinsmen in his article, 'The ætheling: a study in Anglo-Saxon constitutional history', *ASE*, 8 (1979), 2–9.

[98] F. M. Stenton, *Anglo-Saxon England*, 3rd edn. (Oxford, 1971), pp. 364–7, 372–4.

[99] Barlow, *Edward the Confessor*, pp. 90–1, 99–101, 233–9.   [100] S 877.

[101] S 1462; *ASC*, s.a. 1046 (E) (*recte* 1049); 1049 (C). Other examples of family difficulties can be found. For mothers and their children squabbling over land see S 1429, 1462; for widows fighting with their in-laws see S 1497; for uncles in conflict with their nephews' children see S 1507.

ships were used, relied upon, and were very often effective. This network imposed a kind of institutionalized amity at the highest level of society and worked hand in hand with the Church to unify England. An investigation of the most important members of English society during this period recalls similarities with the better known and better understood Norman aristocracy of the eleventh century, an aristocracy in which kinship and other associations were central to the success of the Norman dukes.[102] Both aristocracies were, for the most part, united in their purpose and in their interests; both were closely allied to their rulers; and both helped propel their ruling dynasties to success. Like Normandy's duke and his kinsmen, England's kings and aristocrats were able to ensnare new men into their tangle of relationships. And like the Norman aristocracy, English aristocratic kindreds had the advantage of including, after some judicious and at times brutal pruning, no branch that could present competing claims for the kingdom,[103] but whose interests nonetheless moved in tandem with those of the king.

It is difficult to determine the effects of these extended kindreds and family alliances on the governance of England, but it does seem clear that the community of interests fostered by English kings and their closest associates were used in the running of the kingdom. Witness lists from the period's royal diplomas demonstrate how important personal ties were in the governance of the realm. This is clear, for example, in the charters surviving from the happiest portion of Æthelred the Unready's reign. Witness lists appended to diplomas dating from the first quarter century of Æthelred's regime give pride of place to an array of royal and ealdormanly relations. Indeed these lists glory in nepotism. From the beginning of the boy-king's reign to 982, six related ealdorman witnessed all royal *acta*, suggesting that the running of the kingdom rested on the shoulders of a small cabal of close kinsmen.[104] The ealdormen who had responsibilities for

---

[102] David C. Douglas, *William the Conqueror* (Berkeley, 1964), pp. 83–104; Eleanor Searle, *Predatory Kingship and the Creation of Norman Power*, pp. 98–107.

[103] David Dumville argues that in order to be considered kingworthy, one had to have a royal grandfather (Dumville, 'The ætheling', pp. 6, 12).

[104] The periods used here are based on clear breaks in ealdormanly attestations. Attestation lists from the following charters are used for this period: S 834, 837–42. The ealdormen who attest commonly in this period are Ælfhere, Æthelmær, Æthelweard, Æthelwine, Bryhtnoth, and Eadwine. Thoræd attests one of the surviving charters of this period (S 834). He was the king's father-in-law.

Essex, Mercia, Northumbria and Wessex were related through blood or marriage to one another, and Ælfhere, Æthelweard and Æthelmær were members of the royal kindred. Ælfheah was closely allied to the king's mother, and Æthelwine was the foster brother of the king's father. Thus, with the possible exception of Ealdorman Edwin, for whom no genealogical information has survived, the king ruled from the Channel to the Humber with the aid of a close circle of kinsmen. During the course of the year 982/83, ealdormanly attestors changed.[105] Æthelmær, Ælfhere, and Edwin retired or died and two new men – Ælfric of Hampshire and Ælfric Cild – were elevated to the office of ealdorman. Bryhtnoth and Æthelweard were kinsmen both to one another and to Ælfric Cild. Both Ælfric Cild and Bryhtnoth had married Æthelred's kinswomen, Æthelweard was a cousin of the West Saxon kings, and Thoræd, another attestor in these years, was the king's father-in-law. From c. 993 to 1006, that period described by Simon Keynes as Æthelred's 'years of maturity',[106] the king's chief attestors were once again his kinsmen – Æthelweard and Æthelmær (the latter at this point still attesting as a thegn), Ealdorman Ælfhelm, his brother and sons, men who were closely connected to King Æthelred's children; and the thegn and royal kinsman Beorhtweald.[107] In each of these periods the running of the kingdom north and south was facilitated by a single group of kinsmen. Ealdormen of the period have been portrayed as leaders of local sentiment and as 'erstwhile opponents' of the king.[108] But until c. 1000 it appears that the friends and kinsmen who fostered or sponsored one another's children, who were buried in the same sacred grounds, and who left bequests to one another in their wills, formed the backbone of a successful secular administration. The interests of many of them must often have been more closely allied to the king or to their kinsmen who were ealdormen in other parts of the kingdom than to local families in the regions they ruled.

This habit of kings patronizing kinsmen with gifts of high office on the one hand and ruling with the aid of their cousins on the other made the aristocracy more resilient, more cohesive in

---

[105] The attestation lists from the following charters are used for this period: S 843, 845, 848, 850–852, 855–858, 860–862, 864–865, 867–870, 872, 874, 877, 942, 944.

[106] Keynes, *Æthelred*, p. 189. The charters used for this period are S 876–878, 880, 893, 895–907, 909–912, 914–916, 918, 921–922, 926–927, 931, 933–935, 1379.

[107] Either Beorhtweald or his wife was related to the king (*Liber Vitae of New Minster*, p. 58). [108] Stafford, 'The limitations of royal policy', pp. 18, 21.

troubled times. This is particularly clear in three of the great political crises of the tenth century – the two succession disputes between Eadwig and Edgar, and Edward and Æthelred, and the attacks on the monasteries, most notably in Mercia after Edgar's death. Each of these incidents represented dangerous splits in aristocratic opinion, and all three threatened the fragile unity of the English kingdom. But in each case the break was brief, and after peace was restored, factions disappeared. On all three occasions, moreover, no one in the end was dispossessed or deprived of his office. In 957 the Mercians and Northumbrians withdrew from Eadwig's rule and chose his younger brother Edgar as king.[109] Ealdorman Ælfheah remained with Eadwig, as did two other ealdormen, Edmund and Æthelsige, whose families cannot be identified.[110] Another new ealdorman, the king's kinsman Bryhtferth, also appears as an attestor of Eadwig's charters after the kingdom was partitioned.[111] Æthelweard the Chronicler, a kinsman of Ælfheah, almost certainly remained with Eadwig as well.[112] Edgar's court, however, was composed of Ælfheah's brother Ælfhere, Ælfheah's and Æthelweard's kinsman Bryhtnoth, Bryhtnoth's brother-in-law Æthelstan 'Rota', and Æthelwold, Ealdorman of East Anglia.[113] At Eadwig's death in 959 the Mercian ealdormen rejoined the West Saxon court and Edgar became king of all of England. Eadwig's ealdormen were not excluded from power nor were they penalized for their adherence to him. Instead they retained their offices under Edgar. Indeed in Edgar's earliest charters as king of all England, Ælfheah attests second only to his brother Ælfhere and Edmund signs before Æthelwold.[114] During the remaining years of Edgar's reign there was no indication of trouble between Ælfhere, Æthelweard, or Edmund, and any of their ealdormanly friends and kinsmen who were on the opposite side of the succession dispute.

The troubles which arose over the competing claims of the æthelings Edward and Æthelred once again brought to the fore a serious rift in aristocratic opinion, ending in an assassination and a coup.[115] Yet in spite of these troubles, Æthelred's *witenagemōt*

---

[109] *ASC*, s.a. 957 (B, C).   [110] S 650, 653, 654, 656, 657, 658, 660.   [111] S 653.
[112] Æthelweard remembers Eadwig favourably in his chronicle (*The Chronicle of Æthelweard*, p. 55), and his sister was probably married to the king. (See above, n. 56.)
[113] S 674–9.   [114] S 682, 687, 685.
[115] *Vita Sancti Dunstani auctore Osberno*, in *Memorials of Saint Dunstan*, p. 114; Keynes, *Æthelred*, pp. 166–7.

looks very much like those of his martyred brother and revered father, and Edward's appointees Æthelweard, Æthelmær and Edwin maintained their positions after Edward's murder. Once again, after a near-disastrous split, divisions within the aristocracy were healed.

The outcome of the 'anti-monastic reaction', that puzzling episode which followed on the heels of Edgar's death, also suggests that ties of kinship helped protect the kingdom from civil war. Ælfhere, the leader of attacks against Mercian monasteries, was opposed by the sons of Æthelstan Half-King and by Ealdorman Bryhtnoth.[116] Bryhtnoth, however, was a kinsman and associate of Ælfhere's, and they continued to have the closest of dealings after the hostilities had ceased. Edgar's widow, moreover, was one of the champions of the monastic movement, yet she remained an intimate of Ælfhere.[117] That this potentially divisive incident was put to a halt with no major aristocratic rebellions or exiles indicates that relationships within that class could be set right without civil war. Remarkably, then, the kingdom survived two succession disputes and two royal minorities without purges and without the rise of permanent and disruptive factions.

The aristocracy from which these ealdormen were drawn, however, underwent a profound change over a period extending from the latter half of Æthelred's reign to the opening years of Cnut's regime. In these years, under the pressure of renewed and serious Viking attack, the social tendons that drew this class together and bound it to the house of Cerdic loosened and then were severed. An examination of the fate of the members of England's first families and their lands suggests that the old aristocracy was stripped of its wealth and influence, and that the profiteers of this disruption formed a class very different from the one they succeeded. Witness lists clearly illustrate that all but one of this group of men vanished from the court during the period c. 991–1017.[118] Ealdormen, however, grow old, retire and die, so the disappearance of the greatest secular attestors over the course

---

[116] *Vita Sancti Oswaldi*, i, pp. 445–6.

[117] According to the late source, *Liber Monasterii de Hyda*, ed. Edward Edwards, RS (London, 1866), p. 206.

[118] For an analysis of Æthelred's ealdormanly attestations see Simon Keynes, *Æthelred*, table 8. For the attestations of Cnut's earls' see Larson, 'Political policies of Cnut', pp. 725–8.

of twenty-six years is hardly in itself proof of the destruction of the old tenth-century aristocracy. Other more sinister indications of the fate of ealdormen and their families, however, are preserved by chroniclers, who describe these years as an endless tale of exile, mutilation and murder. Ealdorman Ælfric Cild was disinherited and exiled,[119] and Ealdorman Æthelweard and Eadwig the Ætheling were outlawed by King Cnut.[120] Ealdorman Bryhtnoth died in 991 at the Battle of Maldon with a nephew of Ealdormen Ælfheah and Ælfhere.[121] At Ringmere, in 1010, Æthelstan, who was both King Æthelred's brother-in-law and Ealdorman Thoræd's son, was killed along with his own son Oswig. The same encounter took the life of Wulfric, probably the son of Ealdorman Leofwine.[122] Six years later, the Battle of *Assandun* cost the lives of Godwine Ealdorman of Lindsey; Ulfketil Snilling, son-in-law of King Æthelred; Ealdorman Ælfric, the brother-in-law of Ælfhere and Ælfheah; and Æthelweard, the son of Ealdorman Æthelwine 'Friend of God'.[123] Other members of ealdormanly families were mutilated or murdered by order of Æthelred or Cnut. In 993 Ælfgar, Ealdorman Ælfric's son, and in 1006 the sons of Ealdorman Ælfhelm were blinded at King Æthelred's orders.[124] Eight years later, when Cnut was driven from England, the Dane mutilated his aristocratic hostages before setting them ashore.[125] Probably among them was a grandson of Eadorman Leofwine.[126] Wulfric Spot's brother Ealdorman Ælfhelm was killed on Æthelred's orders, as were two important thegns closely connected to his family.[127] Ealdorman Uhtræd, one of King Æthelred's sons-in-law, was murdered at Cnut's command in 1016.[128] In the following year the treacherous Eadric Streona was killed along with sons of Ealdorman Leofwine, Ealdorman Æthelmær, Ealdorman Ælfheah, and King Æthelred.[129] Charters and chronicles, then, record the ealdormen's loss of life, limb, sight and office. Nonetheless, this evidence falls short of proving that

[119] S 937.   [120] Fl. Wig., i, p. 183; *ASC*, s.a. 1017 (C, D, E).
[121] *ASC*, s.a. 991 (A, C, D, E); *Battle of Maldon.*
[122] *ASC*, s.a. 1010 (C, D, E). Æthelstan is so identified by Whitelock, *ASC*, p. 90, n. 4.
[123] *ASC*, s.a. 1016 (C, D, E).   [124] *ASC*, s.a. 993, 1006 (C, D, E).
[125] *ASC*, s.a. 1014 (C, D, E).   [126] Hemming, i, p. 259.
[127] *ASC*, s.a. 1006, 1015 (C, D, E).
[128] *ASC*, s.a. 1016 (C, D, E); *De Primo Saxonum Adventu*, in Sim. Dur., *Opera Omnia*, ed. Thomas Arnold, RS, 2 vols. (London, 1885), ii, p. 383; *DOD*, p. 218.
[129] *ASC*, s.a. 1017 (C, D, E); Fl. Wig., i, p. 182.

the tenth-century aristocracy was stripped of its lands and offices, establishing only that certain of its most influential members were purged. The history of these men's lands, however, and the lands of their kinsmen, strongly suggests that many forfeited their wealth and local influence long before the Norman Conquest.

Hard times dominated the period on either side of Cnut's accession, years which were the ruination of countless landholders. A number of England's most important thegns lost their lives and their land during this period,[130] apparently among them Saint Wulfstan's parents,[131] as well, perhaps, as a number of Kentish thegns, who took refuge after their impoverishment with the community of Christchurch.[132] Monasteries, too, were despoiled, in part through the opportunism of local thugs making the best of bad times, but also because of these communities' inability to pay the heavy taxes levied on their ravaged estates.[133] One suspects that impoverished aristocrats may have lost land because of the heavy burden of geld as well,[134] but many men were deprived of their estates for other reasons. The commonplace of the purge under Kings Æthelred and Cnut suggest that endemic suspicion and widespread treachery may have played some role in aristocratic ruin, especially since treason was a *botleas* crime.[135] Ealdorman Ælfric, for example, committed offences

---

[130] Katharin Mack, 'Cnut's conquest and the English Aristocracy', *Albion*, 16 (1984), pp. 375–87. [131] *Vita Wulfstani*, pp. 7, xxiii.

[132] Brooks, *The Early History of the Church of Canterbury*, p. 261.

[133] Hemming, i, pp. 248–9, 254, 277. For an important discussion of geld and the loss of church land see M. K. Lawson, 'The collection of danegeld and heregeld in the reigns of Æthelred II and Cnut', *EHR*, 109 (1984), pp. 721–38. Sometimes opportunism and the financial embarrassment caused by the inability to pay one's taxes were combined. A grant of King Æthelstan to Crediton, for example, is accompanied by an endorsement dating from Cnut's reign, which notes that a man named Beorhtnoth was granted part of this land by the Bishop of Crediton because the former had lent the bishop 30 mancuses of gold 'for the redemption of his land'. (See S 405 and 1387, printed together in *Crawford Collection*, n. 4 and pp. 76–7).

[134] In Edgar's reign the thegn Ælfric, burdened with a heavy tax, entered into a not all together advantageous agreement with Bishop Æthelwold in which the thegn exchanged some of his land for the cash to pay his taxes (*LE*, ii, c. 11).

[135] V Æthelred 28–31; II Cnut 64. Treachery, not only against king but against lord, was punishable by death (Alfred 4; II Æthelstan 4; III Edgar 7§3). As Alfred had written in the introduction of his laws; after the English converted to Christianity, 'they then established for that mercy which Christ taught, that secular lords might with their permission receive without sin compensation in money for almost every misdeed at the first offence... only for treachery to a lord they dared not declare any mercy' (Alfred, Introduction, 49.7. Text and translation in *Councils and Synods*, 2 vols., ed. D. Whitelock, M. Brett and C. N. L. Brook (Oxford, 1981), pp. 19–20). For examples of forfeiture for treason see S 414, 918, 927, 934, 937, 939.

'both against God and against King', so lost his property,[136] and the biographer of Cnut's wife, Ælfgifu Emma, also records that Cnut executed 'multos principum' for their deceit.[137] In their place arose a number of new men. Some, like Earl Godwine, who was able to amass an enormous estate after his rise to power, were English adherents of the Viking king risen from the dust.[138] Other important landholders were Cnut's Scandinavian followers. Numbering among them were doubtless the powerful Osgot Clapa and his son-in-law Tovi the Proud,[139] as well as their neighbour Thorkil of Harringworth[140] and the housecarl Orc, the founder of Abbotsbury Abbey.[141] Like Earl Godwine, all four of these men were major landholders in the first half of the eleventh century, and the question arises: Where did they get their land?

The purported treachery of the old guard and the rise of new men were doubtless related. Indeed, a story recorded in the *Chronicle of Ramsey* in describing how one of Cnut's important followers came to possess a certain piece of property links the two explicitly:

When King Cnut the Dane acquired the monarchy and was ruler of the English, certain English nobles [having been] traitors to the ancestors of their king [i.e. the English kings before Cnut], were proscribed and exterminated by Cnut's judgement and they relinquished the hereditary right of their posterity and succession ... to the Danish military followers of the king.[142]

Late Anglo-Saxon wills seem to indicate that accusations of treachery commonly caused the overturning of aristocratic

---

[136] S 896.

[137] *Encomium Emmae Reginae*, ed. A. Campbell, Camden Third Series, 72 (1949), p. 30.

[138] For Earl Godwine's rise and holdings see below, chapter 3, pp. 53–69.

[139] The names of both men are included in a list of those who had entered into confraternity with Thorney Abbey alongside King Cnut and his jarls (London, BL Add. 40,000, fol. 10r). The two appear at the top of a list of thirty-one Scandinavian names, names Dorothy Whitelock has argued represent the retinue of Cnut and his earls (Dorothy Whitelock, 'Scandinavian personal names in the *Liber Vitae* of Thorney Abbey', *Saga Book of the Viking Society*, 12, pt 2 (1937–38), pp. 135–6. See also Cecily Clark, 'British Library Additional MS. 40,000 ff lv–12r', *Anglo-Norman Studies*, 7 (1985), pp. 50–68).

[140] According to the Red Book of Thorney. (*Mon. Ang.*, ii, p. 604; identified by Whitelock, '*Liber Vitae* of Thorney', p. 140). After the Conquest Thorkil joined the Danes, 'who were his kinsmen'. (*Mon. Ang.*, ii, p. 604). For further details of Thorkil's career, see C. R. Hart, *The Early Charters of Eastern England* (Leicester, 1966), pp. 236–7).

[141] S 1064; Simon Keynes, 'The lost Abbotsbury cartulary', *ASE*, 18 (1989), p. 230.

[142] *Chron. Rams.*, p. 129.

bequests. A document, preserved at Canterbury, records the suit of a widow who petitioned King Æthelred for the restoration of her husband's will. It had not stood because

the King was told that [her husband] was concerned in the treacherous plan that Swegn should be received in Essex when first he came there with a fleet...[but his] widow begged Archbishop Ælfric, who was her advocate, and [Ealdorman] Æthelmær, that they would beseech the king...[to] give up the terrible accusation, and [that] Æthelric's will might stand.[143]

The King relented, doubtless swayed by the arguments of the Archbishop, hardly a disinterested party, since the will in question included a bequest to Christchurch. Such happy endings, however, were rare. The bequest of another woman, Æthelflæd, shows clearly that the wills of many suspected of treachery were never honoured.[144] Only two estates are recorded in Æthelflæd's bequest and both were left to St Paul's. By the time of the Conquest, however, these lands were in secular hands.[145] A court case preserved in one of King Æthelred's charters suggests that Æthelflæd's estates were forfeited to the King because she illegally gave aid to her brother, Ealdorman Leofsige, who was banished in 1002.[146] If this is the case, not only was the banished ealdorman destroyed, but so too were other members of his family.

The history of the lands of Ælfgifu, the sister of the powerful Ealdorman Æthelweard the Chronicler, suggests that her family, too, suffered in the decade on either side of Cnut's conquest. Ælfgifu's will was drawn up in the heyday of her family's power and disposed of a number of valuable properties.[147] The fate of the lands which Ælfgifu left, however, suggest that her bequest was overturned sometime between the date she made her will and the Norman Conquest. By 1066 two of her estates were being held by the family of that great nouveau, Earl Godwine,[148] and two others were in the hands of Godwineson retainers.[149] All of her pious donations – to Old Minster, New Minster, Romsey,

[143] S 939.   [144] S 1495.

[145] The two estates are Laver, Essex, and Cockhamstead, Hertfordshire. According to evidence in Domesday Book, Cockhampstead was held by Gauti, a well-to-do thegn and housecarl of Harold Godwineson. Laver in 1066 was divided between several secular holders. There is no indication that any of this land had been leased by St Paul's to their 1066 holders (DB, i, 137v; ii, 30b 31a; and below, chapter 3, n. 155).

[146] S 926; Fl. Wig., i, pp. 155–6; and *Wills*, p. 176.   [147] S 1484.

[148] Haversham and Princes Risborough, Buckinghamshire, were held, according to Domesday Book, by Countess Gytha and Earl Harold. (DB, i, 148r, 143v.)

[149] Wing, Buckinghamshire, and Berkhamsted, Hertfordshire. (DB, i, 146r, 136v.)

Abingdon, and Bath – were in secular hands by 1066.[150] It is clear, then, that Ælfgifu's bequests were never honoured, either because her will did not stand, or because her kinsmen received a life interest in these estates, and then lost them when they were dispossessed. Ælfgifu's grandnephew was murdered at the orders of King Cnut in 1017, and her grandniece's husband exiled in 1020.[151] It is likely that their débâcles were accompanied by the ruin of dependants and close family. These deaths and exiles may have precipitated the division of the land in Ælfgifu's will among Cnut's new favourites, particularly Earl Godwine.

The will of Wulfric Spot, the brother of Ealdorman Ælfhelm, tells a similar tale. Of the dozens of estates which Wulfric bequeathed to his kinsmen, one was part of the *terra regis* by 1066 and another nine were in the hands of King Edward's earls, none of whom were related to Wulfric's family. At least five other estates, which Wulfric had granted to his foundation, Burton Abbey, were also in the earls' hands by 1066.[152] Wulfric Spot's brother, Ealdorman Ælfhelm was murdered and his sons blinded by King Æthelred's orders in 1006, and nine years later two of his family's closest allies were assassinated.[153] These men were beneficiaries in Wulfric's will, but the majority of the land left to them fell to Cnut's earls. Moreover, the Abbot of Burton by the middle of the Confessor's reign was Abbot Leofric of Peterborough, the nephew of Earl Leofwine, and pluralist extraordinaire.[154] Much of Ætheling Æthelstan's will was overturned as well. Marlow, Buckinghamshire, which he had bequeathed to Old Minster, was divided by 1066 between Earl Ælfgar, Queen Edith, a man of the Confessor's, and a man of Ansgar the Staller. Earl Godwine held Rotherfield, Sussex, and Chalton, Hampshire, and Compton was held from him.[155]

---

[150] There is no indication that any of this land was leased to these men by ecclesiastical communities (DB, i, 143v, 144r, 144v, 146r, 150v, 151v, 153r).

[151] *ASC*, s.a. 1017 (C, D, E); 1020.

[152] S 1536. Edward the Confessor's earls held the following estates bequeathed to members of Wulfric's family: Conisborough, Rolleston, Wirral, Harlaston, Elford, Wales, Doncaster and Tonge. Estates he had bequeathed to ecclesiastical institutions that were possessed by the king or the earls are Longford, Sutton Maddock, Tathwell and probably Sharnford (DB, i, 263r, 248v, 246v, 321r, 246v, 321r, 246v, 319r, 379r, 307v, 253v, 257v, 259r, 363v, 236r).   [153] *ASC*, s.a. 1006, 1015 (C, D, E).

[154] Knowles, *Heads*, p. 60.

[155] S 1503; DB, i, 16r, 44v, 24r. Similarly, Ealdorman Æthelmær of Hampshire (not the Fat), left land in Cottesmore, Rutland, to his son, but it was in the possession of the sister of Edward the Confessor TRE (S 1489; DB, i, 293v).

44

In another will, Ealdorman Ælfheah left two estates, Faringdon in Berkshire and Aldbourne in Wiltshire, to his brother Ealdorman Ælfhere. Both were held by Earl Godwine's family by 1066.[156] The two brothers were also the beneficiaries of a number of royal grants. Only a few of the lands involved in these transactions can be traced forward to Domesday Book. Of these, several were held by the Church in 1066.[157] The history of the remaining land suggests that the fortunes of the family declined markedly after the brothers' deaths. Merton, granted to Ælfheah in 967, was in Earl Harold's hands TRE.[158] The earl also held Henstridge in Somerset, which had been granted to Ælfheah in Eadred's reign.[159] Westbury-on-Severn in Gloucestershire, one of Ælfhere's estates, was part of the *terra regis* by 1066.[160] In total, 130 hides of land granted to these brothers can be identified as land held by the King or the Godwinesons in Domesday Book. This is almost a fifth of the hidage which Ann Williams estimates that Ælfhere held during his lifetime.[161] In 1016 the family of Ælfhere's kinsman Æthelweard the Chronicler was ruined. It is hardly surprising that large amounts of land slipped through the family's fingers. A few of these estates may have been attached to the office of ealdorman and simply reverted to the king when the ealdormen died. But manors, like Aldbourne and Faringdon, bequeathed to Ælfhere in his brother's will or the four estates which Wulfric Spot left to his brother Ælfhelm, were heritable. Aldbourne was held by Earl Godwine's wife in 1066, and she was not an office holder, and Ælfhelm's land was held by earls TRE. These must have become available after Ælfhelm's and Ælfhere's deaths, not because they then no longer held an office, but because their lands, including those held personally, had fallen to the king.

The history of estates that another family of ealdormen bequeathed to its own monastic foundation also suggests

---

[156] S 1485; DB, i, 57v, 65r.

[157] Sunbury, Middlesex, was in Westminster's hands (DB, i, 128v). The charter is preserved in a Westminster manuscript. (S 702; Westminster Abbey WAM X). Knoyle, Wiltshire, was held by Wilton TRE (DB, i, 68r). The charter is preserved in the Wilton cartulary (S 531; BL Harley 436, fols. 1–3).   [158] S 747; DB, i, 30r.

[159] S 1736; DB, i, 91v.

[160] S 1747; William of Malmesbury, *De Ant. Glast.*, c. 62; DB, i, 163r. The two other estates held by laymen TRE, which can be traced to Domesday Book, are Compton Beauchamp, Berkshire, held by Almær in alod (S 564; DB, i, 61r) and Olney, Buckinghamshire, held by Burgræd (S 834; DB, i, 145v).

[161] Williams, 'Ælfhere', p. 151.

dispossession at the highest level. Ealdorman Ælfgar and his two daughters, Æthelflæd and Ælfflæd, who were also the wives of ealdormen, were major benefactors of a monastery at Stoke by Nayland in Suffolk. Wills left by these three record the family's generous benefactions over the course of half a century.[162] Ælfgar's will, closing with a prayer and a curse, warned that anyone altering his bequest could 'never repent it except in the torment of hell'. But neither the fires of hell, nor the advocacy of the powerful Ealdorman Æthelmær, promised to one of the benefactresses of Stoke when she made her will, could save the family's foundation. By 1066 the monastery of Stoke had disappeared without a trace.[163] The vill in which it had been located was held by Robert fitz Wimarc. Robert, a Breton, was certainly one of the new men who accompanied Edward the Confessor from Normandy when he was made heir to the English throne.[164] Besides the vill of Stoke, Robert also held a number of other estates which the family of Ælfgar had left to the Abbey – Mersea, Polstead, Stratford St Mary, Peldon, Balisdon and Withermarsh.[165] Although Robert was no relation to Ælfgar's family he profited greatly from the demise of its *eigenkloster*. In the forty years between the time the youngest of Ælfgar's daughters made her will and the accession of Edward the Confessor, a likely time for the bequest to have fallen was 1017, when the son and successor of Stoke's advocate and a kinsman of its founders was murdered by King Cnut.[166] Around this same time the will of Ælfhelm Polga, a close associate of Æthelflæd's husband, was also compromised.[167] He bequeathed Cockayne Hatley and Potton, Bedfordshire, to the brothers Almær and Alstan. Both estates were held by Earl Tostig in 1065.[168] Similarly, the land Ælfhelm had left to his wife in Baddow, Essex,

---

[162] S 1483, 1494, 1486. For the identification of Stoke see *Wills*, p. 105.
[163] Simon Keynes, 'A tale of two kings: Alfred the Great and Æthelred the Unready', *TRHS*, 5th series, 36 (1986), p. 207, n. 43.   [164] DB, ii, 401a.
[165] DB, ii, 42b, 46b, 401a, 402a.
[166] *ASC*, s.a. 1017 (C, D, E). A similar situation may lie behind all the lands described in Hemming as lost by Worcester during the reign of Æthelred (Hemming, i, p. 251). Clifton on Teme was a royal manor by 1066 (DB, i, 176v), while Kyre, Hamcastle and Tenbury were all held by another of the Confessor's new men, the Norman Richard fitz Scrope (DB, i, 176v; Fl. Wig., i, p. 210). It looks suspiciously as if an aristocratic bequest to Worcester was confiscated *in toto* during Æthelred's reign, absorbed into the royal fisc before the arrival of the Confessor, and then granted out to a royal favourite.
[167] S 1487.
[168] DB, i, 217v. The *Chron. Rams.* claims that Ælfhelm left these estates to Ramsey (c. 30).

was in the hands of the Edwardian Earl Ælfgar by the middle of the century.[169]

Not all the descendants of ealdormen were dispossessed, and not all of their bequests failed. Two families of great importance during the late tenth century, those of ealdorman Uhtræd and Ealdorman Bryhtnoth, survived with their estates and their religious houses more or less intact. Ealdorman Bryhtnoth, his wife, children and grandchildren, were generous, indeed enthusiastic, patrons of Ely.[170] The bulk of their gifts made over a century of donation were still in Ely's hands at the time of the Norman Conquest.[171] The family also probably retained a large portion of its land across the decades. In 1066 the wife of Bryhtnoth's great-grandson, invariably described by the Domesday scribe as *Alid quaedam femina*, was one of the wealthiest landholders in East Anglia.[172] In the far north, Ealdorman Uhtræd's offspring from his union with King Æthelred's daughter retained wide estates and a lively interest in the community of St Cuthbert's. Neither of these families, however, were involved, as their ancestors had been, in high politics. None of their descendants ever, so far as we can tell, attested a single charter of Edmund Ironside, Cnut, Harold, Harthacnut or Edward the Confessor, although, admittedly, few charters survive. These families, so the period's scant charter evidence suggests, were effectively disenfranchised. Unlike their more famous ancestors, they did not attend the king's court; nor did they give him council. Instead, still holding many of the estates they had gained in their glory days, they sank back into the local aristocracy. Indeed, Earl Uhtræd's offspring expended much of their considerable resources and energy disrupting northern society with a bloody sixty-year feud and charting an independent course for Northumbria.[173] The ousting of these two families from court may in some way explain the periodic uprising of at least some

---

[169] DB, ii, 21b; Cyril Hart, 'The Ealdordom of Essex', *An Essex Tribute. Essays Presented to Frederick G. Emmison*, ed. Kenneth Neale (Colchester, 1987), pp. 70–1.

[170] *LE*, ii, c. 62–4, 67, 88, 89.

[171] *LE*, pp. 422–3. It is little wonder that the monks of Ely sang so merry during Cnut's reign.

[172] Mack calculates that she held about £100 of land ('Kings and Thegns', appendix I).

[173] The feud is described in detail in *DOD*. William E. Kapelle, however, has developed an elaborate theory to discount the famous feud *as* feud, and explains the killings as pure politics (*The Norman Conquest of the North: The Region and its Transformation 1000–1135* (Chapel Hill, 1979) pp. 16–24).

East Anglian and Yorkshire thegns as well as the extreme independence of Northumbria during this period. It may also, in part, explain why resistance against the Normans after 1066 was most effective in Northumbria and in eastern England. The Danish Conquest came to pass only after the greatest of England's families were destroyed. It took thirty years. The chilling rapidity of the Duke of Normandy's take-over stands out in stark contrast to this lumbering defeat, and it was made possible by this carnage of Cnut. The men who William fought, even including England's king, had gained power, estates and a following in the half century after Cnut's conquest, but they did not have time to consolidate their power. So they fell quickly. Only in Northumbria and the east were English aristocrats able to carry out a large-scale rebellion against the Normans, and it was here that we have evidence for the survival of the tenth-century aristocracy. Perhaps it was not only the soggy ground around Ely or the north's long tradition of independence that accounts for such hard-fought resistance.

Thus an examination of the surviving vernacular and Latin wills illustrates that many of the lands of those closely associated with Ealdormen Ælfgar, Bryhtnoth, Leofsige, Æthelmær, Æthelweard, Uhtræd, Ælfheah, and Ælfhere fell to the king or his new secular officials in the decades surrounding the millennium, or that the survivors of these once great kindreds disappeared from the *witenagemot*.

The new men who rose under Cnut differed fundamentally from the ealdormen they replaced. In the years immediately following his accession, Cnut ruled, as medieval kings so often did, with the aid of his kinsmen. Between the years 1017 and 1024 he packed the ranks of the earls with his cousins, brothers-in-law and ritual kin.[174] But he gradually abandoned this practice when rebellions in Denmark and Sweden compromised the loyalty of his relations.[175] In their stead, he promoted Englishmen short on family histories but long on personal loyalty. The antecedents of one of these men, Earl Godwine, are so obscure that his family cannot be traced back a single generation.[176] Another of Cnut's lieutenants, Earl Leofric, had a slightly more distinguished family. Leofric's father Leofwine had risen under Æthelred to become

[174] Larson, 'Political Policies of Cnut', pp. 725–8, 730–1.
[175] *Ibid.*, p. 734; Thorkil the Tall was exiled in 1021 (Fl. Wig., i, p. 183), Hakun in 1029 (Fl. Wig., i, p. 184; *ASC*, s.a. 1030 (C)).   [176] Freeman, *NC*, i, pp. 475–82.

Ealdorman of the Hwicce, but his connections to the king and to other ealdormen cannot be traced.[177] Leofric's brother, Northmann, who initially succeeded his father, was murdered by King Cnut in 1017.[178] After 'Florence' notes Northmann's innocence and his murder, he adds disapprovingly that Cnut 'appointed Leofric ealdorman in his brother's place, and afterwards treated him with great kindness'.[179] Earl Siward, a Dane and the third man in Cnut's new triumvirate of earls, was married to a granddaughter of Ealdorman Uhtræd.[180] His wife's grandmother, however, was not Uhtræd's third wife, the daughter of King Æthelred, but the ealdorman's first wife, so Siward had not even the most distant of relations with the old royal kindred.[181] Thus, in the span of a decade and a half the leading members of England's dominant kindreds were disgraced or killed, and their families' power and possessions arrogated by three new men. The same close ties that allowed extensive families to prosper together in good times tended to bring them all down in a heap in periods of decline. Moreover, the strength of these bonds appear to have been sorely tested from 1000 onwards, as the greatest men in the kingdom were defeated in battle or were killed, and as King Æthelred began promoting too many new men, too quickly; men whose interests were not always in line with those of the old guard.[182] Even ties within families seem to have weakened under the strain of prolonged invasion. In the 990s Ælfric the Homilist, envisioning the end of the world and pondering on a text in Matthew,[183] described how fathers, sons and brothers would

---

[177] For Leofwine, see Robertson, *Charters*, p. 396.   [178] *ASC*, s.a. 1017 (C, D, E).
[179] Fl. Wig., i, p. 182.
[180] *DOD*, i, pp. 215–17.

Bishop Aldhun		Styre	King Æthelred	
Ecgthryth = (1) Uhtræd = (2) Sige			= (3) Ælfgifu Edulf Cudel	
Ealdræd Eadulf Gospatric			Eadlgyth = Maldred	
Ælffæd = Siward				

This was not the cosiest of families. Siward killed his wife's step-uncle Eadulf on Harthacnut's orders (*ASC*, s.a. 1041 (C, D); Sim. Dur., *Opera Omnia*, i, p. 91). Eadulf, before his death, fought against his step-sister's brother-in-law, Duncan I of Scotland (Sim. Dur., *Opera Omnia*, ii, p. 198).   [181] *Ibid.*, i, p. 217.
[182] As old families were disgraced, new men and their kin began to appear among the *witan* of King Æthelred's councils. Eadric Streona's new prominence at court, for example, was accompanied by the appearance of his kinsmen high on the witness lists of Æthelred's charters (Keynes, *Æthelred*, pp. 212–13).   [183] Matthew 10:21.

destroy themselves by turning against one another.[184] This picture of the social order gone awry perhaps reflected Ælfric's own world, a world increasingly dogged by pagan armies and local defeats. One of Ælfric's older contemporaries's rendition of the story of the Seven Sleepers, a salutary tale of pagan persecution, must have reminded its hearers of modern times:

Kinsmen beheld how their kinsmen were martyred and hung as a spectacle on the borough walls. And a brother beheld his sister in torment and a sister watched her brother in misery. The father forsook his child and the child forsook his father, and at last each friend and kinsman abandoned the other because of the great horrors they saw ...[185]

Archbishop Wulfstan, fastening on to this theme and the same text in Matthew after a dreadful decade of defeat and humiliation, explicitly linked the unravelling of traditional association with the troubles of Æthelred's reign, lamenting in his *Sermo Lupi ad Anglos* that ties of kinship had lost their power, much to the detriment of the kingdom:

For many years now there have been in this land many injustices and unsteady loyalties among men everywhere. Now very often kinsmen will not protect a kinsman any more than a stranger, nor a father his son, nor sometimes a son his own father, nor one brother another...Many are forsworn and greatly perjured, and pledges are broken over and again; and it is evident in this nation that the wrath of God violently oppresses us.[186]

The deaths and purges under Æthelred and Cnut did not, of course, foreclose the possibility of future kings governing in association with royal kinsmen. But the last Anglo–Saxon monarchs appear not to have seized this opportunity. The Confessor's grandnephew Cospatric, for example, was a powerful Northumbrian thegn, but the Confessor never exploited this tie by appointing him to high office.[187] He was passed over first in favour of a distant relative who was not a member of the royal kindred, and second in favour of one of the sons of Earl

---

[184] Ælfric, *De Oratione Moysi*, printed in *Ælfric's Lives of the Saints*, ed. Walter W. Skeat, *The Early English Text Society*, 2 vols. (Oxford, 1881–85), i, p. 304.

[185] The text is printed in *ibid.*, i, p. 494. For the date and authorship of this work see P. Clemoes, 'The chronology of Ælfric's works', in *The Anglo-Saxons: Studies in Some Aspects of their History and Culture presented to Bruce Dickins*, ed. P. Clemoes (London, 1959), p. 219, n. 2.

[186] Wulfstan, *Sermo Lupi ad Anglos*, lines 61–8 (trans. *EHD*, i, n. 240).

[187] *DOD*, pp. 215–17; Kapelle, *The Norman Conquest of the North*, p. 26.

Godwine.[188] Odda of Deerhurst, perhaps a descendant of Ealdorman Ælfhere, was elevated to the office of earl, but only briefly during the Godwine clan's year of exile.[189] Ealdorman Bryhtnoth's family ceased attesting royal charters, even those made in favour of Ely, the centre of their religious benefactions.[190] Ealdorman Æthelwine's descendants sank into obscurity, their names no longer listed in Ramsey's *Chronicle* as benefactors. Only a grandnephew of Ramsey's founder is listed, and then as a novice of that house.[191] The survivors of the ealdormanly kindred had fallen on hard times indeed.

The decimation of the old royal kindred in the last years of Æthelred's reign and the opening years of Cnut's regime changed England profoundly. By King Cnut's death, the great office-holding aristocracy had been transformed. The differences between these new aristocrats and their tenth-century predecessors were great. At the time they róse to prominence, the three new families from which the earls were drawn were related to one another neither by blood nor by marriage, and they continued unallied by ties of kinship for three generations.[192] The new families were not interested in the same ecclesiastical foundations, and they did not share the same ecclesiastical friends.[193] More serious still, none of these families owed their position to the Confessor, nor traced their descent back through former West Saxon kings. Only the Godwinesons were joined to the king through marriage, but since this alliance was without issue, the bond remained tenuous.[194] The lands and authority of the ancient

---

[188] *Ibid.*, p. 217; *VER*, p. 31.   [189] *ASC*, s.a. 1051, 1052 (E).

[190] S 958, in favour of Ely, was not attested by any of Bryhtnoth's wealthy kinsmen.

[191] *Cart. Rams.*, iii, 165–7.

[192] It was not until Earl Harold was elected king that the families of Earl Leofric and Earl Godwine allied themselves through marriage (OV, ii, pp. 138–40).

[193] Frank Barlow, *The English Church 1000–1066*, 2nd edn (London, 1979), pp. 56–62. Leofwine's family, for example, was a dispoiler of Worcester (Hemming, i, pp. 259, 260, 264, 278), while the sons of Earl Godwine were Wulfstan's close allies (*Vita Wulfstani*, pp. 13, 16). The Godwinesons were also allied to Stigand and the Bishop of Hereford. Harold was remembered as a patron of Durham. (Harold Godwinesons's obit is recorded in the *Liber Vitae Ecclesiæ Dunelmensis*, ed. Joseph Stevenson (London, 1841), p. 146. The names of Harold's father and brother Tostig at one time appeared in gold letters in the list of kings and earls who were commemorated in the *Liber Vitae*, but an attempt was made to erase their names some time after they were written (*ibid.*, p. 2). Earl Leofric, the son of Earl Leofwine, and his family were particularly close to Leofric's simoniac nephew Abbot Leofric, and patronized his churches (Barlow, *The English Church*, pp. 56–7).   [194] See below, chapter 3.

aristocracy were thus passed to men who were neither closely bound to the king nor linked to the kingdom's other great families. As a result, the ruling oligarchy no longer shared that community of interests or pursued those same familial strategies that the earlier aristocracy had. Its breaches and factions became more dangerous, its enmity more intense. A quick glance at the rebellions of the last fifteen years of the Confessor's reign exemplifies the rift between aristocratic families and between the king and his earls. Earl Godwine and his sons, Harold, Swein and Tostig, were exiled in 1051, only to be reinstated in 1052 when they returned to England and intimidated King Edward with a show of force.[195] Swein and Tostig rebelled on other occasions;[196] Earl Ælfgar, the son of Earl Leofwine, rebelled twice;[197] Osgot Clapa and Eadric of Laxfield, two of the greatest thegns of Edward's reign, each rebelled at least once;[198] a great number of Wessex thegns rose against the king in 1051 and again in 1052 in support of Earl Godwine and his sons;[199] and the Northumbrian aristocracy rebelled against Earl Tostig in 1065.[200] This was indeed an aristocracy without cohesion and a monarchy in crisis.

[195] *ASC*, s.a. 1051, 1052 (C, D, E).   [196] *ASC*, s.a. 1048 (E); 1065 (C, D).
[197] *ASC*, s.a. 1055, 1058 (C, D, E).
[198] *ASC*, s.a. 1046 (C); Fl. Wig., i, p. 202; DB, ii, 286b.
[199] *ASC*, s.a. 1051, 1052 (C, D, E).   [200] *ASC*, s.a. 1065 (C, D).

Chapter 3

NEW MEN AND THE WANING OF THE WEST SAXON MONARCHY

Edward the Confessor's reign is not an easy one to study. The twenty-three years Edward ruled are represented by only sixty-four charters,[1] and of these, twenty-nine are dubiously worded, highly interpolated, or outright forgeries.[2] There is a fine run of writs, a hundred in all,[3] but half are addressed to just three monasteries – Westminster Abbey, Bury St Edmunds and Wells – and unlike their Norman successors, these instruments include no witness lists and so preserve no record of the king's advisers. The narrative sources for the reign, however, are quite full by English standards. The various versions of the *Anglo-Saxon Chronicle* give interestingly divergent and biased accounts of important events in the reign, in particular Earl Godwine's rebellion in 1051, his family's reinstatement in 1052, and the 1065 Northumbrian revolt. There is also a contemporary biography of the Confessor, the *Vita Ædwardi Regis*, which provides a glimpse of the English court and its habitués on the eve of the Norman Conquest. Both the chronicles and the biography preserve disturbing hints of the overweening power of Cnut's most famous creation, Earl Godwine, and of the weakness of the Dane's eventual successor, King Edward. Other evidence, however, presents a different picture. The coinage of the Confessor's reign, terrible in the early years, but impressively reformed in the early 1050s, points to the peace and prosperity of the period and highlights the remarkable efficiency of late Saxon royal administration.[4] The fine and showy manuscripts produced in Edward's lifetime, such as the Harley Psalter, the Prayer Book of Ælfwine, New Minster's *Liber Vitae*, and the Tiberius and Winchcombe

---

[1] S 998–1062.

[2] S 1000, 1002, 1011, 1018, 1026, 1029, 1030, 1035, 1036, 1037, 1038, 1039, 1040, 1041, 1042, 1043, 1045, 1047, 1048, 1049, 1051, 1052, 1054, 1055, 1056, 1058, 1059, 1060, 1062.　　　　[3] S 1063–162.

[4] H. Bertil A. Petersson, *Anglo-Saxon Currency* (Lund, 1969), pp. 226–32.

Psalters, are indications, too, of a prosperous era. English victories against the Scots, the Welsh and the occasional Viking raider in the 1040s, 50s, and 60s, and the kingdom's intervention into international affairs suggest a confident and forward-looking monarch.

Because our evidence is patchy at best and contradictory in the most confounding of ways, two very different interpretations of Edward's reign have emerged. Some assert that the Confessor's England prospered under a sophisticated and successful royal administration. The leader of this historical camp, Professor Frank Barlow, in his studies of the Confessor's reign, *vita*, and Church, concludes that Edward's tenacious ability to hold on to his kingdom, despite his troubled beginnings as an exile and as the son of a failed king, suggests a competent, manipulative and active ruler.[5] As evidence, Barlow points to the kingdom's prosperity, the court's effective machinery of government, and the native Church's occasional distinction. Other historians, particularly Normanists such as David Douglas and R. Allen Brown, but also pre-Conquest scholars such as Eric John, maintain that England under the Confessor suffered from fundamental 'structural problems' and view the reign as the first act of the Norman Conquest, which they see not as 'a sudden bolt from the blue [but] the climax of a crisis that had been going on for generations'.[6]

The puzzle of Edward's reign is unlikely to be resolved with another careful examination of the well-worn narrative sources. Such reassessments have tended to produce elaborate theories, woven from the inadequate accounts of laconic, sometimes devious, and usually under-informed chroniclers. If, however, the mass of evidence for the period's alliances and landholding preserved in Domesday Book, its satellites, and pre- and post-Conquest charters is investigated, a clearer representation of Edward's reign is possible. These sources allow us to ask questions of fundamental importance: Who held what land, how did they hold it, and why; and where did the loyalty of landholders, both thegns and ecclesiastics, lie? Answers to these questions suggest that Cnut's formation of a new dependent following had profound and disturbing effects on the politics of Edward's reign. An investigation of landholding and alliance on the eve of the

---

[5] Frank Barlow, *Edward the Confessor* (Berkeley, 1970), p. 287.
[6] Eric John, 'Edward the Confessor and the Norman succession', *EHR*, 94 (1979), pp. 247, 267.

Norman Conquest suggests that England, wealthy and well-administered though it was, had been hijacked by members of an overreaching oligarchy that arose from the shambles of the Viking Wars.

The numerous near-contemporary accounts of the period's aristocratic exiles, rebellions, and coups make it clear that any debate over the success or failure of Edward's reign should centre on the relationship between the king and his leading aristocratic families, in particular those of Earls Siward, Leofric and Godwine, who one contemporary observed 'had been exalted so high, even to the point of ruling the King and all England'.[7] Godwine Earl of Wessex and Siward Earl of Northumbria were involved in English politics long before Edward's coronation in 1043. Indeed, both came to power under Cnut. The former was an Englishman, possibly a South Saxon, who was made Earl of Wessex and Cnut's brother-in-law shortly after the Dane's accession.[8] Despite his impressive marriage and important office, Godwine was a new man, described as such even by his family's apologist.[9] Earl Siward, one of Cnut's Danish followers, was put in charge of Northumbria and York.[10] Once established there, he married into one of the north's grand families, defended the Scottish march and kept the peace, activities advantageous to both the king and himself.[11] Leofric Earl of Mercia sprang from older stock. His father Leofwine and brother Northmann had been ealdormen under Æthelred, although neither were among the wealthiest or most distinguished of Unræd's ealdormen, and Northmann was purged early in Cnut's reign.[12] Leofric, however, prospered under the new king, and both his position at court and his landed wealth surpassed those of his father and brother. By 1043 all three of Cnut's appointees were well established at court. They had

---

[7] *ASC*, s.a. 1052 (D) (*recte* 1051).

[8] *VER*, p. 6. He first attests as *dux* in a charter dated 1018 (S 951). On Godwine's possible South Saxon origins, see Freeman, *NC*, i, pp. 475–82.

[9] '...among the new nobles of the conquered kingdom attached to the king's side [was] Godwine' (*VER*, p. 5). For a synopsis of Godwine's career, see C. E. Wright, *The Cultivation of Saga in Anglo-Saxon England* (London, 1939), pp. 213–17.

[10] Siward first attests as *dux* in 1033 (S 968), but did not gain authority north of the Tees until c. 1041 (Sim. Dur., *Opera Omnia*, ii, p. 198). For the details of Siward's life, see Harmer, *Writs*, p. 572.   [11] *DOD*, p. 219; *ASC*, s.a. 1054 (D).

[12] On Leofwine's place in the hierarchy of Æthelred's attesting ealdormen, see Keynes, *Æthelred*, pp. 213–14 and table 6. For the murder of Northmann, see *ASC*, s.a. 1017 (C, D, E).

played a crucial role in the government of England during Cnut's extended absences.[13] They had kept the kingdom and its administration intact during his sons' short and lack-lustre reigns.[14] Together and separately they engineered the dynastic transition from Harold to Harthacnut to Edward,[15] and they were present at court, willing and able to manage the Confessor's affairs when the new king began his rule as a returning exile.[16]

Each of these men, moreover, had sons who were able to build on their careers and who would come to hold important positions at court and large tracts of land in the shires.[17] Godwine's family included his daughter Edith, Edward the Confessor's wife; and his sons, Swein Earl of the southwest,[18] Harold Earl first of East Anglia and then of Wessex,[19] Tostig Earl of Northumbria,[20] Leofwine Earl of the southeast,[21] and Gyrth Earl of East Anglia and Oxfordshire.[22] Leofric's son, Ælfgar, was made Earl of East Anglia in 1053 and translated to his father's earldom of Mercia in 1057.[23] After Ælfgar's death his eldest son Edwin replaced him as Earl of Mercia.[24] Ælfgar's second son, Morcar, was made Earl of Northumbria after Tostig's disgrace in 1065.[25] Siward's son Waltheof was a child at Siward's death.[26] Although Waltheof never succeeded his father in Northumbria and only obtained an

---

[13] *VER*, pp. 5–6; Fl. Wig., i, pp. 182, 184, 185.

[14] Fl. Wig., i, pp. 191–96; *ASC*, s.a. 1041 (C, D); Stenton, *Anglo Saxon England*, pp. 419–23.

[15] Concerning King Edward's election, the author of the *VER* states that 'Earl Godwine…took the lead in urging that [the English] should admit their king to the throne…and since Godwine was regarded as a father by all, he was gladly heard in the witenagemot' (*VER*, p. 9). Fl. Wig. concurs with this opinion, noting that King Edward became king 'mainly through the exertions of Earl Godwine and Lyfing Bishop of Worcester' (Fl. Wig., i, pp. 196–197). See also William of Malmesbury, *GR*, i, p. 237. For Godwine's support of Harthacnut see *ASC*, s.a. 1035 (E, F); 1040 (C, D). For Leofric's support of Harold, see *ASC*, s.a. 1035 (E).

[16] Fl. Wig., i, p. 197; *VER*, p. 9; William of Malmesbury, *GR*, i, p. 238; *ASC*, s.a. 1043 (D); S 993, 994; Barlow, *Edward the Confessor*, pp. 56–7.

[17] In this, Freeman portrays Godwine as a kind of Victorian papa: 'It is hardly possible to acquit Godwine of being, like most fathers who have the chance, too anxious for the advancement of his own family' (*NC*, ii, p. 21).   [18] *ASC*, s.a. 1046 (C).

[19] *ASC*, s.a. 1053 (C, D, E); *VER*, p. 30. Harold first attests as earl in 1045 (S 1008). For his appearance on East Anglian and Wessex writs, see below, n. 29.

[20] *VER*, p. 31.   [21] S 1130, 1132–1137.

[22] *VER*, p. 33; S 1083–1085, 1139, 1147, 1148.

[23] *ASC*, s.a. 1053 (C, D, E), 1057 (D, E); S 1075–1082, 1156, 1157.

[24] S 1140; Barlow, *Edward the Confessor*, p. 210.

[25] *ASC*, s.a. 1065 (C, D, E); *VER*, p. 50.

[26] Kapelle, *The Norman Conquest of the North*, p. 49. Siward's older son, Osbeorn, died fighting against the Scots in 1054, shortly before Siward's own death (*ASC*, s.a. 1054 (C, D)).

earldom centred on Huntingdonshire and Northamptonshire at the end of Edward's reign, he was able nonetheless to maintain a considerable holding across the northern Danelaw.[27] All of these families, to judge from their attestations on royal charters[28] and from their appearances as addressees on royal writs,[29] played a decisive role in the governance of the realm for half a century. All, moreover, were involved with England's defence and helped to protect the kingdom from increasingly troublesome Welshmen and Scots. For their troubles, the three families were able to accumulate immense fortunes in land and treasure. Godwine and his family were inordinately wealthy. The earl twice gave gilt and manned warships as gifts,[30] and four of his sons made expensive pilgrimages to Rome or the Holy Land.[31] Harold was the second founder and generous benefactor of Waltham Holy Cross.[32] The family had cash enough to purchase the loyalty of a number of

[27] For Waltheof's earldom, see Barlow, *Edward the Confessor*, p. 194, n. 3. For his lands, see below, table 3.1.   [28] See below, appendix 3.1.

[29] Earl Godwine is addressed in a Kentish and a Hampshire writ (S 1091, 1153). Harold appears as the addressee of writs for East Anglia (S 1073, 1074), Essex (S 1128), Dorset (S 1063, 1064), Berkshire (S 1066), Kent (S 1090, 1092), Surrey (S 1093–1095), Herefordshire (S 1101, 1102), Somerset (S 1111–1116), Hampshire (S 1129, 1154), Middlesex (S 1142), Gloucestershire (S 1156) and Devonshire (S 1161). Tostig appears in writs for Yorkshire and Nottinghamshire (S 1067, 1160), and a spurious Northamptonshire writ (S 1110). Leofwine was the addressee on a spurious Kentish writ (S 1120) and writs for Surrey (S 1136, 1137), Hertfordshire (S 1134, 1135) and Middlesex (S 1130, 1132). Beorn, Godwine's nephew, was addressed in two dubious Hertfordshire writs (S 1122, 1123); Gyrth for writs concerning East Anglia (S 1083–1085) and Oxfordshire (S 1139, 1147, 1148); Siward for Huntingdonshire (S 1107), Ælfgar for East Anglia (S 1075–1082) Worcestershire and Warwickshire (S 1156, 1157); and Edwin for Staffordshire (1140).

[30] Fl. Wig., i, p. 195; *VER*, pp. 13–14. The family also had a large fleet of its own (e.g., *ASC*, s.a. 1049 (A)).

[31] For Tostig's pilgrimage see William of Malmesbury, *Vita Wulfstani*, pp. 16–17; *ASC*, s.a. 1061 (D). For Harold's travels see *VER*, p. 33. For Gyrth accompanying Tostig, see *VER*, p. 34. For Swein's pilgrimage see *ASC*, s.a. 1052 (C). On the lavish lifestyle of the English earls see Goscelin of Canterbury, *Miraculi Swituni*, Migne, *Patrologia Latina*, 155, cols. 79, 80.

[32] For Harold's refoundation of Waltham, see *De Inventione Sanctae Crucis nostrae ... apud Waltham*, ed. William Stubbs (Oxford, 1861), pp. 40–9. Both this tract and the *Vita Haroldi* describe the lavish gifts of plate, vestments, reliquaries and tapestries given by Harold (*ibid.*, pp. 40–6; *Vita Haroldi*, printed in *Original Lives of Anglo-Saxons and Others*, ed. Rev. Dr Giles, *Caxton Society*, 16 (1854), pp. 50–1). These sources may exaggerate the generosity of their hero, but an inventory of Waltham's possessions made in 1540 includes at least two items that must have come from the earl: 'A Gospeler of the Saxon Tongue, having thone syde plated with sylver parcell gilte, with ye ymage of Cryst, [and] an other Gospler of the Saxon Tonge, with the Crusifixe and Mary and John having a naked man holding up his hands of sylver gilte' ('Inventory of church goods, a.d. 1540', printed in *The History of the Ancient Parish of Waltham Abbey or Holy Cross*, W. Winters (Waltham Abbey, Essex, 1888), p. 138).

ship crews in 1052,[33] and, according to William of Poitiers, Harold bought himself some expensive Continental alliances.[34] Gytha, Godwine's wife, moreover, is said to have offered the Conqueror Harold's weight in gold for the return of his body.[35] Leofric's family, too, was rich. The earl and his wife founded a Benedictine monastery at Coventry, an extravagantly expensive act of piety,[36] and they granted a number of large estates to other ecclesiastical institutions.[37] Less is known about Siward, but he did found a church in York[38] and seems to have been accompanied on his travels around the north by a legion of paid household retainers.[39]

These suggestions of wealth can be made more specific through a systematic accounting of the earls' and their families' lands, most of which are recorded in Domesday Book. That the estates listed in the Conqueror's survey reflect in some meaningful way the wealth of great landholders on the eve of the Norman Conquest cannot be doubted. The survey is far from perfect. It contains its share of omissions, mistakes and textual difficulties but provides us, nonetheless, with the first, the best and the most systematic survey of landed wealth in medieval Europe. Because Domesday Book is concerned with the holders of land, the location of their estates, and the wealth which accrued from them, it enables us both to estimate the resources of great men in Edward's reign and to determine the areas in which their influence lay. Land, moreover, was the primary source of wealth in this period. The boroughs, coinage and taxation were other sources of revenue, more often for the king than his earls, but both pocketed profits from them.[40] Great lords collected a variety of customary dues, judicial fines and labour services as well, such as sesters of honey, blooms of iron, cartage and the third penny of justice, but these dues were associated with particular estates, and their cash value is usually included in the manorial values given at the end of Domesday entries, in much the same way as are the revenues from

[33] Harold came with nine ships from Ireland in 1052, and Godwine raised a larger fleet at Bruge (*ASC*, s.a. 1052 (C, D, E)).
[34] William of Poitiers, *Gesta Guillelmi*, p. 156.   [35] *Ibid.*, p. 204.
[36] Fl. Wig. i, p. 216; *Mon. Ang.*, iii, p. 192.
[37] S 1232, 1478; Hugh Candidus, *Chronicle*, p. 70; *ASC*, s.a. 1066 (E); DB, i, 252v; Hemming, i, pp. 261–2.
[38] *VER*, p. 31; *ASC*, s.a. 1055 (C, D); Bruce Dickins, 'The cult of S. Olave in the British Isles', *Saga Book of the Viking Society*, 12 (1937–38), pp. 56–7.
[39] *ASC*, s.a. 1054 (D).   [40] Barlow, *Edward the Confessor*, p. 141.

Table 3.1 *The values of estates attributed to comital families in Domesday Book*

County	Godwinesons	Leofricsons	Siwardsons
Bedfordshire	60	—	—
Berkshire	180	—	—
Buckinghamshire	140	30	—
Cambridgeshire	70	60	—
Cheshire	10	140	—
Cornwall	110	—	—
Derbyshire	—	50	5
Devonshire	390	—	—
Dorset	280	—	—
Essex	1970[a]	940[a]	20
Gloucestershire	80	—	—
Hampshire	430	—	—
Herefordshire	140	20	—
Hertfordshire	80	20	—
Huntingdonshire	70	40	5
Kent	340	—	—
Leicestershire	40	30	10
Lincolnshire	200	290	30
Middlesex	90	120	30
Norfolk	760[a]	30	—
Northamptonshire	10	30	20
Nottinghamshire	10	70	—
Oxfordshire	60	60	—
Ribble and Mersey	—	—	—
Rutland	10	—	30
Shropshire	10	210	—
Somerset	290	—	—
Staffordshire	10	160	—
Suffolk	50	40	—
Surrey	220	—	—
Sussex	880	—	—
Warwickshire	—	30·	—
Wiltshire	450	—	—
Worcestershire	30	100	—
Yorkshire	230	810	220
Total	7,700	3,280	370

[a] Includes renders of night's farm, calculated at £105.

pastures and fisheries.[41] Although some of the cash from these holdings went to reeves and other estate farmers, totals of Domesday's manorial renders give an indication of the comparative wealth of great landholders. Thus, the manorial values recorded in Domesday suggest the value and extent of great men's landed wealth for the latter part of the Confessor's reign.

In a perfect eleventh-century polity one would find a handful of aristocratic families in control of estates of about equal value, estates that would provide them with sufficient resources to implement the king's will in the shires, but not enough to overshadow other great kindreds. One would expect to find, as well, the king in possession of a noticeably larger holding than his important lieutenants. This ideal, however, does not describe England in the decade or so before the Norman Conquest. The geographic reach of each of England's *eorlisc* families was dramatically different by the end of the Saxon period. In England proper Siward's son of Waltheof held estates in Bedfordshire, Derbyshire, Essex, Leicestershire, Lincolnshire, Northamptonshire and Rutland, but the bulk of his land lay in Huntingdonshire and Yorkshire. (See table 3.1.) Leofric's family controlled estates in every shire in the kingdom north of Berkshire and Gloucestershire except Bedfordshire, Rutland and the nascent Lancashire. (See table 3.1 and figure 3.1.) The bulk of the Leofricsons' land cut a 'U' across England, running along the border of north Wales, swinging south through Warwickshire, Oxfordshire and Middlesex, and then moving up through Essex, Cambridgeshire, Lincolnshire and Yorkshire. The Godwinesons' greatest holdings lay in the southwest and southeast, in counties in which Leofric's and Siward's families held not a single ploughland. Here their estates rendered more than £100 a year in every shire. (See table 3.1 and figure 3.2.) Their lands, however, were not confined to the south. The family had substantial interests in English Mercia, East Anglia, Lincolnshire and Yorkshire. Only in the northern midlands and along the border of North Wales were their holdings inconsequential. In 1065 the Godwinesons surpassed Siward's family in every county in England from Cornwall to

[41] Much Cowarne, Hereford, for example, had the third penny of three hundreds attached to it TRE. The judicial rights were taken away from this estate after the Norman Conquest. As a result, the value fell by 20 per cent (DB, i, 186r). For a discussion of the manorial resources that make up Domesday values, see John McDonald and G. D. Snooks, *Domesday Economy: A New Approach to Anglo-Norman History*, pp. 85, 94, 108–16.

60

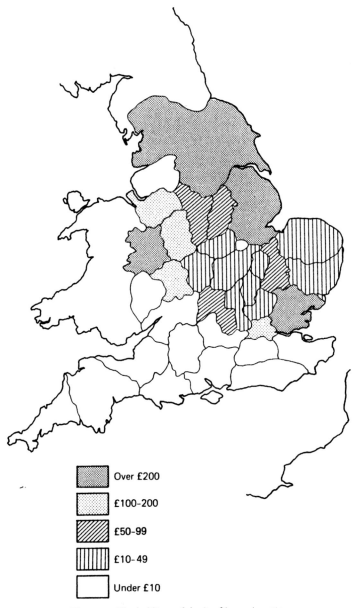

Figure 3.1 The holdings of the Leofricsons in 1065

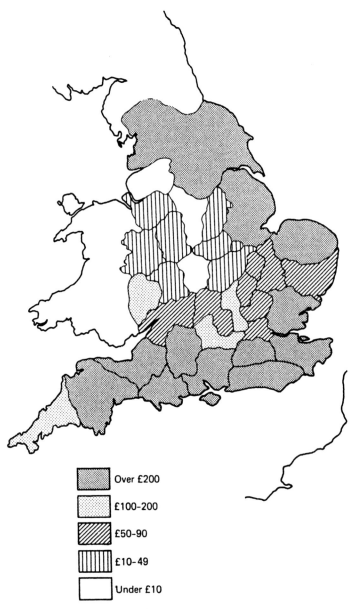

Over £200

£100–200

£50–90

£10–49

Under £10

Figure 3.2 The holdings of the Godwinesons in 1065

Yorkshire, and although they had accumulated less land than the Leofricsons in nine counties, they held more in twenty-three. (See figure 3.3.) The Godwinesons' scattered demesne was worth about £7,500 a year in 1066.[42] Just six months before the Confessor's death, prior to Tostig's rebellion and disinheritance, the family held over £8,400 of land.[43] The Leofricsons for their part held about £3,500 in demesne at the death of the Confessor, and something in the order of £2,700 in 1065. Siward's son Waltheof held about £450 of land in the counties surveyed by the Domesday commissioners TRE. He doubtless held more land north of Yorkshire around Durham and in the Scottish lowlands. Certainly, his father had wielded wide powers in Strathclyde before his death.[44] In England proper, however, he held much less, something on par with the holdings of the kingdom's wealthiest thegnly families like those of Ansgar the Staller and Wulfweard White, who held lands valued respectively at about £480 and £350, nothing near the estate of either the Leofricsons or the Godwinesons.[45] There was, then, by the end of Edward's reign, a wide disparity of wealth among England's comital families. If the lands that all three earls' families held in 1066 are pooled together to form a kind of upper-aristocratic endowment, we find the Godwinesons holding 66 per cent of the total, the Leofricsons 31 per cent and the Siwardsons only 3 per cent. In other words, the Godwinesons had over twice the Leofricsons' landed wealth and seventeen times that of Earl Siward's family. In 1065, before Tostig's fall, the Godwinesons held almost three-quarters of this land, or three times the Leofricsons' holdings. The family's landed wealth can instructively be compared to that of other important landholders. In 1065, for example, the value of

---

[42] This figure was calculated by subtracting the lands attributed to Tostig in Yorkshire, which were doubtless given to Morcar when he replaced Tostig as earl. Values have been calculated on the basis of the following criteria: All values have been added together, whether they are states as values or renders, or given in pounds by tale or by weight. If TRE values are recorded, as is the case for the vast majority of comital holdings, this figure is taken. For those lands which are given no TRE value, the TRW value is taken. Manors that have not been assessed in money, but rather render night's farm, have been valued at £105 (*FE*, pp. 111–12). The results are, of course, only approximations.

[43] This figure is calculated by including Earl Morcar's £560 of land in Yorkshire.

[44] Land which he had most likely gained himself in his war against Macbeth (S 1243 and Harmer, *Writs*, p. 572).

[45] Katharin Mack, 'Kings and thegns: aristocratic participation in the governance of Anglo-Saxon England' (unpublished research paper, University of California, Santa Barbara, 1982), appendix I.

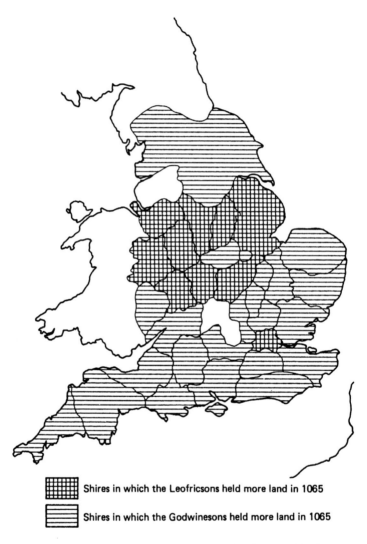

Shires in which the Leofricsons held more land in 1065

Shires in which the Godwinesons held more land in 1065

Figure 3.3 The balance of wealth between King Edward's comital families in 1065

their land was roughly equivalent to the sum total of all land held by England's non-episcopal Benedictine monasteries.[46] Similarly, the family's holdings were greater than those of the wealthiest seventy thegns in England combined.[47] Their estates, moreover, were more valuable and widespread than any aristocratic holdings that came before or after them. Although it is impossible to calculate exactly the landed wealth of tenth-century ealdormen, the impression given by scattered evidence is that even the richest among them had endowments which paled in comparison. Ann Williams has estimated that Ealdorman Ælfhere and his wife held about 750 hides of land.[48] It is not unreasonable to believe that, with his brothers and children, his family held two or even three times this amount. Æthelstan Half-King, his sons and brothers, who had enough land to found a major Benedictine monastery, seem to have been as flush as Ælfhere's family.[49] Even so, the resources of the two mightiest kindreds in Edgar's reign were modest in comparison to those of the Godwinesons, whose holdings were more immense than the unimaginatively large 7,000 hides that Hygelac had granted Beowulf.[50] After the Conquest, too, no single aristocratic family came close to holding what the Godwinesons held. William's two half-brothers, Odo Bishop of Bayeux and Robert Count of Mortain, and Roger de Montgomery and his sons, the largest landholders in post-Conquest England, together commanded fees roughly equivalent in value to the Godwinesons' demesne holdings alone.

The value of the Godwinesons' lands can also be compared to the value of the king's estates. (See tables 3.2 and 3.3.) Before the Confessor's death the size and value of the *terra regis* varied from county to county, but was often exceeded by the land of the Godwinesons.[51] The king did possess more manors, berewicks

---

[46] According to my own calculations the forty-two such houses held just under £8,000 of land TRE. Knowles prints the values of each monastery's holdings TRW in *The Monastic Order in England* (Cambridge, 1963), pp. 702–3.

[47] All those thegns Mack identifies as holding lands valued at £60 or more (Mack, 'Kings and Thegns', appendix I). [48] Williams, 'Ælfhere', p. 151.

[49] For the lands of Æthelstan and his family see Hart, 'Æthelstan Half-King', pp. 136–7.

[50] *Beowulf*, lines 2152–99.

[51] In this study Queen Edith's holdings have been included neither with the *terra regis* nor with the lands of the Godwinesons, since her resources and loyalties are so difficult to determine. Her Domesday property consisted of land in about ninety vills, assessed at some 550 hides and valued at just over £400. As such it was an impressive holding, but its inclusion with the *terra regis* or the land of the Godwinesons makes little difference in the ratio between the two. For Edith as a fully fledged member of the Godwinist camp see Kenneth E. Cutler, 'Edith, Queen of England, 1045–1066',

Table 3.2 *Lands attributed to the Godwinesons in Domesday Book*

County	Numbers of vills in which the family holds	Ploughlands	Value in £s	Night's farm
Bedfordshire[a]	5	50	60	—
Berkshire	15	170	180	—
Buckinghamshire	15	170	140	—
Cambridgeshire[b]	10	50	70	—
Cheshire	5	10	10	—
Cornwall	20	440	110	—
Derbyshire	—	—	—	—
Devonshire[c]	35	920	390	—
Dorset	15	150	280	—
Essex	35	450	290	16
Gloucestershire[d]	5	90	80	—
Hampshire	25	290	430	—
Herefordshire	40	320	140	—
Hertfordshire	10	120	80	—
Huntingdonshire[e]	10	120	70	—
Kent	15	330	340	—
Leicestershire	20	80	40	—
Lincolnshire	65	310	200	—
Middlesex	5	90	90	—
Norfolk[f]	45	230	130	6
Northamptonshire	5	20	10	—
Nottinghamshire[g]	15	30	10	—
Oxfordshire[h]	10	80	60	—
Ribble and Mersey	—	—	—	—
Rutland	5	10	10	—
Shropshire	5	30	10	—
Somerset[i]	20	420	290	—
Staffordshire	5	10	10	—
Suffolk[j]	10	90	50	—
Surrey[k]	10	130	220	—
Sussex[l]	40	730	880	—
Warwickshire	—	—	—	—
Wiltshire[m]	40	350	450	—
Worcestershire	5	40	30	—
Yorkshire	235	230	230	—
Total	800	6,560	5,390	22 (= £2,310)

[a] Domesday only gives TRW values for Bedfordshire *terra regis*. Revenues from these estates were increased by Ivo between 1066 and 1086, but it is unclear by how much (DB, i, 209r–209v).

66

[b] Besides rendering money, Soham, Fordham, Isleham, Cheveley, Wilbraham, Haslingfield, and Chesterton also rendered a partial farm TRE, valued at c. £4 (e.g. Wilbraham) (DB, i, 189r–189v).

[c] The values are taken from Exon DB whenever possible.

[d] The Domesday values for the Gloucestershire *terra regis* are very unsatisfactory. On the one hand Cheltenham, Barton, and Cirencester hundreds rendered £9 5s. each along with a variety of unvalued customary dues (DB, i, 162v). On the other hand, the only value given for Berkeley, Upper Clopton, and Dymock is the amount of cash rendered to King William by Roger of Berkeley, who farmed the three manors in 1086 (DB, i, 163v, 164r). In 1086 he was paying £206 for the three estates. The cash extracted from royal estates in this shire after the Conquest, however, in every case for which we have both TRE and TRW values, more than doubled between 1066 and 1086. Accordingly, I have assigned Berkeley, Dymock, and Upper Clopton a TRE value of £100.

[e] Eynesbury and Paxton have been included among the Godwinesons' holdings, although both are attributed to the Confessor in Domesday Book. It is clear that the two estates were held by Tostig before his fall. Cotton, attributed to Tostig, was assessed in Eynesbury and Buckworth, also attributed to Tostig, was a berewick of Paxton (DB, i, 206v, 205v, 208r).

[f] The values for many royal estates include farms of honey, which are not given a cash value.

[g] The extensive royal estate of Mansfield is not valued in Domesday Book (DB, i, 281r–281v).

[h] King Edward's name is never mentioned in the *terra regis*, but it is clear that Benson, Headington, Kirtlington, Wootton, Shipton-under-Wychwood, and Bampton were all royal manors TRE (DB, i, 154v).

[i] Values are taken whenever possible from Exon DB which, unlike the Exchequer DB, gives 'olim' values.

[j] Two royal estates include honey renders, which are not valued.

[k] The Surrey figures include Ewell, an estate listed under the TRW *terra regis*. No TRE holder is given, but it was doubtless held by Edward (DB, i, 30v).

[l] The two Steyning entries in Sussex are counted as Godwineson holdings (DB, i, 17r, 28r). The first entry clearly notes that Harold held Steyning at the end of Edward's reign and notes that 18 hides and 7 acres of Steyning lay in another Rape. These hides are recorded later in the MS. under Bramber Rape, and are attributed accidentally to King Edward. Other of the king's estates were also divided between two or more Normans after the Conquest, because they included outlying property in rapes other than the one in which the head of the manor lay. Because of this, the king must have held in more vills than is reflected in table 3.3.

[m] The royal estates of Amesbury and Chippenham included unnamed and unnumbered dependencies (DB, i, 64v).

and farms in nine shires; Berkshire, Derbyshire, Dorset, Gloucestershire, Leicestershire, Northamptonshire, Nottinghamshire, Shropshire, and Staffordshire. Two of these, not surprisingly, are in Wessex, the core of Edward's patrimony and the

Table 3.3 *Lands attributed to Edward the Confessor in Domesday Book*

County	Number of vills in which the king holds	Ploughlands	Value in £s	Night's farm
Bedfordshire	5	160	60	1.5
Berkshire	20	380	560	—
Buckinghamshire	5	70	70	—
Cambridgeshire	10	80	130	—
Cheshire	—	—	—	—
Cornwall[b]	5	20	10	—
Derbyshire	45	170	100	—
Devonshire[c]	25	410	250	—
Dorset	20	380	70	4
Essex	—	—	—	—
Gloucestershire	40	220	130	2.5
Hampshire[d]	25	280	340	1
Herefordshire[e]	15	110	30	.25
Hertfordshire[f]	—	—	—	—
Huntingdonshire[g]	10	180	100	—
Kent[h]	5	250	350	—
Leicestershire	35	120	40	—
Lincolnshire	—	—	—	—
Middlesex	5	0	0	—
Norfolk[i]	20	130	70	—
Northamptonshire	40	290	260	—
Nottinghamshire	75	80	70	—
Oxfordshire	5	190	370	—
Ribble and Mersey	40	a	130	—
Rutland	—	—	—	—
Shropshire	70	210	50	—
Somerset[j]	15	420	0	4.75
Staffordshire	10	60	20	—
Suffolk	5	120	90	—
Surrey	5	100	110	—
Sussex[k]	5	220	240	—
Warwickshire	5	110	a	—
Wiltshire[l]	10	350	30	6
Worcestershire	5	40	20	—
Yorkshire[m]	85	160	140	—
Total	665	5,310	3,840	20 (= £2,310)

[a] Information not available.
[b] These figures do not include the twenty-one places attached to Winnianton, which were more likely held by Harold's thegns than by Harold himself.

These lands are valued at £20 10s. (DB, i, 120r).

ᶜ The values are taken from Exon DB whenever possible.

ᵈ Beside these twenty-five vills, the Godwinesons held unnamed and un-numbered dependencies in Hampshire.

ᵉ These figures include the lands in Wales surveyed with Hereford, twenty-six of which are waste with no information on hidation, ploughlands, or value.

ᶠ Hertfordshire figures include only that part of Hitchin held directly by Harold, and not the nine vills loosely associated with it. (DB, i, 132v–133r).

ᵍ Eynesbury and Paxton have been included among the Godwinesons' holdings, although both are attributed to the Confessor in Domesday Book. It is clear, however, that the two estates were held by Tostig before his fall. Cotton, attributed to Tostig, was assessed in Eynesbury and Buckworth, also attributed to Tostig, was a berewick of Paxton (DB, i, 206v, 205v, 208r).

ʰ These figures include £38 of land attributed to Christchurch in Domesday – Sundridge, Langport, and Saltwood (DB, i, 3r, 4v). All three, according to the *Dom. Mon.*, were held by Earl Godwine (*Dom. Mon.*, fos. 3r, 4r).

ⁱ The figures for Norfolk are extremely tentative. In Norfolk it is difficult to distinguish between demesne holdings and the holdings of a lord's man.

ʲ Values are taken whenever possible from the Exon DB which, unlike the Exchequer DB, gives 'olim' values.

ᵏ The two Steyning entries in Sussex are counted as Godwineson holdings (DB, i, 17r, 28r). The first entry clearly states that Harold held Steyning at the end of Edward's reign and notes that 18 hides and 7 acres of Steyning lay in another Rape. These hides are recorded later in the MS, under Bramber Rape, and are attributed, probably accidentally, to King Edward.

ˡ The number of vills does not include a number of unnamed and unnumbered dependencies attached to Gytha's manor of Rushall and Tostig's estate at Corsham (DB, i, 65r).

ᵐ The number of vills includes numerous sokes and berewicks. The value and ploughland figures reflected in this chart are much lower than they actually were TRE, because Domesday does not value nor does it give ploughland information for Tostig's extensive holdings in Amounderness (4 manors and 124 berewicks) (DB, i, 301v).

General notes on tables 2 and 3:

1 The number of vills, rather than the number of Domesday entries, are given in the first column of each table.

2 If no figures for ploughlands are given in Domesday, the figures for ploughteams have been substituted.

3 Totals for each county's ploughlands and values are rounded to the nearest 10, the number of vills to the nearest 5, in order to reflect the approximate nature of these statistics.

4 All figures are based on the 1086 counties.

5 Estates attributed to the Godwinesons in Domesday satellites, but not in the Exchequer Domesday or Little Domesday, are included in these calculations.

Medieval Studies, 35 (1973), pp. 222–31. For Edith as an untrustworthy spouse during periods of conflict between the king and her family, see Barlow, *Edward the Confessor*, pp. 115–16. For Edith as devoted wife, see *VER*.

heartland of the old West Saxon kingdom. In Bedfordshire, Cambridgeshire, Hampshire, Huntingdonshire and Worcestershire the king and the Godwinesons possessed land in about an equal number of villages, but in the kingdom's remaining twenty shires Earl Godwine's sons held more estates in more vills than the king himself. The discrepancy is evident, for example, along the Channel coast from Cornwall to Kent. Here King Edward held land in about 90 vills and the Godwinesons in 150. In Cheshire, Essex, Hertfordshire, Lincolnshire and Rutland, where there were no royal estates, the family held land in anywhere from a handful more vills, as in Cheshire, to sixty-five more in Lincolnshire. In Gyrth's earldom of East Anglia, the family held land in forty more vills, and in Leofwine's southeastern earldom they held land in seventy more.[52] The Godwinesons possessed land in about 70 more villages than the king in Harold's earldom of Wessex and 180 more in Tostig's northern territories.[53] Throughout England the family held land in approximately 200 more villages than the king on the day he died.

The Godwinesons' greater number of farms and villages were accompanied by a greater number of ploughlands and larger annual values. Although the family possessed 180 less ploughlands than King Edward in the East Anglian earldom, they held 870 more in the southeastern earldom, and about 1,100 more in the West Saxon counties. The greater amount of arable land, reflected in ploughland figures, was paralleled by the higher value of Godwine holdings. Although the family's holdings in Wessex were valued at £370 less than Edward's, their estates in the East Anglian earldom were worth £280 more. In the southeastern earldom their estates exceeded the king's by over £2,310, and the family's lands in the Northumbrian earldom rendered about £600 more each year before Tostig's fall. Included among the holdings of both the king and his earls are a number of manors that were not valued in pounds, but rather rendered nights' farm, a customary food rent that was equivalent to approximately £105 per annum.[54] In Norfolk the Godwinesons' manors yielded six nights' farm and in Essex sixteen. Royal estates valued in this manner rendered a total of twenty nights' farm.[55] In all, the estates

---

[52] The configuration of the Confessor's earldoms TRE is taken from Freeman, *NC*, ii, pp. 374–83.   [53] Before Tostig's fall, this figure was closer to 700 more vills.
[54] See above, n. 42.
[55] The king's Cambridgeshire estates of Soham, Fordham, Isleham, Chesterton, Cheveley, Wilbraham and Haslingfield were valued in pounds, but they also rendered

of Harold, his brothers and his mother were valued at £5,400 and twenty-two nights' farm, or about £7,500, and the king's estates about £3,900 and twenty nights' farm, or approximately £5,950. The Godwinesons' lands, therefore, exceeded the total value of the *terra regis* in January of 1066 by £1,550 and slightly exceeded the king's estates in nights' farm. Prior to Tostig's fall in 1065, the value of Godwine estates was probably closer to £8,400, a figure more representative of Godwine holdings during the late 1050s and 1060s than Domesday's figures for 'the day King Edward was both alive and dead'. Thus, the king's lands rendered about £2,500 less revenue each year than the lands of his leading family and were valued at only 70 per cent of the Godwinesons' manorial revenues. (See figure 3.4.) The stretch of the family's territory, the expanse of acres under their ploughs, and the cold, hard cash derived from their estates far exceeded those of the king.

This extraordinary land base not only enriched the Godwinesons, but gave them real power, enabling them, over the course of a couple of decades, to acquire the loyalty of masses of men in the territories where their estates were concentrated. Harold and his brothers attracted a large following, in part because their prodigious holdings allowed them to alienate property to thegns and housecarls hungry for land,[56] but they could also proffer their aid in court and help their dependents to stave off attacks from neighbours or bully local churches into leasing them land.[57] The greater the family's resources and the more offices they held, the more effective and more hotly sought after their lordship was. In return for protection and support, the Godwinesons were

a partial farm of corn, malt and honey (DB, i, 189r,–189v). However, since these Cambridgeshire dues were not valuable like the night's farm rendered by other royal estates, they have not been included in figures for nights' farm.

[56] For example, Harold gave one of his housecarls, Scalpi, two and a half hides in Leighs, Essex, which had been given to the earl by one of his most important men and allies, Ansgar the Staller (DB, ii, 59a). His housecarl Tovi held land in Gloucestershire from him (DB, i, 164r), and Gauti, yet another housecarl, held land from him in Hertfordshire (DB, i, 137v). For other of the earls' housecarls, see Nicholas Hooper, 'The housecarls in England in the eleventh century', *Anglo-Norman Studies*, 7 (1985), pp. 172–4.

[57] Earl Leofric's man, Sigemund, received his lord's help in attaining Crowle from the Church of Worcester (Hemming, i, pp. 264–5), and Earngeat son of Grim got Hampton Lovett from Worcester with Leofric's aid (Hemming, i, p. 260). Æthelnoth Cilt of Kent was able to cheat the canons of St Martin's Dover out of two estates with Harold's help (DB, i, 2r), and Eadnoth the Staller held land in Dorset which Harold had taken from a clerk (DB, i, 80r).

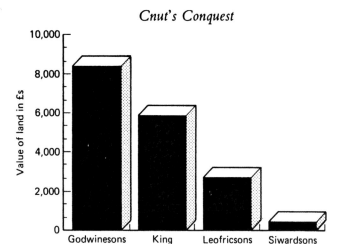

Figure 3.4 The value of lands held by the king and his earls in 1065

provided with service, cash and land.[58] Thegns and freemen in
Hitchin Hundred (Herts.), for example, owed riding and carting
services to Earl Harold,[59] and the freemen of Witham, Essex,
rendered £5 each year to the earl.[60] A number of retainers
bequeathed estates to the Godwinesons, and it is likely that the
heirs of many of the family's men paid a cash heriot to them.[61]
Lordship, therefore, was profitable. It was also a necessary
component of political success because dependents rendered
loyalty and support to lords in their own times of need, swearing
to 'live and die' with them.[62] Not surprisingly, the Godwinesons'
extensive network of men played a crucial role in the family's
political machinations. According to the *Anglo-Saxon Chronicle*

[58] For a general discussion of the obligations of men to their lords, see T. M. Charles-Edwards, 'The distinction between land and moveable wealth in Anglo-Saxon England', *English Medieval Settlement*, ed. P. H. Sawyer (London, 1979), p. 100.

[59] DB, i, 132v–133r.   [60] DB, ii, 2a.

[61] Many must have left family members lands, as did the prosperous East Anglian lady Wulfgyth, who bequeathed Fritton to Earls Godwine and Harold. She may have left Harold land because he was earl of East Anglia, but Godwine was not. It is likely that Wulfgyth granted him land because he was her lord (S 1535). Wulfgyth's son Ketil left Harold a half an estate at *Moran*. He also left Stigand *mine louerd* Harling and his heriot, as was customary among minor thegns who apparently paid relief to their lord and not to the king (S 1519; *Wills*, pp. 202–3). Appended to a Domesday description of the city of York is a list of customary rights belonging to the king and the earl. Included among these, we are told that those thegns with six manors or less 'give to the Sheriff three marks of silver for relief' (DB, i, 298v). When the sheriff did not receive this payment, then perhaps the lord that stood between these men and the king received their relief, as is suggested by II Cnut, 71§1–71§5.

[62] *ASC*, s.a. 1052 (C, D); Rosemary Woolf, 'The ideal of men dying with their lords in *Germania* and in *The Battle of Maldon*', *ASE*, 5 (1976), pp. 69–81.

and the *Vita Ædwardi Regis*, family retainers came to Godwine's aid in 1051, when the earl and his sons challenged the king and his chief Norman adviser Robert of Jumièges, and again in 1052 when Godwine returned from exile in triumph.[63] These two narratives, however, speak of the family's adherents only in the most general of terms, and never bother to estimate their number or identify any by name. Diplomatic evidence from the reign cannot supplement these narratives' vague descriptions. Not a single charter survives that preserves a grant of land or commemorates an act of commendation involving any Godwineson and a retainer. What little information exists is in Domesday Book.

Although the survey's record of late Saxon lordship is far from complete, we find hundreds of individuals holding as 'men of' or 'thegns of' Earl Godwine and his sons. References to the family's men are scattered across eighteen Domesday counties.[64] In some shires, like Berkshire and Essex, there are only infrequent references to Godwineson men, but in seven counties men listed as dependants of the family are recorded holding over £50 of land. The Domesday jurors included among these some of the wealthiest thegns in late Saxon England: Alwine Horne,[65] Ansgar the Staller,[66] Alweald of Stevington,[67] Azur,[68] Æthelnoth Cilt of Kent,[69] Cypping,[70] Eadmær Atre,[71] Eadnoth the Staller,[72] Edward Cilt,[73] Engelric,[74] Gauti the Housecarl,[75] Godwine the Priest,[76]

---

[63] *VER*, pp. 18–28.

[64] In parts of the survey – Hertfordshire, Bedfordshire, Cambridgeshire, Suffolk and Norfolk in particular – evidence on lordship is very good, and the names of almost all TRE holders are preserved in these counties alongside the names of their lords. In the remainder of Domesday, however, information is less complete, and some shires, such as Yorkshire, Lincolnshire and Nottinghamshire, do not preserve the name of a single man's lord. (See below, chapter 4, pp. 111–14.) Working, however, between the survey's best evidence and its more haphazard information, we can form some notion of what kinds of men entered into dependent relationships with the Godwinesons and in what regions these men could be found.   [65] DB, i, 7v, 8r.   [66] Db, ii, 59a.

[67] DB, i, 137r, 137v.   [68] See below, n. 213.

[69] DB, i, 21v. In Kent, Æthelnoth was able to force the canons of St Martins to lease him land in *Merclesham* and Hawkhurst 'for inadequate compensation...through the forcefulness of Harold' (DB, i, 2r).   [70] DB, i, 47r.

[71] Eadmær held the valuable manor of Berkhamsted from Earl Harold. That this individual is Eadmær Atre is made clear in DB's description of one of Berkhamsted's berewicks, Little Gaddesden, where Eadmær is given his by-name (DB, i, 136v).

[72] DB, i, 60r. Earl Harold gave Eadnoth the Staller his aid in stealing land from a clerk in Dorset (DB, i, 8or).   [73] DB, i, 146r, 148r.   [74] DB, ii, 26b.

[75] See below, n. 139.

[76] DB, ii, 343a. He was also associated with Bosham, one of Godwine's chief estates (DB, i, 17v).

Leofwine Cilt[77] and Thorkil the White[78] were all, according to testimony given at the Domesday inquest, thegns of Godwine's sons or held land or received some special aid from them.[79] All of these thegns were powerful men of at least regional importance, and all held lands valued at over £40 per annum,[80] the amount according to the *Liber Eliensis* that set apart thegns of middling rank from the more important *proceres*.[81] Furthermore, some of these men, such as Æthelnoth Cilt, Ansgar the Staller, and Eadmær Atre, held hundreds of hides of land and dozens of men across the kingdom, and attended the king regularly at court.[82]

Godwine's sons offered their lordship to lesser landholders as well. Among the modest thegns who commended themselves to a Godwineson were the brothers Sæwulf and Siward. The two

---

[77] DB, i, 139r, 141r, 142v. For a detailed description of Leofwine's relationship with Earl Harold see Ann Williams, 'Land and power in the eleventh century: the estates of Harold Godwineson', *Anglo-Norman Studies*, 3 (1981), p. 179.

[78] DB, i, 184r, 184v, 185v.

[79] We can add to this list one of the Yorkshire Gospatrics, who accompanied Earl Tostig to Rome (*VER*, pp. 35–6). Another important ally was Eadric *rector navis regis Edwardi*, who, Ann Williams convincingly argues, commanded the ship provided by St Benet of Holm for the king's ship *fyrd* (Williams, 'Land and power', pp. 179–90). If Plumstead, an estate held by the wealthy thegn Beorhtric Cilt TRE, was taken by Godwine from St Augustine's, as a post-Conquest source claims, then it is possible that Beorhtric was given the estate by Earl Godwine, and so may have been one of the family's adherents. (See below, n. 118).

[80] The value of the estates of all the thegns listed above have been taken from Mack, 'Kings and thegns', appendix I with the exception of the following: (1) Azur of Sussex is identified by Mack as three individuals because of Azur's three distinct antecessors in the county. This, however, is more likely a function of the Sussex Rapes than the fact that there were three different Azurs. There is no reason to believe that the Azurs of Sussex, all of whom hold large estates and who have close ties with Earl Godwine, were not a single individual. (2) I have identified the East Anglian landholder Godwine the Priest with the southeastern landholder of the same name. (See Barlow, *English Church*, p. 156.) (3) Gauti, Harold's housecarl, who does not appear on Mack's list, held something on the order of £50 of land in Essex, Suffolk, Middlesex and Hertfordshire. (4) Thorkil the White, Hugh the Ass's antecessor in Hereford, has been identified with Thorkil who was the antecessor of Roger de Lacy in Hereford. Roger's endowment TRW was based on territory rather than tenure, thus breaking the pattern of antecessorial inheritance in the county, and tearing Thorkil's lands apart. (For Roger's Herefordshire endowment, see Fleming, 'Domesday Book and the tenurial revolution', *Anglo-Norman Studies*, 9 (1986), pp. 95–6).

[81] *LE*, ii, c. 97, and references p. 424, n. 9.

[82] Æthelnoth Cilt's name appears among the attestors in two spurious charters (S 1025, 1043); Ansgar is a common attestor (S 1029, 1031, 1033, 1034); and Eadmær Atre attests one surviving charter (S 1034; Tryggvi J. Oleson, *The Witenagemot in the Reign of Edward the Confessor* (Toronto, 1955), p. 123). Godwine the Priest and Engelric were royal priests (Barlow, *English Church*, pp. 156, 190). Eadnoth the Staller is an attestor on two of Osbert of Clare's forgeries (S 1041, 1043), so in all likelihood his name appeared on genuine witness lists which served as Osbert's models.

held eighteen hides and a virgate in Buckinghamshire; the former as a man of Earl Leofwine and the latter as a man of Earl Harold.[83] In Hertfordshire Harold's man Wulfwine of Eastwick worked a couple of farms nestled between two of Harold's large estates, and had a man of his own.[84] In Cambridgeshire a local thegn named Siward with five hides of land is described in Domesday both as holding land from Harold and as one of his men.[85] But more obscure men than these were clients of the family, in particular the well-to-do sokemen of the eastern Danelaw. These men are often unnamed in Domesday, and are recorded in the company of men like themselves, as the proprietors of modest plots of land. Twenty-two freemen in Hevingham, Norfolk, for example, with two carucates between them, were Harold's men,[86] as were two freemen with fifteen acres in Westley Waterless, Cambridgeshire.[87] Four freemen in Runham near Ormesby, Earl Gyrth's large Norfolk estate, were Gyrth's men.[88] Harold and Gyrth, who were both in their time earls of East Anglia, had clients, according to Little Domesday, in almost eighty Suffolk vills and in over one hundred Norfolk villages. It is possible to identify the regions within these two counties in which the brothers were successful in attracting men to their lordship. In the former the family's men were concentrated in the Broadlands of northeastern Suffolk and in the region just west of the Suffolk Sandlings. (See figure 3.5.) In Norfolk their men were especially evident in the north central portion of the shire. (See figure 3.6.) In both of these cases the regions into which Godwineson lordships spread were among the poorest in their respective shires.[89] They were also, and perhaps this is no coincidence, just those districts in which the great eastern abbeys had made so few inroads. Indeed, the areas in which Godwineson men and the men of Benedictine abbots were most commonly found are quite distinct. As a result, there seems to have been little competition between the Godwinesons and eastern abbeys for the hearts, minds and dues of local thegns and freemen. Some East Anglian secular lordships were entangled with the lordships of ecclesiastics. Eadric of Laxfield's men in Norfolk, for example, were found in the same neighbourhoods as the men of eastern abbots and the pattern of their alliances, preserved in Domesday, were probably organized at the same

[83] DB, i, 152v.   [84] DB, i, 140r, 140v.   [85] DB, i, 190r, 190v.   [86] DB, ii, 241b.
[87] DB, i, 197v.   [88] DB, ii, 116a, 115b.
[89] Darby, *Eastern England*, pp. 204–7; 147–52.

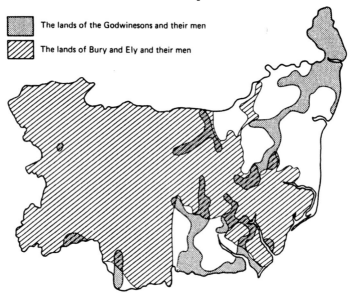

The lands of the Godwinesons and their men

The lands of Bury and Ely and their men

Figure 3.5 Suffolk lordships in 1066

time – that is, in the tenth century. (See figure 3.7.) Since Godwineson lordships tended to skirt around well-established ecclesiastical lordships, they look as if they were formed later. If this is true, Harold's and Gyrth's lordships were newly constructed rather than inherited *en masse* from a single tenth-century predecessor. The fact that the family attracted men in the East Anglia backwater, where the great abbots had so little interest, may explain why family members, so often portrayed in Norman sources as the despoilers of monks, had such good reputations at some eastern abbeys, and why the remaining Fenland houses fostered little animus towards them.

Evidence in Domesday is not accurate enough to allow us to calculate with any certainty the size of the family's following across the kingdom. The survey does, nonetheless, catalogue some £1,200 of land held by the family's men. Figures from Hertfordshire, where evidence on lordship is consistently good, suggest the magnitude of the family's following. Godwineson retainers are recorded on over 50 different occasions in the shire and are said to have held about 125 hides of land. Earls Harold, Leofwine and Gyrth together held just over 50 hides in the county. Thus, the family's men held two and a half times again

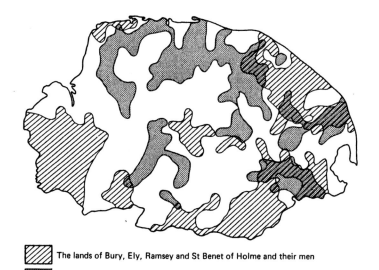

The lands of Bury, Ely, Ramsey and St Benet of Holme and their men

The lands of the Godwinesons and their men

Figure 3.6 Norfolk lordships in 1066

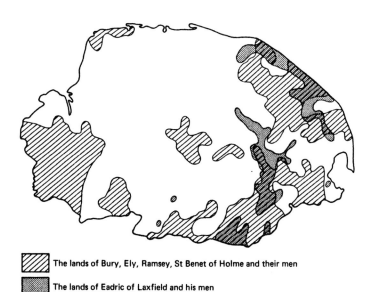

The lands of Bury, Ely, Ramsey, St Benet of Holme and their men

The lands of Eadric of Laxfield and his men

Figure 3.7 Norfolk lordships in 1066

77

as much as did the brothers in demesne, and together the
Godwinesons and their followers held almost a fifth of the
county's assessed land. In Buckinghamshire, another county with
a store of information on pre-Conquest lordship, about fifty
thegns and freemen are described as the men of Earls Harold,
Tostig or Leofwine. These men held just under 200 hides of land
in the shire, almost one and a half times the amount that the
Godwinesons held in demesne. Together the Godwinesons and
their hangers-on held 15 per cent of Buckinghamshire. There
were regions in England where the family doubtless attracted
more men than in Hertfordshire and Buckinghamshire, in
particular in southeastern England and in Wessex, where a family
member had been earl for nearly half a century.[90] If, however,
these two counties, where evidence for pre-Conquest lordship is
most complete, are in any way representative of the size of the
family's following in relation to its demesne holdings, we can
perhaps posit that something over 15,000 hides of land were held
by thegns and freemen who described themselves as Godwineson
men. This is a hazardous extrapolation, but if the figure is
anywhere near correct, the Godwinesons and their men combined
controlled about a third of England's arable. Of course many of
these landholders were king's thegns as well, or were the men of
abbots, thegns or other earls.[91] The conflicts of allegiance that
arose from a man having more than one lord had important
ramifications on the politics of the period. Many of Godwine's
thegns, who joined him at Beverstone in 1051 on the eve of his
revolt, later slipped away to the king, whose men they also
were.[92] By the same token, king's thegns who were Godwine's
men as well, threw in their lot with the family in 1052 and 1066.
Whatever the strengths or weaknesses of these variable and
sometimes conflicting bonds of commendation and lordship, they
played a crucial role in the politics of Edward's reign.

   The Godwinesons' following, cultivated in a mere two
generations, was larger than any other aristocratic entourage.

---

[90] The author of the *VER* states that when Godwine returned from exile, 'all the eastern
and southern English who could manage it met his ship...like children for their long
awaited father' (*VER*, p. 26). Fl. Wig. informs us that Godwine's allies in 1052 were
the men of Sussex, Essex, Surrey and Kent (Fl. Wig., i, p. 208).

[91] My figure of £15,000 is an estimate, based on those lands Domesday specifically
ascribes to men of, thegns of, or sokemen of the Godwinesons. Thus only the £5 of
land Cypping held from Harold in Hampshire is included in these figures and not his
other estates in·the shire.   [92] *ASC*, s.a. 1051 (E).

Men of Earl Leofric's family, according to Domesday Book's uneven information, were holding some £130 of land. The shires where the family was strongest, however – Shropshire, Nottinghamshire, Derbyshire, Cheshire and Warwickshire – record no information on lordship. But their smaller demesne, coupled with the youth of Earls Edwin and Morcar and with their more geographically limited earldoms, suggest that the number of Leofricson dependants paled in comparison to those of the Godwinesons. Similarly, although it is difficult to compare the Godwinesons' following with those of the families of great tenth-century ealdormen, the impression given by the period's scanty evidence is that the ealdormen's more modest and compact holdings were accompanied by fewer dependants. The number of Godwineson allies, therefore, seems out of proportion with that of their aristocratic predecessors or contemporaries. The huge holdings of the family not only supplied them with land and cash but also in some way determined the size of their entourage and their power in the shires and at court.

The Godwinesons formed close alliances, not only with the thegns and freemen of their earldoms, but with important ecclesiastics.[93] The family had a long-standing relationship with the sees of Worcester and York. Godwine and Archbishop Ælfric, who held Worcester for a time, were both supporters of Harthacnut.[94] Wulfstan Bishop of Worcester was a friend and confidant of Earl Harold and was supported by Harold in his election to the see.[95] Wulfstan's predecessor at Worcester, Ealdræd Archbishop of York, was also a friend of the family.[96] He

[93] The family also formed alliances abroad. Among the most important of these was their alliance with the Count of Flanders (Philip Grierson, 'The relation between England and Flanders before the Norman Conquest', *TRHS*, 4th ser., 23 (1941), pp. 97–101). William of Poitiers insinuates that Harold engaged in expensive, high-level diplomacy with a number of Continental princes (William of Poitiers, p. 156). Swein Godwineson allied himself with Gruffydd ap Llewelyn in 1046 (*ASC*, s.a. 1046 (C); Lynn H. Nelson, *The Normans in South Wales 1070–1171* (Austin, 1966), p. 16). Harold had close relations with powerful men in Ireland (Ben Hudson, 'The family of Harold Godwineson and the Irish Sea Province', *Royal Society of Antiquaries of Ireland*, 109 (1979), pp. 92–100). Tostig had an alliance with Malcolm of Scotland c. 1059, when the two became 'sworn brothers' (*VER*, p. 43).

[94] Both men saw to it that King Harold's corpse was mutilated (Fl. Wig., i, p. 194). Ælfric, moreover, may have encouraged Harthacnut to ravage Worcester in 1041, after two of the king's housecarls were killed (William of Malmesbury, *GP*, pp. 250–51). [95] *Vita Wulfstani*, pp. 13, 18.

[96] For a detailed discussion of Ealdræd's career see Barlow, *English Church*, pp. 87–90 and Janet M. Cooper, *The Last Four Anglo-Saxon Archbishops of York* (York, 1970), pp. 23–9.

went with Earls Tostig and Gyrth to Rome,[97] and may have traveled to the Holy Land with Godwine's ne'er-do-well son, Earl Swein.[98] The archbishop lent his aid to the family in a number of delicate matters. He persuaded the king to allow Swein to return from exile, no small feat, since the earl had abducted a nun, murdered his cousin, and 'ruined himself with the Danes'.[99] The archbishop was a friend to Godwine and his sons during the English revolution of 1051, apparently allowing Harold and his followers to slip out of England, although he had been sent to arrest them.[100] He also co-operated with Harold in the pacification of the Welsh march in 1056[101] and may have been in league with the family when he negotiated for the return of Edward's distant Hungarian cousin, Edward the Exile, two years earlier.[102] Ealdræd's support was rewarded in kind. It was through Earl Tostig's efforts that Ealdræd was given his *pallium* in Rome,[103] and it may be that he was not elevated to the archbishopric of York in 1051, when Godwine's power was in eclipse, but was given the see in 1060, after the family's re-establishment, because he was their candidate for the appointment.[104] Several of Canterbury's archbishops were also supporters of the family. Cnut's Archbishop Eadsige, like Earl Godwine himself, supported Harthacnut's first unsuccessful bid for the English crown,[105] and he used Earl Godwine's clout to assure the appointment of his would-be successor and *chorepiscopus* Siward Abbot of Abingdon.[106] The monks of Christchurch, too, were allied to Godwine. After Eadsige's death they attempted to elect a member of their community, the earl's own kinsman Ælfric, as archbishop.[107] Stigand, consecrated archbishop after Robert of Jumièges was forced to flee, must have been a satisfactory candidate to the

[97] *VER*, pp. 34–7; *Vita Wulfstani*, pp. 16–17; *Fl. Wig.*, i, p. 218.
[98] Barlow, *English Church*, p. 88.
[99] Fl. Wig., i, p. 203; *ASC*, s.a. 1049 (D); Cooper, *Anglo-Saxon Archbishops of York*, p. 25.   [100] *ASC*, s.a. 1052 (D) (*recte* 1051).
[101] *ASC*, s.a. 1056 (C); Fl. Wig., i, p. 215.
[102] If we are to believe Eric John, who argues that Edward the Exile was the Godwinesons' candidate for heir to the throne (Eric John, 'Edward the Confessor and the Norman succession', p. 257; Fl. Wig., i, p. 212). For Ealdræd's mission see Freeman, *NC*, ii, pp. 436–9.   [103] *VER*, pp. 36–7.
[104] Barlow feels that Ealdræd, like so many of his predecessors at Worcester, would have been elevated to the Archbishopric of York after Archbishop Ælfric died, had he not had such close connections with Godwine, who was expelled from England that year (*English Church*, p. 87).
[105] *ASC*, s.a. 1036 (E) (*recte* 1035); *Encomium Emmae Reginae*, p. 40.
[106] *ASC*, s.a. 1044 (C).   [107] *VER*, p. 18.

Godwinesons, since it was the appointment of Robert as archbishop that precipitated the family's revolt in 1051, and it was his replacement by Stigand in 1052 that ended it.[108] Certainly, Stigand was friendly enough to Godwine and his sons to act as a go-between during the crisis.[109] Stigand and Ealdræd like Archbishop Eadsige before them, were two of the wealthiest prelates of their day and both wielded considerable power in the Confessor's court.[110] They were men of the world who protected their sees, not only through the shining example of their piety (at least in the case of Ealdræd) and a vigilant watch over their property, but by purchasing the aid of great men with political favours and loans or gifts of their communities's land. During Eadsige's archiepiscopate, for example, Earl Godwine acquired a number of Christchurch estates – Richborough, Sundridge, Langport, Newenden, Saltwood and Folkestone. Some of these lands may have been appropriated from Canterbury, but it is likely that most were given to the family with the approval of either Archbishop Eadsige or Stigand.[111] At Edward's death Godwine's

---

[108] Robert publicly accused Godwine of taking land from Christchurch, and even the partisan author of the *VER* admits that in these matters 'the right was on the bishop's side'. Canterbury's pursuit of its lost lands, however, was abandoned after Robert's deposition and replacement by Stigand (*VER*, p. 19).

[109] *VER*, p. 22. Stigand's personal holdings were immense, and most were concentrated in Godwineson earldoms. For details of his relationship with the Godwinesons see John, 'Edward the Confessor and the Norman succession', p. 245.

[110] Ealdræd was sent on a number of important missions abroad, deeply involving himself both in negotiations with the papacy and in discussions concerning the return of Edward the Exile. Stigand held lands stretching from Norfolk to Kent to Hampshire.

[111] All these estates were recovered by Archbishop Lanfranc in William's reign, and they appear in a report of the pleas held at Penenden Heath (BL Cotton Vespasian A. xxii, fos. 120r–121r, designated as 'Penenden Heath C', in John Le Patourel, 'The reports of the trial on Penenden Heath', *Studies in Medieval History presented to Fredrick Maurice Powicke*, ed. R. W. Hunt, W. A. Patin and R. W. Southern (Oxford, 1948), p. 16. This text is printed in M. M. Bigelow, *Placita Anglo-Normannica* (London, 1879), pp. 5–9. The portion of 'C' which differs significantly from the other texts is printed in Le Patourel, pp. 24–6). According to BL Cotton MS Aug 11 36, it was Archbishop Eadsige who gave Richborough, Sundridge, Langport and Saltwood to Godwine. Eadsige probably also granted Godwine Statenborough (*Dom. Mon.*, fo. 3v). He also gave him Folkestone (Eadmær, *Historia Novorum in Anglia*, ed. M. Rule (London, 1884), p. 5; Douglas, 'Odo, Lanfranc, and the Domesday Survey', *Essays in Honour of James Tait*, pp. 47–57). Lanfranc claimed other Godwineson property at Penenden Heath; 225 burgesses in Hythe (DB, i, 4v; *Dom. Mon.*, fo. 4r) and Harrow (DB, i, 127r; *Dom. Mon.*, fo. 5v). For a discussion of Godwine's crimes against Canterbury, see David Bates, 'The land pleas of William I's reign: Penenden Heath revisited', *Bulletin of the Institute of Historical Research*, 51 (1978), pp. 14–16. Bates, however, sees outright encroachment on the part of Godwine, rather than land in return for political favours.

sons were in legal possession of Haddenham and Halton in Buckinghamshire, valued at £48, although Christchurch and Rochester had some claim to them.[112] Similarly, losses to the family sustained by the sees of Hereford and Worcester were taken in stride until after the Conquest.[113] This kind of activity was not extraordinary, but represents common English practice. Other great lords acquired monastic land during Edward's reign. Archbishop Stigand held Methwold, Croxton, Snailwell and Wood Ditton on lease from the abbot of Ely,[114] and Abbot Ælfwig of Bath gave Stigand a life-lease for thirty hides in Tidenham.[115] Archbishop Ealdræd kept twelve of Worcester's vills after he was elevated to the archiepiscopate, and although Bishop Wulfstan and his community were not pleased with this turn of events, there was little they could do.[116] During the Confessor's reign complaints were generally made against the family only by implacable political enemies, such as Robert of Jumièges, or by reforming Continental bishops, such as Giso of Wells and Leofric of Exeter, who knew little of English custom and owed nothing to Earl Godwine and his offspring.[117] From the little evidence that is given in Domesday, it seems likely that formal accusations of wrong-doing against the Godwinesons were uncommon before 1066, and that the majority of high ecclesiastics bit their tongues and acquiesced when the Godwinesons pressed them for land, in order to maintain cordial relations.

---

[112] For Haddenham, see 'Penenden Heath C', p. 26; DB, i, 143v. William Rufus confirmed Haddenham to the monks, which his father had restored to them. The price of reseisin, however, was stone for the building of the Conqueror's castle at Rochester (*Textus Roffensis*, ed. Peter Sawyer, 2 vols., *Early English Manuscripts in Facsimile*, 7, 11 (Copenhagen, 1957–62), ii, fo. 173r). [113] See below, pp. 85–6, 198–200.

[114] Stigand held Methwold and Croxton TRE (DB, ii, 136a, 136b). Concerning these two manors, the *IE* notes that 'Methwold was for the victualing of the monks, TRE The Abbot leased it to Archbishop Stigand on condition that after his death it would return to the abbey...and Croxton [was held] similarly (*IE*, p. 138). Snailwell, Cambridgeshire, was also in Stigand's possession TRE: 'The manor lay in the demesne of the Church of Ely TRE in the demesne farm, but the Abbot who then was, leased it to the Archbishop, as the hundred testifies. Now Abbot Simeon reclaims it through his antecessors' (DB, i, 199v). According to the *ICC* Stigand paid a food rent to the monks of Ely for Wood Ditton (*ICC*, p. 195). [115] S 1426.

[116] 'At Wlstanus qui nichil apud eum viribus agendum nosset' (*Vita Wulfstani*, p. 20). It was not until after the Conquest that Wulfstan made a formal complaint (*ibid.*, pp. 24–5).

[117] For Giso's problems see *Historiola de Primordiis Episcopatus Somersetensis*, in *Ecclesiastical Documents*, ed. Joseph Hunter, Camden Society (1840), pp. 15–18. For Leofric's problems see Robertson, *Charters*, post-Conquest document n. 1.

The family was successful in its influence peddling. It acquired scores of hides of land in this manner and still managed to receive good press from most of its monastic victims. Godwine had a very good reputation at Saint Augustine's Canterbury,[118] Worcester[119] and Peterborough, whose abbot fought at Harold's side in 1066 and remembered the earl's benefactions.[120] Winchester, Durham and possibly Abingdon were also patronized by the family.[121] The cartularies of Ely and Evesham, two communities with a burning obsession for their patrimonies, say little about the Godwinesons, probably because the family did these houses little harm and perhaps some good.[122] Thus, the unshackled growth of the family's power and its rapid accumulation of earldoms and estates, enabled Harold and his brothers to procure an outsized allotment of land, an immense following and mighty allies, which in turn allowed the family to gather to it more land, more power, and more influence.

The Godwinesons, then, were able to appropriate sizeable chunks of territory with the aid or consent of their aristocratic and

---

[118] The version of the *ASC* from St Augustine's Canterbury is a pro-Godwine source, in spite of the fact that Godwine may have taken land from St Augustine's (*Historia Monasterii S. Augustini Cantuariensis*, ed. Charles Hardwick, RS (London, 1858), p. 350). The Abbot of St Augustine's had also leased or granted a third of Fordwich, which had been given to his community by King Edward (S 1092). He gave it to Earl Godwine 'or allowed [it] to be taken out of fear, folly, or covetousness'. (The accusation is made in *Historia Monasterii S. Augustini*, p. 352). Godwine's share went to Odo Bishop of Bayeux and was then subinfeudated to Haimo the Sheriff. Odo, however, for the good of his soul and the soul of his brother, granted his portion of Fordwich back to St Augustine's (*ibid.*, p. 351; DB, i, 12r).

[119] The family not only received good press in Coleman's life of Saint Wulfstan, but the 'D' version of the *Anglo-Saxon Chronicle*, written at Worcester between c. 1050 and 1073, was friendly to the family. Worcester's fondness for the family was maintained in spite of the fact that Earls Swein and Harold had taken some of Worcester's land (Hemming, i, pp. 275–6; DB, i, 174r).

[120] *ASC*, s.a. 1066 (E). According to Hugh Candidus, Harold granted Clifton and lands in London near St Paul's to Peterborough (*Chronicle*, p. 70).

[121] For Godwine's gifts to Old Minster Winchester, see *VER*, p. 30; For the family's relations with Durham, see Simeon of Durham, *HDE*, p. 94; *Liber Vitae of Durham*, p. 146; *De Miraculis et Translationibus Sancti Cuthberti* in Sim. Dur., *Opera Omnia*, i, p. 245). Harold helped restore some thegnland to Abingdon (*Chron. Ab.*, i, p. 475), and Earl Godwine may have given Sandford-on-Thames to that abbey (S 1022, 1025). Abingdon, however, also lost land to the family (see below, n. 141). For a detailed discussion of Harold's relations with Abingdon, see Williams, 'Land and power' pp. 183–4.

[122] Although none of the Godwinesons seem to have given land to Ely, Gytha gave the monastery a 'wonderfully wrought red chasuble' (*LE*, iii, c. 50).

ecclesiastical allies, but they also pursued both less legal and more royally controlled forms of acquisition. The histories of a number of their prize holdings make it clear that a portion of their land was attained through bare-faced seizure, a portion alienated to them by the king from his own demesne, and a portion acquired as part of an age-old group of estates set aside for royal officials.[123] An examination of the proportions of each type of procurement provides us with a more complete picture of the family's *modus operandi* and reflects directly on royal power in the Confessor's reign. The manner in which the Godwinesons built their estates could indicate on the one hand that the Confessor, in endowing his leading family, was simply following a traditional practice of granting his officials lands set aside specifically for them, or on the other that the king was able to protect neither the *terra regis* nor the patrimony of the Church from his predatory in-laws.

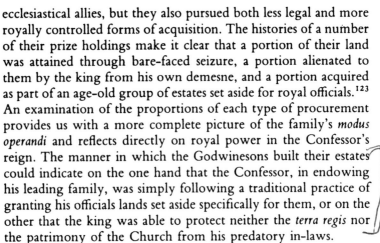

Although some of the estates held by Harold and his brothers had been leased or granted to them by ecclesiastical neighbours, it is clear that they seized a share of their land without churchmen's consent. Steyning, Sussex, had to be restored to Fécamp after the Conquest because the borough, originally presented to the Norman monastery by Edward, had been wrenched from the abbey's grasp by Earl Harold in the last years of the king's life.[124] Harold's seizure constituted the perfect crime: Steyning, worth a small fortune, lay in the heart of Godwine country. It was granted by the aging Edward to Harold despite the king's earlier gift, and belonged by right to a far-off monastery with little power at court and no local advocate. Harold wrested other valuable estates away from communities closer to home. He took Topsham, for example, away from Exeter. The bishop regained it temporarily, but only through hard pleading and cold cash (as a legal notice from the period puts it 'with the help of God and through [Bishop Leofric's] advocacy and his treasure').[125] The earl seized

---

[123] As both Maitland and Barlow would have it (F. W. Maitland, *Domesday Book and Beyond* (Cambridge, 1907), pp. 167–8; Barlow, *Edward the Confessor*, pp. 142–4).

[124] DB, i, 17v. An original confirmation by William the Conqueror of Edward's grant survives. (Printed in facsimile in Chaplais, 'Une charte originale de Guillaume le Conquerant pour L'Abbay de Fécamp', plate 1).

[125] Robertson *Charters*, post-Conquest document n. 1. A charter of King Æthelstan, granting Topsham to Exeter was concocted c. 1070, at just the time that Bishop Leofric was writing his description of Harold's encroachment in the *Exeter Book* (S 433; Pierre Chaplais, 'The authenticity of the royal Anglo-Saxon diplomas of Exeter', *Bulletin of the Institute of Historical Research*, 39 (1966), pp. 4–9). Exeter, no doubt, was trying to meet the same requirements King William placed on Abingdon,

Banwell and Congresbury from an angry Bishop of Wells.[126] Harold preyed upon smaller fry, too, especially nuns and clerks. He took four hides in Allington away from Amesbury.[127] He stole Melcombe Horsey, Cheselbourne and Stour from Shaftesbury,[128] and seized one hide of land from Saint Petroc's in Cornwall[129] and another from Chatteris Abbey in Hertfordshire.[130] The earl also annexed a virgate in Parrock from St John's (Lewes?),[131] and he built a mill in Surrey illegally on one of St Paul's farms.[132] A few of these annexations may have occurred after Edward the Confessor's death, and could have been nothing more than the lawful resumption of royal demesne, but it is clear that many, including the most audacious seizures – Steyning, Banwell and Congresbury – were made before January of 1066.

Harold's siblings took land from the Church as well. In Essex Earl Gyrth's estate of Little Warley belonged by right to St Paul's,[133] and he took land at Poringland, Norfolk, from the monks of Bury 'by force'.[134] Swein took Cleobury, Hopton Wafers and Maesbrook from Worcester.[135] The brothers learned their predatory habits from their father, who 'did all too little reparation about the property of God which he had from many holy places'.[136] Godwine appropriated estates from Wilton Abbey and Sherborne and pilfered ecclesiastical lands in Herefordshire during the 1040s and 1050s.[137] Some of these lands, like

when he promised to confirm all lands and customs to the abbey that it could prove 'through writ or charter' (*Chron. Ab.*, ii, p. 1). Such skulduggery was not always wise. Westminster, was made to forfeit a hide in Fanton, Essex, at the Domesday inquest, 'because it had come to the Church by a false writ' (DB, ii, 14a). In spite of Exeter's efforts, Topsham was not recovered by 1086 (DB, i, 101r). Freeman suggests that since Topsham was the port of Exeter, Harold may have taken this land to aid him in the defence of the coat (Freeman, *NC*, ii, p. 368).

126 For the pre-Conquest complaint, see *Historiola de Primordiis Episcopatus Somersetensis*, pp. 15–18, and Harmer, *Writs*, pp. 275–6. For William's post-Conquest restitution of Banwell, see *Regesta*, i, n. 23.

127 DB, i, 69r. Amesbury recovered this land by the time of the Domesday inquest.

128 DB, i, 75v, 78v. 'King William reseised [Shaftesbury] because the Church itself found a writ with the seal of King Edward ordering that the land should be restored to the Church.'   129 DB, i, 121r.   130 DB, i, 132r.   131 DB, i, 21v.

132 DB, i, 31r.

133 St Paul's claim was strong enough to enable the community to recover Little Warley after the Conquest (DB, ii, 10b).

134 DB, ii, 210a. 'The Feudal Book of Abbot Baldwin', printed in Douglas, *Feudal Documents from Bury St Edmunds*, i, p. 13, also notes that 'Gyrth the very powerful earl had it in the time of good King Edward.'   135 Hemming, i, p. 276.

136 *ASC*, s.a. 1052 (C).

137 For Wilton, see DB, i, 72v. For land in Hereford, see 186r. For Sherborne, see William of Malmesbury, *GP*, ii, pp. 179–80.

Poringland, were taken from the Church through a kind of ham-fisted seizure, but other estates, like Stoke in Kent, were acquired with more finesse, through shady business dealings. Stoke had been part of the bishopric of Rochester, 'but TRE Earl Godwine bought it from two men who held it of the bishop, and this sale was made without [the bishop's] knowledge'.[138] Some of these ill-gotten estates were used to endow family retainers. Thus, Harold's thegn Orthi [*sic*?] held Freckenham Suffolk, which was adjudged to the Bishop of Rochester after the Conquest,[139] and his thegn Thormod held Colwall, Herefordshire, from the earl after Harold had appropriated it from the bishopric of Here-ford.[140] Domesday records that Blæchmann the Priest held Chilton from Earl Harold, even though the *Abingdon Chronicle* insists that the priest leased the estate from the monks of Abingdon.[141] Because the Godwinesons were so powerful in the shires and at court and were such close allies of England's leading bishops and abbots, an environment was created in which their assaults were more often met with whimpers than with lawsuits.

Dozens of other former ecclesiastical estates were also in the family's possession in 1066, but these estates had probably been given to them by the king. A mass of land had been taken over from the Church by the West Saxon kings during the Viking Wars and then granted out to their military followers.[142] An

---

[138] DB, i, 5v; *Textus Roffensis*, ii, fo. 216r.

[139] DB, i, 381r. According to a writ preserved in the *Textus Roffensis*, Freckenham was held not by Orthi but by Harold's thegns Gauti and Thorbert. It is possible that 'Orthi' (which occurs only once in DB) is a mistranscription of Gauti, the name appearing in the Rochester writ, and the name of one of Harold's housecarls (*Textus Roffensis*, ii, fos. 170v–171r; Feilitzen, *Pre-Conquest Personal Names, sub nomine*). After the Conquest Odo and his men took Freckenham, but it was restored to Rochester by Lanfranc (*Textus Roffensis*, ii, fos. 171r–171v; DB, i, 381a). Freckenham's apper-tenance, Isleham in Cambridgeshire, had to be restored to Rochester as well. It had been taken over by Picot the Sheriff for the King's use (DB, i, 190v; *Textus Roffensis*, ii, fos. 175v–176r). Picot seized it, however, either without knowing or without caring about Rochester's claim. After all, in 1066 the bulk of Isleham had been held by twelve sokemen under Thorbert, presumably Harold's man who held Freckenham. It is likely, therefore, that Harold took both the caput and the berewick, and then granted them to two of his followers. Both lands were the centre-piece of a proported charter of King Alfred to Rochester, which was forged in the twelfth century to bolster Rochester's claim (S 349). This charter does not appear in the *Textus Roffensis*, but can be found in Rochester's fourteenth-century *Liber Temporalium*, fo. 10r, printed in *Registrum Roffense*, ed. J. Thorpe (London, 1769), pp. 357–8.　　[140] DB, i, 182r.

[141] *Chron. Ab.*, i, pp. 474, 478; ii, p. 283; DB, i, 59r; *VCH, Berkshire*, i, pp. 298–9. Eadnoth the Staller held land in Dorset, that Harold had taken from a clerk (DB, i, 80r).

[142] Robin Fleming, 'Monastic lands and England's defence in the Viking Age', *EHR*, 100 (1985), pp. 247–65.

example of this is the district of Amounderness, which was given by King Æthelstan to Archbishop Wulfstan in 934 as a bulwark against the Norse-Irish.[143] By 1065 the whole of the district was firmly and apparently legally in Earl Tostig's hands and used as a territorial anchor for his northern activities.[144] Tostig also held Cartmel, a vast estate that lay along the vulnerable northern coast of Morecambe Bay. It had once belonged to St Cuthbert's.[145] Hoo, Folkestone,[146] Battersea, Isleworth, Childerditch,[147] Southwark,[148] Callington[149] and Harrow[150] had similar historic entanglements with monastic patrimonies before the Viking Wars, and yet all were in Godwineson hands by 1066. The bulk of the aforementioned estates were immense and profitable; thus they were valuable plums to be given out by the king to his favoured lieutenants. But these one-time ecclesiastical estates were not only valuable, but vulnerable. Isleworth, Harrow and Battersea lay along the march established by Alfred and Guthrum in the ninth century and may represent marcher estates used by West Saxon kings and their ealdormen in the fight to reconquer the Danelaw.[151] Battersea was the site of an important ford across

---

[143] Dorothy Whitelock, 'The dealings of the kings of England with Northumbria in the tenth and eleventh centuries', *The Anglo-Saxons*, ed. Peter Clemoes (London, 1959), p. 85.

[144] *Ibid.*, pp. 72–3, 85–7; DB, i, 301v. For the organization of the northern estates of Tostig and his followers, see *VCH, Lancashire*, i, p. 272.

[145] DB, i, 302r; *Historia de Sancto Cuthberto*, in Sim. Dur., *Opera Omnia*, i, p. 200; Edmund Craster, 'The patrimony of St Cuthbert', *EHR*, 69 (1954), p. 181.

[146] Both had been dependencies of Peterborough before the ninth century, but were held by the Godwinesons in the eleventh (Frank M. Stenton, 'Medeshamstede and its colonies', reprinted from *Historical Essays in Honour of James Tait* (Manchester, 1933) in *Preparatory to Anglo-Saxon England*, ed. Doris Mary Stenton (Oxford, 1970), pp. 189–90; DB, i, 8v, 9v).

[147] All these estates were part of Barking's early endowment, but by 1066 all were held by Godwinesons. (S 1246. Although this charter is spurious, its author had access to early material. See S 1248.) DB, i, 31r, 130r; ii, 5a; A. Giraud Browning, 'The early history of Battersea', *Surrey Archaeological Society*, 10 (1891), pp. 212–15).

[148] Southwark was divided between the King and Earl Godwine in the mid-eleventh century, but Chertsey had held it earlier (DB, i, 32r; S 1165; Tony Dyson, 'London and Southwark in the seventh century and later. A neglected reference', *London and Middlesex Archaelogical Society*, 31 (1980), pp. 83–95).

[149] Callington, one time part of Lawhitton, was granted to Sherborne by King Egbert, 'and that lasted many years, until the heathen armies overran and occupied this land' (S 1296, 1248). It was held in 1066 by Earl Harold (DB, i, 120r).

[150] Christchurch had a claim to Harrow (S 106, 1414), and these claims were pressed after the Conquest ('Penenden Heath C', p. 126). TRE it was held by the Godwinesons (DB, i, 127r).

[151] Fleming, 'Monastic lands', pp. 261–2; R. H. C. Davis, 'Alfred and Guthrum's frontier', *EHR*, 92 (1982), pp. 803–10; Alfred and Guthrum, 1.

the Thames, and Southwark was the location of a vital bridge by
c. 1000, making it a crucial part of London's defence.[152] There
was a major harbour at Folkestone, and it was subject to Viking
attacks.[153] Other estates may have escheated to the king because
of the heavy gelds levied on them during Cnut's reign, or may
have been bequeathed to monasteries by aristocrats whose wills
were never honoured. For example, Æthelflæd's bequest of
Navestock and Laver, Essex, and Cockhampstead, Hertfordshire,
to St Paul's was compromised, probably because she gave aid to
her brother, the banished Ealdorman Leofsige.[154] These lands
were likely confiscated by the king and then used to endow more
favoured aristocrats. By 1066 Laver was held by Earl Harold, and
Cockhampstead was in the possession of Gauti, a thegn of
Earl Harold, and his housecarl.[155] Other estates in this category
may be Princes Risborough,[156] Ringwood,[157] Rotherfield,[158]
Bincombe,[159] Singleton[160] and Kirtling.[161] All these estates, held

[152] IV Æthelred 2§4; Dyson, 'London and Southwark', p. 91.
[153] *ASC*, s.a. 991 (A).   [154] S 1495, and above chapter 2, p. 43.
[155] DB, i, 137v, 129r. The witness list for Æthelflæd's bequest is unsatisfactory, but
Whitelock notes that 'there is nothing in the phrasing of the bequest to suggest that
it is spurious, and we know no motive for its forgery, as there is no trace that either
Laver or Cockhampstead were ever owned or claimed by St Paul's' (*Wills*, p. 175).
St Paul's, however, certainly claimed the estates in Æthelflæd's bequest after the
Conquest. One spurious charter attributed to Æthelred was cooked up to confirm
Æthelflæd's claim, and another spurious grant, a supposed charter of William the
Conqueror 'made on the first day of his coronation', reseised St Paul's with these lands
'unjustly taken from it' (S 908; William Dugdale, *The History of St Paul's Cathedral
in London* (London, 1658), appendix xiii). The monks were not satisfied with the help
they got from the Conqueror in their attempt to gain back this land and took matters
into their own hands. Under the first of two entries for Navestock, Domesday tells us
that the monks claimed that 'they had it by the king's gift'. In the second entry, we
are told that 'now St Paul's has annexed this land and it is with the other land' (DB,
ii, 13a–13b).
[156] Princes Risborough was bequeathed to Old Minster in Edgar's reign but was held by
Earl Harold TRE (S 1484; DB, i, 143v). In the description of the borough of Oxford,
Domesday suggests that this estate was Earl Ælfgar's. After he died, the estate went to
Earl Harold (DB, i, 154r).
[157] Ringwood was given to Abingdon in Edgar's reign (S 690), but was in Tostig's
possession in the mid-1060s (DB, i, 39r).
[158] Rotherfield was granted to the nunnery at Winchester by Ætheling Æthelstan
(S 1503). It is attributed to Godwine in Domesday Book (DB, i, 16r).
[159] Bincombe was given to Cerne in Æthelred's reign (S 1217). Harold held it TRE (DB,
i, 78v).
[160] Dean, part of Singleton, was given to Wherwell in 1002 (S 904). It is attributed to
Godwine in Domesday (DB, i, 23r).
[161] Kirtling was granted to Ely by Oswig and his wife Leofflæd, the daughter of
Ealdorman Bryhtnoth (*LE*, ii, c. 67). Oswig died at Ringmere (*ASC*, s.a. 1010 (C, D,
E). The estate was held by Harold TRE (DB, i, 202r).

by monasteries or intended for their patrimonies, were likely given out to the Godwinesons as part of their allotment as earls.

From Domesday and its satellites we know of other land handed over to family members along with their earldoms. The most obvious example of this can be found in the *Liber Exoniensis'* description of the Somerset *terra regis*: in its list of King William's holdings TRW, former Godwineson lands are enumerated under the rubric 'mansiones de comitatu'.[162] A number of their other estates have the tell-tale mark of comital holdings, the third penny of justice, a fiscal privilege of the earl. Godwine's wife Gytha, for example, held Over Wallop with the third penny of six hundreds.[163] Gyrth had the third penny for two Suffolk hundreds and the half hundred of Ipswich,[164] and his father had this right for Fordwich and Dover.[165] Harold's manor of Moreton-hampstead possessed the third penny for the hundred of Teignbridge[166] and Molland for three hundreds along with 'the dues of every third beast pastured on the moors'.[167] Puddletown had this privilege for the entire shire of Dorset.[168] The family's Somerset estates of Old Cleeve and Brompton Regis also had third penny rights appended to them.[169] The third penny of five Herefordshire hundreds pertained to Harold's manors of Much Cowarne and Burghill,[170] as did the third penny of the borough of Winchcomb in Gloucestershire.[171] Although there are no other direct references to comital holdings, the histories of some Godwineson estates show them to have been previously in the possession of stallers, ealdormen or other earls, and so may, therefore, have been reserved for royal officials. Lambeth, once held by Cnut's staller Tovi the Proud, was held during Edward's reign by Harold; and Harold was granted Tovi's son's estate at Waltham.[172] Earl Godwine may have received some of another staller, Osgot Clapa's, land after the latter was outlawed.[173] Swineshead, so Domesday records, was given to Earl Siward, 'with sake and soke, and so Earl Harold had it'.[174] Similarly Earl Siward had held Hemingbrough while earl, and Tostig possessed it after him.[175] Earl Ælfgar had held Shipton-under-Wychwood

---

[162] DB, iii, 99a. [163] DB, i, 38v. [164] DB, ii, 290a. [165] DB, i, 12r, 1r.
[166] DB, i, 101r. [167] DB, i, 101r. [168] DB, i, 75r. [169] DB, i, 86v.
[170] DB, i, 186r. [171] DB, i, 162v.
[172] DB, i, 34r; Fl. Wig., i, p. 196; *De Inventione Sanctae Crucis...apud Waltham*, p. 14.
[173] Countess Gytha held Wroxall on the Isle of Wight, which Osgot may have held (S 1391; Robertson, *Charters*, p. 433; DB, i, 53r). [174] DB, i, 208r.
[175] EYC, ii, 303; DB, i, 299r.

and Princes Risborough when Earl of Mercia, but Harold, who probably gained some authority in Oxfordshire and Buckinghamshire after Ælfgar's death, held both estates in 1066.[176] Hitchin, Harold's chief manor in Hertfordshire may have also been an old official estate.[177] The name of Aldermaston, one of Harold's Berkshire estates, means 'tun of the ealdorman', and so may have been attached to an ealdordom.[178] The appearance of estates like these in Domesday as property of the family suggests that a number of Godwineson estates had a traditional connection with local administration and were in some sense official.

Other estates came to the family as the result of the massive confiscation of land which occurred on either side of the millenium. The Godwinesons possessed a number of estates that had once been held by ealdormen or their families, not as part of their official endowment, but as bookland.[179] Princes Risborough, Buckinghamshire, was held by Harold TRE, and his mother held Haversham. Both had been the property of the sister of Æthelweard the Chronicler in the late tenth century.[180] The family also held two estates ealdorman Ælfheah had bequeathed to his brother in Faringdon, Berkshire and Aldbourne, Wiltshire.[181] They also held Merton and Henstridge, two of Ælfheah's other pieces of bookland.[182] Other Godwineson estates were once part of the royal demesne. Several are not given annual values in

---

[176] DB, i, 154r, 154v, 151v; Freeman, *NC*, ii, pp. 377–83.

[177] Hitchin in Hertfordshire was Harold's chief estate in the region, and was the caput of an extensive estate that covered almost the entire hundred of Hitchin. It was valued at £60 and £40 *ad numerum* from the freemen who held Hitchin's associated lands (DB, i, 133r). Harold made a concerted effort to expand the estate's territory and rights. Wymondley, a manor of eight hides, had been held in demesne by Chatteris Abbey, but Harold took it and added it to the neighbouring Hitchin 'three years before the death of King Edward' (DB, i, 132r). The same is true of Hexton, which belonged by right to a man of the Abbot of St Albans, but Harold placed it illegally in his manor (DB, i, 133r). Other men in the neighbourhood were forced to render cartage and escort to Hitchin (e.g. Temple Dinsley; DB, i, 132v). Three men who held Leygreen, a part of Hitchin, were described in DB as 'Earl Ælfgar's men'. This may simply reflect outdated information, and preserve a memory of the time when Ælfgar held the whole manor (DB, i, 133r). Before that Hitchin was held by Tovi the Proud, who granted the church of that vill to his foundation of Waltham (*De Inventione Sanctae Crucis...apud Waltham*, pp. 11–12). Before Hitchin was granted out to royal officials, it may have been royal because of its rights of cartage and escort, dues typically owed to the king (*VCH, Hertfordshire*, i, pp. 273, 278).

[178] Margaret Gelling, *The Placenames of Berkshire, English Placename Society*, 49 (Cambridge, 1973), p. 198. [179] See above, chapter 2.

[180] DB, i, 143v, 148r; S 1484. [181] S 1485; DB, i, 57v, 65r.

[182] DB, i, 30r, 87r; S 747; S 1736.

Domesday, but render nights' farm, a characteristic of the ancient demesne.[183] Included in this group are four of Harold's Essex estates – Writtle, Brightlingsea, Lawford and Newport, and one of his Norfolk estates, Necton.[184] Three Godwineson estates, Chalton, Catherington and Hambledon, had been bequeathed by Ætheling Æthelstan to his father King Æthelred or to his thegn Ælfmær.[185] Other Godwineson lands, Angmering, Candover, Hartland, Rotherfield, Steyning and Tiverton, appear in King Alfred's will.[186]

The reason that the Godwinesons were granted old ecclesiastical estates, holdings of fallen ealdormen, and land from the *terra regis* appears to have been twofold, income and defence. Large estates granted to Harold, such as the one at Writtle, which was valued at ten nights' farm, or Puddletown, with its extensive profits of justice, were enormously valuable, and helped both to defray the expenses of the earl and to encourage his loyalty.[187] Other property, however, like the tracts of waste land held by Harold in Herefordshire, or Tostig's Amounderness, situated at the edge of the world, provided no such economic advantages, and were more likely granted to them because they lay in regions where the kingdom's security was at risk. Godwineson estates, then, came from a variety of sources. Rather than endowing their earls with the lands of a particular family or with large pieces of the *terra regis*, King Edward and his predecessors granted them a combination of ancient ecclesiastical, ealdormanly, and royal estates that would provide the earls with the income and territory necessary to act effectively as the wielders of delegated royal authority. This new amalgamation of estates, amassed to form the comital holdings of the mid-eleventh century, were most likely organized after Cnut's accession. This tenurial revolution was at once facilitated by the disintegration of various important tenth-century kindreds and by the financial embarrassment of a number of monasteries.

The interplay between royal grants to the Earl of Wessex and his family's own subsequent acquisition of land and building of

---

[183] *VCH, Essex*, i, p. 336.   [184] DB, ii, 5a–b, 6a–b, 7a, 235a–b.

[185] DB, i, 44v; S 1503, *Wills*, pp. 167–74.

[186] DB, i, 24v, 100v, 16r, 17r, 100v; S 1507.

[187] Eric John has convincingly argued that profits of justice were granted to earls and other great lords to help defray the cost of maintaining and mustering the local fyrd (*Land Tenure in Early England*, p. 117).

alliances can be seen when Godwineson holdings are examined regionally. The Godwinesons accumulated a vast number of estates on the south coast of England, in the Welsh marches, and along the Essex waterways. Godwine's murky past and his early association with Wessex make it unlikely that this scattering of land came to his family through inheritance alone. Furthermore, a number of the family's most important estates in these regions had independent histories before the eleventh century, making it unlikely that their combination pre-dates Cnut's conquest.

Cnut spent much of his youth working the Southampton Waters in his father's pirating and military operations.[188] By the time he ascended to the English throne, he was familiar with the area's defensive weaknesses. Moreover, the increasing importance of London under his rule as an administrative and military centre lent the city's southern approaches increasing strategic importance.[189] Because Cnut's overseas commitments prevented him from supervising the region's defence,[190] he created the earldom of Wessex in 1017, and within a year he appointed Godwine as the district's earl. One of Godwine's chief military chores, once established there, was the defence of this coast, its rivers and its roads, and it is likely that Cnut gave his earl a sizeable territory in coastal Sussex and Hampshire in order to aid him in this task.[191] Few grants to Godwine survive, but Domesday, with its record of English landholding in the Confessor's reign, shows his family in possession of a hundred hides on the Isle of Wight and along the southwest coast of Hampshire in 1066.[192] The family also held hundreds of hides further inland, on either side of the shires' shared border.[193] Indeed, in January 1066, the family held about £1,200 of land in Hampshire and Sussex alone, just under a sixth of their entire

---

[188] *ASC*, s.a. 1001 (A), 1006 (C, D, E), 1009, 1011.

[189] Nightingale, 'The origin of the court of Husting', p. 571.

[190] *ASC*, s.a. 1019 (C, D, E), 1022 (C, D, E, F), 1028 (D, E, F) 1031 (*recte* 1027).

[191] Nightingale seems to attribute Earl Godwine's acquisition of land in Sussex to the Confessor's rather than Cnut's generosity ('The origin of the court of Husting', p. 571). Ann Williams, on the other hand, argues that from 'the vast accumulation of land in Sussex belonging to Harold and his family ... one is driven to the conclusion that most of his land in the south-east came to him by inheritance' ('Land and power', pp. 176–7).

[192] DB, i, 38r–54r. Two of the mainland estates, Holdenhurst and Ringwood, had extensive outlying property on the Isle of Wight (DB, i, 39r).

[193] DB, i, 16r–53r.

endowment and about double the value of the *terra regis* in the same region.[194] It seems likely that a number of these estates were granted out of the royal demesne. Angmering, Rotherfield and Harting in Sussex, and Chalton and Hambleton in Hampshire, all Godwineson estates in 1066, were part of the ancient West Saxon royal demesne before the year 1000, as was Dean, which formed part of Godwine's huge manor of Singleton.[195] Other valuable estates, like Holdenhurst in Hampshire and Hurstpierpoint in Sussex, valued together at £92 10s., did not pay geld, an indication that both were at one time part of the *terra regis*.[196] In western Sussex, where Hambleton, Chalton, Harting and Angmering lay, only one estate, Lyminster, continued under royal control.[197] The remainder of what at one time had been a sizeable royal holding had fallen to Earl Godwine and his sons. Other estates, like the valuable manor of Washington, Sussex, held in the tenth century by two ealdormen in turn, may have been confiscated from one of the great tenth-century aristocrats during the purges under Æthelred or Cnut, and then handed over to Godwine to further supplement his holdings in the region.[198] Over Wallop in Hampshire, with the third penny of six hundreds, was likely an old official estate as well. Other properties may have been taken from monasteries and bishoprics by Cnut, when they were unable to meet the period's heavy burden of geld.[199]

Royal, ecclesiastical, and aristocratic estates given over to Godwine along the Channel appear to have been rationally organized for defence. In the area between Hayling Island and Selsey and then north along the Sussex–Hampshire border, the family controlled a whole complex of huge, beneficially hidated

---

[194] This was approximately the same amount of land held by Roger de Montgomery in demesne throughout the kingdom in 1086. Roger was the third wealthiest baron of the Conqueror.

[195] Angmering and Rotherfield appear in the will of King Alfred (S 1507). Harting was given to King Edgar by Bishop Æthelwold as part of an exchange (S 779). Chalton and Hambledon, Hampshire and Rotherfield, Sussex, are mentioned in the will of Æthelred the Unready's son Ætheling Æthelstan (S 1503). According to Domesday, all these lands were held directly by Godwine or his sons, except Hambledon, which was held from Godwine by the thegn Edward. Since Edward 'could not go where he would' this looks like land temporarily alienated by Godwine (DB, i, 44v).

[196] DB, i, 39r, 27r.

[197] DB, i, 24v. Lyminster, like these other estates was part of the ancient West Saxon demesne (S 1507).

[198] Washington was granted by Ealdorman Æthelwold to his brother Ealdorman Eadric (S 1504).   [199] See above, chapter 2, pp. 40–1.

estates that included almost all the region's impressive Iron Age hillforts.[200] Wolstanbury Camp lay on an outlying spur of the South Downs above Hurstpierpoint, Godwine's manor of forty-one hides which was exempt from geld.[201] Further west, at Singleton, one of the largest and most valuable manors in the southeast, was The Trundles,[202] a camp which offered the best view of the South Downs in Western Sussex, with clear sight of Chichester Harbour, the English Channel, and the coast of the Isle of Wight.[203] Just east of Singleton, in Godwine's beneficially assessed manor of Stoughton, lay another promontory fortress, Bow Hill; and near Washington, the vill in which Bramber Castle was constructed after the Conquest, there was Chancton-bury Camp. Both were impressive plateau enclosures, built on the edge of the chalk downs.[204] Harrow Hill lay near the Godwineson manor at Angmering;[205] outside Rotherfield lay Kirdford and Saxonbury Camps;[206] and Beacon Hill was situated near Harting.[207] Just west in Hampshire, Harold held Quarley, which included Quarley Hill[208] and Nether Wallop, which included Danebury Camp, the most impressive of Wessex's hillforts after Maiden Castle.[209] The location of the family's manors along the south coast and the inclusion in their estates of all but one of the downland hillforts with their wide views and high ground would have aided the West Saxon earls in their protection of the vulnerable stretch of coast between the Isle of Wight and

---

[200] Leofwine's family was similarly endowed with large estates that included within their bounds massive hillforts. In Shropshire, for example, Morcar held Great Ness, Worthen and Caynham (DB, i, 253v, 255v, 256v). Great Ness included Oliver's Point, a promontory fortress that rose 250 feet above the surrounding countryside (*VCH, Shropshire*, i, p. 356). Worthen was the site of Oakhill Castle Ring, a promontory fortress 750 feet above the surrounding countryside (*ibid.*, i, p. 358). Caynham included Caynham Camp (*ibid.*, i, pp. 360–1). Edwin held Wellington, Ditton Priors and Church Stretton (DB, i, 253v, 254r). Wellington was the site of The Wrekin, a hillfort built on an isolated hill 900 feet above the surrounding territory (*ibid.*, i, pp. 369–70); Church Stretton, Caer Caradoc and Castle Hill (*ibid.*, i, pp. 360–2); Ditton Priors was near a large hillfort 1,200 feet above the Clee Brook (*ibid.*, i, p. 359). Castle Hill was fortified by the Normans (W. J. Varley, 'The hill-forts and the Welsh marches', *Archaeological Journal*, 105 (1948), pp. 57, 65).

[201] Wolstanbury camp lies in Hurstpierpoint parish.

[202] The Trundles lies in West Dean, which was part of Singleton.

[203] *VCH, Sussex*, i, p. 88.

[204] DB, i, 24r; *VCH, Sussex*, i, pp. 92, 103; Cunliffe, *Iron Age Communities*, p. 18.

[205] *VCH, Sussex*, i, p. 91; Cunliffe, *Iron Age Communities*, pp. 17–19.

[206] *VCH, Sussex*, i, pp. 106, 116.

[207] *VCH, Sussex*, i, p. 113; Cunliffe, *Iron Age Communities*, p. 330.

[208] *VCH, Hampshire*, i, p. 91.   [209] *VCH, Hampshire*, i, pp. 103, 115.

Southampton and enabled them to guard the mouths of the Test, Meon and Itchen Rivers.

The land granted to Earl Godwine and his sons in Hampshire and Sussex not only enabled them to protect the coast from pirates and invaders, but allowed them, as we have seen elsewhere, to settle in and consolidate their power. Dozens of Sussex thegns, particularly in the western part of the shire, had become their men by 1066. Some, especially lesser thegns, commended themselves to members of the family because of the effective lordship they could offer. Æthelheard, for example, who leased eleven hides in Treyford from the Abbot of Winchester, just three miles east of Countess Gytha's eighty hide estate of Harting and a couple of miles north of Godwine's vast estate of Singleton, found it prudent to make himself a man of Earl Godwine.[210] Other men became Godwine's allies because the earl had the landed resources with which to cultivate an aristocratic following. A minor thegn named Beorhtric was given a five and a half hide estate at Brighton by Earl Godwine,[211] and the more prosperous Cola held Poynings from the Earl 'because he gave it to him'.[212] Both Azur and Æthelnoth Cilt of Kent – two of the wealthiest men in England and Sussex's most powerful thegns – held some of their lands in the shire from Earl Godwine as well, so must have counted among his allies.[213] The family's power had also infiltrated the county towns by 1066. The borough of Chichester, encircled by a ring of estates held by the Godwinesons and their men, was thoroughly Godwinist by 1066. Although the borough continued to render King Edward £10 a year until his death, the earl got a third of the borough's customary dues. The family had also taken control of most of Chichester's urban property. The borough was made up of 97 and a half *hagae*.[214] Of these, 54 were held directly by the Godwinesons,[215] and another six were held by their men.[216] The Godwinesons and their men held over a hundred *hagae* in Lewes – something like half of Lewes's burgages.[217] and Steyning, with its 118 *masurae*, was held by Earl Harold at the end of the Confessor's life.[218] Thus, in the towns

---

[210] DB, i, 23r. [211] DB, i, 26v. [212] DB, i, 27r.

[213] Azur held Taring Neville, Barcombe, Wantley and Shermanbury from Earl Godwine (DB, i, 21v, 27v, 28v), and Æthelnoth held Wilmington from him (DB, i, 21v).

[214] So the description of the borough tells us (DB, i, 23r). The TRE holders of 88 *hagae* along with 9 burgesses (presumably with 9 *hagae*) are identified in the county's survey of rural property. [215] DB, i, 16r, 23r, 23v, 24r. [216] DB, i, 23r, 23v, 24r, 25v.

[217] DB, i, 26r, 26v, 27r, 27v; Darby, *South East*, p. 467. [218] DB, i, 17r.

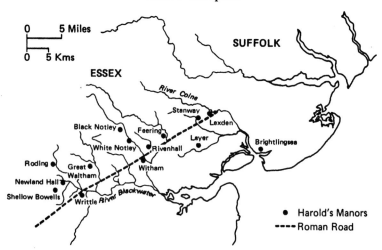

Figure 3.8 Earl Harold's eastern Essex estates TRE

and in the countryside of the south coast, Earl Godwine's family dominated.

Essex, like Sussex, was vulnerable to invasion and became a Godwineson stronghold in the 1040s, 50s and 60s. Its coast, facing east towards Denmark, is riddled with inlets, and its rivers provided Vikings with access to the interior.[219] During the course of the tenth century, royal burhs were built in the county, and the ealdormen of eastern England, perhaps empowered by the sad state of their region, played an increasingly important role in English politics.[220] The defence of Essex continued to be important after the year 1000. Swegn and Cnut invaded the county more than once,[221] and as late as 1049 Essex was ravaged by Scandinavian pirates.[222] Domesday Book indicates that Essex's earl held estates granted to him to insure the shire's protection. Although Harold gave up the earldom in 1053, it is clear that he maintained a number of comital estates until his death. In 1066 Harold held a concentration of land which drained into the Rivers Colne and Blackwater and from there into the sea.[223] (See figure 3.8.) Along the River Colne and its tributary the Roman, Harold held Stanway, Lexden, Layer and Brightlingsea, manors assessed

[219] E.g., *ASC*, s.a. 894, 895, 912, 984, 1004, 1009, 1010, 1100.
[220] Hart, 'Æthelstan Half-King', pp. 115–44.
[221] *ASC*, s.a. 994, 1004, 1009, 1010, 1011.   [222] *ASC*, s.a. 1049 (C), 1050 (D).
[223] Harold's other estates in Essex are near the rivers Lea and Roding, both of which run from the north into the Thames.

at twenty-two hides and valued at £44 and two nights' farm.
Further south, along the Blackwater drainage system, the earl
held Witham, White Notley, Black Notley, Rivenhall, Feering,
Writtle, Newland Hall, Great Waltham, Shellow Bowells and
Roding, valued at £91 10s. and ten nights' farm.[224] Both
Brightlingsea and Writtle were doubtless old royal estates because
they, like other manors of the ancient demesne, rendered night's
farm.[225] As such, they were likely comital in nature, granted out
of the *terra regis* when eastern royal and comital holdings were
reorganized for the defence of the shire. Lexden, another of
Harold's Essex manors, included the Lexden Ramparts, a defensive
dyke two miles in length – running from north of the Bergholt
Road, through Lexden, and then southward to the Old London
Road.[226] Both Lexden and Stanway, which had been combined
by 1066, were bequeathed to King Æthelred by Ælfflæd in
1002.[227] It is significant that Harold, as Earl of East Anglia, was
holding a portion of Ælfflæd's land, since she and her family had
been intimately connected with the defence of Essex. Ælfflæd was
the daughter of Ealdorman Ælfgar of Essex and the sister of
Æthelflæd, which made her sister-in-law in turn to the East
Anglian ealdorman Æthelstan and to King Edmund. Ælfflæd was
also the wife of Bryhtnoth, the Ealdorman of Essex who lost his
life at the Battle of Maldon.[228] Her two Colne estates, which
Harold held TRE, were within two miles of Colchester and were
connected to it and each other by the Great Road, the principal
Roman road in East Anglia, joining Colchester to London. The
road linked these two manors along the Colne with two of
Harold's Blackwater estates, Witham and Feering, allowing easy
access between the two groups.[229] Witham's proximity to Essex's
main roads and its ties to other Godwine lands enhanced its
capabilities for defence, for it was here that Edward the Elder had
constructed a double ring defensive work in 912 to protect and
dominate the area northwest of Maldon.[230] Similarly, Harold's
estate at Benfleet, which lay off the Thames estuary, was fortified
by an earthwork thrown up by the Dane Hæsten and taken over
by the English in 894.[231] The origin, location, and strategic

---

[224] DB, ii, 4b, 6a, 1b, 26b, 84a, 27a, 14b, 5a, 31a, 58a, 3a.   [225] DB, ii, 6a, 7a.
[226] *VCH, Essex*, i, p. 276.   [227] S 1486.   [228] See above, chapter 2, pp. 23–4.
[229] Ivan D. Margary, *Roman Roads in Britain*, 3rd edn (London, 1973), pp. 243–52.
[230] *ASC*, s.a. 912 (A, B); *VCH, Essex*, i, pp. 288–99.
[231] *ASC*, s.a. 895 (C, D) (*recte* 894). It is significant, perhaps, that Benfleet and Witham
are the first two entries in Domesday for Essex (DB, ii, 1b).

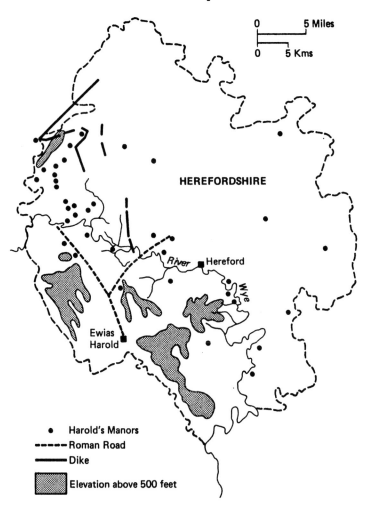

Figure 3.9 Earl Harold's Herefordshire estates TRE

importance of these Essex estates suggest strongly that many were indeed comital and had been provided to Harold in return for his defence of the shire. Harold, however, had not been earl of Essex since 1053. His ability to keep hold of official estates for a dozen years after he had given up his official duties there suggests that the newly reorganized estates of the earls were rapidly becoming familial under Edward the Confessor.

The land with which Harold was entrusted in Herefordshire

seems, as well, to have been organized for defence. Although safe from Viking attack, the shire was harried by the Welsh, who raided periodically from 1049 until the Confessor's death.[232] First, Swein Godwineson, then Ralph the Timid, and finally Harold held the troublesome shire.[233] Ralph attempted to increase the security of Herefordshire by establishing a number of castles and garrisons along the March, in much the way his fellow Normans defended the Duchy's own borderlands. As Ralph's by-name suggests, however, his labours were not a success. When Harold added the shire to his earldom, he appears to have reorganized it yet again. By January 1066 Harold controlled about half the territory west of Offa's Dyke and east of the present Welsh border.[234] (See figure 3.9.) The vast majority of these holdings lay in the lowlands of the Wye Valley, the vulnerable and oft-used route from South Wales to the shire town of Hereford. Harold had twenty-three holdings in this frontier, all of little monetary value. Although together they were assessed at seventy-seven hides, all but two were waste, and in total these lands were valued at only 70s. Harold's estates just east of the Dyke on the other hand – Pembridge, Stretford, Brinsop, Burghill and Sugwas – were profitable. Assessed at twenty-five hides and three virgates they were stocked and cultivated and rendered almost £50 a year.[235] From the location of both the Herefordshire waste and Harold's own holdings it is clear that the Welsh were especially intent on harrying land west of the Dyke, perhaps in an attempt to reassert claims to land which had traditionally been defined as Welsh, and that the English were determined to defend their territory.

Although the Dyke was primarily designed to define the frontier between Mercia and Wales it included tactically strong positions, many of which were held by Harold.[236] Rushock Hill, one of Harold's waste manors, was one such point. Protected by the Dyke, it lay on high ground, offering a view of the surrounding countryside.[237] Burghill, one of Harold's manors just

---

[232] Fl. Wig., i, p. 203; *ASC*, s.a. 1053 (C), 1055, 1056 (C, D), 1058 (D), 1065 (C, D); Nelson, *The Normans in South Wales*, pp. 17–19.
[233] Barlow, *Edward the Confessor*, pp. 93–4.   [234] DB, i, 182r–187r.
[235] DB, i, 186r, 182r. Burghill, moreover, was in possession of the profitable third penny of two hundreds.   [236] Sir Cyril Fox, *Offa's Dyke* (London, 1955), p. 279.
[237] *Ibid.*, p. 280. For Herefordshire and its defence after the Conquest, see Christopher Lewis, 'The Norman settlement of Herefordshire under William I', *Anglo-Norman Studies*, 7 (1985), pp. 195–213.

east of the Dyke and one of the most valuable in Herefordshire,[238] was equally situated for defence. Its name means 'hill of the fort',[239] and during the Godwinesons' year in exile, when Ralph was put in charge of the county, Burghill was given to Osbern Pentecost, one of Ralph's Norman followers, doubtless because of the site's strategic importance.[240] Burghill, moreover, lay on the Roman road from Kenchester, which ran southwest towards Wales to the River Dore and then branched south to Ewias Harold and north through the wasteland to the banks of the northern Wye.[241] Easy access from less vulnerable estates east of Offa's Dyke, like Burghill, to the area subject to raids helps to explain the pattern of Harold's holdings in the shire.

Harold supplemented whatever comital holdings he was given in the county through bold private enterprise. Some of Herefordshire's wasteland may simply have fallen to him by right of conquest. Other, more profitable estates came to him through shakedown operations that he ran against local churches. The canons of the Bishopric of Hereford were despoiled of eight of their manors by Earls Godwine and Harold,[242] the canons of St Guthlac lost an estate worth £16,[243] and the Bishopric of Hereford was stripped by the earl of Inkberrow in Worcester.[244] There is no evidence that these communities complained about the family's encroachments before the Norman Conquest, although it is certainly clear they were impoverished by them. Perhaps at the time, with the Bishops of Worcester and Hereford as close allies of the family, and with their own lands vulnerable to Welsh attack, communities grudgingly gave up some of their property in return for protection.

A study of comital landholding in Sussex, Essex and Herefordshire suggests that eleventh-century kings commonly endowed their earls with land in England's most vulnerable regions. In exchange, the king received services of defence from the earls, whom contemporaries habitually describe as fighting 'in the king's name'.[245] Thus, while circumstances arising from

---

[238] The estate was worth £20 and had 26 ploughteams (DB, i, 186r).
[239] Eilert Ekwall, *The Concise Oxford Dictionary of English Place-Names*, 4th edn (Oxford, 1960), p. 75.   [240] DB, i, 186r.   [241] Margary, *Roman Roads*, pp. 342–3.
[242] Holme Lacy, Hazle, Colwall, Coddington, Hampton Bishop, Sugwas (in Stretton Sugwas), Collington and Bridge Sollers (DB, i, 181v, 182r, 182v).
[243] Pembridge (DB, i, 186r).   [244] DB, i, 174r.
[245] *ASC*, s.a. 1051 (D), 1052 (C), 1055 (C); Richard Abels, *Lordship and Military Obligation in Anglo-Saxon England* (Berkeley, 1988), pp. 169–70.

Cnut's conquest created an opportunity for earls to rise as a new class of mighty subjects, English kings did not necessarily make the worst of a bad situation. They did not have bureaucracy enough to transform the profits from their estates directly into a means of kingdom-wide defence. Domesday statistics do suggest that a greater percentage of geld and fyrd-service could be gathered from lesser thegns, but there was a tremendous need for organizers and leaders who had both large numbers of thegns commended to them and personal sway over local areas.[246] Gifts of land were the primary means of purchasing the loyalty of such men, and were vital in districts outside of Wessex, where the West Saxon kings had less influence. It was wise, therefore, for the monarch to turn some of the burden of geld and fyrd-service over to families of local magnates.[247] When Edward became king in 1042 he found himself saddled with a system of delegated royal authority that enabled his earls to exert great influence in their territories; but his three most important families were of about equal wealth and influence. But the years following Edward's accession witnessed the meteoric rise of Godwine's family. Within a decade Godwine and his sons had extended their authority and landed resources. They were able to acquire wealth which outstripped the king's own, even in parts of Wessex. Except for a brief interlude in 1051–52, Edward was unable to curb the family's growing power in the shires.[248] By the late 1050s the sons of Godwine were dominant at court as well. Not so, the sons of Siward and Leofric, who, if the few charters that survive are any indication, were less often with the king.[249]

Not only were earldoms falling to the Godwinesons, but many of the estates attached to them were changing into private

---

[246] In Cornwall, for example, the Godwinesons paid on the average 3d. geld per ploughland (based on 2s. a hide), but the county average was 4d. In Somerset, they paid an average of 9d. per ploughland, but the county average was 1s. 3d. per ploughland.

[247] Indeed this had been royal policy for several generations. By tying local aristocrats to his family and uniting their interests with his own, King Alfred had been able to assert royal authority over traditional rivals of Wessex (Hart, 'Æthelstan Half-King', pp. 115–44). He and his immediate successors found local allies imperative for the reconquest of England, and thus their wise policy of empowering local lords as royal representatives contributed to their success. The Danish conquest under Swein and Cnut witnessed a continuation of this policy (*ASC*, s.a. 1016 (C, D, E), 1017 (C, D, E)). Cnut's trans-sea empire necessitated such an arrangement and the Danish king was able to develop the Anglo-Saxon political system of ealdordoms to his own advantage.   [248] Barlow, however, disagrees. *Edward the Confessor*, p. 127.

[249] See appendix 3.1.

holdings. In Hampshire, for example, the entire west end of the Isle of Wight along with three great estates along the southwest coast, all vital to the region's safety, belonged to Tostig in 1065, even though Harold and not Tostig was earl of Wessex and in charge of the area's defence. Over Wallop in Hampshire and Brompton Regis in Somerset, with the third penny of justice attached to them, were in possession of Gytha, the earl of Wessex's wife,[250] and Harold continued to hold what were most likely comital estates in Hertfordshire, Essex and Norfolk long after he had given up authority in eastern England.[251] Hartland and Tiverton, Devonshire, were held not by the earl of Wessex in 1066, but by his mother,[252] and Washington, Sussex, was held by his brother.[253] Other manors, like Haversham, Buckinghamshire, Aldbourne, Wiltshire, and Lexden and Stanway in Essex, confiscated from fallen ealdormen and their families and then granted out to earls, were transformed into familial property.[254] In all, the lands just enumerated were worth a fortune – more than £450 and twenty-two nights' farm.[255] Although the tendency for official lands to become personal in the Middle Ages was natural, it was by no means inevitable. In Herefordshire and Gloucestershire, which fell under Harold's jurisdiction sometime after 1053, the earl held a large number of estates. Yet Harold son of Earl Ralph, whose father was succeeded by Harold Godwineson, held only ten hides there TRE; and in Yorkshire, where Earl Siward had once held sway, Waltheof Siwardson held only a fraction of his father's property. Minors when their fathers died and without much influence at court, Harold fitz Ralph and Waltheof had neither power in the shires nor support at court to maintain their father's official endowments.

The fact that the Godwinesons could permanently alienate land set aside for the endowment of royal officials is a sure sign that the West Saxon monarchy was in serious trouble. If the Confessor approved of the family's rapid aggrandizement and its vast network of allies, he was a fool; if he acquiesced he cannot have been in full control of his kingdom. Domesday Book, therefore, offers damning evidence against the competence of Edward the Confessor and the stability of his regime. A systematic investiga-

[250] DB, i, 38v, 86v.   [251] DB, i, 38v, 86v.   [252] DB, i, 100v.   [253] DB, i, 28r.
[254] DB, i, 148r, 65r.
[255] Harold may have held so much in Yorkshire in January 1066 because he had been able to maintain a number of his brother's comital estates.

tion of the information contained within the survey suggests that Edward was a weak king, pushed and bullied by a family of highly competent and slightly unscrupulous earls, and carried along by a well-established royal bureaucracy. Edward's position was certainly not helped by the circumstances of his election. Having spent his boyhood in exile, he owed a huge debt to those of Cnut's aristocrats who pushed for his return, including Godwine, a man implicated in the murder of the king's own brother. Edward's position, never strong, eroded during the course of his reign, worsening with the passing of each year by his inability to stop the growing power and wealth of Earl Godwine and his sons. The Confessor, therefore, was never able to extricate himself from the dangerous changes in the relationship between the monarchy and the aristocracy that were put into motion in the years on either side of Cnut's conquest. The clientage, moreover, built by Harold and his family or by the families of other new men was only two generations old at most in 1066. When this rootless elite lay dead at Stamford Bridge or at Hastings, the fragile structure of eleventh-century secular lordship collapsed, and it became nearly impossible to organize effective resistance, especially against a man who had simply expropriated the recent expropriators. These things combined to give the Battle of Hastings its decisive character.

APPENDIX 3.1

	S 998 (1042) Sherborne	999 (1043) Abingdon	1001 (1044) Old Minster	1003 (1044) Abbotsbury	1004 (1044) Exeter	1005 (1044) OM	1006 (1044) OM	1007 (1045) OM	1012 (1045) OM	1008 (1045) OM	1010 (1045) Wilton	1012 (1046) OM	1014 (1046) Peterborough	1015 (1046) Rouen	1016 (1046) OM	1017 (1048 × 9) Burton	1018 (1049) OM	1019 (1049) St Petroc	1020 (1050) Abingdon	1021 (1050) Exeter	1022 (1050) Abingdon	1025 (1050?) Abingdon	1023 (1052) Abingdon
Godwine	x	x	x	x	x	x	x	x	x	x	x	x	x	x	x	x	x	x	x	x	x	x	x
Leofric	x	—	x	x	x	x	x	x	x	x	x	x	x	x	x	x	x	x	x	x	x	x	x
Siward	x	x	x	x	x	x	x	x	x	x	x	—	x	x	—	x	—	x	—	x	—	x	x
Swein	—	x	x	x	—	x	x	x	x	x	x	—	x	x	—	—	—	—	—	—	—	—	—
Harold	—	—	—	—	—	—	—	—	—	x	—	—	—	—	x	—	x	—	x	x	x	x	x
Beorn	—	—	—	—	—	—	—	—	—	x	x	—	x	x	—	x	—	x	—	—	—	—	—
Ralph	—	—	—	—	—	—	—	—	—	—	—	—	—	—	—	—	—	—	x	x	x	x	x
Sihroð	—	—	—	—	—	—	—	—	—	—	—	—	—	—	—	—	—	x	—	—	—	—	—

Attestations of the Confessor's earls from 1042 to 1052

	S1027 (1059) Exeter	1028 (1059) St Denis	1029 (1060) Peterborough	1031 (1060) Westminster	1033 (1061) Rouen	1034 (1061) Bath	1038 (1065) Malmesbury	1060 (1055 × 1060) Peterborough	1059 (1061 × 1066) Peterborough
Harold	x	x	x	x	x	x	x	x	x
Tostig	x	x	x	x	x	x	x	x	—
Gyrth	x	x	—	x	x	x	x	—	—
Leofwine	x	x	—	—	x	—	x	—	—
Ælfgar	x	x	—	x	x	x	—	—	—
Waltheof	—	—	—	—	x	—	—	—	—

Attestations of the Confessor's earls from 1059 to 1066

II THE NORMAN CONQUEST

Chapter 4

DOMESDAY BOOK AND THE TENURIAL REVOLUTION: LORDSHIP, KINSHIP AND THE VILL

Orderic Vitalis, after completing his long and compelling account of the perils overcome by William the Conqueror in 1069–70, paused to describe the hard-won rewards of some of the new king's most loyal followers. Hugh d'Avranches, so he tells us, received the county of Chester, Roger de Montgomery Arundel and later Shropshire, and Eudo of Champagne Holderness. Orderic goes on at length about the new lands of 'earls and magnates too numerous to name'.[1] He ends his catalogue of earldoms and fees, however, with a sobering remark, to remind his audience upon what hardships Norman prosperity in England was founded:

So foreigners grew wealthy with the spoils of England, whilst her own sons were either shamefully slain or driven as exiles to wander hopelessly through foreign kingdoms.[2]

The Peterborough Chronicler, too, describes the lands acquired by William's companions. As the monk recounts the plagues, fires and famines of 1087, he writes:

The king sold his land on very hard terms – as hard as he could. Then came somebody else and offered more than the other had given, and the king let it go to the man who had offered him more. Then came the third, and offered still more, and the king gave it into the hands of the man who offered him most of all, and did not care how sinfully the reeves had got it from poor men, nor how many unlawful things they did.[3]

These two narratives testify that through grant, purchase and rapine, Norman lords, with their retainers in tow, gained the bulk of England's farms and villages – holdings which had, until the

---

[1] OV, ii, pp. 260–6.   [2] OV, ii, p. 266.   [3] *ASC*, s.a. 1086 (E) (*recte* 1087).

Conquest, supported an altogether different aristocracy. Neither the historian nor the chronicler, however, records enough information to piece together the means by which such land transferences were made. This is unfortunate, since the formation of new honours in England paired with the establishment of Norman families in the kingdom is the most important feature of the Anglo-Norman period, and since a familiarity with these families and their lands is essential for an understanding of the Conquest's impact. Certainly, descriptions of these fees and investigations into the histories of the families who held them lie at the heart of much important scholarship. The lands of the Mowbrays, the Clares, the Beaumonts and the Lacys, to name but a few, have been charted and studied with care.[4] The focus of these recent studies has necessarily been on the particular rather than the general, and on these families throughout the whole of the Anglo-Norman and Angevin periods. Works on post-Conquest families, moreover, are concerned with the fee at hand rather than the legion of fees carved out in William I's reign. And like Orderic Vitalis himself, few of these historians have wondered, at least in print, how the land transferences necessitated by the Conqueror's tenurial revolution actually occurred.

The kingdom William conquered was made up of some 44,000 square miles. There were something like a quarter of a million peasant households, 14,000 settlements, and over half a million ploughing animals. Thousands of mills, fisheries and churches enriched the holders of English lands, and hundreds of thousands of acres of woodland and meadow were part and parcel of England's proprietary landscape.[5] The fields and copses, the livestock and peasants had all, before the Conquest, been controlled by an extensive and economically varied aristocracy composed of perhaps four or five thousand thegns.[6] The almost

extensive + economically varied + not as much economic variation post conq[?]

[4] D. E. Greenway, *Charters of the Honour of Mowbray 1107–1191*, Records of Social and Economic History, new series, 1 (Oxford, 1972), pp. xvii–xxxii; Richard Mortimer, 'The beginnings of the honour of Clare', *Anglo-Norman Studies*, 3 (1981), pp. 119–41; J. C. Ward, 'The place of the honour in twelfth-century Society; the honour of Clare 1066–1217', *Proceedings of the Suffolk Institute of Archaeology and Natural History*, 35 (1983), pp. 191–202; David Crouch, *The Beaumont Twins: The Roots and Branches of Power in the Twelfth Century* (Cambridge, 1986), pp. 115–32; W. E. Wightman, *The Lacy Family in England and Normandy, 1066–1194* (Oxford, 1966), pp. 17–54, 117–66.
[5] For tabulations of Domesday Book's agrarian information by county see H. C. Darby, *Domesday England* (Cambridge, 1977), pp. 336–44.
[6] Henry Loyn, *Anglo-Saxon England and the Norman Conquest* (London, 1962), p. 320.

complete transference of all these lands, men and beasts in less than twenty years is astonishing, especially when it is remembered that there were few good roads, that communications were haphazard, and that royal administration, even when assessed by the most optimistic of historians, was rudimentary. Certainly there was no absolute and systematic record in the royal archives detailing each and every property throughout the kingdom.[7] Yet in spite of England's daunting size and the limits of William's bureaucracy, within twenty years of Hastings the overwhelming majority of land, with its vineyards, beekeepers and swine pastures, had been transferred from one lord to another. By 1086 most peasants paid their dues and worked their land in aid of a different lord, and the English freemen and lesser aristocrats who had survived the difficult decades following the Conquest, looked to a different set of men for protection.

How could all of this have transpired in a mere twenty years? The reasons for solving this puzzle are compelling. An understanding of how post-Conquest fees were constructed would inform our ideas about royal power in the generation after Hastings. It would give us a notion of how much control was exercised by the king in restructuring England's landed wealth, and how much was due to the great men who surrounded him. It would also allow us to posit what administrative devices, old and new, were used to effect such a massive resettlement. Answers to these questions could give us some notion of how uniform, speedy and regulated the progress of the Conquest was. It would allow us to form opinions about the effects of the Norman Conquest on tenure and economics and, finally, it would cast new light on that old but central issue of the impact of the Norman Conquest. Was England's tenurial pattern in the period of Norman settlement marked by continuity or marred by change?

The standard answer given to this puzzle of land transference was established by scholars such as E. A. Freeman, Frank Stenton, James Tait, John Horace Round, and R. R. Darlington. Their understanding of the evidence preserved in private charters, royal grants and especially Domesday Book led them to conclude that by and large the transference of land took place through the rules of inheritance and succession. An individual Anglo-Saxon lord,

---

[7] For the administrative documents that lie behind Domesday see S. P. J. Harvey, 'Domesday Book and its predecessors', *EHR*, 86 (1971), pp. 753–73.

ancecessors

when dispossessed, was made the antecessor of one of William's favourites, who succeeded to the Englishman's lands across the kingdom.[8] Great fees, as Stenton noted, could be constructed from the lands of a number of different men, but 'the best reply that a lord could make to a claim upon his property' was the production of sworn evidence that the land or the rights in dispute had belonged to his antecessor on the day King Edward was alive and dead'.[9] There is a legion of supporting evidence for this assertion in Domesday Book. The studies of Stenton and others, particularly in the *Victoria County Histories*, have brought fame to obscure but wealthy pre-Conquest landholders such as Wigot of Wallingford and Ansgar the Staller, because these men were indeed the antecessors of less shadowy Norman lords.[10]

Beyond the evidence for antecessors and successors in Domesday Book, this orthodoxy has a certain administrative elegance. The written administration needed for such a transfer is placed at a minimum, and the responsibility for determining landed rewards is neatly placed on the grantee rather than on the representatives of royal government. A single writ, passed from one hundred court to the next to demand an accounting of a disseised thegn's land, would be all the written government

---

[8] The terms 'antecessor' and 'inheritance' are used in their Domesday senses. The word antecessor describes an Englishman with a clear Norman successor. Inheritance refers to a Norman's acquisition of the bulk of the lands of a particular English predecessor.

[9] Stenton, *Anglo-Saxon England*, p. 626.

[10] The tendency of a few of William's followers to inherit all the lands of a wealthy pre-Conquest lord was long ago observed. Henry Ellis noted, as early as 1833, that Ansgar the Staller's land fell to Geoffrey de Mandeville (Henry Ellis, *A General Introduction to Domesday Book*, 2 vols. (London, 1833), ii, p. 43, n. 1), and Walter de Grey Birch, some fifty years later, noted that Wigot of Wallingford's land came, through marriage, to Robert D'Oilly (Walter de Grey Birch, *Domesday Book: A Popular Account of the Exchequer Manuscript* (London, 1887), p. 124). E. A. Freeman, in one of his famous, rambling appendices, discussed a number of instances of inheritance through antecessor (Freeman, *NC*, v, pp. 769–78). Inheritance through a well-defined antecessor, however, was not systematically studied until *The Victoria County History* began its publication of 'Domesday Introductions'. The following are especially valuable: J. H. Round, 'Introduction to the Hertfordshire Domesday', *VCH, Hertfordshire* (London, 1902), i, pp. 274–86; 'Introduction to the Essex Domesday', *VCH, Essex* (Westminster, 1903), i, pp. 342–52; 'Introduction to the Buckinghamshire Domesday', *VCH, Buckinghamshire* (London, 1905), i, pp. 212–20; F. M. Stenton, 'Introduction to the Leicestershire Domesday', *VCH, Leicestershire* (London, 1907), i, pp. 289–300, and 'Introduction to the Huntingdonshire Domesday, *VCH, Huntingdonshire* (London, 1926), i, pp. 331–6; R. R. Darlington, 'Introduction to Wiltshire Domesday', *VCH, Wiltshire* (Oxford, 1955), ii, pp. 65–71; A. Williams, 'Introduction to the Dorset Domesday', *VCH, Dorset* (Oxford, 1968), iii, pp. 31–5.

necessary to effect a change of possession in each shire. Domesday
Leicestershire gives clear evidence of inheritance from a single
antecessor, and the manner in which the results of the inquest are
recorded in this county preserves a hint of such single accountings.
The list of the Count of Meulan's fee ends with the statement,
'Saxi held all these lands'; Earl Aubrey's fee with 'Hearding held
all these lands with his men'; Robert de Vessey's with 'Æthelric
son of Mærgeat held these lands of Robert's TRE'; and
Geoffrey Alselin's with 'Toki held all this land with sake and
soke'.[11] From time to time the Domesday scribe also notes when
a Norman acquired land that was not his antecessor's, as if to
highlight the exceptional nature of such acquisitions. In Somerset,
for example, Humphrey the Chamberlain, the successor of a West
Country thegn named Beorhtric, inherited land in Lyte's Cary
which had been held by Lyfing before the Conquest. The scribe
notes, however, that 'this land has been joined to Beorhtric's
land'.[12] In the same county in Nether Stowey, Alvred d'Epaignes
held land once belonging to Osweard and Æthelweard, but 'this
land [so the manuscript says] has been added to Alwig
[Bannesune's] land which Alvred holds'.[13] From these entries and
dozens of others like them, it is easy to form a tidy picture of
continuity in land tenure between the deaths of the Confessor and
the Conqueror.

Peter Sawyer, in his article '1066–1086: A Tenurial Revolution?', has extended this theory of inheritance by antecessor.
He argues that many of the lands of minor English thegns and
sokemen could be found in the hands of a particular Norman
tenant-in-chief, not because they themselves were the antecessors
of great Norman lords, but because they had been the men of such
lords' antecessors. Sawyer provides several dozen examples of this
and maintains that these scattered hints of continuity in lordship
are typical of much post-Conquest land transference.[14] Paired

---

[11] DB, i, 231v, 234r, 235v.   [12] DB, i, 98v.
[13] DB, i, 97r. For other examples see Ridgehill (DB, i, 98r), Woodcocks Ley (DB,
i, 97r) and Witham Friary, Somerset (DB, i, 97v); Clapham, Wanborough (DB, i, 36r)
and Chessington, Surrey (DB, i, 36v).
[14] Peter Sawyer, '1066–1086: A tenurial revolution?', in *Domesday Book: A Reassessment*,
ed. Peter Sawyer (London, 1985), pp. 76–8. Carl Stephenson also believed that pre-
Conquest lordship in the form of commendation, 'at least from the Norman point of
view...might determine the allocation of [an Englishman's] land to a particular
manor' ('Commendation and related problems in Domesday', *EHR*, 59 (1944), p.
296).

argument for continuity of land tenure [handwritten marginalia]

with this argument is Sawyer's further claim that evidence for tenurial continuity is limited simply because Domesday's commissioners or its scribes ignored the bulk of information on Anglo-Saxon overlords. He concludes that although many Old English lordships are concealed by Domesday Book, it is along these pre-Conquest lines that the Norman tenurial pattern emerged.[15] Hence he proposes that 'such examples suggest that pre-Conquest England had fiefs very much like those of 1086', and that 'the changes in tenurial structure after the Norman Conquest were less than revolutionary'.[16]

change in Norman period [handwritten marginalia]

Both the traditional theory of inheritance by antecessor and Sawyer's hypothesis of inheritance of antecessors' lordships emphasize tenurial continuity, and advocates of both theories support the notion that England's tenurial pattern in the period of the Norman settlement was set long before William's victory at Hastings. A systematic investigation of all Domesday's tenurial information, however, suggests that despite some inheritance through antecessors, a great deal of England, including the most important post-Conquest fees, were formed in some other way than succession by antecessor. An examination of Domesday's TRW honours in every circuit and every shire suggests that tenurial patterns, in spite of patchy continuity, were radically altered by the Norman settlement, and that the tendency for Normans to inherit their land from a particular Saxon antecessor, although important for imparting a veneer of legality on the dispossession of the English aristocracy,[17] has been exaggerated by historians. If one actually performs the dreary but necessary task of going through Domesday Book and identifying antecessors and successors and totting up the value of their lands, one finds that from Domesday Book's four or five thousand secular landholders TRE, little more than one hundred significant antecessors can be identified.[18] Thus, inheritance by Normans from well-defined and well-to-do antecessors accounts for a minority of secular land transference – just over 10 per cent in all.

---

[15] Sawyer, 'Tenurial revolution?' pp. 82–4.   [16] *Ibid.*, pp. 78, 85.

[17] One of the techniques used by Normans to legitimize their succession to antecessors' lands is carefully examined by Eleanor Searle in 'Women and the legitimization of succession at the Norman Conquest', *Anglo-Norman Studies*, 3 (1981), pp. 159–70.

[18] According to Mack, there were approximately 115 Anglo-Saxons south of the Humber holding £25 of land or more with well-defined successors (Mack, 'Kings and thegns', appendix I).

This suggests that many post-Conquest fees were the result of a studied disregard for the Saxon past. Furthermore, Domesday's exhaustive data on landholding provides more than enough evidence to unravel the various other ways in which honours were constructed.

In some shires and in certain fees the organization of pre-Conquest landholding and lordships did indeed survive the first twenty years of Norman rule. The 'Domesday Introductions' in *The Victoria County Histories* provide a lengthy catalogue of antecessors and their successors, and, as Peter Sawyer has shown, large numbers of a Saxon antecessor's men could also, on occasion, be found in his Norman successor's fee. Sawyer's example of Count Alan of Richmond's land in Cambridgeshire is an excellent case in point,[19] and numerous other examples can be found, particularly in eastern England. In Essex, for example, Richard fitz Gilbert inherited both Wihtgar's land and the lands of Wihtgar's men,[20] and in Suffolk the Malets inherited the majority of their antecessor Eadric of Laxfield's men.[21] In Middlesex Walter fitz Othere inherited both Azur the Housecarl's land and the land of some of his men,[22] and in Hertfordshire Geoffrey de Mandeville came into the lands of Ansgar the Staller as well as the land of a number of Ansgar's sokemen.[23] On a smaller scale, we can see a variety of lords pressing claims to bits and pieces of land once held by men of their antecessors. Ranulf Peverel added a sokeman to his holding at Willingale Doe in Essex, because the man had been held by Ranulf's antecessor.[24] Ralph de Tosny claimed a freeman in Oxborough, Norfolk 'because his antecessor held him with sake and soke',[25] and Robert Malet claimed Ingham and Stalham in Norfolk 'because TRE his antecessor Eadric [of Laxfield] had the commendation of those men who held [them]'.[26] At first glance, such examples weigh very much in favour of Sawyer's hypothesis, especially in light of his argument that the bulk of Old English lordships,

---

[19] Sawyer, 'Tenurial revolution?', p. 78; L. F. Salzman, 'Introduction to the Cambridge-shire Domesday', *VCH, Cambridgeshire*, i, pp. 354–5.

[20] DB, ii, 38b–40b; Mortimer, 'The honour of Clare', pp. 128–9. But for Wihtgar's relationship with Richard fitz Gilbert before his fall, see below, p. 204.

[21] *Feudal Documents from the Abbey of Bury St Edmunds*, ed. D. C. Douglas (London, 1932), p. xc, n. 3. An analysis of the Suffolk folios of Domesday reveals that the land of just under 70 per cent of Eadric's men was held by Robert Malet. The remainder devolved on to twenty-six other fees.   [22] DB, i, 130r.   [23] DB, i, 139v–140r.

[24] DB, ii, 73a.   [25] DB, ii, 245a.   [26] DB, ii, 148b.

unrecorded in most parts of the survey, follow the model of these successions. This is, however, a dangerous assumption. A comprehensive examination of evidence provided by the Exchequer Domesday in the few counties for which information on Anglo-Saxon lordship is consistently recorded suggests that these examples represent only one type of succession, and not the most important one. Entire shires in Domesday Book rarely or never record pre-Conquest overlords. No Saxon overlords, for example, are recorded in Domesday's folios for Cheshire, Derbyshire, Huntingdonshire, Leicestershire, Nottinghamshire, Somerset and Wiltshire[27] and a dozen or less are recorded in Devonshire, Dorset, Lincolnshire, Northamptonshire, Oxfordshire, Shropshire, Staffordshire, Surrey, Warwickshire and Yorkshire.[28] And in southern counties such as Sussex, Cornwall and Berkshire, typically the only English overlords recorded are the king or his earls. This lacuna in the survey makes it dangerous to speculate on pre-Conquest lordships in these shires. Only Domesday Book's Circuit III provides consistent evidence for Anglo-Saxon lordship, particularly in Hertfordshire, Cambridgeshire and Buckinghamshire. In these three counties especially, nearly every minor Anglo-Saxon tenant is given a lord. When we concentrate our efforts here where the evidence is most complete, we witness the breakdown of Saxon patterns of lordship on a grand scale.

In Hertfordshire, Archbishop Stigand had more men than any other great lord in the shire; his followers are recorded holding nearly forty-five hides of land in thirty-three different instances 'on the day King Edward was both alive and dead'.[29] About half the land of Stigand's men could be found in the fee of Odo Bishop of Bayeux after the Conquest,[30] but the remainder was partitioned between thirteen of the shire's other tenants-in-chief.[31] Thus, in Hertfordshire, the county's greatest lordship did not survive the Conquest. Since Stigand was an ecclesiastic of sorts, he is perhaps not representative. Ansgar the Staller, with his obvious successor

---

[27] DB, i, 262v–268r, 272r–278r, 203r–207v, 230r–237r, 280r–293r, 86r–99v.
[28] DB, i, 112v, 83r, 228r, 229r, 159r, 254r, 249r, 31v, 34r, 35v, 36r, 243v, 72v, 73r.
[29] DB, i, 132r–135r, 137r, 140v, 141v–142r.   [30] DB, i, 134r–134v.
[31] These are King William, the Archbishop of Canterbury, the Bishop of London, the Bishop of Chester, Count Alan of Richmond, Eustace of Boulogne, Ralph de Limesy, Geoffrey de Bec, Hardwin de Scales, Edgar the Ætheling, Sigar de Chocques, and the wives of Richard fitz Gilbert and Hugh de Grandmesnil.

Geoffrey de Mandeville, may be a better example. As Sawyer points out, the bulk of the land of Ansgar's men in Essex was in the hands of his successor Geoffrey by 1086,[32] but in Hertfordshire and Buckinghamshire, this is simply not the case. In Hertfordshire, Ansgar's men held almost forty hides of land. Less than half of these hides were in Geoffrey's hands by 1086 – the other twenty were in the fees of Maurice Bishop of London, Odo Bishop of Bayeux, Eustace of Boulogne, Robert Gernon, Ralph Baynard, Geoffrey de Bec, Edgar Ætheling, and a king's thegn named Alwine Doddason.[33] In Buckinghamshire fourteen hides once held by Ansgar's men were found in Geoffrey's fief,[34] but ten or so others were divided between Walter Giffard and Henry de Ferrers.[35] In these two counties, over half the land once held by Ansgar's men had been scattered by 1086 among eleven new lords. This same pattern (or lack thereof) can be discerned with the land of the men of Eadgifu the Fair, Count Alan of Richmond's antecessor. In Cambridgeshire and Hertfordshire Alan kept firm control over nearly all the lands that had once pertained to Eadgifu's men.[36] In Buckinghamshire and in Suffolk, however, the count was less successful. In the former the lands of Eadgifu's men devolved on to the fees of Jocelyn the Breton, William fitz Ansculf, and Earl Hugh,[37] and in the latter Count Alan received the land of one of Eadgifu's men,[38] but the rest was incorporated into the *terra regis*, or alternatively into the fees of Hugh de Montfort or the Countess of Aûmale.[39] In Buckinghamshire, when we trace the disposition of the lands of Alric son of Goding and his men, we find that Walter Giffard's fee consisted both of Alric's demesne land and eleven and a half hides of land which had been held by Alric's men.[40] Nonetheless, almost fifteen other hides of men once pertaining to Alric's lordship were spread between the Count of Mortain, who had eight and a half of these

---

[32] Sawyer, 'Tenurial revolution?' pp. 73, 74; *VCH, Essex*, i, p. 343.
[33] DB, i, 133v–134v, 137r–138v, 139v–140r, 142r.   [34] DB, i, 149r.
[35] DB, i, 147v, 148r, 151r.
[36] For Hertfordshire see DB, i, 136v–137r. The exceptions are 24 acres in Wallington which Gosbert de Beauvais held, probably illegally (the text is ambiguous on this point), and some land in Berkesdon, held illegally by Hardwin de Scales (DB, i, 140v, 141v). For Cambridgeshire see DB, i, 193v–195v. The exceptions appear on fols. 196v, 198r, 198v, 199v, 200r, 200v, 201r, 201v.
[37] DB, i, 152r, 148v, 146v. None of the land of Eadgifu's men was held by Count Alan in this county.   [38] DB, ii, 295a.   [39] DB, ii, 284b–285a, 410a, 431a.
[40] DB, i, 147r, 147v, 148r.

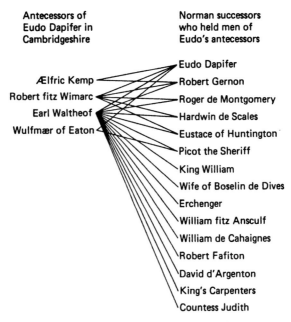

Figure 4.1 Eudo Dapifer's antecessors in Cambridgeshire and their Norman successors

hides, and Miles Crispin, Countess Judith and Leofwine of Nuneham.[41] Moving on to Cambridgeshire and turning to Eudo Dapifer's fee, we find the Steward holding the lands of the men of Ælfric Kemp, Robert fitz Wimarc, Earl Waltheof, and Wulfmær of Eaton.[42] But in the same county the land which Ælfric Kemp himself had held was in the hands of Robert Gernon; the lands of Robert fitz Wimarc's men were subsumed into the fees of Earl Roger, Hardwin de Scales, Eustace of Huntington and Picot the Sheriff; and the lands of Earl Waltheof's men had fallen into the hands of fourteen Cambridgeshire tenants-in-chief.[43] (See figure 4.1.)

Another illustration of this breakdown can be found by tracing the fate of the men of Anglo-Saxon earls in Circuit III counties. The Confessor's earls, with the exception of Waltheof, had no clearly defined successors. It is not surprising, therefore, that the land of comital retainers was spread to the four winds. Cambridgeshire evidence well illustrates the typical disruption of

[41] DB, i, 147v, 150v, 153r.   [42] DB, i, 197v.   [43] See below, n. 46.

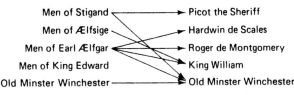

Figure 4.2 The lordships of Abington Pigotts TRE and TRW

comital lordships. Earl Tostig and Earl Gyrth together had only ten men recorded in the Cambridgeshire folios, and yet the lands of these ten were distributed by 1086 between the fees of Eudo Dapifer, Hardwin de Scales, Picot the Sheriff, Countess Judith and Robert Fafiton.[44] The thirteen recorded holdings of Earl Harold's men were meted out to seven tenants-in-chief.[45] The lands of Earl Waltheof's men – assessed at about thirty-five hides and found on thirty-one different occasions – were spread among fourteen tenants-in-chief.[46] Finally, the lands of Earl Ælfgar's forty-four men were by the time of the Domesday survey in the hands of twelve different tenants-in-chief.[47] These earls' men had held their land by a whole spectrum of tenures.[48] The fragmentation of comital lordships, therefore, was not simply the product of pre-Conquest tenurial arrangements. Moreover, King William succeeded to the earls' demesne estates more often than not, and yet only three hides formerly in the possession of earls' men in Cambridgeshire were incorporated into the *terra regis*.[49] These earls' men in Cambridgeshire held in total nearly 120 hides of land, about 10 per cent of the shire's total.[50] Nearly two-thirds of all Cambridgeshire tenants-in-chief in 1086 – 25 to be exact – held a portion of these men's lands. Furthermore, almost half of all recorded Cambridgeshire settlements – 64 out of 141 – witnessed the wholesale fragmentation of lordships once controlled by England's great earls. Even those honours composed of

[44] DB, i, 202r, 197v, 198r, 200v, 202r.

[45] DB, i, 190r, 193r, 196r, 196v, 197v, 198r, 200r.

[46] DB, i, 189v, 193r, 193v, 197r, 197v, 198v, 200v, 201v, 202r, 202v.

[47] DB, i, 189r, 190r, 193r, 193v, 194r, 194v, 195r, 196r, 196v, 198r, 198v, 199r, 199b, 200r, 200v, 201v, 202r.

[48] Some 'could grant' their land (DB, i, 193a), and some 'could grant and sell' (DB, i, 196v), while others 'could not withdraw' (DB, i, 201v). Some held 'under' an earl (DB, i, 201v), some 'of' an earl (DB, i, 193r), and still others were described as 'men of' or 'sokemen of' the earls. (DB, i, 198b).   [49] DB, i, 189v, 190r.

[50] H. C. Darby, *The Domesday Geography of Eastern England*, 3rd edn (Cambridge, 1971), pp. 274–7.

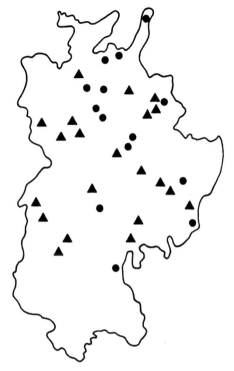

● Land inherited through Eskil of Ware and his men

▲ Land from other men

Figure 4.3 Hugh de Beauchamp's Bedfordshire holdings

vast tracts of land belonging to a single predecessor and his men were often expanded significantly by other acquisitions. Hugh de Beauchamp's fee in Bedfordshire was centred on the holdings of Eskil of Ware and his men. But Hugh's lands in the county were double those of Eskil and his men, supplemented first by the inclusion of the lands of minor aristocrats who had been thegns of King Edward, Earl Waltheof, Earl Ælfgar, Godric the Sheriff, Queen Edith and Earl Tostig, and second with lands of dozens of sokemen who had pertained to other lordships.[51] (See figure 4.3.) When we chart the movement of land across an entire county between 1066 and 1086 it is difficult to find much continuity at all.

---

[51] Unlike Buckinghamshire, Hertfordshire and Cambridgeshire, Bedfordshire does not consistently record the names of the lords of sokemen. In the Beauchamp fee, however, those who were Eskil's are recorded as such. This nonetheless leaves dozens

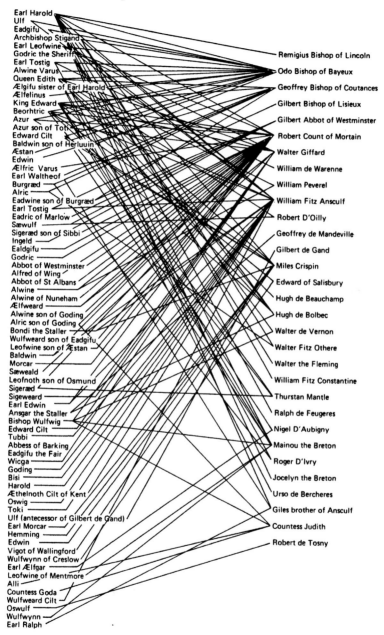

Figure 4.4 The disposition of the lands of Anglo-Saxon lords' men in Buckinghamshire

In Buckinghamshire, for example, the men of pre-Conquest lords often devolved onto more than one fee, and the bulk of post-Conquest honours had incorporated the men of a number of English lords. (See figure 4.4.) Few patterns emerge from this jumbled Buckinghamshire distribution.

This analysis of Circuit III lordships is not based on a series of perfect examples, but rather on a representative sample of post-Conquest successions. In Hertfordshire some 300 hides of land – that is between a quarter and a third of all assessed land in the county – once belonging to the *men* of identifiable Saxon lords, could not be found in the honours of their lord's successor or were not dispersed in any discernible pattern. In Cambridgeshire, a rough calculation based on the same criteria reveals that almost 25 per cent of all lands in the county, once belonging to the men of English overlords, was scattered among several Norman lords by 1086. In Buckinghamshire this figure is about 20 per cent; in Bedfordshire it is approximately 15 per cent, and in Middlesex about 12 per cent.[52] These statistics represent an enormous amount of disruption in secular lordships, particularly when it is remembered that this does not include the great mass of land which TRE was held in demesne by the king, the earls or important thegns, or that land which remained undisturbed in the hands of ecclesiastical corporations. Therefore, on the basis of information supplied to us by the Domesday counties which consistently preserve such evidence, it is certain that Anglo-Saxon lordships tended to fragment, the land of the lord breaking free in part from the lands of his men, and to devolve in different ways on the Conqueror's tenants-in-chief.

This rapid decay of old lordships had a startling effect on the vill and on the local economy. When we compare the shape of lordships within Circuit III vills in 1086 with those of 1066, the disintegration of pre-Conquest patterns is everywhere evident. By 1086, for example, the Cambridgeshire vill of Abington Pigotts was divided between King William and his tenants-in-chief Walkelin Bishop of Winchester, Roger de Montgomery, Hardwin de Scales and Picot the Sheriff.[53] These five men had

---

of unassigned sokemen in his fee. One of the seven sokemen holding in Houghton Conquest (DB, i, 213r) we are told later 'could grant or sell where he would', and his lands lay in the portion of the vill which Adelaid wife of Hugh de Grandmesnil held (DB, i, 217v).

[52] These figures are the result of an analysis of hide information in the Domesday Book Database.   [53] DB, i, 190r, 193r, 198r, 200v.

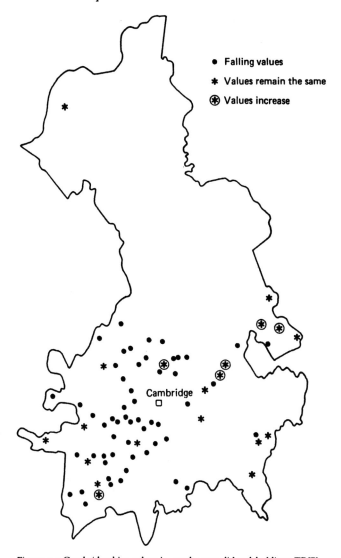

Figure 4.5 Cambridgeshire values in newly consolidated holdings TRW

inherited the lands of the men of Earl Ælfgar, Archbishop Stigand, Ælfsige and King Edward, but they were reorganized along completely new lines. In this vill, the land of Stigand's men went not only to Walkelin, his successor to the bishopric, but also to Picot the Sheriff. The land of Earl Ælfgar's men was divided

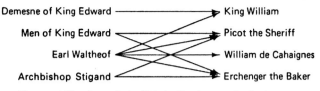

Figure 4.6 The change in lordship in Comberton, Cambridgeshire

between King William, Earl Roger and Hardwin de Scales. Or looking in the opposite direction at the disposition of Abington Pigotts' lordships, Hardwin de Scales held land of Earl Ælfgar's and King Edward's men, while King William held the land of Earl Ælfgar's and Ælfsige's men. Every component of this Cambridgeshire vill was either broken down after the Conquest or used to form a new composite lordship. The vill of Comberton follows a similar pattern of reorganization – the tenancies of its Norman lords are absolutely unrecognizable as the descendants of pre-Conquest lordships.[54] Indeed, a one and a half hide portion of this land, at one time divided among four of Earl Waltheof's sokemen, descended into the hands of each of the four new Norman lords of Comberton. Thus, no lord in Comberton at the end of the Conqueror's reign held a tenancy exactly equivalent to the lordship of one of his predecessors. (See figure 4.6.)

In Barrington Robert Gernon's seven hides three and a half virgates were composed not of a single predecessor's land, nor of the land of his predecessor's men, but the land of fifteen sokemen of Edward the Confessor, four sokemen of Earl Ælfgar, three men of Ansgar the Staller, and a man who held under (*sub*) King Edward.[55] Thus, while the land of the twenty-three men of Ælfgar, Ansgar and King Edward each descended to just one lord, they all descended to the same lord. Because the lines of lordship were redrawn in these vills, resources within them often underwent a radical redistribution as well. Picot the Sheriff's five and a half hides and sixteen acres in the Cambridgeshire vill of Kingston was made up from the holdings of sixteen sokemen, ten of them of King Edward's soke, four Earl Ælfgar's men, one Archbishop Stigand's man, and one the Abbot of Ely's man. No one before the Conquest had held this combination of hides, men and fields.[56] Beyond the amalgamation of small holdings like those found in Kingston into more viable economic units, many holdings, particularly in the east of England, had demesne

[54] DB, i, 189v, 200v, 201v, 202v.   [55] DB, i, 196v–197r.   [56] DB, i, 200v.

imposed upon them for the first time, which required a division of ploughteams and ploughlands and the imposition of new labour services as well.[57]

This reorganization of estates, a commonplace in Circuit III vills, has broad economic implications, and seems in some areas of England to explain the steady decline of Domesday values between 1066 and 1086. Cambridgeshire values provide a clear example of this. Across the shire value fell overall by 14 per cent between the Conquest and the Inquest, but the devaluation was particularly severe in the southwest of the county, where they plummeted by about 25 per cent.[58] The holdings hardest hit correlate very closely with the vills where the pattern of Anglo-Saxon tenure had been disrupted. (See figure 4.5.) This provides a sounder explanation for falling values than William the Conqueror's armies[59] or the retreating forces of the treacherous Earl Ralph,[60] both of which have been used to explain the shire's slumping values. The waste, so pronounced in other areas where armies inflicted serious damage, cannot be found in Cambridgeshire, and much of the value of these estates was maintained until after the period for which Domesday's interim value was given when King William gave the land. This suggests that the time between Domesday's *post* and *modo* values marks the period of greatest decline, and that land held its value until it was acquired and reorganized by a new lord. In Hertfordshire values followed a similar pattern, generally dropping throughout the county between the Confessor's death and the time of the Domesday survey. On the average by 1086 values in the shire had shrunk by about 15 per cent, and many historians have once again pointed a finger at William's harrying armies.[61] But the slumping land

---

[57] D. C. Douglas, *The Social Structure of Medieval East Anglia*, Oxford Studies in Social and Legal History, 9 (Oxford, 1927), pp. 110–11.

[58] R. Weldon Finn, *The Norman Conquest and its Effects on the Economy, 1066–1086* (London, 1971), pp. 98–9.

[59] Finn, followed by Darby, argues that the Conqueror's army, operating in Bedfordshire late in 1066, must have moved into Cambridgeshire because of that county's diminishing values. (Finn, *The Norman Conquest and its Effects*, p. 99; Darby, *Domesday England*, p. 246.)

[60] Finn suggests that the land values in western Cambridgeshire fell because of Earl Ralph's revolt. He believes that the rebellious earl's retreat from Cambridge to Norwich in 1075 accounts for this late devaluation (Finn, *The Norman Conquest and its Effects*, p. 100). And yet the areas in which values fell most markedly after the TRE date are much too far west and south for Earl Ralph's journey.

[61] Francis H. Baring, *Domesday Tables for the Counties of Surrey, Berkshire, Middlesex, Hertford, Buckinghamshire, and Bedford, and for the New Forest* (London, 1909), p. 211;

values were not distributed equally across the county. Those estates that transferred intact to new lords fell by about 13 per cent of their pre-Conquest value; those estates which were reconstituted and made up from the lands of more than one pre-Conquest landholder, fell much lower – on the average by about 22 per cent of their previous value. This pattern can also be found in Nottinghamshire, where Norman armies did inflict fairly serious damage.[62] In holdings which passed from an English to a Norman lord intact, values fell to about 88 per cent of their previous value, or to about 17.5 shillings to the pound. In composite holdings made up of more than one Anglo-Saxon tenancy, values fell to about 75 per cent of their TRE value, or 15 shillings to the pound.[63] This pattern can even be discerned in shires where the pre-Conquest manorial structure was relatively untouched. In Dorset, the vast majority of estates passed from one holder to another, without much consolidation of minor holdings within the vill. The exception to this general rule is the fee of the wife of Hugh fitz Grip, one-time sheriff of Dorset.[64] In 1086 this woman held forty-eight of her deceased husband's lands in-chief. Fourteen of these, or about one third, were created by combining the holdings of several pre-Conquest landholders. These composite holdings typically suffered falling values. (See tables 4.1 and 4.2.) It appears, therefore, that the diminishing value of land in some regions reflects the economic strains caused by a massive manorial reorganization.[65] From these examples it is clear that

The Domesday Geography of South-East England, ed. H. C. Darby and E. M. J. Campbell (Cambridge, 1962; reprinted with corrections 1971), pp. 569–75. The following figures are based on an analysis of the values of all holdings in the Domesday Book Database for Hertfordshire.

[62] OV, ii, p. 230; *The Domesday Geography of Northern England*, ed. H. C. Darby and I. S. Maxwell (Cambridge, 1962, reprinted with corrections 1977), pp. 263–8. The following figures are based on an analysis of the values of all holdings in the Domesday Book Database for Nottinghamshire.

[63] In severely devastated counties, however, such as Yorkshire and Bedfordshire, the manorial reorganization seems to have had the same devastating effect on Domesday valuations as the harrying armies. In Bedfordshire, for example, the value of vills which passed from one lord to another unchanged dropped between 1066 and 1086 to about 15s. 10d. to the pound, while the reconstituted estates dropped on the average to 15s. to the pound. (The former figure is based on Finn, *The Norman Conquest and its Effects*, pp. 93, 94. The latter figures have been derived from the Domesday Book Database for folios 209r–218v.) [64] DB, i, 83v–84r.

[65] To the Norman lords of these composite holdings, the fall in value could not have been of great concern. The profits they received from their English estates must have been beyond anything they had imagined before the Confessor's death whether their new lands yielded 17s. to the pound or not.

Table 4.1 *Values in the fee of the wife of Hugh fitz Grip in Dorset*[a]

	Reconstituted %	Single holding %
Same value	11	45
Rising value	22	23
Falling value	67	32

[a] Holdings which are given only a value TRW have not been used when making this table. If, however, it is assumed that estates for which we are provided with one value maintained a constant value between 1066 and 1086, a significant difference can still be discerned. See table 4.2.

old, commonplace notions that the economic structure of England, in spite of the Conquest, was relatively stable; and that 'there is no evidence that the new lords made drastic changes to their estates', must be reevaluated.[66] Indeed, here may lie some evidence in England for Georges Duby's 'feudal revolution', that assault of the knightly order against the rights and property of peasants. William's tampering with ancient tenurial patterns, not only on the level of the fee, but also on the level of the vill, had huge repercussions for the kingdom.

Thus, the chipping away of pre-Conquest lordships in the years following Harold's defeat had a dramatic impact on the shape of new fees and on the configuration of old villages. There were still places in England which maintained their ancient forms. Robert de Tosny's three estates in western Bedfordshire were exactly the lands held a generation earlier by his antecessor Oswulf son of Frani, and, except for the installation of a couple of *milites* on two of his holdings, little had changed except the name of the lord.[67] In nearby Cainhoe lay a vill that continued to have two lords, albeit two different ones, as it had had on the day King Edward was both alive and dead;[68] and at the core of Count Alan's holdings in Cambridgeshire lay the lands of Eadgifu the Fair and her men.[69] But abutting such isles of continuity were great blocks of reorganized territory, such as Countess Judith's Bedfordshire fee, made up of thirty-six holdings patched together from the

[66] Barlow, *William the Conqueror*, p. 104. He continues: 'in this lower stratum of the kingdom's economy there was massive continuity' (p. 105). A similar point is argued by Loyn in *Anglo-Saxon England and the Norman Conquest*, p. 323.
[67] DB, i, 215r.   [68] DB, i, 214r, 218r.   [69] DB, i, 193v–195v.

Table 4.2 *The fee of the wife of Hugh fitz Grip in Dorset*

	Reconstituted %	Single holding %
Same value	35	49
Rising value	14	30
Falling value	43	21

lands of eighty-four men.[70] It was these reorganized fees and vills, built across wide stretches of countryside, that marked the new England.

There are a number of reasons for this tenurial breakdown. Certainly, the nature of Anglo-Saxon lordship itself put barriers in the way of an orderly dispersal of land based on pre-Conquest personal relationships. Minor aristocrats in pre-Conquest England, if we are to believe the Anglo-Saxon dooms, had lords, and their lords commonly had lords as well,[71] and in Domesday we often find men like the one in Hasketon, Suffolk, who was 'a man commended to he who was commended to Eadric'.[72] The resulting tangle of rights and obligations could create havoc when lands were shared out after the Conquest. In Bedfordshire, for example, one of William de Warenne's predecessors was a man named Augi. William received a hide and a virgate of Augi's land, and another virgate which had belonged to Blæch, Augi's man. A third virgate, however, was in dispute because Augi had held it as a man of Eskil of Ware, Hugh de Beauchamp's antecessor.[73] Such cases of disputed tenure were common in these counties where our evidence for Anglo-Saxon lordships is best, and their *ad hoc* resolution did much to mar old lordship patterns. Anglo-Saxon lordship, moreover, was found in a variety of guises; in the form of personal commendation, or as a tenurial tie, as a set of judicial rights over inferiors, or as the rights to various customary

---

[70] DB, i, 217r–217v. Several of these previous holders had been earls and a score more king's thegns. Some had been housecarls, some the men of earls, and a number had been commended to abbots or thegns.

[71] For example: Alfred 42§5, 6; II Æthelstan 2; III Æthelstan 4§1, 7; V Æthelstan 1§1; I Edgar 7§1; III Edgar 73; II Cnut 78.

[72] DB, ii, 346b. Or again, on the same folio in Clopton (near Woodbridge), not only did Wulfric, a freeman commended to Harold, hold land, but a freeman commended to the same Wulfric held land there as well. [73] DB, i, 211b.

labour services, dues in kind, and money rents.[74] Some of these relationships need not have involved land at all; thus Englishmen before the Conquest commonly practised a kind of serial lordship. Lesser aristocrats and freemen entered into a variety of relationships with a number of powerful men for land, for protection in the local courts or for personal safety.[75] As a result, some ties were tenurial and others were not.[76] These complicated arrangements with their clinical distinctions between personal and tenurial bonds often befuddled Norman lords and kept the hundred and shire courts busy untangling conflicting yet legitimate claims over the same land. Eadric *Pur*, for example, a petty landholder in Cambridgeshire, held two and a half hides in Meldreth as a thegn of King Edward.[77] In Barrington the same man not only held a couple of virgates under (*sub*) King Edward, but half a virgate which lay in the lands of Chatteris Abbey.[78] A woman named Ælfflæd held Bolnhurst in Bedfordshire from King Edward and 'could grant to whom she would'. Nonetheless, her land lay in Thorney TRE.[79] In Otley, Suffolk, land was held jointly by Eadweald, a freeman of Harold and by Eadweald's wife who was 'commended to E'.[80] Eadwig, who held a hide in Eversden, Cambridgeshire, TRE, was 'a man of the Abbot of Ely. He could grant or sell without [the Abbot's] permission, but Earl Ælfgar had the soke'.[81]

The problems arising from serial lordship in the 1070s and 1080s were particularly acute for the Church, because so much of their land before the Conquest was loaned out as thegnland. Great Benedictine houses such as Bury, Abingdon and Glastonbury fought, after Hastings, to regain thegnland held from their houses by disgraced thegns. After the Conquest, monasteries had to worry as well over lands held of them by the commended men

---

[74] Maitland, *Domesday Book and Beyond*, pp. 66–79.

[75] In the 1050s, for example, Ælfric Modercope, with permission of the king, commended himself both to the Abbot of Bury and the Abbot of Ely (*bugan to þo tueyen abboten*) (S 1081).

[76] For a general discussion of pre-Conquest personal and tenurial bonds see Maitland, *Domesday Book and Beyond*, pp. 66–79; Stevenson, 'Commendation and related problems in Domesday', pp. 289–310; Barbara Dodwell, 'East Anglian commendation', *EHR*, 63 (1948), pp. 289–306.   [77] DB, i, 200r.

[78] DB, i, 196v–197r.   [79] DB, i, 211r.

[80] DB, ii, 347a. Husbands and wives were often commended to different lords. In Sibton, Suffolk, a freeman named Blæchmann was commended to Eadric of Laxfield but his wife was 'Bishop Stigand's man' (DB, ii, 331a). In Heckingham, Ulfketil had 'the whole commendation of the wife of Bondi, but only half of Bondi's commendation' (DB, ii, 182b).   [81] DB, i, 199r.

of fallen lords. In Norfolk Hugh de Montfort acquired land held by a freeman of his antecessor Guthmund in Wick,[82] but the *Inquisitio Eliensis* makes it quite clear that although the man was Guthmund's, his land was Ely's[83] Geoffrey de Mandeville entered into a dispute with Barking over Abbess Roding in Essex. Although a man of Geoffrey's predecessor had held land in the village TRE, 'he could not put that land to any place except the Abbey'.[84] In both instances the successors of the personal lords were in possession of the land in 1086, but in each case their acquisition was judged illegal by the local courts; in some cases the tenants' rights were limited to a term of lives; never, apparently, more than three.[85] Complaints brought by ecclesiastical houses against various tenants-in-chief, like the ones discussed above, were generally settled in favour of the Church, although these decisions could not always be enforced.[86]

Parallel suits which sprang up between secular lords in which one of the plaintiffs based his case on acquisition via a tenurial bond and the other on an acquisition based on a personal one, so far as our fragmentary evidence shows, resulted in similar judgements. In Prested, Essex, for example, Ranulf Peverel held five acres once belonging to a freeman commended to Ranulf's

---

[82] DB, ii. 238b–239a. [83] *IE*, p. 140.

[84] DB, ii, 57b. For other examples see Maitland, *Domesday Book and Beyond*, pp. 71–2.

[85] A similar judgement was reached in the case of Eadric *Pur's* half virgate, which lay in Chatteris (DB, i, 197r). In the following examples, Domesday Book makes the existence of such leases explicit: 'In Wadborough [Worcestershire] there is also one hide of land which was the monks' cow pasture. Godric, a thegn of King Edward, bought it for the life-span of three heirs... the third heir has this land, namely Urso [the Sheriff] who holds it. After his death it has to return to the Church' (DB, i, 175r). Ralph de Mortimer was the last of three heirs in Headbourne Worthy, Hampshire (DB, i, 46v). Earl Roger had given Bayston, Shropshire, to William Pantulf. The grant, however, was illegal because Bayston's TRE holder Eadric 'held it from the Bishop of Hereford. He could not alienate it because it was for [the Bishop's] victualing, and he had leased it for his life only' (DB, i, 257r).

[86] Many disputed estates adjudged to Lanfranc at Penenden Heath were still recorded in Odo's fee TRW (David Douglas, 'Odo, Lanfranc, and the Domesday Survey', pp. 54–5), and the favourable judgements Ely received in 1071 x 1075 against Hardwin de Scales were only moderately successful. Under the lands of Hardwin de Scales in Cambridgeshire six holdings are recorded as part of his tenancy-in-chief, but the same six lands are found earlier in the survey under Ely. In Ely's fee Hardwin appears as the Abbey's tenant (DB, i, 190v). When the lands are recorded a second time under the rubric of Hardwin de Scales, the sokemen who held them TRE are often simply described as sokemen who 'could not withdraw' or 'could not sell', but in the Church's fee is added the notice that they 'held of the Abbot' (DB, i, 199r). These men were not simply commended to the abbot, but they held their land from him. See E. Miller, 'The Ely land pleas in the Reign of William I', *EHR*, 62 (1947), pp. 438–56, for a further discussion of Ely's battle to maintain its lands.

antecessor. The jurors, however, were quick to note that the man 'could go where he would with the land', implying that Ranulf's acquisition was illegal because the land he acquired had belonged to a man who was simply commended to Ranulf's antecessor, but who had not held any land from him.[87] In other words, his relationship was the 'mere commendation' of Maitland, expressed by the Domesday scribe with phrases such as *non habuit nisi commendationem, tantum commendatos,* or *commendatio sine soca,* and not the more binding relationship of commendation accompanied by obligations of service and soke which the *Inquisitio Eliensis* characterizes with the phrase *saca et soca et commendatio et servitium.*[88] In a case similar to the one involving Prested, Ranulf held Vange in Essex, which a freeman of his antecessor had held. Again, the jurors reported that the freeman 'did not give his land [to the antecessor]. However, when the king gave the land [of the antecessor] to Ranulf, he seized [Vange] with the other land'.[89] In Cambridgeshire Aubrey de Vere held six hides, five of which he inherited from his antecessor Wulfwine. The sixth hide was held by a priest of Eadgifu the Fair. Because the priest 'could not withdraw without her permission', Count Alan, Eadgifu's successor, claimed the hide.[90] In Lincolnshire Gilbert de Gand claimed a meadow held TRE by his antecessor, but the wapentake would not support his claim because 'Gilbert's antecessor did not have any of it except through leasing it with money'.[91] Or again, the hundred court challenged Aubrey de Vere's lordship over half a hide and thirty acres in Wilbraham because Godric, the man who had held the land TRE, 'did not hold [it] of Aubrey's antecessor' (*non tenuit de Antecessore Alberici*).[92] Taking these decisions as our models, it appears that Hugh de Port's right to five hides in Amport, Hampshire were indisputable, in spite of another tenant-in-chief's possession of them, because the man who held the land TRE 'held it under an agreement that as long as he behaved well towards [Hugh's antecessor], he would hold the land from him; if he wished to sell, he was not permitted to sell or grant it to anyone except to the man from whom he held it'.[93] In short, the antecessor had leased out the land, so Hugh's

---

[87] DB, ii, 74b. [88] Cf. *IE*, pp. 121–2.
[89] DB, ii, 71b. Similarly, under the Suffolk *invasiones,* Domesday notes that 'in Lavenham Aubrey de Vere holds three freemen. Wulfwine, Aubrey de Vere's antecessor, had the commendation only. [They lay] in the soke of St Edmund's' (DB, ii, 449a). [90] In Abington. DB, i, 199v. [91] DB, i, 377r. [92] DB, i, 199v.
[93] DB, i, 45v. The hundred supported Hugh's claim.

rights to it were greater than the successor of the man who had held the lease. William de Warenne's possession of a virgate of his antecessor Augi's land in Little Staughton, on the other hand, was not legal, since the land had lain in Colmworth, an estate of Eskil of Ware, Hugh de Beauchamp's antecessor, and was therefore held by Augi 'de' Eskil. Indeed, 'all the sworn men of the sheriffdom bear witness that this land does not belong to William'.[94] Tenurial arrangements, like the ones described above, appear to represent temporarily alienated demesne land, land which looks very much like the thegnland of great ecclesiastical establishments.[95]

Like ecclesiastical tenancies, pre-Conquest secular tenancies were not always granted in perpetuity, but could he held on lease for one life or for three, for money or for service, before reverting back to the lord.[96] It is clear from Domesday that such lease arrangements were preserved after the Conquest whenever possible. When Gilbert Crispin, Abbot of Westminster, enfeoffed William Baynard on some of his house's Middlesex land, he preserved one of the tenurial arrangements which dated to the Confessor's reign. Despite the innovations of imposed knights' service and feudal aids, William promised, as part of his agreement, 'that he will not sell this land nor will he mortgage or alienate it to anyone', the familiar 'could not grant or sell' of Domesday Book.[97] Cypping, Ralph de Mortimer's antecessor, had held land in Headbourne Worthy on a three-life lease from Old Minster Winchester. Ralph accordingly only inherited the lease and not the land.[98] Thus, when Normans succeeded to an Englishman's land, if that Englishman held it on lease, his landlord's successor was often able to press for reversion. The

---

94 DB, i, 211v, 213v.

95 See Dodwell, 'East Anglian commendation', p. 301, for further discussion of secular thegnland.

96 *Ibid.* No secular leases have come down to us, although dozens of leases between ecclesiastics and thegns survive (e.g., S 1297–1374). A vernacular purchase agreement made during the Confessor's reign between thegns, however, does survive, and specifically notes that the land purchased is to be held in perpetuity (*æfre in his cynn to fane 7 to syllanne þam þe him æfre leofost beo*) (S 1469). Such a distinction would hardly be necessary unless land was sometimes given only for a generation or two.

97 'Nec terram prefatam vendet nec in vadium ponet nec alicui ad dampnum ecclesie nostre dimittet'. Charter printed in J. Armitage Robinson, *Gilbert Crispin Abbot of Westminster* (Cambridge, 1911), p. 38.

98 'This manor TRE was bought out of the Church with a compact and agreement that after the third heir, Old Minster Winchester would have it back with all its stock. Now this Ralph who holds it is the third heir' (DB, i, 46v).

lords most able to do this were ecclesiastics, whose houses had long memories, good records, and unbroken tenures. Most new secular lords were no match for the bishops and abbots who came to local inquests waving their old *landbocs* and threatening hellfire and damnation, but there is no reason to believe that lands which had been leased by secular lords before the Conquest would have been treated any differently by hundredal courts than lands leased by ecclesiastical corporations.

All of this suggests that the absolute and crucial connection between lordship and land transference after the Conquest was not an antecessor's relation to his men, but his connection to any land that they might hold. This certainly explains why the lands of those Englishmen whose relationship with their lords could be characterized by Norman commissioners at the Domesday inquests as 'mere commendation' were so frequently dispersed. In Grundisburgh, Suffolk, for example, Roger the Poitevin's land descended to him from nine freemen commended to Ely, a man of King Edward, a man commended to Beorhtric, two commended to Æthelric of Burgh, and one commended to Healfdane.[99] In Hudeston, Norfolk, Roger Bigot inherited land held by Æthelwig of Thetford. He also held land there which had pertained to five sokemen. 'Æthelwig had only the commendation of two ... and the antecessor Robert Malet of the third, and the antecessor of Ralph Berling of the fourth, and the antecessor of Eudo son of Spearheafoc the fifth'.[100] In these villages and in hundreds of others like them in East Anglia and in the south midlands commendation did little to determine post-Conquest landholding patterns. Still, the delineation between loan rights and commendation rights was often impossible. A complicated suit recorded in Domesday took place in Warwickshire c. 1080 between Archbishop Ealdraed of York and Bishop Wulfstan of Worcester.[101] From this, it is easy to see how convoluted pre-Conquest relationships could be and how the short memories of those testifying precluded fair judgement of them:

T.R.E. Beorhtwine held seven and a half hides in Alveston. [Archbishop] Ealdraed had the sake and soke and toll and team and churchscot, and

---

[99] DB, ii, 346a–346b. Grundisburgh typifies Roger's Suffolk holdings, which were composed of the lands of over 250 men commended to approximately thirty lords TRE (DB, ii, 346a–353a). Roger's land, in turn, typifies the disposition of land in Suffolk.   [100] DB, ii, 181b.   [101] For the date of this case, see *Regesta*, i, n. 185.

all other forfeitures [from this land] except those four which the King has throughout his whole kingdom. [Beorhtwine's] sons Leofwine, Eadmaer and four others testify to this, but they do not know from whom he held this land – perhaps the Church or Earl Leofric, whom he served. They say, however, that they themselves held it of Earl Leofric and could turn where they would with the land. Beorhtnoth and Alwig held the remaining seven and a half hides, but the county does not know from whom they held.[102]

Lack of information and perhaps a limited understanding of Old English land law were other reasons for the transformation of English landholding in William's reign.

The attempt by hundreds of Englishmen to find themselves some sort of security after the Battle of Hastings by seeking new and more powerful lords chipped away at pre-Conquest tenurial patterns as well. Nevertheless, a careful study of 1086 suits and landholding patterns suggests that a lord's power over another man's land was taken into account with some frequency when the lands of disinherited thegns were granted out, but his power over the man himself, through simple commendation, was often ignored. Immediately after the Conquest there was a scramble by minor landholders for protection in the face of massive disinheritance. In Surrey, for example, Walter de Douai held two hides in spite of the fact that no one had 'seen a writ or an injunction (*nunciam*) of the king which put him in possession it'. Instead he got a grip on these hides because a freeman who held the land 'and could go where he would, put himself in Walter's hands for his own protection'.[103] In Trowse a sokeman of Stigand, probably after 1070, commended himself to Alfred. As a result, his ten and a half acres ended up in the fee of Aitard de Vaux, Alfred's successor.[104] And Roger Bigot picked up a collection of lands from men, including a thegn of Earl Harold, who had commended themselves to his antecessor Æthelwine of Thetford in the months immediately following the Conquest and were 'seised there' when the king granted Roger Bigot the land.[105] We can see the gradual erosion of old landholding patterns in the face of new deals struck in the months after Hastings between Englishman and Englishman and Englishman and Norman.[106]

[102] DB, i, 238v.   [103] DB, i, 36r.   [104] DB, ii, 124b.
[105] DB, ii, 182a, 181b, 187b.
[106] For a further discussion on the extension of lordship in William's reign, see below, pp. 204–9.

Soke-right, too, played a more prominent role in land disposition than personal lordship over men, probably because rights of soke were territorial in a way that 'mere commendation' was not. Peter Sawyer argues that 'the Norman conquerors put much greater weight on commendation than on soke'.[107] This proposition seems unlikely, however, in light of the rather arbitrary scattering of the lands of the men commended to prominent pre-Conquest lords but who 'could go where they would with their land'.[108] Moreover, the Yorkshire and Lincolnshire *clamores*, which preserve a considerable portion of Domesday's legal disputes, never once report a claim on the basis of commendation, but record such claims on the basis of soke on over one hundred occasions. Whole folios in Domesday Book are given over to the recording of information on caputs with their attached berewicks, sokes and inland, and in the vast majority of cases, the appurtenances of great estates remained tied to their heads. Thus, the attachments between the bulk of berewicks and soke, inland and caputs in Derbyshire, Nottinghamshire, Shropshire, Staffordshire, the nascent Lancashire, Yorkshire and Lincolnshire – the counties whose agrarian settlement was most marked by these complex estates – testify to the continued importance of such ties during the course of the Norman settlement. Furthermore, the pre-Conquest tenurial arrangements enveloping this web of estates and sokes were maintained when forfeitures were granted to a new set of lords. Decisions made by the local Domesday inquests held in Yorkshire and particularly in Lincolnshire verify this assertion. The *clamores* appended to these shires are concerned almost exclusively with untangling the rights

---

[107] Sawyer, 'Tenurial revolution?', p. 80. In this opinion Sawyer echoes Round, who believed that commendation was more important for land division after Hastings than soke (*FE*, pp. 30–4).

[108] Moreover, soke was valuable, and control over an estate's soke was maintained in the pre-Conquest period whenever possible, by whatever means, including the curse. Three principle estates of the Archbishopric of York – Sherburn-in-Elmet, Otley, and Ripon – along with their vast collection of sokeland, were lost to the church in the mid-tenth century (S 1453), but recovered during the episcopacy of Archbishop Wulfstan. To protect these estates and their soke, a survey of each was drawn up and entered into the York Gospels. The sokeland recorded in these surveys dating from c. 1020 matches closely with information recorded in Domesday Book, three generations later. (Text printed in W. H. Stevenson, 'Yorkshire surveys and other eleventh century documents in the York Gospels', *EHR*, 27 (1912), pp. 1–25; commentary by S. D. Keynes, 'The additions in Old English', *The York Gospel*, Roxburghe Club (London, 1986), pp. 81–91). There is no reason to believe that secular lords would treat their sokes differently.

over soke, inland and berewicks from rights over caputs, with the assignment of TRE holders for each of these elements; and based upon this information with the parceling out of these individual components to their legal 1086 proprietors. A typical case dealing with these problems is found in a dispute between Archbishop Thomas and Rainer de Brimeux, both of whom claimed rights to ten bovates in South Willingham.[109] Koddi, Rainer's antecessor, held these bovates as soke of Barkwith, a manor Rainer had also inherited from Koddi.[110] But elsewhere in Domesday Book, the archbishop too is assigned land in South Willingham, in the form of two manors with attached soke in Barkwith.[111] The wapentake court, however, noted that Koddi's soke in South Willingham was mortgaged for £3, probably before the Conquest and probably to the archbishop or his predecessor. Thus, the men of the South Riding of Lindsey adjudged the ten bovates to Archbishop Thomas, but only until Rainer paid the £3 mortgage to him.[112] It was also decided that the archbishop had soke over the land which the Bishop of Bayeux held in South Willingham and which Odo had inherited from his antecessor Eskil, because one of 'the Archbishop's own antecessors had sake and soke over the same land, and the Bishop [of Bayeux]'s men wrongfully took the same soke away from the same Archbishop'.[113] In the case of all these South Willingham disputes, we can see rights over soke and rights over land had to be separated carefully for a judgement to be reached; and in all three cases pre-Conquest soke-right was carefully preserved by the Norman settlement.[114] Similarly, in a Lincolnshire dispute over the soke of a fishery and a toft in Coningsby, the wapentake court made a careful delineation between rights over land and rights over soke. Robert Dispensator, according to a notice in the *clamores*, ought to have had soke over these two appurtenances because Robert's antecessor Aki had held their soke before the Conquest.[115] Instead, Ketilbiorn was in possession of them TRW. Yet it is easy to see how Ketilbiorn came to hold soke over the fishery and the toft; he already held a manor in West Keal as well as West Keal's berewick and inland in Coningsby.[116] Robert Dispensator also held land in Coningsby

[109] DB, i, 375v. [110] DB, i, 364r. [111] DB, i, 339v. [112] DB, i, 375v.
[113] DB, i, 375v, 343r.
[114] Sawyer maintains that only the sokes of the king and very great men had any chance of preservation in William I's reign (Sawyer, 'Tenurial revolution?', 81), but information in Domesday's northern circuit suggests otherwise. [115] DB, i, 375v.
[116] DB, i, 370v.

– nine bovates – which formed a berewick to his manor of Thornton, inherited from Aki.[117] The complex relationship between these three vills is understandably confusing, but after the jurors abstracted the rights over soke from those over land, the relationships between these lands and their holders were restored to their pre-Conquest form. Or again, the wapentake assigned one bovate of land in Mablethorpe to the Bishop of Durham, three bovates to William Blunt and two bovates in Huttoft to Alvred of Lincoln, because the land had belonged to their antecessors. Earl Hugh, nonetheless, had held these bovates until 1086; but through his accession to Earl Harold's manor in Greetham, he was only entitled to the soke and not the lands.[118] In other words, Hugh had seized these lands when he had only seised of the soke. Norman d'Arcy was holding both land and soke in Brocklesby, but the men of the North Riding, after separating who held the land TRE from who held the soke, decided that 'the land ought to be [Hugh fitz Baldric's] and the soke Norman's through their antecessors'.[119] Thus, Domesday's treatment of soke belongs very much to the world of the *Leges Henrici Primi*, where we are told that soke did not automatically pass with the granting of the manor, but depended on 'personal arrangement', and that soke could be 'acquired by purchase, or exchange or in any other way'.[120] The importance of controlling such valuable appurtenances was hardly new with the Normans. Edward the Confessor's generous gifts of judicial rights to Westminster and Bury St Edmunds have shown historians that soke was as suitable a benefaction for monastic houses as seigneurial rights.[121] Such acquisitions of soke independent from the acquisition of land, to judge from Domesday's *clamores*, had also been occurring among several generations of prosperous thegns. In 1086 the wapentake jurors spent a great deal of time sorting through the tangle of rights that resulted from this practice in order to determine the validity of competing claims; and it is clear from their judgements that the sokes of both greater and lesser lords were carefully preserved.

Berewicks tended, as well, to adhere to their manorial centres

---

[117] DB, i, 363v.   [118] DB, i, 375r, 349r.   [119] DB, i, 375v, 361v.

[120] *Leges Henrici Primi*, ed. L. J. Downer (Oxford, 1977), 19§3, 20§2.

[121] Westminster's rights are described in DB, i, 172. The grant is preserved in three Westminster writs – S 1125–27. Notification of Bury's grant is recorded in S 1069, 1078, 1084.

after the Conquest. The 141 berewicks recorded in Shropshire tenaciously clung to their caputs, whether they were granted directly to Roger de Montgomery by the king or subinfeudated by Roger or by one of his tenants.[122] Potton, one of Countess Judith's chief manors in Bedfordshire, carried with it a number of outlying properties; a half a virgate in Potton itself, a manor of three hides two and a half virgates in Cockayne Hatley, and five hides in Everton. These lands had all pertained to Potton while Earl Tostig held the manor, and continued to do so in 1086. The wife of Hugh de Grandmesnil's manor of Chalton, which had been one of Potton's berewicks TRE, however, had broken free from its caput some time after the Conquest, but the tone of the entry suggests her tenure was not legitimate because it ends with the statement: 'This land was a berewick of Potton, Countess Judith's manor TRE, so that it could not be separated.'[123] Hugh de Port claimed a hide in Hampshire, in the possession of Gilbert de Breteuil because 'it belongs to his manors of Charford and *Eschetune*, and his antecessors held there'.[124] Or again, among Adelaide's Bedfordshire lands, we read that Hugh de Beauchamp held half a virgate and thirty acres which was held by a man who could 'grant or sell to whom he would' but which 'lay with the other land which Adelaide holds'.[125] The hundred testified in her favour and the landholding regained its TRE configuration.[126] The continued importance of the rights over soke and over outlying properties can also be seen in a Lincolnshire claim. Baldwin the Fleming's entire holding in Lincolnshire was composed of the soke and berewicks of Doddington,[127] but

---

[122] DB, i, 253r–255r, 257v–258v, 260r. There are two notable exceptions to outlying property transferring with a caput. The first occurs with the establishment of the Sussex Rapes. For a detailed discussion of the Count of Eu's treatment of outlying property see Eleanor Searle, 'The abbey of the Conqueror: defensive enfeoffment and economic development in Anglo-Norman England', *Anglo-Norman Studies*, 2 (1979), p. 158. The second is the establishment of Richard fitz Gilbert's lowey of Tonbridge. See Richard Mortimer, 'Clare', pp. 120–1. [123] DB, i, 217v. [124] DB, i, 48r.
[125] DB, i, 217v.
[126] In a Westminster charter dated c. 1083, the Abbot enfeoffed one of his knights with a berewick of Tottenham Court. One of the stipulations of the knight's tenure was the recognition that he could not separate this land from its caput, thus preserving pre-Conquest manorial arrangements (Charter printed in Robinson, *Gilbert Crispin*, p. 38). Westminster asserted that this land formed a berewick of Tottenham in Edward the Confessor's reign in one of the house's forged charters. (S 1043 records land which likely represents Tottenham and its berewick. Robinson, *Gilbert Crispin*, p. 40).
[127] DB, i, 370r.

Ælfric, Doddington's Edwardian holder, had granted this land to Westminster before 1066, and the abbot made a claim to it. In a suit recorded concerning this fee, we are told that those who testified

> say that they heard that the same Ælfric gave it to St Peter, but they do not know whether he gave the whole or the half. They say, however, that in Haddington there are 8.5 carucates which are soke and inland pertaining to Doddington, and in Hykeham 4 carucates of land, which are soke pertaining to Doddington, and in Skellingthorpe 12 carucates which are soke pertaining to Doddington, and in Whisby 6 carucates of land which are inland and soke of Doddington. *The Abbot of Westminster claims the whole of this because the chief manor was given to St Peter.*[128]

In other words, the abbot demanded any outlying properties attached to Doddington before the Conquest, as well as Doddington itself.

A last example, that of the much disputed vill of Hail Weston in Huntingdonshire, serves to illustrate the Conquest's preservation of territorial patterns of soke and berewicks but not pre-Conquest lordships. Of the four manors in Hail Weston in 1086, Eustace the Sheriff had two. One was held by Algeat TRE and the other by an unnamed Englishman. Both the sheriff's manors were in dispute. Countess Judith claimed the former because after the Conquest Algeat had been held by her husband Waltheof.[129] Eustace's other manor was claimed by Robert Fafiton, but the jurors decided against Robert, pointing out that the manor had not belonged to Robert's antecessor Saxi.[130] Robert may have been confused about the limits of his rights in Hail Weston, since he already held a manor of Saxi's in the vill.[131] He held yet another manor in Hail Weston once belonging to Wulfwine *Chit*. This last holding was also in dispute and was claimed by William de Warenne. The jurors stated that Wulfwine *Chit* was a man of Earl Harold, whose lands William had inherited in the shire. William's bid, however, was unsuccessful, because although Wulfwine had been a man of Earl Harold's, his estate had not pertained to Harold's manor of Kimbolton, an estate William held in 1086.[132] What does all this tell us? It informs us that

---

[128] DB, i, 377r; under the lands of Westminster Abbey, the scribe records how expensive the loss of Doddington's outlying property and judicial rights were: 'TRE with all things pertaining to this manor it was valued at £20. Now what Saint Peter has is valued at £4' (DB, i, 346r). Alric's grant is confirmed in *Regesta*, i, n. 212.

[129] DB, i, 206v.   [130] DB, i, 208r.   [131] DB, i, 208r.   [132] DB, i, 208r.

Norman lords attempted to exert claims over their predecessor's men, but this rationale was not always deemed sufficient by the local courts, and that in William's case, the jurors decided he only had rights to the *land* which pertained to the estates he had inherited from Harold, and not to Harold's men. It also shows that claims based on pre-Conquest territorial arrangements, like the ones governing Kimbolton, helped dictate land division after Hastings. Lordship over men, therefore, was a fragile thing which survived only unevenly after the Conquest. At the same time, territorialized rights were more tenacious and had a more noticeable impact on the formation of Anglo-Norman honours.

From scattered evidence it seems likely that rules governing the redistribution of land as often disregarded Anglo-Scandinavian kinship as they did Anglo-Scandinavian personal lordship. England's pre-Conquest kindreds can rarely be pieced together. Nonetheless, it is clear from those that can, that English families regularly had their landed wealth partitioned between a number of William's followers.[133] Gamal son of Osbern, a substantial Yorkshire thegn who had a brief career under William the Conqueror, held a large number of estates in the East Riding before his disinheritance to Hugh fitz Baldric.[134] Gamal's brother Forni, however, whose chief manor lay in Skirpenbeck, was also dispossessed, yet his lands went to another lord – Odo the *Balistarius*.[135] The lands of another group of brothers, Alnoth, Fenkell, Eskil and Sigvatr, were similarly divided after the Conquest – the first three men's lands descended to the fee of the Bishop of Durham,[136] but the lands of the last brother, Sigvatr 'the king's man', went to Eudo son of Spearhavoc.[137] In Lincolnshire two brothers, Ketil and Thorfrothr, divided their

---

[133] The most notable exceptions to this are Ralph fitz Hubert's succession to the lands of the brothers Leofnoth and Leofwine (DB, i, 277r–277v, 289v), Richard of Clare's succession to the lands of Wihtgar Algarson, his son Ælfric, and his priest Leodmær (DB, ii, 38b–41b, 389b), and Hugh the Ass's succession to most of the land of Thorkil the White and his wife Leofflæd (DB, i, 187r–187v). For an opposing view on the effects of family landholding on the redistribution of land, see Sawyer, 'Tenurial revolution?', p. 75.

[134] *EYC*, i, n. 88, p.86; DB, i, 327r–328r. We can identify this Gamal as Gamal son of Osbern because a notice in the description of the city of York identifies Gamal son of Osbert (*sic*) as holding sake and soke over Cottingham, one of Hugh's chief estates (DB, i, 328v).   [135] *EYC*, i, p. 87; DB, i, 329v.

[136] So stated the wapentake court (DB, i, 375v, 376r). Their lands can be found in the bishop's fee in DB, i, 340v–341r.   [137] DB, i, 359v, 360r.

father's land after his death so that Ketil, 'while doing the service of the king, should have the aid of his brother'.[138] After the Conquest Ketil was made an antecessor of William de Percy, but Thorfrothr's land went to Ansketil, described rather enigmatically as 'a certain cook'.[139] An Anglo-Scandinavian couple's land in Yorkshire's East Riding descended to two different successors. The wife Asa's land initially went to William Malet,[140] while her husband Biornwulf's land, as well as Biornwulf himself, who survived to 1086 as an undertenant, descended to the fee of William de Percy.[141] Geoffrey de la Guerch came into the lands of Leofwine of Newnham, while Osbern fitz Richard came into those of Leofwine's mother.[142]

Anglo-Saxon kindreds, however, extended beyond siblings, spouses and parents, and often a man's proprietary rights in pre-Conquest England were dependent on his cousins, uncles and in-laws as well. These extended families can never be reconstructed by evidence in Domesday alone, suggesting that such relationships were of no interest to the Domesday commissioners and, therefore, had little or no bearing on land division after 1066. Several late Saxon wills, however, used in conjunction with Domesday Book, can aid in piecing together two of these extended families and their lands. The lands of the kindred of Abbot Brandr of Peterborough show all too well the dismemberment of what had, before the Conquest, been a sizeable group of family estates. Although Brandr had been prior of Peterborough before his election in the first bitter weeks after Hastings,[143] his elevation to the office of abbot must have been motivated in part by his powerful family connections. How else could the monks of Peterborough hope to protect their house in such dangerous times? Brandr's family was large, rich, and influential. (See figure 4.7.) His brothers and his other more distant kinsmen held land scattered throughout Lincolnshire and across the Humber into Holderness. His brothers and cousins probably leased some of the lands ascribed to them in Domesday Book from Peterborough,[144] and Peterborough, in turn, profited

---

[138] DB, i, 354r.
[139] DB, i, 354r. In 1086 William de Percy held both brothers' land, but only because he had bought Thorfrothr's land from Ansketil.   [140] DB, i, 373r.
[141] DB, i, 322r–323r.   [142] DB, i, 244r.   [143] ASC, s.a. 1066 (E).
[144] The Lincolnshire *clamores* describes Ansketil brother of Brandr's land of Scotton, Scotter and Raventhorpe as land held by Ansketil of King Edward. Nonetheless, all were held by Peterborough TRW, suggesting that they had been held on loan. The

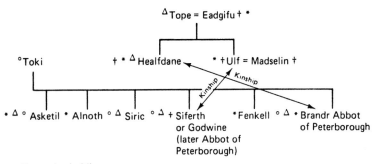

* Domesday holdings
† Will of Ulf and Madselin
Δ Chronicle of Hugh Candidus
o Brevi Cartula (Society of Antiquaries MS 6 fol. 72v-73r.)

Figure 4.7 The family of Abbot Brandr of Peterborough

from the benefactions of the abbot's kinsmen.[145] Although his family's wealth was centred in Lincolnshire, its attentions were drawn ever southward by its constant involvement with Brandr's abbey. The family's fortunes, however, like the fortunes of so many others, soured soon after the Conquest. Brandr's kinsman Ulf son of Tope may have had to redeem his lands from the Conqueror soon after Hastings and his will, made prior to 1068, did not stand.[146] Within two years of the Conquest Ulf's brother Healfdane was dispossessed and Abbot Brandr had died.[147] These events and the native rebellions which followed, led to the parceling out of individual holdings within the family's lands to half a dozen different tenants-in-chief. The lands of Eadgifu, the mother of Ulf and Healfdane, went to Erneis de Buron;[148] Ulf's land went to Drogo de la Beuvrière;[149] Healfdane's went to Remigius Bishop of Lincoln;[150] the land of Ansketil, Brandr's brother,[151] descended to Odo Bishop of Bayeux;[152] and Alnoth's

claim further notes that Ansketil leased Manton 'from his·brother Brandr the monk' (DB, i, 376v, 345v–346r).

[145] TRW Peterborough held £28 of land in Lincolnshire which had been held by Ansketil before the Conquest (*Brevi Cartula*, Society of Antiquaries, MS 60, fols. 72v–73r; Hugh Candidus, pp. 35–6). Ulf son of Tope and his wife Madselin left land in their will to both Peterborough and Abbot Brandr (*Wills*, n. 39).

[146] *Wills*, n. 39, and pp. 207–12; A. E. C. Welby, 'Ulf of Lincolnshire, before and after the Conquest', *Lincolnshire Notes and Queries*, 14 (1917), pp. 196–200.

[147] Hugh Candidus, p. 35; *ASC*, s.a. 1069 (E).   [148] DB, i, 362r–362v.

[149] DB, i, 360r–360v.   [150] DB, i, 344r–344v; Hugh Candidus, p. 35.

[151] Ansketil is described as 'Ansketil son of Toki and brother of Siric and Sigvartr' in the *Brevi Cartula*, fols. 72v–73r, and he is described in DB as the 'brother of Brandr the monk' (DB, i, 376v).   [152] DB, i, 342r, 343r.

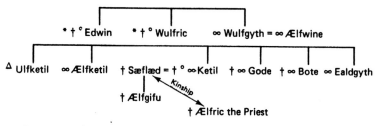

Figure 4.8 The family of Ketil *Alder*

land was inherited by the Bishop of Durham.[153] For at least a generation prior to the 1060s the bulk of these lands had supported a group of kinsmen who had acted in concert – endowing their favourite monastery together, transacting business together, attesting one another's charters, and lending each other a helping hand in troubled times.[154] This activity and the landed wealth which had supported it was destroyed within a half decade of the Conquest, and five new, independent fees in Lincolnshire had at their core members of this kindred's land. Drogo de la Beuvrière, as mentioned above, was Ulf son of Tope's successor – but the Fleming's holdings were supplemented by the lands of other lesser men, particularly in Holderness, where his inheritance from Ulf was greatly increased. Here Drogo received every available piece of land in three hundreds, that is the entire territory, except for the farms, peasants and woodlands which the Archbishop of York possessed by right and by custom.[155] Because of this, Drogo's newly enriched fee was very unlike Ulf's holding. It was not part of a loose network of local holdings controlled by Drogo's kinsmen, but was more compact, and the entire fee was oriented towards the north, centred as it was on the Humber and that stretch of coast from Spurn Head to Bridlington.[156]

Of more modest means was Ketil *Alder*, who deposited his will

---

[153] DB, i, 340v–341r. According to Hugh Candidus, Brandr's immediate successor, Thurold, 'badly broke up his compact estate and gave lands to his kinsfolk and the knights who came with him' (Hugh Candidus, p. 44). Thurold, with his own friends and kinsmen to look after, was not interested in being an advocate for the family of Brandr.   [154] Hugh Candidus, p. 35; Wills, n. 39; *Regesta*, i, n. 8.
[155] DB, i, 323v–325r; Barbara English, *The Lords of Holderness 1086–1260* (Oxford, 1979), pp. 76–7.   [156] See below, chapter 4, p. 150.

along side that of his uncle at Bury St Edmunds during the
Confessor's reign.[157] (See figure 4.8.) Ketil and his two maternal
uncles, Edwin and Wulfric, all of whom are mentioned in these
wills and in the will of Ketil's mother,[158] were still alive in 1066,
and Domesday Book records some two dozen of their estates in
East Anglia, Kent and Essex.[159] The family wills preserve the
complex arrangements that aristocratic kinsmen of pre-Conquest
England contrived to preserve family holdings and postpone
pious donations by a generation or two. In Ketil's will his two
uncles, in accordance with an agreement (*forwarde*) the three had
made, were to succeed him in East Harling, an estate bequeathed
to Ketil and his brother by their mother, if Ketil died before them.
According to the family plan, therefore, the land was to go from
mother to sons and then back, if need be, to the mother's two
brothers. At the same time one of the uncles, Edwin, had formed
an arrangement (*felageschipe*) to give *Thorpe* to Ketil and the other
uncle, Wulfric, so long as another estate in Edwin's will, Melton,
went to St Benedict's at Holme without incident. Or again, Ketil
made an agreement with his sister Bote, that if he outlived her, he
was to have Somerleyton; if she outlived him Bote was to inherit
Ketteringham. Two decades before, Ketil's mother had bequeathed the bulk of her land in a kind of partnership. Her two
sons together inherited a life interest in one estate, and outright
inheritance of three others, while two of her daughters were
granted a joint bequest of two other estates. Clearly this family
had developed a careful strategy to preserve family holdings from
one generation to the next. The purpose of the strategy was not
to secure an offspring's patrimony, but to uphold a compact
kindred's rights to familial land. In a number of ways, therefore,
members of Ketil's family looked upon an important portion of
their heritable lands as familial property. The Norman settlement,
however, was utterly insensitive to the complex family holdings
of such a collateral kindred, made up of property sharing uncles
and nephews, brothers and sisters. The bulk of the land held by
Ketil himself was granted to Ranulf Peverel.[160] Edwin's land went
to Godric *Dapifer*,[161] and Wulfric's land may have descended to
the Countess of Aûmale.[162] The careful bequests of land from

---

[157] S 1516, 1519; *Wills*, pp. 199–204.   [158] S 1535; *Wills*, pp. 197–9.
[159] DB, i, 13r; DB, ii, 8a, 26b, 75b, 151b, 293a, 204a, 223a, 243b, 254a, 355b, 416b, 421a,
   430b.   [160] DB, ii, 75b, 254a–254b, 416b.   [161] DB, ii 204a; *IE*, fos. 54, 213.
[162] DB, ii, 430b.

parent to child and from nephew to uncle were ignored by the Normans and played no part in the redisposition of their landed wealth.

Lordship and kinship, the relationships which governed the lives of landholding people in pre-Conquest England, played no significant role in the parceling out of land to the kingdom's new masters after the Battle of Hastings. These relationships, in their Old English forms, were problematic for Normans because they did not always involve land or patrimony, those things which lay so often at the heart of Norman arrangements. Normans instead, when they looked to divide the spoils, fastened on to ancient territorial bonds – the tenurial relationship between a man and his lord based on a lease of one or more lives or on manorial or jurisdictional rights which a lord held over far-flung estates. As a result, the more important relationships for Englishmen were circumvented almost immediately after the Conquest, as William began to share out the lands of those who fought against him at Hastings or rebelled. Because of the untidy nature of Anglo-Saxon land law and inheritance customs, there was no such thing as a clean and cauterized dispossession. Each time William dispossessed an aristocrat and granted out his land, the king violated the rights of that man's kindred. Healfdane son of Tope, for example, was dispossessed very soon after the Conquest. When his lands fell to Remigius Bishop of Lincoln, the expectations of his kinsmen, who would in more predictable times have inherited rights to them, must have been dashed. His dispossession may well have driven his powerful kindred into action during the eastern rebellion of 1070–71 in an attempt to gain back what was rightfully theirs. That kinsmen had such expectations is manifestly clear, even after the Conquest, when we can on occasion see them attempt to gain back familial land. Domesday's Hampshire folios, for example, preserve the notice of land in *Sudberie* which had been held by Eadnoth and Eadwig from King Edward. 'After his death they also died, but Cola, a close kinsman of theirs, bought the land back from Earl William'.[163] Again in Hampshire, Domesday notes that a certain Alric held land at the time of the survey. 'His father held it of King Edward, but he did not ask the King for it at the death of his uncle Godric who had custody of it.'[164] As Orderic explains

---

[163] DB, i, 50r.   [164] DB, i, 50v.

it, 'fealty, oaths, and the safety of hostages were forgotten by the Anglo-Saxons in their anger at the loss of their patrimonies and the deaths of their kinsmen'.[165] The monk's words should remind us that much of a thegn's future inheritance could be lost before his own dispossession. Commendation accelerated this process.[166] Since English landholders were in the habit of commending themselves to more than one advocate, some thegns sought new lords after the Conquest even though the men to whom they owed service and loyalty had survived the battles of 1066. Powerful Englishmen, observing the world around them, could not have helped but notice that the arrangements between themselves and their dependants were dissolving around their ears, as Normans newly installed in the region actively developed private understandings with their English neighbours, gaining for themselves these men's services and dues, and sometimes their lands as well. Many English lords must have taken strong exception to the rush of minor landholders into the arms of Norman lords for protection. As their dues and retinues shrank, these men were propelled into rebellion. Thus, once the Conqueror and his followers began to restructure landholding without regard to kinship and commendation, little could stop the English aristocracy's terrible slide toward annihilation.

[165] OV, ii, p. 223.   [166] See below, chapter 6, pp. 204–9.

Chapter 5

TERRITORIES AND TIME

The widespread destruction of Old English lordships and kindreds altered the tenurial fabric of England. This metamorphosis of aristocratic landholding was not limited to the counties and vills described in the previous chapter: it was evident throughout the kingdom. In the marches the changes were dramatic.[1] Shropshire, southern Lancashire, and Cheshire, protecting the kingdom's western flank from Welshmen and Norse Irish, and from Anglo-Saxons exiled in Ireland, were reorganized soon after 1066 along new, Continental lines.[2] In Shropshire there was an almost complete abandonment of ancient tenurial, familial and lordship patterns in favour of endowments constructed from consolidated stretches of territory.[3] By the time of the Domesday inquest nearly all the land found in this county's secular fees was listed under the rubric of Roger de Montgomery regardless of Anglo-Saxon antecessors,[4] and his Shropshire honour in no way mirrored tenurial patterns in existence before the Conquest. Ralph de Mortimer's fee in the county was built around his castlery of Wigmore and Osbern fitz Richard's abutted Richard's Castle. Neither can be described as the fossil of an earlier lordship and, furthermore, the compact territories of these two tenants-in-chief could be found in 1086 straddling the Shropshire–Herefordshire

---

[1] For a discussion of the Norman settlement of England's marches see D. C. Douglas, *William the Conqueror* (Berkeley, 1964), pp. 272–3; John Le Patourel, *The Norman Empire* (Oxford, 1976), pp. 41, 63, 65, 308–9; J. F. A. Mason, *William the First and the Sussex Rapes*, The Hastings and Bexhill Branch of the Historical Association (1966).

[2] Douglas, *William the Conqueror*, pp. 272, 294–6.

[3] Only the fees of Roger de Lacy (36.5 hides), Hugh the Ass (10 hides) and Nigel the Physician (5 hides) were constructed from the holdings of individual TRE antecessors (DB, i, 206v).

[4] Roger's fee, covering six folios, is recorded in DB, i, 253r–259v. The fees of the other tenants-in-chief – Osbern fitz Richard, Ralph de Mortimer, Roger de Lacy, Hugh the Ass and Nigel the Physician – can be found on folio 260r–260v. For the date of the establishment of this fee, see J. F. A. Mason, 'Roger de Montgomery and his sons 1067–1102', *TRHS*, 5th ser., 13 (1963), pp. 3–4.

border, a boundary which a generation earlier had separated the Mercian and West Saxon earldoms.[5] Further north, in Cheshire, with the exception of the ancient endowment of the canons of St Werberg and the bishopric of Chester, the entire shire by 1086 had been formed into a great marcher earldom under the authority of Hugh d'Avranches.[6] Earl Edwin, the wealthiest lord by far in pre-Conquest Cheshire held little more than half the amount of hides Hugh had accumulated there by the time of the survey.[7] Finally, in the list of lands compiled under the rubric 'Between the Ribble and the Mersey', Roger the Poitevin, Roger de Montgomery's son, was assigned the entire district including its ancient royal demesne.[8] None of these counties, so far as our surviving evidence reveals, displayed any sort of territorial consolidation before the Conquest.[9] In Shropshire, Cheshire and southern Lancashire, territory and territory alone determined the descent of secular lands after the Conquest.

In shires along the south coast pre-Conquest lordships and tenurial patterns were also ignored in favour of territorial

[5] For a general discussion of Shropshire's post-Conquest fees see J. Tait, 'Introduction to the Shropshire Domesday', *VCH, Shropshire*, i (London, 1908), pp. 279–308; J. F. A. Mason, 'Roger de Montgomery and his sons (1067–1102)', pp. 1–28. For the geography of late Anglo-Saxon earldoms see Freeman, *NC*, ii, pp. 374–83; and Frank Barlow, *Edward the Confessor*, pp. 358–9.   [6] DB, i, 263v–268r.

[7] The valuation of land in Cheshire underwent a sharp decline between 1066 and 1086. Nonetheless Earl Hugh's land was valued at approximately £225 TRW. Earl Edwin's was valued at about £140 TRE.

[8] DB, i, 269v–270r; Mason, 'Roger de Montgomery', pp. 14–15. Herefordshire, too, may have been reorganized after the Conquest under William fitz Osbern. Because of William's early death, however, and because of the disinheritance of his son and heir, the degree to which territory determined the shape of his fee is unclear. For opposing views see W. E. Wightman, 'The palatine earldom of William fitz Osbern in Gloucester and Worcester (1066–1071)', *EHR*, 77 (1962), pp. 6–17, especially p. 8, and Christopher Lewis, 'The Norman settlement of Herefordshire under William I', *Anglo-Norman Studies*, 7 (1985), pp. 195–213.

[9] It has recently been argued that the majority of thegns in Cheshire, a county in which Domesday records no English overlords, were the men of Earl Edwin, and that because of this, 'Earl Edwin's position in Cheshire as a whole was perhaps even closer to that of the Norman earls in size and importance than is suggested by an initial reading of the survey' (*VCH, Cheshire*, i, p. 317). Although some men in Cheshire were doubtless Edwin's men, there is no evidence for this assertion. Certainly nothing in Domesday suggests that Cheshire, unlike every other shire in pre-Conquest England, was completely within one man's lordship. Earl Hugh did, at times, subinfeudate his knights on the land of well-defined antecessors (for a discussion of this, see *VCH, Cheshire*, i, pp. 302–15), but Hugh did not build the fees of his undertenants strictly along pre-Conquest lines. Earl Edwin's land was used by Hugh, for example, to form his own demesne (DB, i, 263v–264r), and was granted out as well to his tenants Robert fitz Hugh (DB, i, 264r), Bigot de Loges (DB, i, 266v) and Gilbert de Venables (DB, i, 267r).

consolidation. Sussex, with its rapes, is an obvious example,[10] and the county of Cornwall, excluding old ecclesiastical interests and less than one other hide of land, was organized into a kind of huge appanage under the lordship of the king's half-brother, Robert Count of Mortain.[11] Kent, too, was divided along new territorial rather than old tenurial lines.[12] Very roughly, these six border or coastal shires constituted about 10 per cent of all the assessed land in William's kingdom.[13] What is particularly striking about the division of these marcher and coastal shires is the Norman tenants-in-chief who held there. Many numbered among Corbet's 'Class A', that is wealthiest, barons.[14] Accordingly, a majority of William's greatest secular lords were in possession of honours centred on territorial divisions that were entirely the Conqueror's creations. The core of these great lords' demesne and enfeoffed land was often founded on new territories that had little to do with the Anglo-Saxon past; these new divisions ignored the great lordships of the Anglo-Saxon earls as well as the Edwardian boundaries between the earldoms of Wessex and Mercia and Wessex and the earldom of the south-east.[15] As a result, the tenurial map of England was turned inside out, as new and valuable territories were formed along the edges of the kingdom and given into the charge of William's most trusted magnates. Yet these new lordships were quite different from the great landed conglomerations of the pre-Conquest era. During the Confessor's reign the sons of Earl Godwine or the grandsons of Earl Leofric had held a minimum of £100 more land than any other family in over half the counties of England, most notably in areas where West Saxon kings had traditionally based their power – in Devonshire, Wiltshire, Somerset, Dorset, Hampshire, Surrey, Kent and Buckinghamshire. (See chapter 7, figure 7.3.) By 1086, however, holdings like these were situated for the most part on the outskirts of the kingdom and no longer existed in the southwest and in the southern midlands. (See chapter 7, figure 7.4.) Great Norman lords, unlike their Anglo-Saxon counterparts, had the seats of their power and a substantial portion of their land

[10] J. F. A. Mason, 'The rapes of Sussex and the Norman Conquest', *Sussex Archaeological Collections*, 102 (1964), pp. 68–93 and *William I and the Sussex Rapes*.

[11] DB, i, 121v–125r.   [12] See below, pp. 152–3.

[13] These statistics are based on figures found in Darby, *Domesday England*, p. 336.

[14] W. J. Corbett, 'The development of the Duchy of Normandy and the Norman Conquest of England', *The Cambridge Medieval History*, ed. J. R. Tanner *et al.* (Cambridge, 1926), v. p. 508.   [15] See above n. 5.

along the edges of the kingdom and not in the heart of England, where Edward the Confessor and his earls had vied for landed wealth and influence.[16] The real precedent for the marcher lordships is to be found in Normandy, not in England.

The formation of tight-knit lordships is evident even in shires where landholding at times devolved neatly from antecessors to successors. In Nottinghamshire, for example, several Norman honours were formed by a strict adherence to antecessors and successors. Gilbert de Gand came into the Englishman Ulf Fenisc's land and Walter d'Aincourt into the holdings of the thegns Swein Cilt and Thori.[17] But the two greatest secular tenants-in-chief in the county – Roger de Bully and William Peverel – were each granted large, consolidated blocks of territory within the county; William held almost all of Broxtow Wapentake and the northern portion of the neighbouring wapentake of Rushcliffe; Roger de Bully held a mass of land in the north-northeast of the shire, especially in the wapentakes of Bassetlaw, Lythe and Oswaldbeck. He also held a block of land in the south central portion of the shire. Furthermore, Roger de Bully's and William Peverel's honours within Nottinghamshire nullified a number of Old English tenancies. Roger, for example, held two estates which pertained to Grimketil TRE in the north county, but William got the remaining four in his territory centred on Broxtow Wapentake.[18] Roger de Bully acquired the thegn Glædwine's estate in the area in which Roger held major interests, while William got the same thegn's lands in Broxtow Wapentake.[19] These territories were new in 1086 and were in no way evident in Edward the Confessor's day. William Peverel's fee was pieced together from the lands of at least thirty-three Englishmen, and Roger de Bully's holding was composed of the lands of a minimum of sixty-eight Anglo-Saxons.[20] There is no evidence in the Nottinghamshire folios that these hundred or so men had, before the Conquest, been the men of any one lord. Nottinghamshire, like the rest of the shires in Domesday's Circuit

---

[16] Robin Fleming, 'Domesday estates of the king and the Godwines: a study in late Saxon politics', *Speculum*, 58 (1983), pp. 987–1007.

[17] DB, i, 290v, 288v, 289r. For Gilbert de Gand's and Walter d'Aincourt's antecessors in other counties see Mack, 'Kings and thegns', appendix I.

[18] DB, i, 285r, 286v, 287v, 288r. On Roger's successions in Nottinghamshire, see F. M. Stenton, *VCH, Nottinghamshire*, ii, pp. 223–5.   [19] DB, i, 286r, 287v, 288r.

[20] DB, i, 287r–288r, 284v–287r. For a description of William's fee, see *VCH, Nottinghamshire*, ii, pp. 228–30.

VI, is silent on pre-Conquest lordships, but the men most likely to have been the lords of Nottinghamshire's minor landholders were powerful thegns like Swein Cilt, Ulf Fenisc, and Thori, men who held major interests in the region. Yet the lands of these great thegns devolved on to Norman lords through a strict adherence to antecessorial inheritance.[21] Therefore, the men most likely to have been lords of Nottinghamshire's lesser landholders are found with well-defined successors, but the lands of the county's minor thegns were appropriated into one of the shire's two territorial fees.

The same mix of new and old landholding patterns can be found in Northamptonshire, where the Bishop of Lincoln's honour was formed from his antecessor Bardi's land, William Peverel's from Gytha's land, and Robert de Bucy's from Northmann's land.[22] Robert Count of Mortain, however, by far the wealthiest lord in the county, held a fee constructed of the lands of at least fifty-one thegns and sokemen who had held farms scattered across the Northamptonshire wolds 'on the day King Edward was both alive and dead'.[23] In Derbyshire, Geoffrey Alselin inherited Toki son of Outi's lands and William Peverel came into Leofric's lands;[24] but the wealthiest man in the shire, Henry de Ferrers, succeeded into the lands of dozens of pre-Conquest tenants whose holdings were clustered in Derbyshire's southern lowlands north of the River Trent.[25] In Kent both Odo Bishop of Bayeux and Hugh de Montfort's fees were made up of the holdings of numerous TRE holders, and both held concentrated territories within the shire.[26] In Yorkshire the lands of many pre-Conquest lords – Mærle-sveinn and Eadgifu to name two – formed the core of small, dispersed post-Conquest tenancies-in-chief.[27] The extensive fees of Drogo de la Beuvrière, Alan of Richmond and Robert Count of Mortain, on the other hand, were each formed from the lands of half a hundred 'antecessors', all of whom had held in a compact district.[28] Drogo de la

---

[21] Toki's lands went to Geoffrey Alselin (DB, i, 289r–289v), Ulf's to Gilbert de Gand (DB, i, 290v), and Thori's to Walter d'Aincourt (DB, i, 288v–289r).

[22] DB, i, 221r, 225v, 226r, 225r, 225v. For the antecessors of these tenants-in-chief in other parts of England, see Mack, 'Kings and thegns', appendix I.

[23] DB, i, 223r–224r.   [24] DB, i, 276v, 276r.   [25] DB, i, 274r–276r.

[26] See below, pp. 152–3.

[27] Mærle-sveinn was Ralph Pagnell's antecessor (DB, i, 325v–326r). Eadgifu was the antecessor of Ralph de Mortimer (DB, i, 325r–325v).

[28] Drogo succeeded to the lands of landholders with forty-four different names in Yorkshire, the Count of Mortain to sixty, and Count Alan to fifty-four.

Beuvrière's fee in Yorkshire, for example, was formed from all the lands in the three hundreds of Holderness that the Church had not held TRE. The Fleming, however, did not hold any land in Yorkshire outside of Holderness. At the heart of his fee lay the lands of his Lincolnshire antecessor Ulf son of Tope, who had held extensively across eastern Yorkshire before the Conquest. But to this inheritance had been added the lands of at least forty-three other Anglo-Scandinavian lords. As is typical with the development of many territorial honours, we see Drogo accumulating all the disparate pre-Conquest estates found in the region's divided vills. He came, for example, into both Thor's and Thorketil's lands in Ottringham, although the two men had held their land as two separate manors before the Conquest, and all of Holmpton, which had consisted of six manors before the Confessor's death.[29] This accumulation of all manors in a single vill occurs in twenty of the fifty-two vills in which Drogo held land; and in these twenty vills, there had, before the Conquest, been sixty-two holdings. Thus Drogo acquired everything in each Holderness vill regardless of who held the land in Edward's reign. Such a sweeping together of land and combining of pre-Conquest divided vills into a single holding is a hallmark of such territorial grants and it leaves a strong imprint on the Domesday Survey. In counties such as Nottinghamshire, Derbyshire and Yorkshire it is common to find entries beginning with notations to the effect that a TRW tenancy was made up of many manors. Roger de Bully, for example, held 'ten manors in Eaton ... [TRE they were held by] ten thegns and each had his hall', or 'four manors in Ordsall. Osweard, Thurstan, Ordric, and Thurstan had [them]'.[30] Such jottings preserve the wholesale grants necessitated by the establishment of compact fees. In all of the counties discussed above the very great secular fees were granted on the basis of territory rather than tenure.

In each of these cases, evidence preserved in Domesday suggested that territorial fees were granted out by county rather than by region or across the kingdom. In Nottinghamshire William Peverel 'inherited' the two estates Stapolwine had held.[31] Roger de Bully, on the other hand, held all three of Spearheafoc's lands, Othenkarl's seven, and Karski's two.[32] But

---

[29] DB, i, 324r.   [30] DB, i, 284v.   [31] DB, i, 287r, 287v, 287v, 288r.
[32] DB, i, 286v, 284v, 285v, 286r, 286v.

Territorial rather than tenurial grants.

across the border and into Derbyshire, Roger's and William's 'antecessors'' lands devolved onto a different set of lords. Stapolwine's and Karski's estates were taken over by King William, and Othenkarl's lands in Derbyshire and Lincolnshire went almost entirely to Gilbert de Gand.[33] Thus Spearheafoc, Othenkarl, Stapolwine and Karski were either antecessors to William and Roger only in Nottinghamshire and not in neighbouring counties, or their land devolved on these particular lords not by principle of antecessor but simply because of the shire in which they lay. Similarly, Robert Count of Mortain's vast expanse of land in Northamptonshire did not extend across the shire's borders, and he did not hold a single ploughland in the neighbouring counties of Leicestershire, Warwickshire or Oxfordshire, although they abutted his Northamptonshire fee. Ilbert de Lacy's compact Yorkshire fee, which skirted along southern Yorkshire's Pennine uplands, did not spill over into Derbyshire or Cheshire. Thus, it appears that when the king granted blocks of territory to important *familiares*, he did so county by county. This suggests that territorial grants, like those discussed above, were implemented in some way by the Old English county courts and officials, particularly the sheriff. Notification could be sent to the sheriff after such a territorial gift was made, and the new tenant-in-chief, the sheriff and the county courts could then implement these grants. The writ was perfectly suited for such a task.

It also seems that within the county, territorial fees were often granted out by hundred or wapentake, and again the organization of Anglo-Saxon government could facilitate such grants.[34] Henry de Ferrers held a block of land cutting a wide swathe across

---

[33] DB, i, 273r, 277v, 355v.

[34] The language of Geoffrey de Mandeville's foundation charter for the Hurley Priory, preserved in two of Westminster's cartularies, may reflect the kind of language used in writs made out for hundredal grants. In his charter, Geoffrey gave the vill of Hurley 'et cum toto circumjacenti nemore, sine particione aut aliqua vel alicujus hominis in ipsa parochia aliquid tenentis; excepta terra Edrici prepositi et excepta terra rusticorum de Parva Waltham, quas retinui in manu mea' (Pierre Chaplais, 'The original charters of Herbert and Gervase Abbots of Westminster (1121–1157)', in *A Medieval Miscellany for Doris Mary Stenton*, ed. Patricia M. Barnes and C. F. Slade (London, 1962), p. 105). There are hints in Domesday Book, as well, that territorial grants were made after exempting the lands of certain holders. In both Cheshire and Shropshire Domesday notes that the lands of ecclesiastical communities were confirmed, but that Earl Hugh and Roger of Montgomery 'hold the remaining land' (DB, i, 262v, 252r; Holt, '1086', *Domesday Studies*, ed. J. C. Holt (Woodbridge, Suffolk, 1987), p. 61).

Derbyshire, the core of which lay in Appletree Wapentake, where Henry held in all but two of the wapentake's sixty-eight vills.[35] In Nottinghamshire Roger de Bully got the bulk of the land in Oswaldbeck, Bassetlaw, Lythe and Thurgarton Wapentakes, while William Peverel received most of Broxtow Wapentake,[36] and in Northamptonshire the Count of Mortain appears to have been granted a territory based on sixteen hundreds.[37] In Lincolnshire Geoffrey de la Guerche inherited land in three West Riding wapentakes from his antecessors Leofric and Leofwine,[38] but the rest of his fee was comprised of Epworth Wapentake, in which he inherited from a dozen or so pre-Conquest tenants.[39] And with three exceptions all the lands not inherited through an antecessor in Holland's wapentakes of Wolmersty and Kirton were held by Alan of Richmond TRW.[40] The Sussex Rapes, too, were formed according to hundredal lines.[41] In Kent, beside the church and the king, the only two secular tenants-in-chief of any importance were Hugh de Montfort and Odo Bishop of Bayeux as Earl of Kent,[42] and the basis of their fees was hundredal. Hugh de Montfort's land lay in a consolidated block in southeastern Kent and was composed of eleven hundreds. The only other secular tenant-in-chief in these hundreds was Odo himself, and he held just over five sulungs of land there.[43] For Odo's part, he gained control over twenty-nine hundreds. Only Richard fitz Gilbert held an estate in demesne in one of Odo's hundreds.[44] No

---

[35] The two exceptions are Hoon, soke of Burton Abbey, and Robert fitz William's holding in Stanley (DB, i, 273r, 278r). For a further discussion of Henry's Derbyshire holdings see F. M. Stenton, 'Introduction to the Derbyshire Domesday', *VCH, Derbyshire*, i, 300–26.   [36] See figure 5.1.

[37] These hundreds are Stoke, Stotfold, Rothwell, Orlingbury, Mawsley, Guilsborough, Nobottle, Gravesend, Warden, Foxley, Towcester, Cleyley, Alboldstow, Sutton, Spelhoe and Hamfordshoe.

[38] DB, i, 369r. His lands from Leofwine descended to Geoffrey through his marriage to Leofwine's daughter (Searle, 'Women and the legitimization of succession at the Norman Conquest', p. 164).   [39] DB, i, 369r–369v.   [40] DB, i, 347r–348v.

[41] Mason, *The Sussex Rapes.*

[42] Odo's land in Kent covers six folios and Hugh de Montfort's a further folio (DB, i, 6r–11v, 13r–14r). The lands of the remaining secular tenants-in-chief are recorded on slightly less than two columns (DB, i, 14r–14v).

[43] Hugh's holdings centred on Longbridge, Newchurch, Worth, Hayne, Aloesbridge, Blackburn, Street, Stowting, Bircholt and Chart. In these hundreds Odo held only four sulungs in Bilsington, one half yoke in Aloesbridge Hundred, three yokes in Hastingleigh, and one half sulung in *Blocheland* (DB, i, 10v, 11v, 9v).

[44] Odo's holdings centred on Axton, Little, Ruxley, Greenwich, Bromley, Larkfied, Toltingtrough, Littlefield, Washlingstone, Eyhorne, Chatham, Rochester, Hoo, Twyford, Maidstone, Shamwell, Milton, Bridge, Downhamford, Folkestone, Longing-

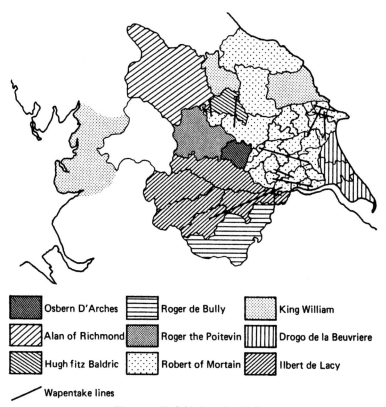

Osbern D'Arches   Roger de Bully   King William

Alan of Richmond   Roger the Poitevin   Drogo de la Beuvriere

Hugh fitz Baldric   Robert of Mortain   Ilbert de Lacy

Wapentake lines

Figure 5.1 Yorkshire's territorial fees

other secular lord did so. The only hundreds in which secular landholding was divided were the districts of Wye and Bewsborough. There is, therefore, an almost perfect correlation between TRW landholding patterns and Kentish hundreds. This was not the case in the Confessor's day.[45]

In Yorkshire, as in Derbyshire, Nottinghamshire, Northamptonshire, Kent, Sussex and parts of Lincolnshire, it looks as if ancient administrative districts played a crucial role in the formation of the most important secular fees. In Yorkshire thirty-six areas, either the wapentake or more ancient *scire* like Craven,

borough, Rolvenden, Eastry, Barham, Whitstable, Faversham, Felborough, Calehill, Oxney, Langport and *Summerdene*. Richard fitz Gilbert held two sulungs in Twyford Hundred and one in Maidstone Hundred (DB, i, 14r).

[45] For example the holdings of Earl Godwine, Esbiorn Bigga and Moleva were split between Hugh and Odo according to the hundred in which they lay.

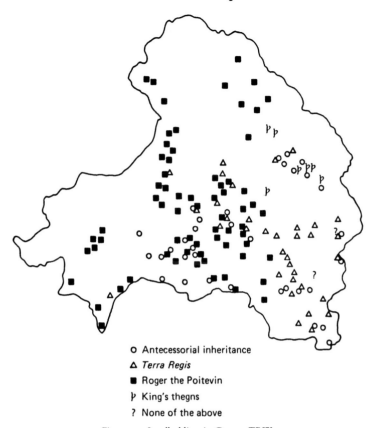

O Antecessorial inheritance
Δ *Terra Regis*
■ Roger the Poitevin
Þ King's thegns
? None of the above

Figure 5.2 Landholding in Craven TRW

Amounderness and Holderness, formed the boundaries of the
shire's eight territorial fees. (See figure 5.1.) Roger the Poitevin,
for example, was placed in charge of Craven. Except for the land
of the king, the property of king's thegns, and the sokeland and
berewicks attached to a caput in another wapentake, all the
holdings in Craven with two minor exceptions went either to the
fees of Normans with well defined antecessors or to Roger, who
came into the land not of one TRE holder, but of twenty-five.[46]
Roger, moreover, held exclusively in Craven and nowhere else in
the shire, suggesting that the district itself formed the basis of his
grant. (See figure 5.2.) Robert Count of Mortain's enormous
holding in Yorkshire was similarly formed. The king's half-

[46] DB, i, 332r.

154

brother was granted virtually all the land not inherited through a well-defined antecessor, absorbed into the *terra regis*, or maintained by the Church in the wapentakes of Langbargh and *Manshowe, Dic,* Hessle, Howden and Hunthrow, Acklam, Burton, Bulmer (*Bolesford*), Driffield, Cave, Pocklington, *Scard, Sneclufcros, Thorshowe, Tubar,* Warter, Weighton and Welton. In these wapentakes or hundreds the count succeeded a minimum of sixty named Englishmen; twenty of these names can be found among his North Riding successions, twenty-five in those of the West Riding, and thirty-three in those of the East Riding. A handful of these names appear over and over again in the folios enumerating Count Robert's Yorkshire fee. Robert received nine or more holdings in Yorkshire from men bearing nine names – Swein, Uhtræd, Northmann, Waltheof, Ulfketil, Orm, Thorketil, Gamal and Ligulfr. All but the last of these names, however, are common north of the Humber and so may represent two or more pre-Conquest landholders.[47] Nonetheless, the holdings of some of these individuals probably came into Robert's possession by rights of inheritance and succession. The remaining fifty-one names, however, appearing as pre-Conquest holders in Robert's fee, cannot in any meaningful way be described as the names of people he succeeded because of who they were, as opposed to where they held. The one carucate holding of Halldor in Brafferton,[48] the three carucates five bovates held by Ealdgyth in Middleton on the Wolds,[49] and the six carucates five bovates in Long Sandall once belonging to Skotakollr[50] all devolved onto the king's half-brother for some reason other than succession by antecessor. Each of these names, along with twenty-nine others, is recorded only once in Robert's honour. It is difficult to envision an administrative device that could oversee the redistribution of the scattered holdings of very minor Anglo-Saxon landholders over a vast expanse of devastated territory on the basis of antecession.

The carucates of land Robert received from Halldor in the vill of Brafferton lay in the North Riding in Bulmer wapentake. In this wapentake the Archbishop of York had managed to maintain his Saint's ancient demesne in twenty-two vills. The king held in thirty-one of the wapentake's vills. A number of secular tenants-in-chief held in Bulmer wapentake as well. Hugh fitz Baldric held

---

[47] von Feilitzen, *Pre-Conquest Personal Names, sub nomine.*   [48] DB, i, 306r.

[49] DB, i, 306v.   [50] DB, i, 307v.

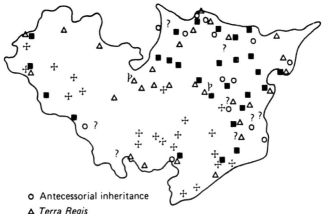

○ Antecessorial inheritance

△ *Terra Regis*

■ Robert Count of Mortain

Þ King's thegns

✢ Ecclesiastical holdings

? None of the above

Figure 5.3 Landholding in Bulmer Wapentake TRW

there, the bulk of his lands deriving from his antecessor Orm;[51] Berenger de Tosny held all the lands in Bulmer once controlled by Gamal and Thorbrandr, his antecessors throughout Yorkshire.[52] Robert Malet held two carucates in the wapentake which had belonged to a man he frequently succeeded named Asketil.[53] The remaining land in the wapentake, ranging across twenty-nine vills and held before the Conquest by over a dozen English landholders including Halldor, was granted to Count Robert. In other words, the count received all the land that remained in the wapentake after the first wave of dispossession and acquisition had occurred. (See figure 5.3.) This pattern is evident not only in the wapentakes which the count thoroughly dominated, but it can also be discerned in wapentakes where the count actually held very little. Domesday records thirty-one holdings in the wapentake of *Scard*. (See figure 5.4.) By 1086 these lands were split between seven honours, and Robert's share was a small one. Three *Scard* holdings remained in ecclesiastical lordships between the Conquest and the Inquest,[54] another eight were incorporated

[51] DB, i, 327v. [52] DB, i, 314r.

[53] DB, i, 320v. The MS says Arnketil, a mistake for the name Asketil.

[54] DB, i, 303r. All three holdings – North Grimston, Birdsall and Sutton Grange – were soke of Weaverthorpe, one of the Archbishop's manors lying in *Thorshowe* Wapentake.

○ Antecessorial inheritance
△ *Terra Regis*
■ Robert Count of Mortain
Þ King's thegns
✝ Ecclesiastical holdings
? None of the above

Figure 5.4 Landholding in *Scard* Wapentake TRW

into the *terra regis*[55] and one other was held by a king's thegn.[56] Three other lands were held by Berenger de Tosny, but these came into his possession, as had those lands in Bulmer Wapentake, through his Yorkshire antecessors Thorbrandr and Gamal.[57] Five other holdings were enfeoffed to Ralph de Mortimer, but they were lands which had been held by Ralph's antecessors Eadgifu and Orm.[58] Another seven were held by Hugh fitz Baldric, but again Hugh received these lands via his antecessors Gamal and Orm, whose lands made up the bulk of Hugh's Yorkshire fee.[59] Robert Count of Mortain held all the remaining land in the wapentake.[60] A similar pattern can be found in *Thorshowe* Wapentake with its thirty holdings. The archbishopric maintained a third of the wapentake,[61] the king had six holdings,[62] and king's thegns were in possession of two.[63] Beside these there were five other tenants-in-chief in the wapentake: Berenger de Tosny held land here as he did in *Scard* Wapentake through his inheritance from Thorbrandr;[64] Ralph de Mortimer held in *Thorshowe* because of his antecessor Eadgifu;[65] Hugh fitz Baldric succeeded to Gamal's and Orm's lands;[66] and Gospatric, one of the few major pre-Conquest tenants to survive as tenant-in-chief,

[55] DB, i, 301r.   [56] DB, i, 331r.   [57] DB, i, 314r.
[58] DB, i, 325r–325v. He also succeeded Eadgifu in Lincolnshire (DB, i, 363r).
[59] DB, i, 327v.   [60] DB, i, 307r.   [61] DB, i, 303r.   [62] DB, i, 301r.
[63] DB, i, 331r.   [64] DB, i, 314v.   [65] DB, i, 325v.   [66] DB, i, 328r.

managed to keep hold of his lands in the wapentake.[67] As in *Scard Wapentake*, we are left with the Count of Mortain, who held the remaining land in the district. In each of these wapentakes or hundreds – Bulmer, *Scard*, and *Thorshow* – the count was the only secular tenant-in-chief with no easily discerned antecessor. It appears, therefore, that Robert's fee in Yorkshire was formed in the same way in which the fees of William Peverel and Roger de Bully had been formed to the south. In all, the Count of Mortain gained control of virtually all the lands not granted out by principle of a well defined antecessor in nineteen Yorkshire wapentakes.

As in Nottinghamshire, Derbyshire and Northamptonshire, the composition of Count Robert's fee appears to have been a territorial one, built from mass confiscations of lesser men, and granted out by wapentake or hundred. Such a pattern of endowment was not limited to Robert's nineteen wapentakes, but can be discerned in every other wapentake in the shire with the exception of Claro. Drogo de la Beuvrière, as noted above, gained control of the three hundreds forming Holderness, and Roger the Poitevin got the lion's share of Craven. Roger de Bully acquired the shire's southernmost wapentake of Strafforth which adjoined his territory in Derbyshire. Ilbert de Lacy gained the bulk of six wapentakes south of the River Ouse,[68] Alan of Richmond was granted the northwestern corner of the shire.[69] Hugh fitz Baldric gained control of Birdforth and Osbert d'Arches Ainsty. In the two remaining Yorkshire wapentakes and in Amounderness, the king maintained all the land not given out by antecessor for his own use.[70] Throughout Yorkshire a single tenant-in-chief was granted all the lands in a wapentake which were not held by the Church, granted out on the principle

---

[67] DB, i, 330r.

[68] W. E. Wightman noted that Ilbert's honour of Pontefract 'formed an almost solid rectangle of over five hundred square miles', but he did not see the wapentakes which lay at his territory's core (W. E. Wightman, *The Lacy Family in England and Normandy 1066–1194* (Oxford, 1966), pp. 17–19).

[69] This territory was later known as Richmondshire (*Calendar of Inquisitions, Miscellaneous*, i, pp. 168–71). For Count Alan's compact fee in Yorkshire see Stenton, *First Century*, pp. 194–5.

[70] The king most likely held this land in reserve to give out to other tenants, but did not grant it out before his death. It is clear that some of the 1086 *terra regis*, however, was used after the Inquest to endow other men. William de Warenne, for example, gained the manor of Wakefield with its extensive sokes and berewicks after 1086 (*EYC*, 8, p. 178). The King held Wakefield at the time of the survey (DB, i, 299v).

158

of antecessor and successor, not sokeland or berewicks of a caput in another wapentake, or which had not been absorbed into the *terra regis*. In all of Yorkshire more than 95 per cent of all successions can be explained by the principle of acquisition by antecessor or by wapentake.

Further evidence of the wapentake's role in the formation of Norman fees can be found by tracking the dispersal of William Malet's fee in Yorkshire, formed within two years of the Conquest and dissolved no later than 1071.[71] This early fee was built along different lines from the Yorkshire honours formed after it. William Malet held something like 200 carucates across Yorkshire's three ridings. Most of his land was in the East Riding, but he had substantial interests in the three West Riding wapentakes of Ainsty, Barkston Ash and *Burghshire*. The Anglo-Saxons from whom he had inherited were an undistinguished lot; certainly none can be identified as members of northern England's high society. Several of William's modestly wealthy predecessors are identified in Yorkshire's *clamores* specifically as his *antecessores*. We are told, for example, that William succeeded to all of Havarthr's, Asa's and Northmann son of Mælcolumban's holdings.[72] Other Englishmen appear more than once as pre-Conquest holders of William Malet's lands. Oddi, sometimes styled 'the Deacon' and sometimes 'the Priest', was succeeded by William in Hornington Manor, Holmpton and Southcoates,[73] and William was frequently endowed with the lands of Cnut and Northmann son of Ulf.[74] The group of men he succeeded in Yorkshire in the first years of the Conquest were probably men who fell at Fulford or Stamford Bridge,[75] or individuals who for one reason or another went into exile in the first months of the Conqueror's reign, since entries in the *clamores* often state that William held a particular piece of land before the destruction of the castle at York, which took place in 1069.[76] With the Yorkshire emergency of 1069–70 and with William Malet's death no later than 1071, the bulk of the Malet fee was redistributed. When it was, it was granted neither to William's undertenants (if he had

---

[71] Freeman, *NC*, iv, p. 473; Round, 'The death of William Malet', *Academy* (26 April 1884). [72] DB, i, 373r. [73] DB, i, 374r, 324r, 325r. [74] DB, i, 373r.

[75] An example of a thegn who died in York in the autumn of 1066 is preserved in DB, where it is recorded that a thegn 'gave this land to the Church [of Westminster] when he went to battle in York with Harold' (DB, ii, 15a).

[76] For example, 'they testify that William Malet held Havarthr's land in Yorkshire before the castle was taken' (DB, i, 373r).

any) nor to his son and heir, Robert.[77] By 1086 men testifying at the wapentake courts believed that this redistribution was illegal, and in cases of disputed tenure they always settled in favour of Robert Malet. Restitution, however, was complicated by the fact that over 200 of William Malet's hides had been divided between the king and nine of his tenants-in-chief, and had been held by them for perhaps a decade or more. Some of William's land was granted out by antecessor to other Normans. William de Percy was granted all the land Malet had acquired from Asa and Northmann,[78] and Landric acquired Malet's possessions once held by a second Northmann.[79] The bulk of William's land, nonetheless, was dealt out by wapentake, and so was used, along with the land of hundreds of minor Anglo-Scandinavian thegns and freemen, to create the new territorial settlement in Yorkshire. Hugh fitz Baldric succeeded to only one piece of William Malet's land – land William had purchased from a man named Sprottr in Sand Hutton (near Thirsk) soon after the Conquest.[80] These seven carucates were found by the commissioners to be part of Hugh's fee in 1086, and found, moreover, in *Gerlestre* (Birdforth) Wapentake, the wapentake Hugh dominated at the end of the Conqueror's reign.[81] Osbern d'Arches, unlike Hugh, picked up a considerable amount of land from the Malet honour – ten holdings in all. But this windfall was confined to Ainsty Wapentake, the wapentake Osbern dominated.[82] Drogo de la Beuvrière, by 1086, held nearly one hundred carucates once pertaining to William, gathering to his fee every one of William's possessions in the three hundreds of Holderness, that is, in his territory.[83] Finally, the Count of Mortain came into William's land in the three East Riding wapentakes of Cave, Howden and Welton, hundreds dominated by that count.[84]

In Nottinghamshire, Derbyshire, Northamptonshire, Kent, Sussex, Yorkshire and parts of Lincolnshire, land redistribution echoed the divisions of shires, wapentakes and hundreds more closely than lines of pre-Conquest tenure. So Domesday reveals two methods or principles whereby the Normans established themselves on the land. One was antecessorial, the other

---

[77] It is interesting to note that the one Norman we do know to have been with William Malet when the castle at York was taken was Gilbert de Gand (Sim. Dur., *Opera Omnia*, ii, p. 188), and he held no land in Yorkshire in 1086.

[78] DB, i, 373r, 322v. [79] DB, i, 374r. [80] DB, i, 373r. [81] DB, i, 327v.
[82] DB, i, 373v, 374r. [83] DB, i, 374r. [84] DB, i, 374r.

territorial. The first founded title in inheritance from an antecessor, the second was based on grants made by county, hundred and wapentake. This created an extraordinarily complicated tenurial patchwork across England and certainly helps to explain why there were so many legal disputes by 1086. The *clamores* of Lincolnshire and Yorkshire preserve a multitude of disputes centred around rival claims to the same holdings, one based on an antecessorial grant and the other on a hundredal one. Geoffrey de la Guerche, for example, possessed everything in Epworth Wapentake not held by the king or the Church, including land in Amcotts, held TRE by Siward Barn and land and soke in Belton (near Epworth), which had pertained to Ulf Fenisc.[85] Ulf was Gilbert de Gand's antecessor elsewhere in Lincolnshire and throughout England, and Siward was Henry de Ferrers' antecessor. Accordingly, Gilbert and Henry claimed these lands against Geoffrey.[86] William de Percy, who was granted Bolton Percy very soon after the Conquest 'while William Malet was alive and held the sheriffdom of York', had to defend himself against a counter claim, probably by Osbern d'Arches, in whose territory this land lay TRW.[87] Similarly Geoffrey Alselin laid claim to ten and a half carucates of his antecessor Toki's land in Strafforth Wapentake – the basis of Roger de Bully's fee – and land which Roger possessed TRW.[88] In Derbyshire Geoffrey Alselin claimed Scropton in Appletree Wapentake because his antecessor Toki had held it, but Henry de Ferrers had granted the tithe of this vill to Tutbury Priory in 1080 because it lay in his territory.[89] Even churchmen had to defend their ancient patrimonies against lords who had been granted territories. Drogo de la Beuvrière claimed a number of Holderness estates held by St John's Beverley, but the canons had the seals of both King Edward and King William to prove their claim to the land.[90] In all these cases the two principles of antecession and territorial distribution were confused or in conflict.

Despite this confusion the distinction between the two principles is of crucial importance in constructing a chronology of dispossession and acquisition. For there can be little doubt that

---

[85] DB, i, 376v.   [86] DB, i, 369v, 376v.   [87] DB, i, 374r.   [88] DB, i, 373v, 319r.
[89] DB, i, 274v; *Mon. Ang.*, iii, 319.
[90] DB, i, 374r. William's confirmation of Beverley's Holderness land is preserved in a writ printed in Benjamin Thorpe, *Diplomatarium Anglicum Ævi Saxonici* (London, 1865), p. 438.

where the two methods of endowment appear side by side, the antecessorial was the earlier and the territorial the later. Such is the inescapable conclusion drawn from Domesday Book. The Nottinghamshire folios provide a clear example. Here, Ralph fitz Hubert must have received his Nottinghamshire land relatively soon after the Conquest. He was made the successor of a very important local thegn named Leofric, whose holdings lay along the south-southeastern border of the shire.[91] These lands of Leofric are virtually the only lands excluding royal or ecclesiastical estates that William Peverel did not eventually inherit in Broxtow Wapentake or that Roger de Bully did not acquire in the wapentake of Rushcliffe. Intruding into their territories as Ralph fitz Hubert does, it appears that Ralph was given his land prior to the formation of either Roger's or William's consolidated, territorial fees. When they were granted their lands, their holdings had to skirt around fitz Hubert's already established honour. Similarly, the Count of Mortain was the successor of another south Nottinghamshire thegn named Stori. One of Stori's old estates, held in 1086 by Count Robert, lay in the midst of some fifty square miles of territory controlled by William Peverel. Further south, abutting Roger de Bully's Rushcliffe holdings, the Count of Mortain also held Stori's property.[92] His succession to Stori's land probably, therefore, like the succession of Ralph fitz Hubert, predated the granting of William's and Roger's fees. Gilbert de Gand, the successor of Ulf Fenisc in this county as elsewhere in England, inherited Ulf's land in five wapentakes, including Bassetlaw, the wapentake which Roger de Bully so thoroughly dominated.[93] Remigius Bishop of Lincoln inherited Countess Godgifu's land, Walter d'Aincourt came into the lands of Thori and Swein Cilt, and Gilbert Tison was granted another Swein's lands.[94] The king maintained the Confessor's lands, and various ecclesiastical establishments managed to keep hold of their Nottinghamshire endowments.[95]

All of these land transferences probably occurred before the Conqueror established his two Nottinghamshire territorial fees. This he did by giving William Peverel all the land in Broxtow

---

[91] DB, i, 289v. [92] DB, i, 282v. [93] DB, i, 290v.

[94] DB, i, 283v, 284r, 288v, 291r.

[95] Edward the Confessor's five estates – Dunham, Grimston, Mansfield, Arnold and Orston – with their extensive sokes and berewicks were still part of the *terra regis* in 1086 (DB, i, 281r–282r). The Archbishop of York's and the Abbot of Peterborough's TRW lands mirrored their TRE holdings (DB, i, 283r–283v; 284r).

Wapentake that had not previously been granted out by antecession and a scattering of land in the bordering wapentake. Roger de Bully similarly was presented with the remaining land in Oswaldbeck, Bassetlaw, Thurgarton and Lythe. This explains why their two fees together were made up of the holdings of over one hundred Anglo-Saxons' lands. It also accounts for the apparent intrusion of other tenants-in-chief into their fees. These others were there first: they were not an intrusion, but a prior establishment on which it was difficult if not impossible to encroach. It is now possible to reconstruct a chronology. It seems likely that the antecessors – the thegns Leofwine, Ulf Fenisc, Thori and Swein Cilt – were killed, outlawed or dispossessed at a relatively early date, and Normans such as Robert Count of Mortain and Gilbert de Gand came into the county soon after the Conquest. Henry de Ferrers also established an early foot-hold in the county through his 'inheritance' of the land of his antecessor Siward Barn after 1071, when Siward revolted for the last time against the Conqueror.[96] But the two greatest Nottinghamshire tenants-in-chief TRW, Roger de Bully and William Peverel, can have held little in the shire at this date. It was only as a second stage, probably (and in some cases certainly) after 1071 that the king granted them each endowments made up of all the remaining land in each wapentake which had not yet been granted out on the basis of succession by antecessor. The implication of this is that William Peverel, put in charge of the Conqueror's hastily built castle at Nottingham in 1067, hung on by his toenails in the county as a royal official in an ostensibly loyal shire for more than half a decade.[97] It was only after England was shaken again and again by serious rebellions that the Conqueror undertook a massive dispossession of lesser thegns and granted his two vassals each a territory and the landed resources to dig in and hold a hostile land.

There was a further result. The two largest and most important secular fees in the county were not only late creations, but they were entirely new – made up of leftovers – created from the holdings of more than one hundred obscure men. The resources

[96] DB, i, 291v; *ASC*, s.a. 1071 (E).
[97] OV, ii, p. 218. William Kapelle, on the other hand, argues that William Peverel's Nottinghamshire fee, was 'formed in the early 1070s' and dates from 'the days when the marcher earldoms had been formed'. Further, he argues that it 'survived as a direct archetype for the fees William created in the North around 1080' (*Norman Conquest of the North*, p. 144).

of the most powerful men in the shire, therefore, underwent a significant geographical shift. Certainly for at least a century before the Conquest, power in Nottinghamshire was rooted in the estates of the brothers Leofnoth and Leofric. Many of their holdings had been in the possession of the powerful thegn Wulfric Spot around the year 1000 and earlier may even have belonged to the Mercian kings.[98] After the Conquest, however, the greatest men in the county no longer had an interest in these estates. The centre of political gravity had migrated by the middle of the Conqueror's reign to estates once belonging to Nottinghamshire's rank-and-file thegns.[99] In total, about a quarter of all land available for secular redistribution in Nottinghamshire after the Conquest was granted out by the Conqueror, probably within six years of Hastings by the principle of antecessor and successor. But the remaining three quarters was distributed territorially following the boundaries of wapentakes.

Something similar occurred in Derbyshire. Here Henry de Ferrers was given a fee composed of all available land in High Peak, Appletree and Morleystone Wapentakes with the exception of lands already granted out to William's followers through their antecessors, and a compact block of land centred on William Peverel's castle at Peak Cavern.[100] Henry's acquisition in Derbyshire necessarily post-dates the creation of William Peverel's castelry and the granting out of Leofric and Leofnoth's land to Ralph fitz Hubert and Ulf son of Tope's land to Geoffrey Alselin, since Henry's lands skirt these three fees.[101] We know that initially Ulf was able to maintain his lands, possibly after paying a heavy fine.[102] He held on to his political position as well for a time,

---

[98] *Charters of Burton Abbey*, pp. xxvi–xxvii, xl.

[99] Many examples of this shifting political geography can be found. Alvred d'Epaigne gained land in twenty-four Somerset vills, eighteen of which had been held by his antecessor Alwine Bannesuna. One of the holdings he acquired that was not Alwine's was Nether Stowey. This estate was to become one of the most important for Alvred's heirs. It was the site of an early twelfth-century castle, so must have taken pride of place among the Somerset estates of Alvred's daughter and heir Isabel (*VCH, Somerset*, v, p. 194). And in 1212 Alvred's great-granddaughter held Stowey in-chief, as the head of an honour of ten fees. Thus, an estate that did not come to Alvred through his antecessor became the *caput* of the fee (Sanders, *English Baronies*, p. 67; *Book of Fees*, i, p. 83; *VCH, Somerset*, v, p. 193). [100] DB, i, 276r.

[101] DB, i, 277r, 277v, 276v.

[102] For an example of such ransoming see DB, ii, 376v. The *Anglo-Saxon Chronicle* records that men paid the new king 'tribute and gave him hostages and then redeemed their lands from him' (*ASC*, s.a. 1066 (E)). *The Feudal Book of Abbot Baldwin* refers to land in Ixworth Thorpe, Suffolk, which Abbot Baldwin 'redeemed (*redemit*) from the

attesting one of the Conqueror's early charters.[103] His brother Healfdane, however, was disinherited before November 1069.[104] Ulf lost his land either around the same time or during the uprising of Hereweard the Wake.[105] Henry's acquisitions, therefore, must date between c. 1071 and 1080, when he founded an alien priory at Tutbury and endowed it from his Derbyshire holdings.[106]

Yorkshire's territorial fees provide clearer evidence than any for the chronology of William's tenurial revolution. In the first year of the new regime there was little land for William to give away in the shire, since northern earls and their contingents did not fight or fall at Senlac,[107] and since many of the leaders of Northern opinion submitted to the new king at Barking around the time of William's coronation.[108] Because of this, Yorkshire's Anglo-Scandinavian aristocracy remained intact throughout 1067. With few of his loyal followers in the shire, William's hold, however, was tenuous. To remedy this dangerous state of affairs he began in 1068 after Whitsuntide to move north, taking hostages along the way, building castles, and leaving trusted *familiares* in their garrisons; first at Warwick, then at Nottingham, York, Lincoln, Huntingdon and Cambridge.[109] But those few

barons of the king' (Douglas, *Feudal Documents from Bury St Edmunds*, p. 8). Domesday Book, in its reference to this transaction, is more genteel, and records that the abbot 'pledged (*invadiavit*) 100 s. against the barons of the king' (DB, ii, 376b). Orderic may possibly imply that land was redeemed as well when he discusses the 'groans of the English' in Book iv (OV, ii, p. 202).

[103] *Regesta*, i, n. 8. He and his wife also made a will after Hastings (*Wills*, n. 39).

[104] Brandr Abbot of Peterborough let Dunsby to his kinsman Healfdane because King William had given Healfdane's estates to Remigius Bishop of Lincoln (*The Chronicle of Hugh Candidus*, p. 43). Brandr died in the autumn of 1069 (*ASC*, s.a. 1069 (E)). For a further discussion of the family's fate after the Conquest see above, pp. 139–41.

[105] His will was overturned. See above, p. 141.

[106] *Mon. Ang.*, iii, p. 392. J. C. Holt and P. E. Golob date Henry's succession to Siward Barn's land to c. 1070 and his holdings in Appletree Wapentake to c. 1071 (J. C. Holt, '1086', p. 58, n. 75). 1071 is the earliest date possible for Henry's hundredal grant. Kapelle dates the formation of the castelry of Tutbury to the period when the marcher earldoms were created, but his only chronological evidence comes from Gaimar, who records that it was knights from Tutbury who killed Hereweard the Wake (Gaimar, lines 5658–92).   [107] Stenton, *Anglo-Saxon England*, p. 589.

[108] *ASC*, s.a. 1066 (D); OV, ii, p. 194.

[109] OV, ii, p. 218. After building his castles and garrisoning them, William took hostages as well. Thorgautr, later Bishop of St Andrews, for example, was kept hostage, according to Simeon of Durham 'for all of Lindsey in the castle of Lincoln', before he bribed his way out and fled as a stowaway, on a ship bound for Norway (Sim Dur, *Opera Omnia*, ii, pp. 202–3). See also Hugh the Chantor, *History of the Church of York*, ed. and trans. Charles Johnson (London, 1961), p. 1; *ASC*, s.a. 1067 (E) and OV, ii, p. 218. For this date see *Regesta*, i, n. 23.

Normans William placed in Yorkshire and beyond during this period settled uneasily and ultimately unsuccessfully. Robert de Commine, placed in charge of the county of Durham and Robert fitz Richard, the guardian of the Conqueror's first castle at York, were slaughtered with their men in the winter of 1068–69. Among the Englishmen involved in the treachery which led to these murders were Mærle-sveinn, the Confessor's sheriff of Lincolnshire, Gospatric, a descendant of the Æthelredian Earl Uhtræd, Edgar the Ætheling, a strong contender for the English throne, Arnketil 'the greatest of all Northumbrian nobles' and the four sons of Karle.[110] All of these men were major landholders in Yorkshire. After William pacified the north, built a second castle in York, and placed it in the hands of the capable William fitz Osbern, some of these men fled to the Scottish Court,[111] but others doubtless retained their possessions and their positions in the north, since William's authority in the shire was too fragile to enable him to clear out all of Yorkshire's powerful traitors. Trouble, predictably, flared up again. Edgar the Ætheling, Earl Waltheof, Siward and 'other English leaders' – once again including Gospatric, Mærle-sveinn, Arnketil and the sons of Karle – rebelled for a second time in conjunction with an invasion led by Swein Estrithson.[112] From 1069 until Easter of 1070, the north, along with the West Country, Staffordshire and southern Cheshire, were in revolt.[113] During the course of a long campaign, William brutally and successfully quashed the northern rebellion and destroyed Yorkshire's agrarian wealth in the process.[114] Massive dispossessions certainly followed William's ruthless winter campaign, after the king, having almost lost his kingdom, realized he could not survive another fifth columnist revolt north of the Humber. These dispossessions would naturally have been accompanied by generous grants of land to a number of the king's military retainers who agreed to settle in the north and defend William's interests there.

Preserved in Domesday's Yorkshire folios is the record of a number of grants which probably date from the spring or summer of 1070. Mærle-sveinn the Sheriff, having revolted twice in two years, certainly lost his lands. Ralph Pagnell came into

---

[110] OV, ii, pp. 222, 218. [111] ASC, s.a. 1067 (D, E); OV, ii, p. 222.
[112] OV, ii, pp. 226–8. [113] OV, ii, p. 228.
[114] Douglas, *William the Conqueror*, p. 220.

them, acquiring almost ninety carucates of the sheriff's lands across the kingdom.[115] Arnketil of Northumbria's lands were probably incorporated into the *terra regis* at this time,[116] since the author of *De Obsessione Dunelmi*, an expert on Arnketil's family, records that he fled after William's harrying of the north.[117] William de Percy, the successor of Gamal, Northmann and Gamalbarn, was active in Yorkshire soon after the rebellion was put down. Domesday Book, in its description of the city of York, notes that William was involved in the seizure of an Englishman's house there 'in the first year after the destruction of the castle' – that is 1070 – and was also involved in the king's Scottish campaign in 1072.[118] It is likely, therefore, that he was settled on his antecessors' lands within a year or two of the Yorkshire rebellion. Similarly, Hugh fitz Balderic, made sheriff of York c. 1070, probably came into the thegns Gamal's and Orm's lands around the same time.[119] Other wealthy Yorkshire thegns, who were the *antecessores* of some of Yorkshire's most powerful post-Conquest tenants-in-chief, may also be identified as victims of the purge of 1070. Berenger de Tosny was probably granted the lands of Thorgautr *Lagr* in Oxfordshire and Nottinghamshire, while his father, Robert de Tosny, received the same Thorgautr's lands in Yorkshire and Lincolnshire.[120] Other thegns who had well-defined successors may have been implicated in the northern revolt as well; among them Gamal son of Osbern, whose lands

---

[115] At the time Ralph 'inherited' fifty carucates of the sheriff's in Lincolnshire, he inherited about thirty hides in Somerset and Cornwall (Mack, 'Kings and thegns', appendix I).

[116] Many of Arnketil's lands were retained by the Conqueror throughout his reign, although a portion of Arnketil's holdings – those laying in the northeast of the shire – were later used to form the core of Count Alan of Richmond's Yorkshire fee. Corroborating evidence in the *Chron. Ab.* suggests that the king himself sometimes took possession of the lands of renegade thegns before granting them out to retainers (*Chron. Ab*, i, p. 482).   [117] *DOD*, i, p. 220.

[118] DB, i, 298r. See also *EYC*, 9, p. 1.

[119] DB, i, 327r–328r. Hugh was sheriff within a year of the destruction of the castle at York (DB, i, 298r). According to a Selby tradition, Hugh was instrumental in the foundation and endowment of Selby Abbey c. 1070 (*Historia Selebiensis Monasterii*, printed in *Coucher Book of Selby*, ed. J. T. Fowler, 2 vols (Durham, 1891–93), i, pp. 1–54.

[120] DB, i, 159r, 291v, 314r, 352v–353r. It is likely that Robert de Tosny was granted all of Thorgautr's lands, and that those estates of Thorgautr's that Berenger held were granted to him by his father. The bulk of Robert's lands in Lincolnshire and Yorkshire that he had inherited from Thorgautr were held of him by Berenger (DB, i, 357v, 314r).

went to Hugh fitz Baldric, Eadgifu, whose lands descended to Ralph de Mortimer,[121] and Gamalbarn, whose holdings fell to Gilbert Tison.[122] Still other Yorkshire thegns, who held extensively in the east of England as well, also had Norman successors. These include three of the Confessor's wealthiest Danelaw thegns – Siward Barn, Ulf son of Tope and Toki son of Outi – and they probably fell either during the Yorkshire debacle, or later in the summer of the following year, after William crushed the revolt centred around the Isle of Ely.[123] Whatever the month of their fall, many of the thegns implicated in the pages of Orderic Vitalis were likely dead or exiled by the summer of 1071. Their lands must have been granted out about this time, after the worst of the northern and eastern rebellions were over, and after the smoke had cleared enough for William to ascertain who had rebelled, whose lands he had rights to because of this, and which of his retainers deserved landed rewards.

There is also more miscellaneous evidence which throws light on the process of settlement. Both Domesday Book and the Conqueror's earliest writs suggest that the lands of outlaws were taken almost immediately into the king's hands and given out rapidly to his followers. The famous writ directed to the Abbot of Bury St Edmund's c. 1067 demanded the lands of thegns who had fought against William at Hastings for the king's own use.[124] This document illustrates how rapidly the new king could act against Englishmen whose actions displeased him. Again, in Foulton Essex, a man named Beorhtsige had held a manor TRE:

---

[121] This Eadgifu is identified by Margaret L. Faull and Marie Stinson as the sister of Earls Edwin and Morcar (*Domesday Book, Yorkshire*, Phillimore edn, ii, n. for 15E1). If this identification is indeed correct, her possessions would not have been protected after her brothers' fall in 1071.

[122] Most of the thegns just mentioned are described at the beginning of the folios for Yorkshire and Lincolnshire as having sake and soke over their land (DB, i, 337r, 298v).

[123] Fl. Wig. specifically notes that Siward Barn participated in the Fenland rising (Fl. Wig., ii, p. 9), and the *LE*, which derives much of its information on the year 1071 from Fl. Wig., but which also has access to local traditions, mentions Siward Barn as well (*LE*, ii, c. 102). According to Simeon, Siward Barn languished in prison until the king, on his deathbed, released him along with Odo and other hostages (Sim. Dur., *Opera Omnia*, ii, pp. 213–14).

[124] This writ demanded that the Abbot of Bury 'alle þo londe *me to hande* þat þo men aihten þe on orreste stoden to ihenes me and þer ofslagen weren' (Douglas, *Feudal Documents of Bury St Edmunds*, p. 47). Similarly, Limpsfield Surrey, which was granted to Battle Abbey by King William c. 1070 was held by Harold TRE (DB, i, 34r). *The Chronicle of Battle Abbey*, however, describes this land, before William's grant as 'antea in dominium suum idem rex redgerat' (*The Chronicle of Battle Abbey*, ed. and trans. Eleanor Searle (Oxford, 1980), p. 80).

'When the King came to this land [Beorhtsige] was outlawed and Robert [fitz Wimarc] received his land.'[125] Since Robert died c. 1070, Beorhtsige's land was almost immediately granted out to one of the king's favourites. Eustace of Boulogne, according to William of Poitiers, forfeited his fees – some of them probably in England – after he attacked Dover in 1067.[126] Eustace, then, must have received land almost immediately after Hastings. Furthermore, the organization of Orderic Vitalis's narrative of 1070 gives some support to the notion that a number of fees were formed at this time. Although Orderic's chronology for the acquisition of lands and titles is not always accurate, he breaks his story after the rebellion of the eastern thegns to give a lengthy description of the rewards that the Conqueror's followers garnered during the course of his reign, suggesting that many Normans came into a substantial part of their holdings in 1070. Although Orderic tends to conflate all the acquisitions of William's great lords over the course of the whole reign, his narrative gives the impression that after the suppression of the eastern revolt a good deal of land exchanged hands.[127] Certainly a large amount of land must have been reallocated by the winter of 1071–72 when William returned to Normandy.[128] Such acquisitions, based on the inheritance of a single thegn's land, at least in Yorkshire and in Lincolnshire, appear to have continued through 1073. In this year Thorbrandr, the eldest son of Karle, one of the rebels of 1069, was assassinated by Earl Waltheof's retainers as a result of a long standing family feud. Since he was killed at his *setl* in Settringham, he doubtless retained his property until his death. By 1086 Settringham, along with Thorbrandr's other Yorkshire and Lincolnshire estates, had found their way into the honour of Berenger de Tosny. It is unlikely, since these lands devolved uniformly on to one fee, that Thorbrandr was stripped of his land a carucate at a time. It is more probable that they were given *en masse* to Berenger c. 1073.[129]

Although charters from William I's reign are scarce and notoriously difficult to date, they are occasionally of some use in determining the chronology of the formation of a particular fee.

[125] DB, ii, 48a.
[126] William of Poitiers, *Gesta Guillelmi Ducis Normannorum et Regis Anglorum*, ed. and trans. R. Foreville (Paris, 1952), pp. 266–8.   [127] OV, ii, pp. 260–6.
[128] Some early northern settlement would certainly have facilitated William's campaign against Scotland in 1072 (Douglas, *William the Conqueror*, pp. 226–7).
[129] *DOD*, i, p. 200; DB, i, 314r.

The diplomatic records make it clear, for example, that the lands of Earl Harold and his family were immediately absorbed into the *terra regis* or granted out rapidly to important *familiares*, pet monasteries and hardworking royal officials. One of the earliest surviving post-Conquest writs, dating from 1067, concerns land granted to Regenbald the Priest at Latton, and shows the conveyance of property once held by Earl Harold to an important curial official.[130] The Abbey at Fécamp was promised Harold's land in Steyning, Sussex, months before Duke William set sail, and the abbey must have received it very soon after Hastings.[131] By 1069 Holy Trinity Rouen, a ducal foundation,[132] was in possession of Earl Harold's only manor in Middlesex.[133] Battle Abbey was endowed with Harold's twenty-five hide estate in Limpsfield, Surrey c. 1070,[134] and Westminster was given Battersea and Pirford before 1070 'as fully and freely as Harold held it'.[135] Westminster was also granted Harold's estate at Woking and Fering on another occasion.[136] King William granted Brooke, a manor held by Earl Gyrth, to Bury 'when he first came to St Edmunds'.[137] Battle Abbey was given St Olave's Church in Exeter, along with land in Sherford, Devon. St Olave's was one of the churches patronized by Harold's mother, and it

[130] *Regesta*, i, n. 9, translated in EHD, 2, n. 35; DB, i, 68v. For Regenbald as William the Conqueror's chancellor see Simon Keynes, 'Regenbald the Chancellor (sic)', *Anglo-Norman Studies*, 10 (1988), pp. 185–222.

[131] *Regesta*, i, n. 1; According to Domesday, Steyning was held by Harold 'at the end of King Edward's [life]' (DB, i, 17r), but the borough had been given to Fécamp by Edward the Confessor. See S 1054, which is most likely a post-Conquest forgery of an Edward the Confessor writ, making just such claims, and a charter of William I, dated 1085, which records Edward's gift. (A facsimile of the charter is printed in Pierre Chaplais, 'Une charte originale de Guillaume le Conquerant pour l'Abbay de Fécamp: La donation de Steyning et de Bury (1085)', in *Essays in Medieval Diplomacy and Administration* (London, 1981), pp. 92–103, and plate 1).

[132] *Mon. Ang.*, vi, p. 1073.

[133] *Regesta*, i, n. 29, printed in *Chartularium Monasterii Sanctae Trinitatis de Monte Rothmoagi*, ed. A. Deville, p. 455; DB, i, 128v.

[134] *The Chronicle of Battle Abbey*, p. 20; DB, i, 34r. Bromfield pertained to Limpsfield and may be the site of the battle (*Domesday Book, Surrey*, Phillimore edn, n. for 11–1). If this is the case, Limpsfield would necessarily form part of the initial endowment. William the Conqueror's grant of Limpsfield to Battle is preserved in *The Chronicle of Battle Abbey*, p. 80. Battle also held Hutton, Essex, TRW, which had been held by Gauti, probably Earl Harold's housecarl of that name (DB, ii, 20b). Since Hutton ended up in Battle's hands, it is likely that Gauti held Hutton on some sort of precarious tenure from Harold, and that after the Conquest it was granted to Battle by William because it was perceived as Harold's land.

[135] *Regesta*, i, n. 45; DB, i, 32r.   [135] *Regesta*, i, n. 86.

[137] DB, ii, 210a. See Douglas, *Feudal Book of Abbot Baldwin*, p. 13, for a description of the ceremony accompanying this grant.

was she who had given Sherford to it.[138] St Stephen's Caen was granted Bincombe and Frampton in Dorset, the former held by Earl Harold and the latter by his mother.[139] Before his death in January 1071, William fitz Osbern had generously endowed his own foundation of Lyre, using land, tithes and churches in Hampshire, Herefordshire, Gloucestershire and Worcestershire which had been granted to him out of the ancient royal demesne or more commonly from that pool of land which pertained to pre-Conquest earls.[140] This suggests that the very early endowment given to him in return for defending the Southampton Waters and the Welsh march was almost exclusively fashioned from old comital or royal estates and that he was not granted an appreciable amount of land from other secular holders because most had not yet been dispossessed. In any case, it would have been difficult for Normans to confiscate and settle land, at least along the southern march, until 1070, when the powerful English thegn Eadric the Wild and his Welsh allies ceased to wage guerilla warfare against William fitz Osbern's garrison at Hereford.[141]

As for the dispossession of the Saxon thegnage, Geoffrey de Mandeville's title of 'port reeve' of London, a position doubtless held by his antecessor Ansgar the Staller, on a writ dated 1067, suggests that the Norman had received not only Ansgar's position by this date, but his lands as well.[142] If this is the case, within a year of the Conquest Geoffrey held over £400 of land in nine English counties, mostly in the midlands and in the east.[143] Eadric of Laxfield, along with Ansgar the Staller one of the richest men in pre-Conquest England,[144] must have fallen at an early date as

---

[138] DB, i, 100v, 104r; S 1236; *Mon. Ang.*, iii, p. 377.

[139] DB, i, 78v; *Regesta*, i, n. 105.

[140] *Gallia Christiana*, xi, p. 1874, App p. 123; *Mon. Ang.*, vi, pp. 1092–3; DB, i, 39v, 52r; S. F. Hockey, 'William fitz Osbern and the endowment of his abbey of Lyre', *Anglo-Norman Studies*, 3 (1980), pp. 96–105.

[141] Fl. Wig. ii, p. 9; Sim. Dur., *Opera Omnia*, ii, pp. 185, 194. The rarity of land grants by William in the first months after Hastings is further suggested by Orderic Vitalis's story of the death of Robert de Vitot. Orderic preserves a grant made by Robert to Saint-Evroul in late 1066 or early 1067, as he lay dying at Dover 'after the English war in which he was wounded in the knee'. In his death-bed grant he relinquished claims to a number of Saint-Evroul's Norman estates, but gave no land in England, probably because he had received none (OV, ii, pp. 120–2 and n. 5).

[142] *Facsimiles of English Royal Writs to A.D. 1100*, ed. T. A. M. Bishop and P. Chaplais (Oxford, 1957), n. 15. For the identification of 'Gosfregth Portirefan', see J. H. Round, *Geoffrey de Mandeville: A Study of the Anarchy* (London, 1892), p. 37, n. 354, 493, but see C. N. L. Brooke and G. Keir, *London 800–1216: The Shaping of a City* (London, 1975), p. 372.   [143] Mack, 'Kings and thegns', appendix I.

[144] Mack, 'Stallers', p. 132.

well, since his lands formed the bulk of William Malet's fee in Norfolk, an honour cobbled together some time before the second Yorkshire rebellion in 1069.[145] William Malet was also established in Yorkshire by 1069, some of his fee formed through his antecession to the lands of Asa, Northmann, Healfdane and Havarthr.[146] Traces of the fee of Fredrick, the brother-in-law of William de Warenne, remain in Domesday Book, although Fredrick was slain by Hereweard the Wake in 1070.[147] He had succeeded to the lands of a king's thegn named Toki in Norfolk, Cambridgeshire and Suffolk.[148] Healfdane son of Tope was succeeded by Remigius Bishop of Lincoln in the same region before the end of 1069.[149] Æthelric, brother of Bishop Beorhtheah of Worcester, and his son were diseised by Ralph de Bernay before 1071.[150] In 1068 William the Conqueror, as a thank offering for his crossing wind, granted the Abbey of St Valéry the lands of Thorkil in Essex.[151] In 1076 Robert de Tosny began

---

[145] Traces of this fee and the date of its formation can be found in Yorkshire and East Anglia, but see especially DB, ii, 133b, which notes that William Malet held one of Eadric of Laxfield's estates 'when he went into the marsh' (*invit in maresc*). Freeman because of this reference believed that William Malet was killed in the Fenland rebellion of 1070–71 (Freeman, *NC*, iv, p. 473), although Round argued that he was killed in 1069 (Round, 'Death of William Malet'). Whether he was killed in 1071 or 1069, one of the largest secular fees in East Anglia, worth about £150, was established in the first couple of years of the Conqueror's rule.

[146] For Robert Malet's claim to all of Asa's lands see DB, i, 373r; for his claim to Northmann and Healfdane's lands see DB, i, 373r; for claims to Havarthr's lands see DB, i, 373r. [147] *EYC*, 8, p. 44; *LE*, ii, c. 105.

[148] DB, ii, 162a, 165b, 170a; DB, i, 196r–196v; DB, ii, 398a. Toki may possibly have fallen in one of the battles of 1066, since DB records under its entry for Trumpington, that 'Toki held this land from Ely and could not grant, sell, or separate. After Fredric, William's brother [sic] had it'. In 1086 it was found in William de Warenne's fee with no reference to Ely (DB, i, 196v). Ely's loss, therefore, may parallel similar losses of thegnland sustained by Bury St Edmunds (Douglas, *Feudal Documents from Bury St Edmunds*, p. 47). [149] *The Chronicle of Hugh Candidus*, p. 35; *ASC*, s.a. 1069 (E).

[150] For the seizure of Æthelric's (a.k.a. Alric) land see Hemming, i, p. 266; DB, i, 172v, 173v. For the seizure of Godric Æthelricson's land, see Hemming, i, p. 255; DB, i, 176r. These dispossessions date no later than 1071 because they were made with the aid of William fitz Osbern.

[151] C. R. Hart, *Early Charters of Eastern England* (Leicester, 1966), n. 85; St Valéry was a TRW tenant-in-chief in Essex. Five of the Abbey's lands, including Takeley, granted by this charter, were Thorkil's TRE (DB, ii, 20b–21a). An original charter of Saint Anselm to St Valéry survives, dated c. 1097, which confirms the Conqueror's grant of twelve hides in Essex. A later description of William's gift is also extant. It notes that the king's grant was made on 19 October 1068 and that the twelve hides include Takeley, Widdington and Birchanger, all held, according to DB, by Thorkil TRE. The king also granted Lidsell, an estate held by Horwulf TRE, and recorded in Domesday as part of St Valéry's fee. The only other land held by a Horwulf in Essex

Belvoir Priory, a church that was to be his burial place.[152] Included among his gifts were tithes from Horninghold and Meolbourn, Leicestershire, and Stoke Albany, Northamptonshire, estates that had belonged to his antecessor Oswulf son of Frani TRE,[153] and Horton, Frampton Mansell, Sapperton and Great Rissington, Gloucester, which had pertained to another of his antecessors, Ulf.[154] Robert, then, was established in Gloucestershire, Leicestershire and Northamptonshire within ten years of the Conquest, through his inheritance of these men's lands. This evidence suggests that fees based on a Norman's inheritance of a well-defined antecessor's land were rapidly established, at least in eastern England, and that many predate the eastern rebellion and may, therefore, help to explain it. Some of these eastern successions were made possible by the fatalities at Hastings. Clearly, the grants of the land of fallen 'traitors' were the earliest made,[155] but the dispossession of the quick probably had to wait until Christmas of 1067, after William's triumphant return from Normandy, when the *Chronicle* records that William 'gave away every man's land', an action that surely lies behind the exile of Mærle-sveinn the Sheriff, reported by the Chronicler with his very next breath.[156] Until this time, the sheriff's promise of fealty had been enough to secure his lands.[157] Certainly, through the end

descended to a royal priest, so Horwulf, too, may have fallen at an early date (*Facsimilies of Early Charters in Oxford Muniment Rooms*, ed. H. E. Salter (Oxford, 1929), n. 27; DB, ii, 3b).

[152] *Mon. Ang.*, iii, pp. 284, 289. For the background to this endowment see *Gesta Abatum Monasterii S. Albani a Thoma Walsingham*, 3 vols., ed. Henry T. Riley, RS (London, 1867–69), i, p. 57; *VCH, Lincs*, ii, p. 125.   [153] DB, i, 233v, 225r.

[154] DB, i, 168v.

[155] For an early writ which demands that the abbot of Bury give up the lands of those 'who stood against me in battle and were slain there', see Douglas, *Feudal Documents from the Abbey of Bury St Edmunds*, p. 42.

[156] ASC, s.a. 1067 (E). According to William of Poitiers the threat of an invasion by Swein Estrithson may have precipitated William's return to England (William of Poitiers, *Gesta Guillelmi*, p. 264). For the date of William's return see OV, ii, p. 208. Henry of Huntingdon reports that in 1067 after the king returned to England he 'divided the lands among his *milites*' (Henry of Huntingdon, *Historia Anglorum*, ed. T. Arnold, RS (London, 1879), p. 204). Orderic Vitalis's description of William's Christmas court, however, matches neither the *Chronicle* nor William of Jumièges. According to Orderic, the King 'made himself very gracious to the English Bishops and lay lords. He was at great pains to appease everyone, invited them to receive the kiss of peace, and smiled on them all, he willingly granted any favours they sought, and gave ear readily to their statements and proposals' (OV, ii, p. 210).

[157] OV, ii, p. 222. There are occasional notices in Domesday of men who lost their land, not immediately after Hastings, but at some later date. For example, Azor, a Worcester thegn, who held his land from Pershore 'was alive on the day of King

of 1067 the Confessor's thegns were still commonly found as witnesses on charters or as the addressees on writs. (See table 5.1.) All but three of the fourteen identifiable Englishmen whose names are preserved in the Conqueror's writs and charters were among the fifty wealthiest thegns in pre-Conquest England, and their survival on our few extant writs and charters, suggests that a legion of other great thegns remained throughout 1068 not only as hot-house captives at William's court, but as prominent local men, whose support and retinues helped implement the new king's will in the shires. Certainly, Eadnoth's defence of William's kingdom against the sons of his former king, Harold, suggest early co-operation and accommodation between the Conqueror and his English subjects.[158] The survival of Eadnoth and other attestors of local prominence for at least fourteen months after the Conquest also informs us that the Normans who would one day be their antecessors had not yet been granted fees based on these Englishmen's holdings. By 1075, however, when the Conqueror demanded an inventory of Ely's moveable wealth, his list of commissioners reads like a page out of Domesday Book Cambridgeshire; among them are Eudo Dapifer, Ralph Taillebois, Picot the Sheriff and Hardwin de Scales, all prominent Cambridgeshire landholders in 1086. All must have been settled in the county at the time of this earlier inquest.[159] Thus, evidence in Domesday, bolstered by a few datable charters, suggests that the dispossession of those thegns who had not fought at Hastings began rapidly after December of 1067, that antecessor grants were continued after the northern and fenland revolts and beyond, at least until 1073, but that by 1075 many Domesday fees based on the holdings of pre-Conquest lords were in place. Certainly, we know that subinfeudation, a sign of solid, assured and permanent settlement, was taking place in Suffolk in 1073, when Godric was granted Breckles by Earl Ralph,[160] and before 1072 on the Bishop of Bayeux's land in Kent.[161] And in Langbargh Wapentake,

Edward's death and held the land in this way. But later, when his wife was dead, he was made an outlaw' (DB, i, 175r).   [158] ASC, s.a. 1067 (D).

[159] LE, ii, c. 114. Furthermore, the summary of land pleas preserved in the ICC and LE dating from 1071 × 1075 mention William de Warren (whose attacks against Ely are rehearsed in the LE in a chapter entitled Quomodo post mortem comes Willelmus Warennie sit damnatus in anima, LE, ii, c. 119), Richard fitz Gilbert, Hugh de Montfort, Geoffrey de Mandeville and Hardwin de Scales. All doubtless were neighbours of Ely before they could encroach upon its lands.   [160] DB, ii, 110b.

[161] Odo's undertenant Thurold of Rochester was forced to restore Canterbury land to Lanfranc in 1072 (Anglia Sacra, i, pp. 335–6).

Table 5.1 *English addressees and witnesses of early post-Conquest writs and charters*

Thegn	Date	*Regesta*	County	£ TRE[a]	Successor
Ælfwine of Gotton	1066/67	16	hrt	45	x
Azur	wtsn 1068	23	so	120	Bishop of Salisbury
Beorhtric Algarson	1067	9	wi, gl	280	x
	wtsn 1068	23	so		
Bondi the Staller	1067	18	ox	150	Henry de Ferrers
	wtsn 1068	23	so		
Eadnoth the Staller	1067	7	so	60	Earl Hugh
Eadric the Wild	1067	9	wi, gl	105	Ralph de Mortimer
Engelric	?1067	21	ha	65	Eustace of Boulogne
	1067	8	li		
	wtsn 1068	22	ex, hrts		
	1069	28	dv		
Gamal son of Osbern	1066 × 1069	88[b]	yr	25	Hugh fitz Baldric
Hearding son of Eadnoth	wtsn 1068	23	so	55	Earl Aubrey
Leofnoth	1069	28	dv	20	Miles Crispin
Mærl-sveinn the Sheriff	1067	8	li	160	Ralph Pagnell
Northmann	1066 × 1070	41	sf	15	Roger de Lacy
Tovi the Sheriff	1067	7	so	20	Hearding s. of Eadnoth
	wtsn 1068	23	so		
Ulf son of Tope	1067	8	li	105	de la Beuvrière

[a] Except for Gamal, the value of these thegns' holdings are from Mack, 'Kings and Thegns', appendix 1. Values have been rounded to the nearest £5.

[b] This is a reference not to *Regesta*, i, but *EYC*, i.

Yorkshire, not only had Earl Hugh granted Whitby to William de Percy by 1078, but William in turn had granted the site of the derelict monastery there to Reinfried in order that it might be refounded.[162]

Establishing dates for the creation of hundredal fees is more difficult than for antecessorial ones. Those in Kent must have been very early. A charter of Hugh de Montfort's, preserved in the cartulary of Bec and made as early as 1067, granted churches in several manors of his hundredal fee that he had 'inherited' from three different Englishmen.[163] But as we have seen, those hundredal territories north of Watling Street, were later, the majority necessarily dating after c. 1073. We have no hints of hundredal grants outside of Kent and Sussex before this date, although admittedly our evidence is so imperfectly preserved and fragmentary that arguments from silence are worthless. We do, however, know that in Derbyshire the monks of St Pierre-sur-Dives held Marston on Dove and Doveridge from Henry de Ferrers by 1086. The two manors formed the original endowment of Tutbury Priory, a dependent priory of St Pierre, and were granted in 1080.[164] These vills lay in the wapentake of Appletree which defined the boundaries of Henry's Derbyshire territorial fee. In Lincolnshire, where the wapentake of Epworth formed the basis of Geoffrey de la Guerch's territorial fee, Geoffrey granted Crowle to Selby before 1082.[165] Since Thorbrandr, who died in

---

[162] DB, i, 305r. William granted the ruined site of Whitby to Prior Reinfried (*EYC*, ii, p. 193). The refoundation legend is somewhat garbled, but suggests that the foundation was underway by 1078 (*Whitby Cartul.*, i, p. xxxiv).

[163] Round, *Cal. Doc. Fra.*, n. 357, printed in *Annales Ordinis S Benedicti* (1739), p. 696; Bradbourne, the site of one of the churches, was held by Godric of Bishopsbourne and Eastbridge, the site of another, by Alsig. Tinton was held by Wulfnoth (DB, i, 13v, 13r). The date of this charter is based on its attestation by Maurilius Archbishop of Rouen's attestation. The Archbishop died on 9 April 1067. For objections to this charter, however, see *Dom. Mon.*, p. 67, n. 1. It is clear from other evidence that Hugh was established very early in Kent and put in charge of Dover (William of Poitiers, *Gesta Guillelmi*, p. 267; William of Jumièges, p. 138; OV, ii, p. 204).

[164] *Mon. Ang.*, iii, p. 392; *VCH, Staffordshire*, iii, p. 331; DB, i, 274r.

[165] *Coucher Book of Selby*, pp. 279–80. The editor dates this grant c. 1084, but the confirmation is made in London, 'in solaro domus Waleramni coram Odone Episcopo Baiocensi', so it necessarily dates before Odo's disgrace. Diana Greenway has suggested that Geoffrey was granted this land in 1069, after the Danes had used the Isle of Axholme as a base from which to harass the Normans (Greenway, *Honour of Mowbray*, p. xxi). This may explain why Geoffrey had succeeded in this area to the lands of Ulf Fenisc and Siward Barn in the Isle, even though Gilbert de Gand was their successor elsewhere in the kingdom. This grant may have predated these two men's fall, but see above, p. 169. This date is probably too early for such a grant.

1073, held extensively in the wapentakes eventually used to build the Count of Mortain's fee, Robert's territory could not have been granted to him within the first eight years of the Conqueror's reign. Drogo de la Beuvrière's fee in Holderness, based in part on William Malet's fee, could not have been formed before c. 1071. Roger the Poitevin, born c. 1060, could not have been granted his territory much before 1080.[166]

Other historians have posited the late creation of fees north of the Humber. W. E. Wightman has made a case for the formation of Ilbert de Lacy's Yorkshire fee c. 1080 in his seminal book on the Lacy family. His chronology hinges on the fact that there is no evidence in Domesday for the castle of Pontefract. Since the castle did not exist in 1086, so Wightman's argument goes, the fee recorded in Domesday was newly formed.[167] Domesday's record of castles, however, is notoriously incomplete, and it is difficult to believe that the castle at Pontefract was not constructed until after the Inquest, in light of the Conqueror's desperate river crossing in the winter of 1069 at the ford marked by Pontefract and his fight to make the crossing there.[168] In order to protect his access into Yorkshire, the king may well have built a castle 'at the broken bridge' as soon as the northern revolt was suppressed. William Kapelle, building on Wightman's argument, believes the proof of the lateness of the Lacy fee in particular, and the Norman settlement of Yorkshire in general, lies in Simeon of Durham's statement that York remained uncultivated and empty for nine years after William's northern campaign, and thus dates the establishment of two Yorkshire castleries and three fees to this time.[169] He further holds that these fees – those of Drogo de la Beuvrière, Roger de Bully, Ilbert de Lacy, Count Alan and Roger the Poitevin (in Lancashire) – were all formed around 1080 to provide security for the Vale of York.[170] His argument is flawed in two respects. First, his hypothesis requires that all these fees be formed in a single instant, although we have much evidence to suggest that Yorkshire honours were developed one at a time, and continued to be formed after the Conqueror's death. William de Warenne, after all, did not receive much in the West Riding until after the Domesday inquest,[171] and Robert de Brus's fee was not

[166] OV, iii, p. 138; *Complete Peerage*, xi, pp. 688–9.
[167] Wightman, *The Lacy Family*, pp. 21–7.   [168] OV, ii, p. 230.
[169] Sim. Dur., *Opera Omnia*, p. 188; Kapelle, *Norman Conquest of the North*, pp. 144–5.
[170] Kapelle, *Norman Conquest of the North*, p. 145.   [171] EYC, viii, p. 178.

established until 'after the Winchester Book was written'.[172]
Second, other territorial fees – like the Count of Mortain's, Hugh
fitz Balderic's and Osbern d'Arches' – were formed in the heart
of Yorkshire, and so do not fit into Kapelle's ingenious argument
about William's policy to ring and destroy the 'free zone' (nor,
for that matter, do the antecessorial grants which would have
preceded them). It is more likely that territorial fees in Yorkshire
and elsewhere were established separately, perhaps at intervals.
The likely date for their genesis is not c. 1080 but rather c. 1075.
The difference is not simply one of five years: it involves the
whole explanation of these territorial honours. For by c. 1075 two
factors were coming into play which may account for a change
in the pattern of endowment. First, by 1075 the majority of
wealthy pre-Conquest landholders were already dispossessed, and
their lands had long ago been given out to other men. It was no
longer possible, therefore, for William to patronize loyal
followers with generous fees based on the lands of a single thegn.
Not only were the holdings of surviving Englishmen too small
to form substantial honours, but the huge number of minor
landholders and the modesty of their estates would make further
antecessorial grants an administrative nightmare. In short, the
Conqueror had run out of antecessors. Second, the Earl's Revolt
of 1075 probably necessitated certain changes in landholding. This
rebellion of young men did not produce the crisis in England that
the earlier Yorkshire rebellion had, and with the exception of
Normanized sycophants like Earl Waltheof and the semi-
Englishman Ralph Wader, did not involve Anglo-Saxons, the
most powerful of whom, as we have seen, were already dead or
in exile. It is unlikely, therefore, that the massive confiscations
necessitated by the formation of hundredal fees, were brought on
by fear of English rebellion, especially since Yorkshire's territorial
fees tended to have listed among their undertenants a high
proportion of natives.[173] Had these surviving thegns represented
a real challenge to Norman rule, they would not have maintained
their lands and help make up the contingents of Norman barons.

The threat of this rebellion to the Conqueror on the Continent,
however, was quite a different matter, and the challenge of Ralph
the Gael's uprising in Brittany, a rebellion in Maine, and the King

---

[172] DB, i, 332v. For the date of 1114 × 1119 for the formation of Robert's fee, see Peter
King, 'The return of the fee of Robert de Brus in Domesday', *YAJ*, 60 (1988),
pp. 25–9).   [173] Wightman, *The Lacy Family*, pp. 40–1.

of France's machinations very nearly toppled the Conqueror. This Continental crisis and the ones that followed kept William occupied to the end of his life, and must have made it clear that if the Anglo-Norman realm were to survive, no time could be spared fighting in England. Thus, William's greatest friends began at this time to be entrusted with compact territories, centred on castles from which they could maintain the Norman hegemony. A likely inspiration for these territorial fees were the hundredal honours of Kent and Sussex, organized in the 1060s. The later, northern hundredal fees may well have been implemented by Odo Bishop of Bayeux, possibly a vice-regent in England in the late 1070s, and one of the profiteers of Kentish hundredal grants.[174] Certainly, two of the beneficiaries of territorial grants in Yorkshire were Odo's men. The first was Ilbert de Lacy, a retainer of Odo's, who held from the bishop in Surrey, Lincolnshire and Oxfordshire, and who had come from Odo's estates in Normandy.[175] The second was Osbern d'Arches, whose family had received the enormously valuable estate of Folkestone from the bishop earlier in the reign.[176]

The confiscation of the land of important but disloyal thegns and its granting away to one successor, therefore, occurred between 1066 and c. 1073. Sometime between 1073 and 1075, however, the Conqueror appears to have changed, at least in part, his practice, and to have begun laying on top of this earlier pattern of antecessor and successor his midland and northern territorial grants such as Roger de Bully's in Nottinghamshire, the Count of Mortain's in Northamptonshire and Yorkshire, and Henry de Ferrers' in Derbyshire. William's distribution of land to his most trusted friends and kinsmen along the outskirts of the kingdom very soon after the Conquest, his granting out of all the land of

---

[174] David Bates, 'The character and career of Odo, Bishop of Bayeux (1049/50–1097), *Speculum*, 50 (1975), pp. 1–20 and 'Justiciarship', pp. 1–12. Stenton, *Anglo-Saxon England*, p. 601. Odo was certainly instrumental in the choosing (and perhaps the endowing of) sheriffs. Judith Green has identified six of the Conqueror's sheriffs as close allies of the bishop (Judith Green, 'The sheriffs of William the Conqueror', *Anglo-Norman Studies*, 5 (1982), pp. 136–7). Other of the king's most trusted associates can be seen dispersing land, particularly Odo's fellow vice-regent in 1067, William fitz Osbern. Hereford Domesday notes that 'Hugh the Ass says that Earl William gave this land to him when he gave out the land of [Hugh's] antecessor Thorkil [the White]' (DB, i, 181r). In Gloucester, Domesday notes that Earl William enfeoffed Ralph de Limesy out of his own fee with fifty carucates of land 'as is done in Normandy' (DB, i, 162r). [175] Wightman, *The Lacy Family*, p. 31.
[176] Folkestone was valued at £145 10s. TRE (DB, i, 9v). For Osbern's family connections see *Dom. Mon.*, pp. 42–4.

an English landholder across the kingdom to one of his tenants, and finally his formation of compact territories from the lands of minor thegns, seriously disrupted pre-Conquest patterns of landholding and lordship. From the evidence in Orderic, we know the names of a number of the most important thegns and landholders involved in the northern and eastern rebellions of 1069–71. In Domesday these thegns all have well-defined successors. It follows that for four or five years after the Conquest the new king was granting out the lands of powerful but disobedient thegns to a single Norman successor. The lands of Normans who received such fees in Yorkshire are generally scattered over the entire county. Ralph Pagnell's inheritance from Mærle-sveinn was spread across all three ridings of Yorkshire, and across Lincolnshire and the West Country as well. These holdings, therefore, typically did not form any sort of compact territory. On the other hand, such antecessorial fees tended to be engulfed, at least north of Watling Street and west of the fens, by more compact and artificial territories held by some of William's greatest men. These tight-knit fees were a Norman innovation. Made up as they were of the lands of dozens of different Anglo-Saxon thegns and freemen, they in no way mirrored pre-Conquest landholding patterns. Impressive amounts of land went into the creation of these hundredal fees. The fees formed from the lands of well-defined secular antecessors in Yorkshire, for example, account for something like 20 per cent of all land granted out in the county by 1086. The remaining 80 per cent of Yorkshire landholdings were either formed by the passing of ecclesiastical lands unhindered to the same religious corporations, the formation of the *terra regis*, or the formation of territories based strictly on the wapentake or the hundred.

If the preceding scenario for land division is correct, several important points emerge for the chronology of Norman settlement. First, antecessorial grants, outside the Welsh March, Sussex and Kent, were made prior to hundredal ones. It follows, therefore, that in counties where William's followers were established by both antecession and by hundred, that hundredal grants often cannot date within the first decade of the Conqueror's rule. The relatively late creation of these territorial fees, often consisting of over half the land held by secular holders in a county, suggests that minor English aristocrats maintained their lands for many years after the Conquest and that the Norman settlement, at least north of Watling Street, was only a very gradual process. Thus, the overwhelmingly Norman character of landholding preserved in Domesday Book was the product of the last decade of the Conqueror's rule. Second, ecclesiastical patrimonies had to be secured, and indeed established, before territorial fees could be assigned. Marjorie Chibnall has suggested that such guarantees were obtained by England's ancient ecclesiastical communities when they struck new bargains with the king for knights' service.[177] The little evidence that survives for this process suggests that such agreements were made within the first half decade of the Conquest. Peterborough secured its holdings, particularly those hastily bequeathed between the death of the Confessor and William's coronation, within a year of Hastings.[178] And sometime before 1072, King William ordered Æthelwig Abbot of Evesham to bring five knights along with those who were owed by his men to Clarendon.[179] Other abbeys likely had quotas of knights imposed at an early date as well,[180] but in so doing they gained warranty for their ancient patrimonies. Such bargains, however, not only provided the Conqueror with knights, but gave his administrators some notion of what lands they could confiscate. Third, the *terra regis* was established before territorial fees were created, since royal officials would have had to set aside land for the king's own use in the county, before overseeing a territorial grant. This suggests careful consideration on the part of royal administrators on how best to harbour the king's resources. Fourth, in the shires where antecessorial and hundredal grants have left a clear imprint, we have evidence of a settlement firmly controlled by the king. Royal grants based on the holdings of individual antecessors or on hundreds were strictly maintained throughout much of England and show that the Norman settlement across large stretches of the kingdom was an act of royal will. Some of the king's early territorial grants, like the Rape of Bramber to William de Braose, were carved out of the holdings of other of the king's followers – in this case William de Warenne – but the willingness of the Conqueror's barons to accept land in exchange elsewhere in the kingdom, to accommodate William's defensive strategies, shows

---

[177] Chibnall, *Anglo-Norman England*, pp. 23, 29–35.   [178] *Regesta*, i, n. 8.
[179] Printed in Round, *FE*, p. 304; Chibnall, *Anglo-Norman England*, p. 34.
[180] For example, Abingdon (*Chron. Ab.*, ii, p. 3).

tremendous royal control.[181] Finally, most great pre-Conquest thegns had well-defined Norman successors, and since so many appear to have relinquished their land by the early 1070s, the lesser thegnage quickly lost its leadership and much of its threat. This suggests that if most hundredal grants do indeed date from c. 1075, the impetus for dispossession came not from threats to William in England, but from the administrative impossibility of dealing with thousands of very small antecessorial grants, and from threats on the Continent.

[181] Chibnall, *Anglo-Norman England*, p. 13.

Chapter 6

PRIVATE ENTERPRISE AND THE
NORMAN SETTLEMENT

Sir Frank Stenton, when describing the destruction of the Anglo-Saxon aristocracy and its replacement by the Conqueror with his kinsmen and his cronies, wrote:

It is remarkable proof of the Conqueror's statesmanship that his tenurial revolution never degenerated into a scramble for land. In every part of England the great redistribution was controlled by the king and carried out by his ministers on lines which [William] himself laid down.

These lines were based on the inheritance of land by a Norman from several well-defined English antecessors: in Stenton's words, 'the best reply [one of the Conqueror's new lords] could make to a claim upon his property was the production of sworn evidence that the land or the rights in dispute had belonged to his *antecessor* on the day when King Edward was alive and dead'.[1] Similarly, it was D. C. Douglas's considered opinion that,

it became usual for a Norman lord in England to find himself endowed within each shire not with a miscellaneous collection of manors but rather with all the lands which had formerly belonged to one or more pre-Conquest landowners... while the transference of possession was of course sometimes accompanied by private violence, it was more often effected without disturbance, and it is wholly remarkable how frequently cases of dispute were settled at the king's command by reference to traditional legal process...[and with a] respect for legal precedent.[2]

The twin assumptions lying at the heart of these and other scholars' works – tenurial continuity after Hastings and firm royal control over a massive legal dispersement of land – have become the central and unquestioned tenets of all modern writing on the

---

[1] Stenton, *Anglo-Saxon England*, p. 626.
[2] Douglas, *William the Conqueror*, pp. 271–2.

Norman settlement. These notions are in part the legacy of William the Conqueror's persuasive apologists – William of Jumièges, William of Poitiers and the creator of the Bayeux Tapestry – who insisted at every turn on William's lawful inheritance of England's crown and his right to the lands of those who fought against him.[3] The most influential voice among William's pack of admirers is William of Poitiers, a contemporary and a chronicler of the Conqueror's early years as king, whose contention that no Frenchman received anything seized unjustly from an Englishman, has taken root in the canon of Conquest writings from William's day until our own.[4] Certainly his claims reverberate throughout Domesday Book and the Conqueror's writs: Harold is *comes* not *rex*;[5] William is Edward's legal heir, not simply England's conqueror; and everywhere we find Normans 'inheriting' Anglo-Saxon tenancies in much the same way that William 'inherited' the kingdom. It is hardly surprising, therefore, that modern historians from Stenton onward have been persuaded by the consistent claims of Anglo-Norman historians and administrators.[6]

There is, however, as we have seen, a stock of contemporary evidence that marks the 1060s, 70s and 80s as a period of jarring

[3] For William of Jumièges' case for William the Conqueror's legal claim see *Gesta Normannorum Ducum*, ed. J. Marx, Société de l'Histoire de Normandie (Rouen, 1914), pp. 132–3, 215. For the Tapestry, see *The Bayeux Tapestry*, ed. F. M. Stenton *et al.*, 2nd edn (London, 1965) and *The Bayeux Tapestry*, ed. David M. Wilson (New York, 1985), especially plates 25–6, 30–2.

[4] William of Poitiers, *Gesta Guillelmi*, pp. 236–8.

[5] Harold is called *rex* only once in the Conqueror's writs. This writ is one of the new king's writs and favors Regenbald the Chancellor, a man who, it has been argued, had much to do with the making of early post-Conquest writs and charters (*Regesta*, i, n. 9; Keynes, 'Regenbald the Chancellor'). For other examples of the Normans' insistence that Harold had never been king, see George Garnett, 'Coronation and propaganda: some implications of the Norman claim to the throne of England in 1066', *TRHS*, 5th ser., 36 (1986), pp. 91–116.

[6] Thus R. Allen Brown, who has written most recently on the Norman Conquest, believes that the 'peaceful' settlement of England was made by Normans who 'conducted themselves as Christians in a Christian land'. Further, Brown states that 'the most noticeable feature of the Norman settlement in England...[was] its orderliness, and the firm control maintained by King William throughout' (R. Allen Brown, *The Normans and the Norman Conquest*, 2nd edn (Woodbridge, Suffolk, 1985), p. 172). V. H. Galbraith emphasized that William won England through the use of violence, but he did not elaborate on the means by which the new king's followers gained land (V. H. Galbraith, *Domesday Book. Its Place in Administrative History* (Oxford, 1974), pp. 175–9). John Le Patourel expressed some doubt concerning the notion of an orderly and lawful reallocation of land after the Conquest. Unfortunately, he devoted only five sentences and little evidence to his discussion of this idea (*The Norman Empire* (Oxford, 1976), pp. 47–8).

and violent tenurial discontinuity. Pre-Conquest landholding patterns in Sussex, Shropshire, Cheshire, Cornwall and southern Lancashire were savaged as great marcher fees were established. Territorial fees were granted out as well by hundred or by wapentake, and lay at the heart of the largest and most important secular fees north of Watling Street and west of the fens. The honours of Pontefract, Richmond and Holderness, formed along hundredal lines in the first generation after Hastings, ignored older tenurial arrangements and preserved throughout the Middle Ages the innovations of William and his *familiares*, and seem to account for something over a third of all land that exchanged hands after the Conquest. While the discovery of such enfeoffments challenges the notion of strong tenurial continuity, the planning and execution of such territorial grants confirm the commonly held notion that William was very much in charge of the settlement of his retainers in England. There is evidence, however, that preserves traces of a land rush in parts of England which more closely resembled a free for all than a centrally sponsored programme of colonization. In counties south of Watling Street, and in the eastern midlands and East Anglia, patterns of land acquisition by antecession and by hundred are less clear and suggest a less controlled, less planned settlement. Domesday evidence for these counties, paired with Orderic Vitalis's dark hints of illegal land seizure,[7] form a strong circumstantial case for a less controlled settlement, and suggests that private enterprise on the part of William's followers played a significant role in the formation of post-Conquest fees.

The only property that the Norman settlers consistently stole, according to standard English historiography, is that belonging to the Church primarily because this activity is so well represented in the materials surviving from monastic archives, particularly from the reports and precepts stemming from the great judicial pleas held in the 1070s and 80s. Documents from Ely, Christchurch, Rochester, Bury, Westminster, Evesham, Worcester, Ramsey and Abingdon, in their preservation of a memory of such pleas, record the relentless encroachments of these communities' Norman neighbours, and the restitutions

---

[7] Orderic tells us that both Gilbert de Heugleville and Guitmund a monk of La-Croix-Saint-Leufroi returned to Normandy because they would not hold ill-gotten lands (OV, iii, pp. 254–6, ii, pp. 270–80).

demanded by the Norman king.[8] No corresponding documents preserve information on the baronial assault against thegns and their land, resulting, naturally enough, in an emphasis in the historiography on the losses sustained by religious houses. The well-documented squabbles over thegnland, the dozens of writs penned to restore church property, and the vitriolic complaints of monastic chroniclers have led us, therefore, to think that despoliation in the Conqueror's reign was limited, essentially, to ecclesiastical victims. Secular English landholders were legally disseised; the English Church was despoiled: such is the picture. But churchmen who appeared at local inquests held on their behalf, accompanied by chests full of charters,[9] by ancient and venerable colleagues dragged to the proceedings in ox wagons,[10] and by the moldering bodies of their founder-saints,[11] were not easy prey. The supernatural arsenal at ecclesiastics' disposal, coupled with churchmen's ability to publicize saintly heroics, did much to protect monastic patrimonies.[12] Those who violated Bury St Edmunds' lands were rewarded with nightmares, tumours, stupidity and madness,[13] and St Ætheldreda rained coronary occlusions upon Ely's despoilers.[14] Furthermore, King William, who took his duties as defender of the reformed Church very seriously, did what he could to protect the property of his bishops and abbots, restoring much of the land that they had lost to Normans, or, for that matter, to Englishmen before the Conquest.[15] Still, abbeys and bishoprics were not immune to the depredations of their Norman neighbours, especially if, like Ely, they had sided with the losing party.[16] Nonetheless, they were not

---

[8] For a convenient, if incomplete, collection of documents relating to these pleas see Bigelow, *Placita*, pp. 2–61.

[9] Domesday often implies that documents were brought to inquests for inspection. In Yorkshire for example, the Canons of St John proved their rights to land in Holderness with 'the seal of King Edward and King William' (DB, i, 374r), and in Huntingdonshire Bishop Remigius brought pre-Conquest writs, which he showed at the hundred courts to prove his claims (DB, i, 208v).

[10] 'Ægelricus episcopus de cicestra, vir antiquissimus et legum terre sapientissimus, qui ex precepto regis aduectus fuit ad ipsas antiquas legum consuetudines discutiendas et edocendas in una quadriga' (Le Patourel, 'Report of the trial on Penenden Heath', p. 23 text 'A').   [11] Hemming, i, p. 75.

[12] Antonia Gransden, 'Baldwin, Abbot of Bury St Edmunds, 1065–1097', *Anglo-Norman Studies*, 4 (1982), n. 45; Susan Ridyard, *The Royal Saints of Anglo-Saxon England* (Cambridge, 1988), pp. 234–52.

[13] *Hermanni Archidiaconi Liber Miraculis Sancti Eadmundi*, in *Memorials of St Edmund's Abbey*, ed. Thomas Arnold, RS 3 vols. (1890–96) i, pp. 76, 59, 79–80.

[14] *LE*, ii, c. 131.   [15] See above, n. 8.

[16] For Ely's revolt against the Conqueror and subsequent losses, see *LE*, ii, cc. 102–23.

nearly as helpless as the small landholders whose lords had fallen at Hastings or in the uprisings which followed. These men were without the protection of more powerful patrons and without recourse to formal inquests.[17] Indeed, Orderic Vitalis writes that the king's vice-regents, Odo Bishop of Bayeux and William fitz Osbern, 'would not deign to hear the reasonable pleas of the English or give them impartial judgement'.[18] The seizure of ecclesiastical land, so well documented, must have been dwarfed by Norman encroachments against the lands and rights of truly vulnerable men. But, while the barons' ecclesiastical victims complained to the king and wrote tracts defending their rights to lost property, lesser English landholders who fell victim to the same set of circumstances were long dead by 1086, or living unhappily, like Russian émigrés, in exile, or surviving in reduced circumstances in England, and were thus in no position to preserve for posterity a list of their losses. Accordingly, our evidence provides us with a sharp image of Norman campaigns against the patrimonies of great ecclesiastical establishments, but only intimations of similar activity against minor characters. Moreover, there had to be a complaint for there to be a claim. The seizure of thegns' and freemen's property may in the early years of the Conquest have sparked rebellion, but is unlikely to have encouraged lawsuits.[19] In order, therefore, to uncover Norman annexations against secular English holders we must move from rock-hard evidence to innuendo and to the hint of violence.

Difficult as this is, we can, from time to time, catch a glimpse of extra-legal encroachment against secular landholders in the

---

[17] Domesday preserves dozens of instances of Normans taking land from men who had lost their lords. In Hemingford Abbots, for example, Sæwine the Falconer, who had held an estate from the Abbot of Ramsey, lost his land when the Abbot fled to Denmark c. 1070, and Osmund father of Ralph fitz Osmund 'took it by force' (DB, i, 208r. For the date of the Abbot's exile, see Freeman, *NC*, iv, pp. 509–11). The complaint was more likely made at the Domesday inquest by Ramsey than by Sæwine, who seems to have disappeared by 1086.

[18] OV, ii, p. 202. Englishmen's pleas are recorded only very rarely in Domesday Book. The most revealing is a claim preserved in the Hampshire folios. There, Ealdræd, the brother of one of the few successful post-Conquest Englishmen, Oda of Winchester, claimed a virgate of William the Archer's manor of Compton. 'He states that he held it TRE and was dispossessed after King William crossed the sea. He established his right to it in front of the Queen. Hugh de Port is witness to this and the men of the whole hundred' (DB, i, 48v).

[19] The institution of *murdrum* fines suggests that there was a more common English reaction to the seizure of land.

Conqueror's reign. There is a mass of information on illegal seizure in Domesday – something over a thousand cases in all – preserved in the *clamores* of Lincolnshire, Yorkshire, and Huntingdonshire, in the *invasiones* of Essex, Norfolk and Suffolk, and in the hundred court testimony scattered throughout the survey's remaining folios.[20] Thus, the most casual turn through Domesday Book exposes Normans helping themselves to property. In Essex, for example, 'Alwynn a free woman held [Childerditch] and it is not known how it came to Robert fitz Wimarc [TRW]'.[21] In Ewell, Surrey, two hides and a virgate were stolen from the king by his reeves who 'made use of it for their friends',[22] and in Bedfordshire William de Warenne seized land and two horses and 'has not yet given them back'.[23] Such anecdotal information is abundant, but in order to form a notion of how common extra-legal seizures were and to what degree they typify the Norman settlement, it is necessary to study systematically such private acts of despoliation and examine land holding across entire counties and throughout whole fees. Surrey provides an excellent starting point for such an investigation.

Whatever the Conqueror's initial plans were for land redistribution in Surrey, they had become blurred by 1086. A few fees in the county remained stable throughout the reign. At the time of the inquest Roger of Montgomery still held his antecessor Osmund's land and nothing more,[24] and William de Braose's lands in the county were limited to those he had inherited from Godtovi.[25] But the history of the two largest honours in the shire suggests that the Conqueror's early intentions had rapidly given way to the aspirations of Richard fitz Gilbert and Odo Bishop of Bayeux. Richard fitz Gilbert succeeded into the holdings of Alnoth, Alwine, Azur, Hearding and Almær. Although the lands of these five thegns formed the core of his honour in Surrey, well over 40 per cent of his fee's value in the county was derived from the lands of at least twenty-two other Englishmen.[26] Odo, for his

---

[20] For the Lincolnshire *clamores* see DB, i, 375r–377v; for Yorkshire see 373r–374r; for Huntingdonshire see 208r–208v; for Essex see DB, ii, 99a–103b; for Norfolk see DB, ii, 273b–280a; for Suffolk see DB, ii, 447b–450a.   [21] DB, ii, 42a.

[22] DB, i, 30v.   [23] DB, i, 211v.   [24] DB, i, 34r–34v.   [25] DB, i, 35v.

[26] DB, i, 34v–35v. Some of the names of Richard's English antecessors may represent more than one individual. Each of the aforementioned names, in any case, appears in Richard's Surrey fee three or more times. Richard Mortimer, in examining Richard's holdings in Surrey, identifies only three antecessors–Azur, Alnoth and Hearding

part, succeeded Æthelnoth Cilt, gaining his predecessor's r
of Bramley and Banstead.[27] He also succeeded into the estates or
Leofwine Godwineson, the Edwardian earl of the southeast, in
Gatton and Cuddington.[28] The four holdings of Leofwine and
Æthelnoth, assessed collectively at 103 hides TRE, paid geld for
only seventeen by the early 1080s, evidence that they formed the
earliest part of Odo's endowment by the king as Earl of Kent. The
acquisition of the remainder of the bishop's Surrey lands,
however, is quite mysterious. By the time of his disgrace, Odo
had gained control over the lands of thirty-two local English
landholders scattered across the county. Both the bishop's and
Richard's fees were formed, therefore, along neither strictly
tenurial nor hundredal lines. What, then, was their basis?

From the county's legal evidence it is clear that many of
Richard's and particularly Odo's acquisitions in the shire were
illegal. There is the strong suspicion that Richard took from
whomsoever he could in the county in order to supplement both
the lands of his antecessors and his lowey of Tonbridge. The
county's hundred courts stated flatly that his possession of App's
Court, Dirtham and perhaps Harthurst was illegal.[29] Furthermore,
Richard's son, apparently pressured during William Rufus's reign
by Archbishop Lanfranc, provided compensation to the community at Rochester for land – in particular for dens – which his
father had appropriated from the Church both in Surrey and
nearby in Kent.[30] For Odo, the evidence is more damning still.
Bramley, Æthelnoth Cilt's old manor, lay at the heart of the
bishop's aggressive expansion in southwestern Surrey. To this
manor he added the holdings of ten thegns assessed collectively at
thirty-two hides.[31] Odo even managed to add a couple of houses
in Guildford to his burgeoning manor with the help of a
dedicated reeve, who married a widow[32] and usurped dead men's

---

('Clare', p. 125) – but Richard did succeed an Alwine four times in his Surrey honour
and an Almær eight times. The differences between my figures and Mortimer's serves
as a reminder of both the difficulties in determining antecessors and the tentativeness
of Domesday figures.   [27] DB, i, 31r, 31v.   [28] DB, i, 31v.

[29] The hundred offered testimony against him concerning his holding at App's Court
(DB, i, 35r), Dirtham (DB, i, 35v) and Harthurst (DB, i, 35v). Mortimer, 'Clare', p.
127.   [30] Mortimer, 'Clare', p. 127; *Mon. Ang.*, i, p. 164.

[31] And one unassessed ploughland. DB, i, 30v, 31r, 31v, 32r, 34r.

[32] 'There is another house that the reeve of the Bishop of Bayeux holds of the manor of
Bramley. Of this, the men of the county say that he has no other right there, but that
the reeve of the vill took a widow, whose house it was, and that the Bishop, therefore,
placed the house in his manor' (DB, i, 30r).

property for the good of his lord.[33] When Bramley's post-Conquest growth is viewed on a map of Surrey, it is clear that the estate, despite rules of succession, absorbed most of the territory in its vicinity, and that it stopped only at the boundaries of royal estates or the estates of Odo's most powerful neighbours.[34] In the northeast of the shire, in Brixton Hundred, Domesday captures Odo busy again. Here he managed to gain a field in Lambeth through nefarious means.[35] Here, also, he and his godson, the Bishop of Lisieux, were acting in some sort of profitable if unholy alliance and expanding their interests together. The Bishop of Lisieux had two hides at Peckham, which lay in Battersea TRE and belonged by right to the church there,[36] and two further sulungs in Kent, which should have been attached to the king's manor of Merton, Surrey. Odo acted as *advocatus* for the bishop and his claims.[37] The Bishop of Lisieux also held Hatcham from Odo, an estate which had apparently been pinched from the antecessor of Walter fitz Othere.[38] Many of Odo's acquisitions were gained without any kind of royal grant, and complaint is often made in the Surrey folios that 'the county states that he has no right there', or that 'he did not have livery or the king's writ for it, so the hundred testifies'.[39] Although Odo doubtless received a portion of his land – that of his antecessors – very soon after Hastings, many of his holdings were gathered over time, and some he acquired very late indeed. We can, for example, date the bishop's acquisition of Farncombe to 1081 or 1082.[40] Thus, over the course of William's reign, Odo's position as Earl of Kent and

---

[33] 'The sworn men say that it is only because the reeve of that vill was a friend of the man who had the house, and when he died [the reeve] converted it to the manor of Bramley' (DB, i, 30r).

[34] I.e. Walter fitz Othere, Earl Roger, Richard fitz Gilbert and William fitz Ansculf.

[35] DB, i, 34r.

[36] This holding is found in Odo's fee under Peckham (DB, i, 31v) and in Westminster's fee under Battersea. In the latter description the manuscript notes that the Church held the two hides after the time of King William, but that Odo had disseised it (DB, i, 32r).

[37] DB, i, 30v. Paul Hyams notes that 'the best defence of tenure was to cite one's grantor, who was usually also the same person who had seised you and ought to protect you' ('Warranty and good lordship in twelfth century England', *Law and History Review* (1987), p. 458).

[38] DB, i, 31v. Before the Conquest the estate was held by Beorhtsige, Walter's antecessor (DB, i, 36r, 36v).   [39] DB, i, 30r, 32r.

[40] 'A certain reeve of the king named Lofus claims this manor (Farncombe) and the men of the Hundred testify that he held it of the king when the king was in Wales, and he held it afterwards until the Bishop of Bayeux came to Kent. The Bishop himself appropriated (*convertit*) Rodsell and Farncombe for the farm of Bramley' (DB, i, 31v; note in Phillimore edn of Surrey for 5–3).

his possession of several key estates gave him the power to acquire a sizeable holding in the county and allowed him to form a substantial honour, much of which he appropriated for himself.

Richard's and Odo's activities in Surrey echo their better-known exploits in Kent. There, Odo made raids against Christchurch's land, and Rochester fell victim to both Richard and Odo. Although the king held a plea at Penenden Heath to adjudicate some of the resulting disputes, the *Domesday Monachorum* leaves one with the strong impression that Odo obstinately held on to what he could after the famous trial.[41] This surely explains the inclusion of Odo's land and the lands of his knights into Christchurch's careful in-house survey of its own Kentish holdings.[42] Stoke, one of the estates Odo acquired that was later adjudged to Lanfranc, answered for five sulungs in Edward's reign, but for only three TRW. Odo got this land as part of his 'inheritance' from the long-dead Earl Godwine, doubtless through Godwine's son Leofwine. Godwine purchased the land illegally from two men, who held the land from the Bishop of Rochester, and had sold it without the bishop's permission. Lanfranc was able to prove Rochester's claim,[43] but even so was only able to repossess a portion of Stoke. The missing two sulungs remained in Odo's fee, and were held TRW by one of Odo's Kentish tenants, Ansgot of Rochester.[44] Similarly Brook was recovered at Penenden Heath for Canterbury, but one of Odo's tenants, Robert of Romney, continued to hold it in 1086.[45]

The misdeeds of Odo and Richard in the southeast were in no

---

[41] The texts stemming from the trial at Penenden Heath are printed in John Le Patourel, 'Reports of the trial on Penenden Heath', pp. 21–6, and David Bates, 'Land pleas of William I's reign: Penenden Heath revisited', pp. 3–6. For a discussion of these losses see Douglas, *Dom. Mon.*, pp. 27–32, and 'Odo, Lanfranc, and the Domesday Survey', pp. 54–5. Many of the estates Christchurch and Rochester claimed over the course of William's reign, claims that are most fully recorded in the 'C' version of the 'report on the trial', have been analyzed by David Bates, who has shown that of the twenty-eight properties listed, eleven were lost before the Conquest and, therefore, came to Odo not through illegal seizure but through legal inheritance (Bates, 'Land pleas', pp. 14–15). Although Odo's reputation declined between the earliest report of the plea and the last, it is nonetheless clear from Domesday Book and the *Domesday Monachorum* that the Bishop continued to hold property which Lanfranc had proven to the King's satisfaction pertained to Christchurch.   [42] *Dom. Mon.*, fo. 5v ff.

[43] DB, i, 5v; Le Patourel, 'Penenden Heath', p. 22, text 'A' and 'D'.

[44] DB, i, 8v. Ansgot also appears as a knight of the Archbishop in Farningham (*Dom. Mon*, fo. 6v).

[45] Robert did, however, hold this land of the monks, and not of Odo. Le Patourel, 'Reports of the trial on Penenden Heath', p. 25, text 'C'; *Dom. Mon.*, fo. 4r. Robert appears as Odo's tenant in a number of places (DB, i, 11r).

way unusual; we simply know more about Odo's, in particular, than those of others because of the monks of Canterbury's and Evesham's painstaking record of them, and because Odo's imprisonment at the time of the Domesday Inquest encouraged testimony against him.[46] Certainly, other of the Conqueror's *familiares* were commandeering whatever they could. A writ issued by King William demanding restoration of ecclesiastical lands, also admonished the great magnates addressed in the document – Geoffrey Bishop of Coutances, Robert Count of Eu, Richard fitz Gilbert and Hugh de Montfort, some of the greatest of the king's tenants-in-chief – to give up any lands they had 'dragged away through violence'.[47] Lesser men, too, stole whatever land or rights they could. Norman sheriffs such as Picot, described by the monks of Ely as a 'filthy pig', are famous for their appropriations.[48] Indeed, every great monastery and bishopric seems to have had its own sheriff-nemesis. Ely had Picot, Worcester had Urse d'Abetot, Canterbury Hugh de Montfort, Glastonbury Hugh fitz Grip and Abingdon Froger. Almost all of the Conqueror's tenants-in-chief were reproached at one time or another by Domesday juries for illegally seizing Englishmen's land. Thus, Geoffrey the Chamberlain was accused of annexing the land of four Winchester *suburbani*,[49] and Hugh de Port was implicated in the theft of a freeman's land in Esher.[50] Robert fitz Corbucion arrogated the land of eight freemen in Tolleshunt Major, Essex,[51] and Eustace of Huntingdon held land in Huntingdonshire, but 'the County denies that they have ever seen a seal or a seisor who put him in possession of it'.[52] Even minor undertenants relieved others of their property. The Bishop of Bayeux's knights, for example, 'appropriated' two freemen along with their forty-seven acres in Dengie, Essex.[53] Nigel, a servant of the County of Mortain, 'annexed' eleven acres of land from Stowmarket,[54] and two nameless marshalls 'seized Northmann's land and held it. The men of the wapentake do not know in what way or for those use, but they saw them holding it.'[55]

An examination of the fees of great men and minor tenants

---

[46] For a summary of Canterbury's opinions of Odo, see Bates, 'The character and career of Odo', pp. 2–4; for Evesham, see *Chron. Ev.*, pp. 96–7.

[47] Printed in Bigelow, *Placita*, pp. 4–5.   [48] *LE*, ii, c. 131.

[49] 'Neither the sheriff nor the hundred have ever seen the King's seal for it' (DB, i, 39r).

[50] 'When Hugh was seised of this land he did not have a feoffer or a King's writ, so the hundred testifies' (DB, i, 32r).   [51] DB, ii, 86a.   [52] DB, i, 208r.

[53] DB, ii, 24a.   [54] DB, ii, 291b.   [55] DB, i, 373v.

alike, preserved in the detailed and complex account of landholding in Norfolk, Suffolk and Essex, suggests that the scale of such appropriations is quite astonishing. The holdings of Roger the Poitevin's Suffolk antecessors Wulfmær, Wulfric, Leofwine Croc and Ælfflæd accounted for something like twenty-three carucates of his fee. These carucates, however, formed only a third of Roger's holding in the county; the remaining two-thirds, scattered across a dozen hundreds, devolved for the most part on to Roger's fee from the small acre parcels of scores of men commended in their turn to twenty-eight pre-Conquest lords.[56] Geoffrey de Mandeville's smaller, more compact holding in the county was centred, as it was elsewhere in England, on the lands of his antecessors Ansgar the Staller and Healfdane. These holdings together account for just a fraction under half of Geoffrey's fee in the shire. The remainder of his land had been held TRE by dozens of freemen.[57] A third of Ranulf brother of Ilger's holding in Suffolk came from his antecessors Beorhtmær and Queneva, but the remaining two-thirds were from a scattering of thegns' and freemen's land.[58] Half of Reginal fitz Ivo's holdings in Norfolk were from the lands of his antecessors Toli, Thorketil and Ketil, the other half from other men,[59] and similar proportions of the lands of antecessors and of other men went into the making of Ranulf brother of Ilger's honour in Essex.[60] These percentages are typical for the fees found in Little Domesday. In the whole of Suffolk, just over a third of all land which changed hands after the Conquest did so through antecession. The remaining two-thirds devolved on to new lords

---

[56] DB, ii, 346a–353a. These lords were the Abbots of Ely and Bury, Earl Harold, Healfdane, King Edward, Beorhtric, Æthelric of Burgh, Wulfric, Eadric of Laxfield, Brown, Lustwine, Eadweald, Grimulf, Earl Gyrth, Wulfmær, Eadric Grim, Earl Ælfgar, Wihtgar, Bishop Almær, Ulf, Stigand, Wulfweard, Leofwine Croc, Alsige nephew of Earl Ralph, Ælfflæd, Leofric, Godmann and Finn the Dane.

[57] DB, ii, 411a–413a. Geoffrey's lands in Suffolk had also been held TRE by Wihtgar, a freeman of the Abbot of Ely; five freemen of the same Wihtgar; a freeman of Eadric of Laxfield; Fridebiorn, a thegn of King Edward; a freeman 'commended to some one commended to Ralph the Staller'; a freeman half commended to Wulfric; six freemen half commended to Ely; a freeman commended to Stigand; Almær commended to Æthelric of Burgh; Beorhtweald *Mufla* half commended to Hervey de Berry's antecessor, half to Eadric of Laxfield; a freeman commended to Ely; and Topi commended to Ely.

[58] DB, ii, 423b–425a. Besides acquiring Beorhtmær's and Queneva's land, he held the land of Godric; Hardwine, 'half commended to N. and half to Eadric'; Beohtric, half commended to Stanmær; Eadweald, a freeman half Eadric's man and half Northmann's; Durand, Robert Malet's antecessor; Wulfric, a thegn of King Edward; and Ælfric of *Wenhou*. [59] DB, ii, 230a–234b. [60] DB, ii, 79b–81b.

for other reasons. In Essex close to 60 per cent and in Norfolk close to 70 per cent of the land found in secular fees was not held because of an antecessor. What these figures suggest is that well over half the land transference which took place in eastern England between 1066 and 1086 did so in spite of pre-Conquest landholder or hundred.

The fate of urban tenancies after the Conquest hints, as well, at the widespread seizure of property, seizure propelled both by military necessity and by opportunity. Some urban holdings did remain in English hands. Onomastic evidence from the *Winton Domesday* suggests that a half a century after the Conquest at least a third of all urban landholders in Winchester were English. Thus burgesses managed to hold on to their property in Winchester at least twice as often as thegns and freemen in the surrounding countryside.[61] Of the urban tenancies that did change hands, a considerable portion passed on to Normans through antecessorial inheritance. In Lincolnshire, for example, the thegns who were stripped of their manors and sokes during the course of the English Wars lost their burgages as well, usually to the same successors to whom they had forfeited their manors.[62] Continuity, too, was marked before and after the Conquest by urban street plans, the location of town churches, and by the materials with which urban tenements were built; all remained for the most part unchanged throughout William's reign.[63] Nonetheless, the hurried construction of castles, the ambitious ecclesiastical building programmes and the rapid settlement of French burgesses, all hallmarks of urban development in the Conqueror's reign, left their imprint on English towns.[64] All, moreover, presuppose the widespread seizure of land. Domesday evidence makes it clear that towns were revamped during the Conqueror's reign, and that large amounts of urban property were consumed to make way for new castles and churches and for Norman traders settling within the towns. Shrewsbury's English burgesses were in

---

[61] *Winchester Studies*, 1, pp. 183–91.

[62] J. W. F. Hill, *Medieval Lincoln* (Cambridge, 1948), pp. 45–52. Such an antecessorial grant is preserved in Domesday's description of York: 'The Bishop of Durham has of the king's gift...the whole of Uhtræd's land and Earnwine's land which Earl Hugh, the sheriff, delivered to Bishop Walcher by the king's writ' (DB, i, 298r). The involvement of the sheriff and the use of a writ was probably common and must typify the way in which antecessorial grants were instituted in the boroughs.

[63] This is certainly the case for Winchester, the most thoroughly excavated English town (Martin Biddle, 'Early Norman Winchester', *Domesday Studies*, i, p. 325).

[64] Le Patourel, *The Norman Empire*, pp. 45–6.

desperate straits in 1086 for just these reasons. They complained bitterly that

> it is very hard for them to render as much geld as they rendered in the time of King Edward... Earl [Roger de Montgomery]'s castle has occupied fifty-one *mansurae* and fifty other *mansurae* are waste, and forty-three French burgesses hold forty-three *mansurae* which were gelded TRE; and the Earl himself has given the Abbey, which he built there, thirty-nine burgesses who once paid geld similarly to the others.[65]

The impression given by this entry is that Normans often appropriated large blocks of territory within the town, rather than settling for piecemeal acquisitions based on antecessorial inheritance. Norwich's burgesses found themselves in a difficulty similar to that of their Shrewsbury brethren, as a royal castle was constructed and later as Herbert Losinga, the bishop of the new Norman see, dismantled a large section of town to accommodate his magnificent new cathedral.[66] Similarly, the defensive measures taken by the Conqueror in the city of York wreaked havoc with burgal holders. The River Foss, dammed to protect the city's southeastern flank, drowned two of the town's mills and a carucate of land.[67] South and west of the River Ouse a whole network of streets was destroyed with the construction of Old Baile in 1068–69,[68] and what had once been a large commercial district was cut in two.[69] Moreover, the archbishop's 'shire' or precinct within the walls witnessed the destruction of nearly half its urban tenements and the king's precincts in 1086 included 540 wasted and 400 partially wasted tenements.[70] Some of these thousand properties were destroyed during the rebellion of 1069–70 when the city first caught fire and then was ravaged, but other tenements were levelled to make way for the city's second castle and to clear a parimeter around the city's walls.[71] *Francigenae*

---

[65] DB, i, 252r.

[66] James Campbell, 'Norwich', *The Atlas of Historic Towns*, ed. M. D. Lobel (London, 1975), ii, pp. 8–9; DB, ii, 117a.

[67] DB, i, 298r; *VCH, Yorks, City of York* (London, 1961), p. 22; *An Inventory of the Historical Monuments in the City of York*, vol. 2, *The Defences, Royal Commission of Historical Monuments in England* (London, 1972), p. 10.

[68] Addyman in *The Anglo-Saxons*, ed. James Campbell (1982), p. 166. D. M. Palliser, 'York's west bank: medieval suburb or urban nucleus?', in *Archaeological Papers from York Presented to M. W. Bailey, York Archaeological Trust* (York, 1984), p. 106. Excavations of the ground surface underneath Old Baile revealed eleventh century occupation debris (*ibid.*, p. 89).   [69] Palliser, 'York's west bank', p. 106.

[70] DB, i, 298r.

[71] Domesday notes that 'one of these shires was wasted for the castle' (DB, i, 298r). For York's fire and its subsequent ravaging see Fl. Wig., ii, p. 4.

were settled in York, as well, and by 1086 they occupied 145 of
the surviving manses, manses once held by Anglo-Scandinavian
thegns and traders. In Winchester twelve burgesses lost their
houses when the royal palace was enlarged c. 1070.[72] A street was
blocked to make way for the king's new kitchen,[73] and the
tenements facing the street were doubtless destroyed. The new
castle at Winchester, too, necessitated the confiscation of property.
The intra-mural street, blocked by the construction of the motte,
had been densely settled before the Conquest, but it and the
tenements built along it were levelled in 1067 to make way for the
castle.[74] Suburban property outside the West Gate was also
destroyed, as an entire extra-mural street and its tenements were
demolished to make way for the castle's foss.[75]

The king's barons, too, were seizing land beyond the tenements
of their antecessors. The Count of Mortain had fourteen
tenements in York by 1086, which had been held before the
Conquest by Sunulf the Priest, Morulf, Sterri, Snarri, Gamel,
Arnketil, Lyfing the Priest, Thorfinnr, Ligulfr and four drengs.[76]
Although Arnketil and Ligulfr probably both numbered among
the Count's thegnly antecessors, five of these names never appear
again in Domesday as holders of the Count's rural property. A
portion of the Count's urban possessions looks, therefore, like a
convenient, and perhaps personal acquisition. In this Robert's
holding is similar to that of Bishop Remigius's in the town of
Lincoln. Half of Toki son of Outi's urban property, including his
two city churches and his hall, went to his successor Geoffrey
Alselin, but the Bishop, who was settling into the town, and
hatching plans for a large cathedral, managed to grab a valuable
chunk of Toki's property – thirty *mansurae* – probably located
between the city wall and the river wharves.[77] Nottingham
underwent radical changes as well. The Norman castle was built
on a sandstone outcropping west of the Old English town.

---

[72] *Winton Domesday*, I, n. 57, 80. For the most recent summary of Winchester in the
Conqueror's reign, see Martin Biddle, 'Early Norman Winchester', pp. 311–31.
[73] *Winton Domesday*, I, n. 60.   [74] *Winchester Studies*, I, pp. 278, 302.
[75] *Winton Domesday*, I, n. 81; *Winchester Studies*, I, p. 303.   [76] DB, i, 298a.
[77] Hill, *Medieval Lincoln*, pp. 131–3; James Campbell, 'The Church in Anglo-Saxon
towns', *Essays in Anglo-Saxon History* (London, 1986), pp. 151–2. When Remigius's
see was moved from Dorchester to Lincoln, the king endowed the new church with
land 'enough to construct a mother-church for the whole bishopric and its buildings'
along with the churches of St Lawrence and St Martin (*Registrum Antiquissimum of the
Cathedral Church of Lincoln*, ed. C. W. Foster and K. Major (Horncastle, 1931), i, p. 3).
Toki's land, however, was not part of the king's endowment.

Between the castle and the old borough a French precinct was developed by William Peverel. This push westward made the northern and western defences of the old Saxon burgh unnecessary, and when the ancient borough ditch was filled in pre-Conquest tenements were destroyed.[78] Canterbury's record in Domesday also suggests widespread seizures against laymen. Forty-five suburban *mansurae* and their associated rights and 113 acres of land – all property of the burgesses' or their guild before the Conquest – were possessed by Ranulf de Colombières TRW.[79] His warrantor for this, and his lord, was the Bishop of Bayeux,[80] a man who was remembered in Domesday Book as a despoiler of Canterbury burgesses.[81]

This redevelopment was disastrous for many Englishmen. In Ipswich the number of burgesses had declined to less than a half by 1086; of these only 110 could render their customary dues, and the hundred others who remained were described as *pauperes burgenses* and were men too poor to pay the king anything but a penny a head.[82] In Norwich things were so desperate that thirty-two of the burgesses fled – 'those fleeing and the others remaining have been utterly devastated, partly because of Earl Ralph's forfeiture, partly because of the fires, partly because of the king's tax and partly through Waleran'.[83] Waleran was a royal official, whose responsibilities included the confiscation of land.[84]

The revolution in urban topography effected during William's reign was often marked by the king's own involvement. The siting of the royal palace at Winchester and the building of the castles at York were doubtless planned and implemented by William himself. But the participation of Norman magnates in the development of large blocks of commercial property and in the construction of urban castles, abbeys and episcopal churches suggests that these men took whatever property was necessary to implement their designs. Some holders of English burgages, like

---

[78] This infilling probably occurred before the Domesday survey, since Domesday records that 23 houses were 'in the ditch of the borough' (DB, i, 280r; W. F. Bailey and I. F. Straw, 'Nottingham', *Atlas of Historic Towns* (London, 1969), i, p. 2).

[79] DB, i, 2r. For the best discussion of the Normans in Canterbury see W. Urry, 'The Normans in Canterbury', *Annales de Normandie*, 8 (1958), pp. 122–3.

[80] White Book of St Augustine's, printed in *An Eleventh Century Inquisition of St Augustine's Canterbury*, ed. A. Ballard, Records in Social and Economic History of England and Wales (Oxford, 1920), fo. 22v.   [81] DB, i, 9v.

[82] DB, ii, 290a–290b.   [83] DB, ii, 117b.

[84] In Sidestrand, Norfolk, Waleran delivered some of Stigand's land to William de Warenne (DB, ii, 170b).

the wealthy thegns of Lincolnshire, were legally dispossessed when they rebelled against the king, and others, particularly ecclesiastics, were sporadically compensated for their losses.[85] But burgesses whose workshops and houses were buried under the rising mottes of Roger de Montgomery and William Peverel or flattened for Bishop Remigius's new episcopal complex, were simply pushed aside. This heavy-handed treatment of burgesses echoes that of thegns and freemen, and suggests that little attention was paid to legal boundaries or precedent. The treatment of both burgesses and thegns points to chaotic and haphazard acquisitions, which often had more to do with local circumstance and opportunity than a carefully implemented royal policy.

Some of the burgages and farms that descended into post-Conquest fees irregularly came to Normans through extraordinary royal grants. Bishop Remigius, for example, was granted two urban churches when his see was moved to Lincoln.[86] Robert d'Oilly received Ludwell from the king at the siege of Sainte-Susanne,[87] and Roger Bigot, after an Englishman named Ælfric was outlawed, 'asked the King for [Ælfric's estate of Mundham] and he ceded it to him'.[88] Nonetheless, many of these holdings were taken without the king's permission. Such acquisitions, according to evidence in Domesday Book and William's charters, came about for a variety of reasons. English freemen and thegns came into the fees of Normans because they themselves had been leased, sold, exchanged or given as gifts. Tenants in Normandy had similarly been exchanged or granted away on occasion. Thus, Saint-Evroul received three customary tenants (*hospites*) and their lands as a pious donation from Ralph de Tosny,[89] and Osbern d'Ectot gave seven knights and their holdings to Saint-Ouen.[90] This practice continued in England, but on a grand scale, and

---

[85] Ecclesiastical institutions were sometimes compensated for urban property taken from them. The king's palace at Winchester required the acquisition of some of Old Minster's property, including its graveyard, so the church was given land outside the city in exchange (*Liber Vitae Hyde*, pp. 110–13, 163–4; *Winchester Studies*, i, pp. 292–4). The Church of St Peter's Shrewsbury, used for the foundation of Shrewsbury Abbey, was held by Odelerius, the father of Orderic Vitalis. Its former English holder, however, was given the church of Cheney Longville in exchange for St Peter's (Chibnall, 'Introduction' to OV, i, pp. 3–4). Such exchanges, however, were not always advantageous to the Church. J. H. Harvey has suggested that Archbishop Ealdræd was compelled to have Old Baile built upon his property and then forced to help with its upkeep ('Bishophill and the Church of York', *YAJ*, 41 (1965), p. 381).

[86] See above, n. 77. [87] DB, i, 158v. [88] DB, ii, 176b.

[89] OV, iii, p. 126. This grant was confirmed by William in 1081 (OV, iv, pp. 232–40).

[90] Fauroux, *Recueil*, n. 210.

often without the king's consent or guiding hand.[91] Thus Domesday notes that Picot the Sheriff loaned three men to Roger of Montgomery,[92] and the reeve of Saham Toney sold five sokemen to one of Earl Ralph's men for a bridle.[93] Miles Crispin held rights over Alwine White and his two hides, claiming that he had got them as part of his exchange with William de Braose for Broadwater,[94] and ten freemen and their sixty acres in Onehouse were traded by an unnamed baron to Humphrey fitz Aubrey for land in Normandy.[95] Richard fitz Gilbert held eighty sokemen – three of whom were given to him as a gift by Bishop Herfast,[96] and Earl Edwin gave rights over a thegn named Sægeat to Robert d'Oilly.[97] This tendency for Englishmen and their land 'to be given away like a horse or an ox',[98] was the result of private arrangements between Norman landholders, and had little to do with the carefully controlled construction of fees. Indeed, the hundred courts sometimes declared that they 'knew nothing' about such dealings,[99] and in none of the cases noted above is there any evidence that the king gave his approval.

Englishmen's lands also taken by Norman barons for their holders' legal infractions. One of Robert Gernon's men confiscated and kept the land of a thief, even though it should have gone to the king.[100] Lisois, not the king, 'appropriated' the land of a freeman in Mundon, Essex, when he became an outlaw,[101] and

---

[91] Such grants in Normandy are usually accompanied by phrases like 'dedit per auctoritatem comitis Willelmi' (Paris, Bibliothèque Nationale, Col. Moreau, vol. 30, fols. 190r–191r).

[92] 'Six sokemen held this land...Picot loaned three of these men to Earl Roger for holding his pleas, but afterwards the Earl's men retained them with their land without seisin' (DB, i, 193v).　　　　　　[93] DB, ii, 110b.

[94] Miles Crispin, in a transaction that must have involved the king, was given land as compensation for the estate of Broadwater, Sussex, an estate he had inherited from his antecessor Wigot of Wallingford, but which he was forced to give up when the Rape of Broase was formed (DB, i, 28v). Miles may, therefore, have been attempting to disguise an extra-legal seizure as a royally sponsored exchange. He claimed that the land was 'delivered by Humphrey Visdeloup in exchange for Broadwater, so he says, but the hundred knows nothing about it' (DB, i, 50v).　　　[95] DB, ii, 436a.

[96] DB, ii, 115b.　　　　　　　　　[97] DB, i, 154v.

[98] So the Count of Evreux felt when Robert Curthose ceded 'his county and all his subjects' to Henry I in 1104 (OV, vi, 58).　　　[99] E.g. DB, i, 50v.

[100] DB, ii, 66b. The king's officials, particularly the sheriffs, profited from their actions against both English and Norman wrong-doers, often keeping land and rights they had confiscated. In Abington, Cambridge, for example, Aubrey de Vere was found to have annexed a half hide of the king's soke. Picot the Sheriff found against him 'and still retains one plough and 380 sheep which Aubrey has from that land' (DB, i, 199v).

[101] DB, ii, 49b. Similarly, Ketilbiorn, one of the few English profiteers of the Norman Conquest, claimed a carucate in Scremby unjustly because 'his antecessor forfeited it'

thirty acres of land in Rackheath, Norfolk, were 'forfeited TRW, but a certain monk gave half a mark of gold for the forfeiture to the reeve ... so had the land without licence of the king'.[102] Reeves in the Conqueror's reign, moreover, were confiscating land for their lords or themselves, as did a reeve of the Abbot of Chertsey because of a feud,[103] or as Ordwig the reeve of Bury did when he took land in Biddenham, Bedfordshire, as a forfeiture, and then held it himself from Bury illegally at the time of the Inquest.[104] Ralph Taillebois confiscated a virgate of land in Sharnbrook, Bedfordshire, and gave it to one of his knights, because its English holder, the antecessor of Osbern *Piscatoris*, refused to pay tax on it.[105] Undertenants appear, as well, to have brought land into the fees of their lords through their marriage to the daughters and widows of minor Saxon thegns and Norman knights. In Darsham Roger Bigot held a carucate of land, including six acres 'which one of his men gave with his daughter, whom a man of Roger Bigot's married TRW'.[106] Similarly, in Norfolk at Pickenham Wihenoc held thirty acres because one of his men 'loved a certain woman on that land and took her'. Later he held that land as part of Wihenoc's fee 'without the king's gift, and without livery'.[107] These sales, confiscations and exchanges clearly bypassed the king and were the result of personal arrangements between barons or the private settlement of lawsuits.

Often, Normans – and for that matter Englishmen who survived the Conquest – simply took land.[108] Before the Conquest a couple of freemen held three hides in Ramsden Crays,

(DB, i, 375v). Again, in Bradwell Quay, 'there was a freeman with 30 acres and he was outlawed. Now Swein [of Essex]'s men have received it and still hold it' (DB, ii, 24a). [102] DB, ii, 217b. [103] DB, i, 32r.

[104] DB, i, 210v. This activity was common in the Confessor's reign as well: 'At that time stolen horses were found in the home of Brungar and so the Abbot, who had sake and soke and Robert who had commendation over him, came to the plea about this theft, as the hundred testifies. They left amicably without a judgement that the hundred has seen.' Since the land is in the fee of Swein son of Robert TRW, Robert must have got this land as a result of the plea (DB, ii, 401a–402b). But the revolts, disruption, and chaos arising from the Conquest must have made this kind of activity more common, and this kind of settlement more likely. [105] DB, i, 216v.

[106] DB, ii, 334b. Robert Malet claimed the land. [107] DB, ii, 232a.

[108] A number of pre-Conquest lords took advantage of the chaos brought on by the invasions, and profited from this disruption until their own fall. Engelric the Priest collected hundreds of acres and rights over dozens of men illegally after the Conquest (*VCH, Essex*, i, p. 354), and Godric the Sheriff, antecessor of Henry de Ferrers, seized land in Berkshire 'against King William after the Battle of Hastings ... he never held it TRE' (DB, i, 60v).

Essex, but after William came to England the hundred court
testified that a certain Ravengar 'took land away from one of
them and Robert fitz Wimarc took the other land away from the
other one'.[109] In Saxlingham a man of Archbishop Stigand was
captured by a man named Waleran in one of the early battles for
England. Domesday records that the Englishman 'so that he
might redeem himself from capture by Waleran...mortgaged
[this land] for one mark of gold and £7 to St Benedict. Now
John, nephew of the said Waleran, holds it from St Benedict in
fee.' The Church, then, in spite of its mortgage, did not hold the
Englishman's land in demesne.[110] It seems that Waleran's capture
of the Englishman entitled him to enjoy the profits of the
freeman's land. This incident, along with the *Anglo-Saxon
Chronicle*'s reports of Englishmen having to buy back their lands,
preserves evidence of unbridled predation.[111]

It appears, moreover, that Normans, once legally established in
a vill, commonly attempted to overrun the lands of any
Englishmen who might remain. In Rainham, Essex, for example,
after Robert the Lascivious was enfeoffed by Robert Gernon, with
land the latter had inherited from an antecessor, Robert the
Lascivious annexed (*invasit*) land in the same vill that a freeman
should have forfeited to the king.[112] William de Percy likely held
Hagendebi in Yorkshire simply because it lay a stone's throw
from Tadcaster, one of his chief manors in the county,[113] and
similarly William picked up the lands of Oddi and Alwine in
Hornington, not because he had legal claim to them – he did not
– but because he held the bulk of the vill already through his
antecessor Healfdane.[114] William d'Ecouis acquired Moreton,
Essex, from his antecessor Saxi, but for good measure annexed the
remaining land in the vill.[115] The Count of Boulogne got eight

---

[109] DB, ii, 23a. It is interesting to note that in this case the extra-legal disseisin concerned
the hundred court not at all. Instead it worried over how the three hides had come into
the Bishop of Bayeux's fee where it lay in 1086.   [110] DB, ii, 217a.

[111] *ASC*, s.a. 1087 (E) (*recte* 1086).

[112] DB, ii, 66b. Anglo-Saxon lay lords did this as well. Before 1066 Crowle,
Worcestershire, was divided in two. One part was held by the monks of Worcester,
the other by Sigemund, a man of Earl Leofric, who first stole the monastery's portion
of Crowle and then forced Worcester to lease it to him (Hemming, i, pp. 264–5).

[113] DB, i, 321v, 374r.

[114] DB, i, 374r. These holdings lay in Aisnty Wapentake, the wapentake that formed the
core of Osbern d'Arches' territory. Both appear in the *clamores* as part of the Malet fee.
Both should have appeared either in Robert Malet's honour or in Osbern's fee. See
above, pp. 159–60.   [115] DB, ii, 88b.

hides and 23 acres in Boreham, Essex, through his antecessor Engelric. After this acquisition the count granted half a hide, eighteen acres, and half a church in the same vill to one of his knights, in spite of the fact that TRE 'Engelric was not in possession'.[116] Such encroachments were widespread in the eleventh century. Before the Conquest, the monks of Saint-Evroul had been plagued by Baldric and Wiger de Bocquencé, who shared the vill of Saint-Evroul with the monks. The two men, to hear Orderic tell it, were constantly 'inflicting all kinds of annoyances' on the community, as the brothers and the Bocquencé competed for the village's fields, rights, and profits.[117] The violence of the Conquest, combined with the vulnerability of the surviving English landholders, provoked such barn-burning and belligerence, and they left their stain on England's post-Conquest landholding patterns.

Powerful Normans not only stole land outright, but developed private understandings with their English neighbours, both lay and ecclesiastical, which appear to have been based on the exchange of land or loyalty in return for protection. These actions must often have been rooted in extortion. Certainly Normans were collecting protection money from English survivors. The burgesses of Yarmouth gave William's new sheriff a payment (*gersuma*) of £4 and a hawk each year 'freely and through friendship'.[118] The burgesses of Cambridge had lent their ploughs to the sheriff three times each year in Edward's reign but 'now they are demanded nine times',[119] and English traders in Lincolnshire found themselves paying new tolls on bread, fish and skins to Gilbert de Gand's coterie.[120] Normans fleeced other men out of their lands. A common refrain in the writs of William the Conqueror is one which berates bishops and abbots for their 'softness, *temerity* or cupidity', because they were granting out their churches' demesne to Frenchmen settling in their neighbourhoods. Temerity does indeed seem to have determined a certain amount of land transference.[121] For example, Urse d'Abetot was

---

[116] DB, ii, 31b. The Count's acquisition of Engelric's land in Boreham is interesting. TRE it had been held by 14 freemen, but Engelric, the Count's antecessor, annexed it 'after the King came into this land', giving Eustace a claim to it.   [117] OV, ii, pp. 80–2.

[118] DB, ii, 118b.   [119] DB, i, 189r.

[120] These were new tolls, originating in the years after the Conquest (DB, i, 375v).

[121] *Placita*, p. 5 ('vel lenitate, vel timore, vel cupiditate') and p. 13 ('vel levitate, vel timore, vel cupiditate'). The king, however, occasionally ignored his own orders. He insisted, for example, that Hermer be placed on one of Abingdon's estates for the

able to intimidate the community of Worcester into leasing him Greenhill and Eastbury because they feared him,[122] and in *Brutge*, Suffolk, Hervey de Bourges held 120 acres in-chief because he 'came to an agreement (*conciliatus*) with the Abbot [of Ely]'.[123] We do not know what this agreement entailed, but it was likely similar to the one drawn up between Hugh de Montfort and the monks of Jumièges in Normandy a generation earlier: Hugh had received one of Jumièges' men and Jumièges, in turn, was promised Hugh's protection.[124] In Surrey Walter de Douai held two hides in spite of the fact that no one had 'seen a writ or an instruction (*nuncium*) of the king who put him in possession of it'. Instead he got a grip on these hides because a freeman who held the land TRE 'and could go where he would, submitted himself into Walter's hands for his own protection'.[125] Queen Matilda had land in Coombe which came into her fee because 'TRW the woman who held this land put herself with [the land] into the hands of the Queen',[126] and in Havering-atte-Bower, Gilbert Abbot of Westminster acquired forty acres because a freeman 'came of his own accord to the Abbey'.[127]

The results of such deals are everywhere apparent. In Oxfordshire, for example, one of Miles Crispin's undertenants, an Englishman named Ordgar, held two lands 'from Miles [but] he ought to hold from the king, because he and his father and his uncle held them freely TRE'.[128] It is likely that Ordgar held land from Miles, long held by his family, in order to guarantee his claim. Similarly, twenty years after the Conquest, Azur, the Confessor's old *dispensator*, was still in possession of land in Berkshire which he had held in Edward's reign, but now Robert d'Oilly was his lord for it. Domesday, however, notes that 'the men of the Hundred testify that he ought to hold from the King, as King William restored it to him at Windsor and gave him a writ for it'. Azur and his lands doubtless devolved onto Robert's

monks' victualing, because his hands had been cut off by pirates (*Chron. Ab.*, ii, 6; DB, i, 59r). Norman demands on Englishmen could be relentless. After the Conquest, the burgesses of Colchester and Maldon were burdened with a £20 payment for their mint, although the fine was so steep that Waleran, who acted as the king's agent in several eastern boroughs, pardoned the burgesses of £10. Nonetheless, Walkelin, Bishop of Winchester, who held rights over the mint, demanded £40 from the burgesses! (DB, ii, 107b).   [122] Hemming, i, p. 257.   [123] DB, ii, 441a.
[124] *Chartes de l'Abbaye de Jumièges (v. 825 a 1204) conservées aux archives de la Seinte-Inferieure*, ed J. J. Vernier (Rouen and Paris, 1916), i, n. 42.   [125] DB, i, 36r.
[126] DB, i, 36v.   [127] DB, ii, 100a.   [128] DB, i, 159v.

fee because of some private arrangement not entirely to Azur's advantage. Indeed the hundred court judged that Robert 'holds unjustly for no one has seen the King's writ or a man who seised him of it'.[129] Such offers of protection could enormously increase the size of a Norman's fee. Richard fitz Gilbert, for example, nearly doubled his East Anglian lands by capitalizing on the value of his lordship. In Cornard, Suffolk, two freemen commended to Ælfric Kemp before the Conquest were annexed after it by Richard fitz Gilbert's antecessor, Wihtgar Algarson, so Domesday tells us, 'with the agreement of Richard [fitz Gilbert] who now holds them'.[130] This statement is astonishing. It suggests that a man who, in the future, was to become the legal antecessor of Richard, came to Richard before his fall to gain his permission or his aid in annexing other men's land. This suggests that Richard fitz Gilbert's chief antecessor and one of the wealthiest thegns in pre-Conquest England had entered into some sort of private arrangement with Richard before his fall, probably in return for protection.

Normans in Normandy had been entering into similar arrangements long before the Conquest. Count Herbert II of Maine, for example, 'fearing to lose all to the tyranny of Geoffrey [Count of Anjou], came to Duke William of Normandy, under whom he would be safe, as a supplicant, and did homage to him, receiving all his [lands] from [the Duke] as a knight from his lord'.[131] Wihtgar may well have commended himself to Richard, or given homage to him. When he fell, in accordance with Norman custom, his lands reverted to his lord. It is very likely, therefore, that Richard came to possess almost £200 of land, not through a royal, antecessorial grant, but as the overlord of a disgraced dependant. Perhaps these two men's relationship was similar to the one between Gilbert de Gand and the Yorkshire thegn Vigleikr. When Vigleikr forfeited his land, it went to 'his lord Gilbert'.[132] Another of fitz Gilbert's 'antecessors', Finn the

---

[129] DB, i, 62r.   [130] DB, ii, 448a.
[131] William of Poitiers, *Gesta Guillelmi*, p. 88. Thus William of Poitiers, in his account of Harold's homage to Duke William, has the duke confirm Harold's rights to his land (William of Poitiers, *Gesta Guillelmi*, p. 104). As a result, when Harold acted treacherously against his lord, his land escheated to the duke. William of Poitiers also notes that Anglo-Saxons after the Conquest, specifically Archbishop Stigand, gave homage to William at Wallingford (William of Poitiers, *Gesta Guillelmi*, p. 216).
[132] So says the claim for Scremby (DB, i, 375v).

Dane, survived for some time after the Conquest, long enough for him to press local men into his own lordship,[133] and Finn's widow according to Domesday was still holding in-chief TRW.[134] It is quite clear, however, that Finn and his wife put themselves under Richard's protection after the Conquest and that their lands came into Richard's hands as a result. In a charter dating from William Rufus's reign, Eudo Dapifer, one of Richard's sons-in-law, was seised of a manor held by Finn's wife, suggesting that Finn and his wife were somehow associated with Richard before the latter's death,[135] and according to Little Domesday Richard had subinfeudated a portion of Finn's land, that at Langham, Essex, to Walter Tirel another of his sons-in-law.[136] Similarly, Roger Bigot's Suffolk antecessor Northmann was the tenant of Roger after the Conquest, as were many of his men.[137] It is likely that Northmann and his men appear in Roger's fee as the result of a bargain struck between Northmann and Roger, rather than between Roger and the king. Thus, it appears that Normans were able to increase their fees not only through seizure, but through the extension of lordship.

This is certainly the case with post-Conquest abbots. Æthelwig, Abbot of Evesham, was able to increase his monastery's holdings in the first decade after the Conquest by extending patronage over his fellow Englishmen. In the words of the Evesham Chronicler, after 'the kingdom had been conquered by the Normans and the region [around Evesham] had been completely abandoned by the most important nobles, the abbot himself received many men', and 'little by little the Abbot spread his protection as many rich men of the province were drawn to him for their protection... Moreover, he attracted *milites* and *homines* to him with their land... promising them protection against the Normans.'[138] Even some of the Bishop of Worcester's men left the lordship of St Oswald for the protective arms of Abbot Æthelwig.[139] By the end of the Conqueror's reign, some of the land of this abbot's men was being treated like the abbey's own property and granted out

by church tenure

---

[133] DB, ii, 393a. Richard did not get all of Finn's land. Robert d'Oilly and a king's thegn were holding between them his land in Cheddington, Buckinghamshire (DB, i, 149v, 153r). [134] DB, ii, 98a–98b.

[135] *Cartularium Monasterii Sancti Johannis Baptiste de Colecestria*, ed. Stuart A. Moore, 2 vols., Roxburghe Club (London, 1897), i, p. 18; *VCH, Essex*, ii, pp. 348–9.

[136] DB, ii, 41a; Round, *FE*, p. 468; *VCH, Essex*, ii, p. 349. [137] DB, ii, 341a.

[138] *Chron. Ev.*, p. 271. [139] *Chron. Ev.*, p. 270; Hemming, i, pp. 80–1, 269–70.

to Norman knights, Norman sheriffs, and the Norman relatives of Æthelwig's successor, the wicked Abbot Walter.[140] That such acquisitions were extra-legal is clear. At the instigation of the heirs of the men who had put themselves under Æthelwig's protection, Bishop Odo, acting in some sort of official capacity, held a local plea, accusing the abbot of 'acquiring much land by force and not by right of law'.[141]

Chertsey, too, profited through its proffer of security. While King Edward was still alive, the vill of Esher in Surrey had been divided between a number of landholders. The only one of any substance was a thegn named Tovi, who held the lion's share of the vill – eleven hides three virgates in all – and was something of a power in the district, with another six hides and a virgate in the neighbouring village of West Molesey.[142] Alongside him in the village were at least one other man and two women who held small estates.[143] After the Conquest, the lords of Esher found their lands and positions tenuous. Tovi was dispossessed; part of his holding in Esher and all of it in West Molesey was taken away from him and granted to Odard the *Balistarius*, and his remaining land in Esher went to the Abbey of St Leufroys 'by gift of the king'. To add to the troubles of Esher, a man of one of the most powerful new lords in Surrey, the Bishop of Bayeux, grabbed a hide in the village without any right to it. With two new Norman lords established legally in the vill and another encroaching upon Esher's lands, the remaining proprietors, to shore up their positions and assure their tenures, turned to the only Anglo-Saxon power left in the region – Wulfweard abbot of Chertsey. Although these thegns were free enough in Edward's reign to 'turn where they would' with their land they now 'put themselves under the abbey for their own defence'. The protection offered to them by the abbot – apparently a wolf in sheep's clothing – proved ephemeral. In Domesday their holdings were entered under the lands of Chertsey and had been subinfeudated to two of the Church's new Norman tenants, William de Watteville and Rainald. Thus, the Church gathered to itself several hides of land which, in all likelihood it would never otherwise have gained, and two Norman *milites*, riding on the

---

[140] Walter, 'not wishing the homage of many good men which his predecessor had received, was able to steal the land of all of them' (*Chron. Ev.*, pp. 96–7).
[141] *Chron. Ev.*, p. 96.   [142] DB, i, 34r, 36v.
[143] One of these had granted land in Esher to Chertsey before the Conquest (DB, i, 32v).

coat-tails of the Conqueror, established themselves and their families in Surrey.

Norman newcomers had great success in gathering to their fees the lands of very minor men who became their dependants. The report on the trial of Pendenden Heath states that 'there was no one in [Kent] who could resist so powerful a magnate [as Odo], and he attached to himself many men... These he annexed wrongfully to his own lordship.' And in 1077 William the Conqueror fired off a writ ordering Peter de Valognes to give back any men commended to Bury that he 'holds in captivity'.[144] Patterns of Norman settlement in Domesday indicate the vast scale of such activity. When we plot TRW fees on a map we can see that the estates Normans held by right of an antecessor acted as magnets, drawing towards them the unapportioned lands of thousand of freemen and thegns. Examples of this process can be found in every hundred in eastern England. It is well illustrated by the Suffolk villages between the Rivers Orwell and Stour. (See figure 6.1.) In *Finesforda* Geoffrey de Mandeville came into his antecessor Healfdane's land.[145] In the neighbouring Tuddenham Hervey de Bourges gained some property attached to his manor of Bealings.[146] To the south Robert Malet inherited the large manor of Playford from his antecessor Godwine son of Ælfhere.[147] Just north, in Clopton, Roger the Poitevin acquired an estate held by his antecessor Wulfric.[148] Grundisburgh, encircled by these villages, housed no large estate and no English antecessors, but was instead formed by the holdings of over thirty men commended to ten different pre-Conquest lords.[149] The lands of these middling landholders were, nonetheless, divided between the new Norman proprietors in Grundisburgh's neighbouring vills. Some of these Normans gained the lands of freemen who had been commended to their antecessors, but more commonly they acquired land from a host of thegns' men. Roger the Poitevin, for example, gained the land of fifteen freemen commended to a variety of pre-Conquest lords, including the Abbot of Ely, William de Warenne's antecessor and Geoffrey de Mandeville's antecessor, and Hervey de Bourges picked up the land of seven freemen, including one commended to Robert Malet's antecessor. (See figure 6.2.) Each of these new lords was

---

[144] Douglas, *Feudal Documents*, pp. 56–7.   [145] DB, ii, 413a.   [146] DB, ii, 442a.
[147] DB, ii, 314b.   [148] DB, ii, 346b.
[149] DB, ii, 300a, 315b, 346a, 386a, 412b, 423b, 441b.

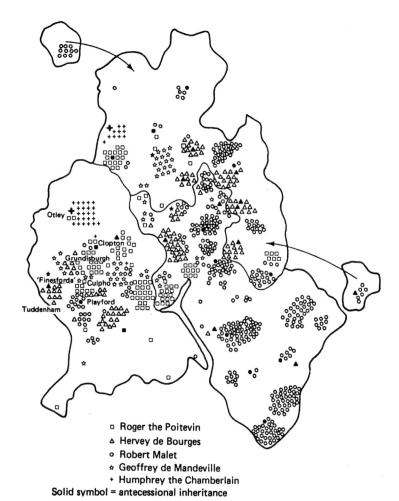

Figure 6.1 TRW lordships in the Suffolk hundreds of Carlford, Loes and Wilford

able, then, through his proximity to Grundisburgh, to attract or terrorize freemen into his orbit. Illegal and extra-legal annexations, coupled with the extension of lordship, make sense of the whole sale compacting of pre-Conquest tenancies, occurring in East Anglia between 1066 and 1086. Roger Bigot's holding at Darsham, for example, is better explained by private enterprise than royal magnanimity. Roger's holding in the vill was made up of the lands of nine men:

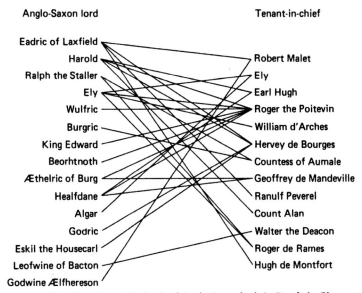

Figure 6.2 The disposition of the lands of Anglo-Saxon lords in *Finesforda*, Clopton, Tuddenham, Grundisburg and Playford

one was Toli's man...Leofric Cobbe [was another] over whom Æthelweard the king's reeve had half the commendation; Thorkil, over whom the same Æthelweard had half the commendation; Alnoth, a man of Northmann the Sheriff; Brunmann Beard, half Northmann's man and half Brunmer's; Wulfric the Deacon, the man of Godwine Algarson; Osmund, the man of Eadric of Laxfield... [Further] sixteen acres and a virgate which Ælfgifu a free woman held TRE. Over her Northmann had commendation. Twenty-four acres less one virgate which Blæchmann held TRE. The same Blæchmann was the man of Eadric of Laxfield.[150]

East Anglia and the eastern midlands were particularly susceptible to such pressures, because of the regions' propensity for modest landholders. It is probable, however, that the high ratio of lands appropriated to lands granted could also be found outside of the Danelaw. Edward of Salisbury's honour in Wiltshire was formed from three estates inherited from his antecessor Wulfwynn, but the remaining land came from the holdings of men bearing twenty-nine names.[151] About half of Judhael of Totnes's land in Devonshire was inherited from his

[150] DB, ii, 334b.   [151] DB, i, 69r–69v.

antecessors Alwine, Ælfric, Algar, Heca and Aubrey, but the rest came to him from thirty-four other thegns.[152] Similarly, in Somerset, Robert Count of Mortain held the lands of something like fifty pre-Conquest thegns, Roger de Courseulles of fifty-three, and William de Mohun thirty-five.[153] Despite all five of these fees' compact nature, hundreds did not act as their building blocks. Each fee ranged over a number of shared hundreds, and none of them were the only fees in the hundreds in which they lay to have been built from a whole collection of pre-Conquest tenancies. Like hundredal honours north of Watling Street, these five West Country fees were fairly compact, but unlike them, they were pieced together much more haphazardly from bits and pieces. And although they were limited to a particular region within a county, they were not as compact as the hundredal fees of Yorkshire or Kent. It is as if barons, given a foothold in the region, conquered the land about them or drove Englishmen with their lands into their fees.

What we have, then, in some fees and in certain parts of England, particularly those regions where holdings were small and freemen and minor thegns were numerous, is the establishment of a kleptocracy, which supplemented royal grants through a self-interested and aggressive private enterprise, based on theft, intimidation and the extension of protection. The actions of this kleptocracy profoundly affected the Norman settlement and were more important in some regions in the formation of Norman honours than was antecession. These acts of private despoliation explain why the overwhelming majority of land of thousands of freemen and thegns fell to the Normans in just twenty years. Neither the Conqueror nor his ministers could oversee the reallocation of the lands and rights held by each and every one of these for the most part obscure men. But given a foothold in neighbourhoods where the old guard had disappeared, Normans were certainly capable, as we have seen, of seeing to such a reallocation, even if they were not legally empowered to do so. And we can see them nibbling away everywhere at the ancient tenurial pattern. In Essex a man of Haimo Dapifer annexed thirteen acres and Domesday Book notes that 'he still has the spoils from them',[154] while in Dorset the Abbot of Cerne's

---

[152] DB, i, 108v–110r.   [153] DB, i, 91v–93r; 93r–94v; 95v–96v.   [154] DB, ii, 99a.

manors of Bloxworth and Affpuddle had been 'plundered' by Hugh fitz Grip.[155] These actions – the spoiling and the plundering – do not sound like the work of the orderly, king-fearing Normans of traditional English historiography, but rather like the crimes perpetrated by Normans in southern Italy and Sicily, where chroniclers complained that Norman bully boys 'seized everything for themselves...plundering without king and without law'.[156]

The case against Norman barons is admittedly circumstantial. Domesday's legal disputes are by and large between Norman and Norman. Even so, they are telling because they serve to remind us that William's new lords acted aggressively against their neighbours as they extended and consolidated their own holdings. Beyond Domesday, evidence suggests that these same barons moved against ecclesiastical communities whenever the opportunity presented itself. The descriptions of pleas held to put right the losses of churchmen and the writs sent out to ensure reseisin are all, without exception, in favour of saints and their communities. Thus, the evidence we possess suggests that Normans grasped what land they could, even if they had to steal from Norman barons and abbots. This habit of predation would clearly have extended to the Normans' more vulnerable English neighbours. Lordless, for the most part after 1071, these men were easy prey. Although Englishmen after the Conquest were rarely in the position to petition the king to redress their grievances or preserve whatever writs or reassurances they might acquire, a case for the extra-legal seizure of their land can be made from sporadic references in Domesday Book and from the patterns of Norman landholding fossilized in the survey. The picture that emerges is one of massive private enterprise on the part of William's barons, many of whom acquired a large portion of their English fees by themselves, without writ or warrant. It is impossible to conjure up exact figures for this kind of activity, but a loose estimate based on landholding patterns in Domesday suggests that something like a fifth of all land in secular fees descended to Normans by antecessorial inheritance. Of this probably just over 10 per cent came from the holdings of antecessors with over £25 of land and the remaining from petty local gentry with perhaps five or six

[155] DB, i, 77v.
[156] John the Monk, *Chronicon Vulternenses*, ed. Vincenzo Federici, 3 vols., *Fonti per la Storia d'Italia* (Rome, 1924–38), i, p. 231.

farms worth something like £10 or £15 a year.[157] Something over a third of all land in England came to Normans through territorial grants often based on hundreds or wapentakes. The remaining land fell to Normans through private acquisitions and was gained through personal conquests or the extension of lordship. The percentage of territorial grants, extra-legal seizures, and antecessorial inheritances were spread unevenly across England, creating a disorderly and confusing tenurial jumble, having far less to do with the Anglo-Saxon past than has previously been thought.[158] (See figure 6.3.)

This essential variety of land settlement serves to emphasize that much in eleventh-century government, even William the Conqueror's government, was ad hoc, or temporary, or the result of a special set of circumstances. When we set forth the diversity of acquisition in William's reign, we find no all-encompassing rule and no single, central plan. Instead, we see that tens of thousands of holdings passed to new lords in the course of twenty years. Many were confiscated by the king from the great Saxon magnates who warred against him and then were granted out to his supporters. Others were used to build compact, defensive fees, centred on a castle, and planted in districts of uncertain loyalty or used to form territories built as spring-boards for further aggression. These acquisitions had at their roots a royal grant. But the amount of land available and the power and aggression of William's own followers meant that much land was acquired outside the king's gift through the extension of lordship, through the private settlement of lawsuits, or through raw aggression. Thus small, private conquests play a central role in transforming the tenurial map of England. This, in the end, brings us to Domesday Book itself, and its reasons for being. J. C. Holt has asked the crucial question: Why did William's great tenants-in-

---

[157] The lands of some of these minor holders could have ended up in the fees they did simply because they put themselves under a single Norman for protection or because their lands lay in a single hundred. Thus, some Norman holdings are disguised in Domesday as antecessorial inheritance, but are in reality extra-legal or territorial grants. See above, pp. 204–7.

[158] Each of these regions takes in counties from different Domesday circuits. The region with the highest percentage of antecessorial inheritance includes shires surveyed in three circuits; the second highest in five circuits. The region with the largest numbers of extra-legal seizures encompasses four circuits, and the region with the highest territorial settlement covers five circuits. Thus, the difference in settlement is not simply a mirage caused by the nature of Domesday evidence, but rather reflects real differences in settlement patterns.

Areas with a high percentage
of territorial settlement

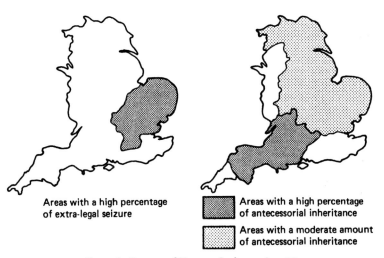

Areas with a high percentage
of extra-legal seizure

Areas with a high percentage
of antecessorial inheritance

Areas with a moderate amount
of antecessorial inheritance

Figure 6.3 Patterns of Norman Settlement in 1086

chief co-operate in the making of Domesday, and has answered
that they did so to obtain a 'record of their tenure, in effect
a confirmation of their enfeoffment'.[159] But his answer is
incomplete. Where he posits that Normans participated in the
making of this *carta regis*[160] to protect themselves against the
encroachments of their neighbours and to gain written title to
lands which had come to them without written order, I would

[159] J. C. Holt, '1086', pp. 41–64, especially pp. 55–6.
[160] So called in Hemming, i, p. 298; Holt, '1086', pp. 56–7.

suggest that they did so to secure their tenures and to gain warranty for lands they had acquired on their own. The advantages for both sides are obvious. The barons, for their part, obtained written rights to their spoils. But William was able to put a cap on private conquests, stopping, with a single kingdom-wide inquest, private acquisition, and transforming every baronial holding into that characteristic English feudal tenancy – that is, of all land in England held 'of the king'. This perfect feudal pyramid was the product not of the Norman Conquest, but the Domesday Inquest.

Chapter 7

ARISTOCRATIC LANDHOLDING
AND ROYAL POWER IN THE
ELEVENTH CENTURY

Contemporary chroniclers found the relationship between Edward the Confessor and his great lords prior to 1066 and that of William I and his barons in the decades after to be compelling subjects. Edward's eulogy in the *Anglo-Saxon Chronicle* was fashioned around the king's piety and his relations with those who helped him rule. It described the king as a 'ruler of heroes', 'strong in council' and 'loyally' obeyed.[1] The Conqueror's eulogist was struck most forcibly by the king's parsimony and his greed, but he was impressed nonetheless with William's ruthless ability to make the mighty heed his will, describing him as 'so very stern and violent a man, that no one dared do anything contrary to his desire. He had earls in his fetters, who acted against [him].'[2] These final portraits present a highly stylized picture of strong monarchs and obedient lords, but there are also numerous accounts from each reign of aristocratic disaffection and revolt.[3] Ambiguous and elusive, the narrative sources alone provide neither a straightforward assessment of royal power in the eleventh century nor the information necessary to judge whether England's most important aristocrats had resources sufficient to allow them to follow a strictly independent and self-interested course. Evidence in Domesday Book, however, furnishes both. Its record of landholding and wealth on either side of the Norman Conquest enables the historian, however tentatively, to compare directly royal and aristocratic resources and allows us to measure the changing economic balance between Edward the Confessor and his greatest aristocrats on the one hand and William the Conqueror and his magnates on the other.

---

[1] *ASC*, s.a. 1065 (C, D).   [2] *ASC*, s.a. 1086 (E).
[3] For Edward's reign see *ASC*, s.a. 1046 (C), 1048 (E), 1049 (C, E), 1050 (D), 1051 (D, E), 1052 (C, D, E), 1064 (E), 1065 (C, D). For William's reign see *ASC*, s.a. 1067 (D), 1068 (D, E), 1069 (D, E), 1071 (D, E), 1075 (E), 1076 (D), 1079 (D, E), 1086 (E).

Information in Domesday, as we have seen, shows emphatically that the eleventh century twice witnessed the refashioning of aristocratic landholding; first in that period on either side of Cnut's accession and then again in the two decades following the Battle of Hastings. In both periods powerful men and their kin were generously endowed with estates and offices, but they helped themselves to land as well, often supplementing dramatically the farms and villages given to them with lands belonging by right to other men. Although the upheavals in landholding and the establishment of new men in the kingdom's highest circles mark each eleventh-century conquest, the results of the two tenurial revolutions were dramatically different. The first of these hamstrung the king and the second empowered him.

To determine how and why this is so, we are compelled to delve briefly and finally into the perilous world of Domesday statistics, because it appears that the qualitative differences between Edward's kingship and William's can be explained in part by the quantitative differences we find in the landed wealth of pre- and post-Conquest kings and their greatest lords. Before doing so, qualifications, as always, must be made. First, the limitations of Domesday, in particular its statistics, make any figures derived from it the grossest of approximations. Second, an absolute comparison of Domesday's TRE and TRW information is impossible, since the Conquest brought about a distinct increase in land values in some regions and a marked decline in others. Third, William the Conqueror's tenants-in-chief tended to enfeoff their own followers with at least half their English lands. Although subtenancies existed in the Saxon period, they were less formal, less often acknowledged by Domesday juries, and were not directly equivalent to Norman subinfeudations. As a result, comparisons of pre- and post-Conquest holdings are imperfect. Fourth, Domesday Book's information is at times temporally confused. Earls Godwine and Ælfgar, long dead by 1066, both appear as major landholders on the day King Edward died; presumably the bulk of their land continued to be held by their sons and wives. Similarly, a number of important Norman magnates, the most famous of whom is Odo Bishop of Bayeux, had fallen on hard times by the Inquest, but appear, nonetheless, as major holders of land. For certain fees, therefore, TRW figures do not represent landholding in 1086, but for some moment earlier in the reign. Finally, when comparing the endowments of pre- and post-Conquest lords it is difficult to decide who exactly to compare. While the Confessor's comital families, especially those of Earls Godwine and Leofric, stand out as an elite whose enormous wealth separated them from all other secular land-holders, it is not clear which post-Conquest families were their political and economic heirs. This last problem is perhaps more easily overcome than the others. It seems reasonable, in an attempt to determine the relation between the king's resources and those of his greatest magnates, to compare the holdings of the families of Edward's earls with those of the families of William's 'Class A' barons, those men identified long ago by William Corbett as the richest and most important of the Conqueror's followers.[4]

The families of William's 'Class A' barons established themselves in England in the late 1060s and early 1070s. Like Edgar the Peaceable's and William Longsword's supporters long before, the Conqueror's wealthiest followers were a mixture of close kinsmen, trusted friends and important officials. These families were the brothers Odo Bishop of Bayeux and Robert Count of Mortain; Roger of Montgomery and his son Roger the Poitevin; Alan of Richmond; Richard and Baldwin of Clare; Eustace of Boulogne and his wife; William de Warenne; Geoffrey de Mandeville; Hugh d'Avranches; and Geoffrey Bishop of Coutances. Of these men, the Count of Mortain and the Bishop of Bayeux were the king's own half-brothers. The Montgomeries, the Clares, Alan of Richmond, William de Warenne, and possibly Bishop Geoffrey were all the king's cousins, or thought they were.[5] Each of these families were important landholders and supporters of the duke's regime before Hastings. Roger of Montgomery and Hugh d'Avranches each supplied Duke William with sixty ships for his English expedition and Odo

---

[4] Corbett, 'The development of the duchy of Normandy', in *The Cambridge Medieval History*, v, pp. 505–13. Corbett's list of 'Class A' barons has been improved since its first appearance. Odo Bishop of Bayeux and Robert Count of Mortain, as brothers of the king, were not included by Corbett in his list of the wealthiest barons in Domesday Book, but they are regularly treated as such by other historians (Le Patourel, *The Norman Empire*, pp. 335–6; Hollister, 'The greater Domesday tenants-in-chief', *Domesday Studies*, p. 220). Alan of Richmond and Geoffrey de Mandeville were excluded by Corbett as well, but both held the requisite £750 of land that set 'Class A' barons apart from other men. (See Hollister, 'The greater Domesday tenants-in-chief', pp. 220 and 242.) I have not included William fitz Osbern's holding in this analysis, since he died so early in the reign.

[5] Cokayne, *Complete Peerage*, xi, pp. 683–7; xii, pt 1, p. 492; Douglas, *William the Conqueror*, pp. 423, 418, 422, 426; Eleanor Searle, *Predatory Kinship*, p. 321, n. 13.

Bishop of Bayeux provided one hundred.[6] Robert Count of
Mortain, Roger of Montgomery, and Roger de Mowbray,
brother of Geoffrey Bishop of Coutances, along with Richard fitz
Gilbert and his brother Baldwin, Sheriff of Devon, were
numbered by contemporaries among the most important of Duke
William's Norman barons in 1066;[7] and Odo, Robert of Mortain,
Roger of Montgomery, William de Warenne and Hugh
d'Avranches were among a small group of magnates who were
William's staunchest supporters in Normandy.[8] The Count of
Mortain controlled a large marcher apanage along the Maine–
Breton frontier.[9] The Montgomeries, in addition to their
considerable holdings in north-central Normandy, had acquired
through marriage the vast inheritance of the lords of Bellême in
southern Normandy and beyond its frontiers.[10] Hugh held the
hereditary vicomte of the Avranchin,[11] Alan of Richmond was a
count in Brittany,[12] and Eustace of Boulogne held three counties
– Boulogne, Guines and Therouanne. The men of these nine
families were also trusted royal *fideles* after the Conquest. Odo,
William de Warenne and Richard fitz Gilbert all served as vice-
regents in England,[13] and Robert Count of Mortain was left in
charge of Lindsey c. 1069, when the area was threatened by
Danish attack.[14] Geoffrey de Mandeville was the Sheriff of
London,[15] Middlesex and Essex,[16] and probably custodian of the
Tower of London.[17] Roger of Montgomery was placed in charge
of the Rapes of Chichester and Arundel in 1067, and the earldom
of Shrewsbury in 1071.[18] Alan was made Lord of Richmond,[19]
Hugh became Earl of Chester, Baldwin of Clare served as Sheriff

---

[6] A facsimile of this text and a transcription of it are printed in Elizabeth M. C. van
Houts, 'The ship list of William the Conqueror', *Anglo-Norman Studies*, 10 (1988),
pp. 175–6. This list, however, has clearly suffered some corruption and is certainly not
comprehensive. On the value and reliability of the list see van Houts, 'Ship list',
pp. 159–84 and Hollister, 'The greater Domesday tenants-in-chief', pp. 221–3, 243.

[7] OV, ii, p. 140.   [8] Douglas, *William the Conqueror*, pp. 272–3.

[9] Jean-François Lemarignier, *Recherches sur l'Hommage en marche et les frontières féodales*
(Lille, 1945), pp. 67–8; Jacque Boussard, 'Le comte de Mortain au xi⁵ siecle', *Moyen
Age*, 58 (1952), pp. 253–79.

[10] John Le Patourel, *Norman Barons*, (rpt, London, 1971), pp. 16–18.

[11] Douglas, *William the Conqueror*, p. 54.

[12] OV, ii, p. 206. However, all members of the ruling family were styled count in the
eleventh century (*EYC*, iv, pt 1, p. 98).   [13] OV, ii, p. 316; *ASC*, s.a. 1066 (D).

[14] OV, ii, p. 230.

[15] *Facsimiles of English Royal Writs to A.D. 1100*, ed. T. A. M. Bishop and P. Chaplais
(Oxford, 1957), n. 15.   [16] *Regesta*, i, n. 181.

[17] R. H. C. Davis, *King Stephen* (Berkeley, 1967), p. 59.   [18] OV, ii, p. 210.

[19] OV, iv, p. 48; *EYC*, iv, pt 1, p. 86.

Table 7.1 *The values of lands of England's wealthiest families TRW*

Family	In demesne	Enfeoffed	Total
King's brothers	£1,690	£3,540	£5,230
The Montgomeries	1,240	1,160	2,400
Alan of Richmond	770	430	1,200
The Clares	620	530	1,150
William de Warenne	550	540	1,090
Eustace of Boulogne	610	300	910
Hugh d'Avranche	430	610	1,040
Bishop of Coutances	230	540	770
Geoffrey de Mandeville	490	240	730
Total	6,630	7,890	14,520

of Devon,[20] and Bishop Geoffrey was one of William's most active justiciars.[21] Thus, between 1066 and 1086 England's greatest aristocratic families had been transformed. Not only were the families themselves different, but their relationship with the king had changed. Most were ducal kinsmen, all had served William long and well, and all owed their English acquisitions in a very real sense to the king.

Of equal importance, the cash these families derived from their English lands was modest compared to that of their Anglo-Saxon predecessors. Combined, the value of the nine wealthiest families' demesne in the last decade of the Conqueror's reign was only about 80 per cent of the value of the Godwinesons' estates in 1065 and about 60 per cent of the holdings of all the Confessor's earls, wives, and children. (See table 7.1 and table 3.1.) If one compares the value of entire fiefs of Norman families, that is, both the demesne and enfeoffed lands, with the demesne holdings and the holdings of the men of Anglo-Saxon comital families (admittedly a problematic comparison), it appears that the 'Class A' families together accrued benefits from only about half as much land as did their English counterparts. The endowments of England's wealthiest lords and their men, then, were reduced significantly between 1066 and 1086, and this in spite of the fact that the number of great families had increased. It has often been observed that the lands of many thousands of Anglo-Saxon landholders

<hr>

[20] DB, i, 105v.   [21] Douglas, *William the Conqueror*, p. 306.

were consolidated and placed into the hands of a mere 144 tenants-in-chief. What has not been recognized, however, is that, as the figures just quoted make clear, this oft perceived consolidation of landholding did not take place in the very greatest estates; instead, the lands of the wealthiest Anglo-Saxon families in England were broken apart, and William's reign, rather than witnessing the growth of this class of endowment, saw to its diminution.

The estates of Anglo-Norman barons, moreover, were more geographically limited. In 1066 the Godwinesons held land in thirty-two counties, the Leofricsons in twenty-one, and the Siwardsons in nine. After the Conquest, the most far-flung constellation of estates, covering twenty-one counties, belonged to the combined holdings of the king's brothers. Next came the holdings of Earl Hugh, which stretched across twenty shires. The bishop of Coutances's fee was spread across thirteen. William de Warenne, Alan of Brittany, Eustace of Boulogne and the Montgomeries were each enfeoffed in twelve counties, Geoffrey de Mandeville in ten, and the Clares in nine. Thus not even the widest holdings had the extent of the Godwinesons' land and none but the king's brothers' fiefs and the fee of Earl Hugh came near to matching the reach of the Leofricsons. Furthermore, the bulk of most post-Conquest fees were confined quite narrowly to a single region. Geoffrey de Mandeville held predominantly around Middlesex, Hertfordshire, and Essex; Hugh Earl of Chester in Cheshire, Yorkshire and Lincolnshire, Eustace of Boulogne in the southeast, Bishop Geoffrey in the West Country, and Count Alan in Lincolnshire and East Anglia.[22] Thus the commonplace notion that Norman honours were more diffuse than similar Anglo-Scandinavian holdings does not apply to the largest English estates.

In Edward's reign there was also a tendency for the most powerful families to accumulate vast holdings in counties where men like themselves held not at all. In 1065 the Godwinesons possessed lands valued at at least twice that of the other comital families in eighteen counties, and the Leofricsons did so in seven. (See figure 7.1.) William's brothers, on the other hand, held twice the demesne of the other great families in only six counties, the

---

[22] Geoffrey de Mandeville held just under three-quarters of his demesne land in these counties, and Eustace of Boulogne just over three-quarters. Earl Hugh held 98 per cent in this region and Count Alan of Richmond 96 per cent.

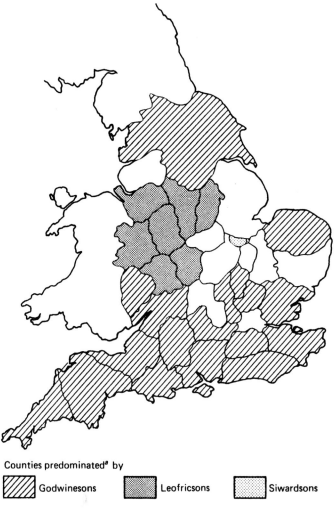

Counties predominated[a] by

Godwinesons   Leofricsons   Siwardsons

[a]Counties in which one of Edward's comital families held a minimum of twice the demesne of the other comital families

Figure 7.1 The balance of landed wealth in 1065

Montgomeries in five, Geoffrey de Mandeville, Alan of Richmond and the Clares in two, and Eustace of Boulogne, Geoffrey Bishop of Coutances and William de Warenne in one. (See figure 7.2.) Furthermore, during the Confessor's reign, one comital family held at least £100 more demesne than the others in

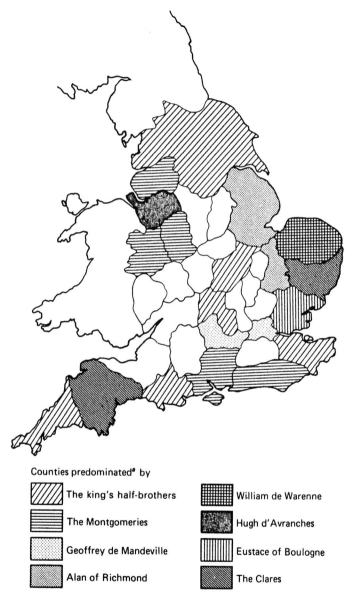

Counties predominated^a by

The king's half-brothers

The Montgomeries

Geoffrey de Mandeville

Alan of Richmond

William de Warenne

Hugh d'Avranches

Eustace of Boulogne

The Clares

^aCounties in which a single family held a minimum of twice the demesne of the other great families

Figure 7.2 The balance of landed wealth in 1086

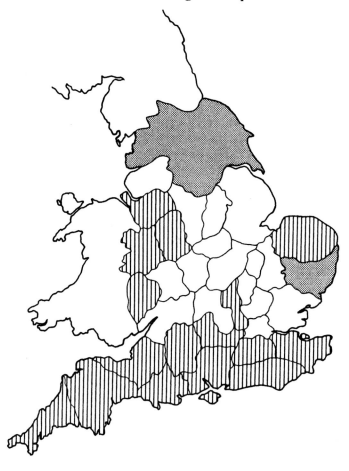

Counties in which one comital family held a minimum of £100 more than the others

Counties in which one comital family held a minimum of £100 more than the others and in which two or more comital families held at least £75 in demesne

Figure 7.3 Comital holdings TRE

eighteen counties. (see figure 7.3.) By the 1080s this state of affairs existed in only twelve counties, and in seven of these at least one other 'Class A' family held extensive tracts of land.[23] (See figure 7.7.) So, it appears that earls in the late-Saxon period were able to

[23] That is, a minimum of £75 of land.

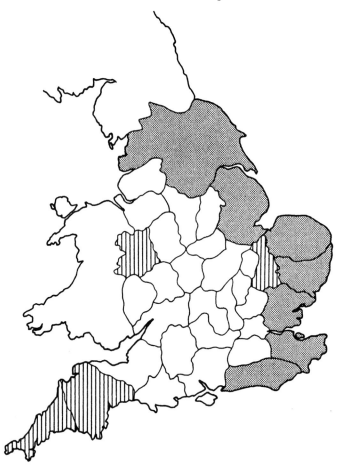

Counties in which one 'Class A' family held a minimum of £100 more than the others

Counties in which one 'Class A' family held a minimum of £100 more than the others and in which two or more 'Class A' families held at least £75 in demesne

Figure 7.4 'Class A' holdings TRW

consolidate their holdings in regions where men of their own class were absent, but Norman barons' opportunities for similar estate building were more limited. A closer examination of aristocratic estates in individual shires shows that during the Confessor's reign, family holdings worth at least £100 more than those of the

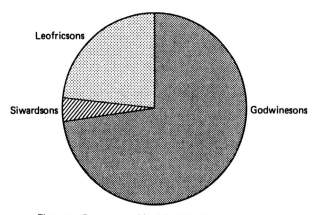

Figure 7.5 Percentage of land held by the earls in 1065

next wealthiest magnate family were found in areas where the king traditionally based his power – in Devonshire, Wiltshire, Somerset, Dorset, Hampshire, Surrey, Kent and Buckinghamshire. By the Norman period similarly compact county holdings were found almost exclusively on the outskirts of the kingdom, especially along the southern and eastern coasts. After the Conquest, then, the expansion of great lords was checked by other mighty barons or the king, whose own jealously guarded interests would have been threatened by the growth of another's local influence.

Not only were the fees of William's wealthiest baronial families more limited geographically, but they were more evenly allotted than the holdings of Edward's comital families. In the last years of the Confessor's life there had been a wide disparity of wealth among England's comital families. (See figure 7.5.) In 1065 the Godwinesons' land was valued at three times that of the Leofricsons' and almost twenty times that of the Siwardsons.[24] In contrast, William's half-brothers controlled only one and a third times the demesne of the next wealthiest family, the Montgomeries. (See figure 7.6.) Although these two families were in possession of approximately 45 per cent of the total 'Class A' demesne, their combined portion was valued nonetheless at about a third less than the Godwinesons' estates. The seven other 'Class A' families controlled the remaining land in fairly even proportions. Thus, while the Montgomeries along with the

[24] See above, chapter 3, pp. 58–63.

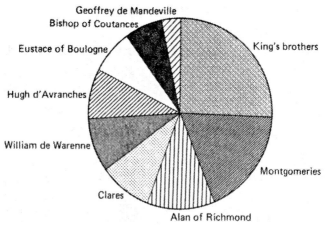

Figure 7.6 Demesne of 'Class A' families TRW

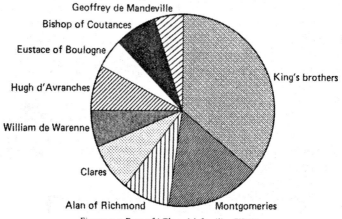

Figure 7.7 Fees of 'Class A' families TRW

brothers Odo and Robert held more demesne than William's other great men, the glaring imbalance of aristocratic wealth found in the Confessor's time no longer prevailed. Similar statistics performed on these men's entire fiefs – both demesne and enfeoffed land – produce similar figures. (See figure 7.7.) The king's half-brothers held about a third of the 'Class A' lands and the Montgomeries just under a fifth. The remaining 50 per cent was divided fairly evenly among the other 'Class A' families. Thus, a general comparison of the holdings of the greatest Anglo-Norman and Anglo-Saxon families illustrates several basic

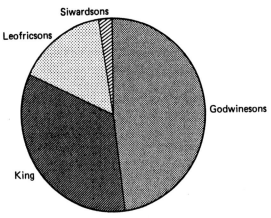

Figure 7.8 Percentage of land held by the king and his earls in 1065

changes between c. 1066 and c. 1086. First, individual Anglo-Saxon families controlled far more land in far more counties than did their Anglo-Norman counterparts; second, the wealthiest baronial families held fees more similar in size than the Confessor's comital families; and third, the total land held directly by England's wealthiest aristocratic families had shrunk as a result of the events of 1066.

The changes the Conquest wrought in the balance of aristocratic resources were echoed in the balance of resources between the king and his greatest lay lords. In the last decade of the Confessor's reign, the Siwardsons's landed wealth was valued at something like 7.5 per cent of the royal demesne and the Leofricsons' land was worth about 60 per cent of the *terra regis*. The Godwinesons' land, however, was valued at approximately 125 per cent of the *terra regis* in 1066 and 140 per cent before Tostig's fall. After the Conquest, the ratio of baronial demesne to royal demesne was reduced dramatically. The value of William's half-brothers' demesne was equivalent to just 15 per cent and the Montgomeries' demesne just 10 per cent of the value of the *terra regis*. The value of the other great Anglo-Norman magnates' demesne lands were worth between 2 per cent and 6 per cent of the royal demesne. The transformation of landholding patterns between 1066 and 1086 can also be approached by considering the values of royal and upper-aristocratic holdings as percentages of the total value of all such holdings. (See figures 7.8 and 7.9.) When the *terra regis* and the demesne holdings of the 'Class A'

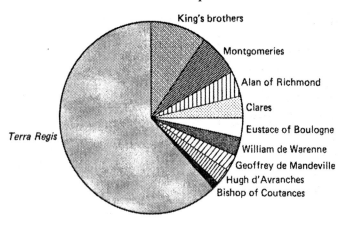

Figure 7.9 The *terra regis* and the demesne of William's 'Class A' families TRW

families are added together, the portion controlled by William's half-brothers is about a tenth. Other great baronial families held from one to 7 per cent of this land. William, however, held approximately two-thirds of this land. By comparison, in 1066 the Godwinesons held 43 per cent (or in 1065 about 48 per cent), the Leofricsons 20.5 per cent, the Siwardsons 2.5 per cent, and the king 34 per cent. Thus, the total percentage of upper aristocratic demesne in 1086 was approximately equal to the percentage of land held by the Confessor in 1066. More importantly, William the Conqueror held 64 per cent of this land by 1086. In 1066 it had been the Godwinesons and the Leofricsons who controlled 64, and King Edward a mere 34 per cent. Thus, within twenty years of Edward's death, the ratio of royal to aristocratic landed wealth had been inverted.

The question remains: was the tenurial revolution effected by the Norman Conquest and settlement the result of a conscious plan initiated by the Conqueror or simply fortuitous circumstance? With regard to the distribution of aristocratic lands TRW, it is clear that the impetus for the greater consolidation of demesne holdings lay with William's barons rather than with the king. Although William insisted on knight's service and the payment of geld in return for land, he had little say over the way in which tenants-in-chief disposed of their English holdings. The duties of some of his men did, in part, determine this. Hugh d'Avranches, as earl of Chester, sensibly maintained the greater part of his lands in Cheshire. William de Warenne and Roger of Montgomery, both in charge of Sussex Rapes, each held over £100 of their Sussex lands in demesne, and Robert of Mortain, as Earl of Cornwall, and Baldwin of Clare, as Sheriff of Devon, kept hold of many of their West County estates. Nonetheless, in regions where they had no official duties, magnates appear to have retained or enfeoffed their lands as they saw fit. Moreover, much of the land gained by William's adherents in England was acquired privately. The shape of a number of honours, therefore, sometimes owed as much to personal initiative as it did to royal favour. Similarly, the difficulties that grew out of the twin problems of an inadequate *terra regis* and over-large comital endowments were solved not by the Conqueror but by the Saxon earls themselves. The Godwineson holdings were shattered when the sons of Godwine lay dead on the field of Hastings. But Harold had already done the important work; on his accession he combined the bulk of his family's West Saxon estates with the *terra regis*. The surviving earls disgraced themselves by 1075. As a result, within nine years of William's victory, every hide and every ox once held by an Anglo-Saxon earl had escheated to the king. Had William come to the throne peaceably, on terms such as he is said to have offered Earl Harold, he would have faced many of the same problems that had plagued the Confessor: a shrunken fisc, over-wealthy magnates who owed him little, and competition for men and estates in the region where the majority of his own holdings lay. Thus, fortuitous circumstance rather than royal policy lead to the dispersion of Anglo-Saxon comital holdings. Finally, the royal demesne was shored up because the Confessor's habit of lavishly patronizing earls' wives, brothers and children was put to a halt. That this happened owes as much to Norman tradition as William's foresight. Aristocratic landholding in Normandy had evolved earlier in the century from the traditional Carolingian pattern of collateral kin-groups to a new, lineage-based pattern characterized by primogeniture, by the association of aristocratic families with a major castle or caput, and by the adoption of a family toponym. Although the Conquest sometimes provided opportunities for Norman aristocratic cadets to establish honours of their own, Normans were clearly less insistent than Englishmen that a ruler should endow every son.[25] The result was that both in Normandy and in England, William was more successful than Edward in balancing wealth and power between a number of lineages. Thus, William's good fortune, so evident at Hastings, played a decisive role in the rebalancing of royal and aristocratic wealth. Still, William and his sons kept close watch on their wealthiest magnates, and those who showed signs of modelling their behaviour on that of the more independent Anglo-Saxon earls were disinherited. Indeed, by 1100 the fees of Odo, Roger the Poitevin, Eustace of Boulogne and Geoffrey of Coutances had escheated, and by the end of Henry I's reign the Count of Mortain's son, the sons of Roger of Montgomery and Geoffrey de Mandeville had disgraced themselves as well.[26] Thus, within two generations of Hastings well over half the land held by William's 'Class A' families had fallen once again to the king, and were broken up and given out to more trustworthy adherents.

Although the dramatic change in landholding witnessed by Domesday Book may not have been the result of any royal scheme, it was, nonetheless, a fact of political life by 1086. Conscious or not, this redistribution of lands had important effects on royal power and aristocratic independence. The extent and value of their lands in 1086 suggest that Norman barons as individuals and as a class were easier to control than their late Saxon counterparts. The regions in which the bulk of their wealth was derived were limited, unlike the holdings of their English progenitors, to the outskirts of the kingdom, placing their resources in areas where invasions were most likely and rebellions least potent. By 1086 the aristocracy, too, was more balanced; no one family could dominate all others, and no single lineage had gained influence throughout the realm. Instead, a number of key families with relatively even resources kept one another in check, jealously guarding their lands, wealth and influence in the shires. More important, proceeds from the *terra regis* had increased

[25] Eleanor Searle suggests that one of the driving forces behind the Norman Conquest was the need of William and his greatest magnates to provide for their many sons (Searle, *Predatory Kinship*, p. 232). She notes that the Duke had three sons, William fitz Osbern had two, and Roger de Montgomery more. But, according to Domesday Book, among all these boys, only one of Roger's sons and one of fitz Osbern's received tenancies-in-chief from the king.

[26] Chibnall, *Anglo-Norman England*, pp. 73–6. And only one of the twenty-five barons of Magna Carta could trace his descent back directly to one of these Domesday families (the Clares) (J. C. Holt, 'Feudal society and the family in early medieval England: I: The revolution of 1066', *TRHS*, 32 (1982), p. 208).

dramatically in the twenty years after Edward's death, providing William with the resources for a strong rule. Thus, the restructuring of both the *terra regis* and baronial landholding contributed significantly to the re-establishment of a powerful monarch and a co-operative aristocracy in the kingdom of England.

BIBLIOGRAPHY

I PRIMARY SOURCES

(A) CHRONICLES, NARRATIVES AND LITERARY SOURCES

Alfred, *King Alfred's Old English Version of Boethius's De Consolatione Philosophiae*, ed. W. J. Sedgefield (Oxford, 1899; rpt Darmstadt, 1968).

King Alfred's Old English Version of Saint Augustine's Soliloquies, ed. H. S. Hargrove (New York, 1902).

Anglia Sacra sive Collectio Historiarum, ed. H. Wharton (London, 1691).

The Anglo-Saxon Chronicle, trans. G. N. Garmonsway, rev. edn (London, 1960).

The Anglo-Saxon Chronicle. A Revised Translation, trans. D. Whitelock, D. C. Douglas, and S. I. Tucker (London, 1961).

Anglo-Saxon Chronicle. *Two of the Saxon Chronicles Parallel*, ed. C. Plummer, 2 vols. (Oxford, 1892–99).

Asser, *Asser's Life of King Alfred*, ed. W. H. Stevenson (Oxford, 1904).

Ælfric, *Ælfric's Colloquy*, ed. G. N. Garmonsway, 2nd edn (London, 1978).

Ælfric's Lives of Saints, ed. W. W. Skeat, 4 vols., Early English Text Society, o.s. 76, 82, 94, 114 (Oxford, 1881–1900).

The Old English Version of the Heptateuch, Ælfric's Treatise of the Old and the New Testament and his Preface to Genesis, ed. S. J. Crawford, The Early English Text Society, 160 (1922).

Æthelweard, *The Chronicle of Æthelweard*, ed. A. Campbell (London, 1962).

B, 'The B Life of Saint Dunstan', *Memorials of Saint Dunstan Archbishop of Canterbury*, ed. W. Stubbs, RS (London, 1874).

The Battle of Maldon, ed. E. V. Gordon (London, 1937).

Bede, *Historia Ecclesiastica Gentis Anglorum*, ed. and trans. B. Colgrave and R. A. B. Mynors, Oxford Medieval Texts (Oxford, 1969).

The Old English Version of Bede's Ecclesiastical History, ed. T. Miller, Early English Text Society, 4 vols. (Oxford, 1890–98).

Beowulf, ed. F. Klaeber, 3rd edn (Lexington, Mass., 1950).

Boniface, *Die Briefe des Heiligen Bonifatius und Lullus*, ed. M. Tangl, MGH, Epsitolae Selectae, vol. 1 (Berlin, 1916).

The Carmen de Hasetingae Proelio of Guy Bishop of Amiens, ed. C. Morton and H. Muntz, Oxford Medieval Texts (Oxford, 1972).

Cartularium Monasterii de Rameseia, ed. W. H. Hart and P. A. Lyons, RS, 3 vols. (London, 1884–93).

Bibliography

Chronicle of Battle Abbey, ed. E. Searle, Oxford Medieval Texts (Oxford, 1980).

Chronicon Monasterii de Abingdon, ed. J. Stevenson, RS, 2 vols. (London, 1858).

Chronicon Abbatiae de Evesham, ed. W. D. Macray, RS (London, 1863).

Chronicon Abbatiae Rameseiensis, ed. W. D. Macray, RS (London, 1886).

Eadmer, *Eadmeri Historia Novorum in Anglia*, ed. M. Rule, RS (London, 1884).

    Vita Sancti Oswaldi, in *The Historians of the Church of York and its Archbishops*, ed. J. Raine, RS, 3 vols. (London, 1879–94).

Encomium Emmae Reginae, ed. A. Campbell, Camden Third Series, 72 (London, 1949).

'Florence of Worcester', *Florentii Wigorniensis Monachi Chronicon ex Chronicis*, ed. B. Thorpe, 2 vols. (London, 1848–49).

Frithegodi Monachi Breuiloquium Vitae Beati Wilfredi et Cantoris Narratio Metrica de Sancto Swithuno, ed. A. Campbell (Zurich, 1950).

Gaimar, Jeffrey, *L'Estorie des Engles*, ed. A. Bell, Anglo-Norman Text Society (Oxford, 1960).

Historia Monasterii S. Augustini Cantuariensis, ed. C. Hardwick, RS (London, 1858).

Historians of the Church of York and its Archbishops, ed. J. Raine, RS, 3 vols. (London, 1879–94).

Historiola de Primordiis Episcopatus Somersetensis, in *Ecclesiastical Documents*, ed. J. Hunter, Camden Society (London, 1840).

Hemming, *Hemingi Chartularium Ecclesiae Wigorniensis*, ed. T. Hearne, 2 vols. (Oxford, 1727).

Henry of Huntingdon, *Historia Anglorum*, ed. T. Arnold, RS (London, 1879).

Hermann, *Hermanni Archidiaconi Liber Miraculis Sancti Eadmundi*, in *Memorials of St Edmund's Abbey*, ed. T. Arnold, RS (London, 1890–96), i, pp. 26–92.

Hugh Candidus, *The Chronicle of Hugh Candidus*, ed. W. T. Mellows (London, 1949).

    Relatio Heddae Abbatis, *Historiae Coenobii Burgensis Scriptores Varii*, ed. J. Sparke, *Historiae Anglicanae Scriptores*, pt 3 (London, 1723).

Hugh the Chantor, *History of the Church of York*, ed. and trans. C. Johnson (London, 1961).

De Inventione Sanctae Crucis nostrae…apud Waltham, ed. W. Stubbs (Oxford, 1861).

John of Glastonbury, *Johannis…Glastoniensis, Cronica sive Antiquitates Glastoniensis Ecclesie*, ed. J. P. Carley, trans. D. Townsend (Woodbridge, Suffolk, 1985).

    Johannis…Glastoniensis Chronica sive Historia de rebus Glastoniensibus, ed. T. Hearne, 2 vols. (Oxford, 1726).

John the Monk, *Chronicon Vulternenses*, ed. V. Federici, 3 vols., Fonti per la Storia d'Italia (Rome, 1924–38).

Liber Eliensis, ed. E. O. Blake, Camden Third Series, 92 (London, 1962).

Liber Monasterii de Hyda, ed. E. Edwards, RS (London, 1866).

Liber Vitae Ecclesiae Dunelmensis, ed. J. Stevenson (London, 1841).

Liber Vitae: Register and Martyrology of New Minster and Hyde Abbey, Winchester, ed. W. de G. Birch, Hampshire Record Society (London and Winchester, 1892).

Bibliography

Memorials of Saint Dunstan Archbishop of Canterbury, ed. W. Stubbs, RS (London, 1874).

Minge, J. P., *Patrologiae Cursus Completus, Series (Latina) Prima*, 221 vols. (Paris, 1844–64).

De Obsessione Dunelmi et probitate Uchtredi Comities, in *Symeonis Monachi Opera Omnia*, ed. T. Arnold, RS, 2 vols. (London, 1882–85).

Orderic Vitalis, *The Ecclesiastical History of Orderic Vitalis*, ed. M. Chibnall, Oxford Medieval Texts, 6 vols. (Oxford, 1969–80).

Registrum Roffense, ed. J. Thorpe (London, 1769).

Roger of Wendover, *Flores Historiarum*, ed. H. O. Coxe (London, 1841–42).

Simeon of Durham, *Symeonis Monachi Opera Omnia*, ed. T. Arnold, RS, 2 vols. (London, 1882–85).

Textus Roffensis, ed. P. Sawyer, 2 vols., *Early English Manuscripts in Facsimile*, 7, 11 (Copenhagen, 1957–62).

Vita Aedwardi Regis. Life of King Edward, ed. F. Barlow (London, 1962).

Vita Haroldi, in *Original Lives of Anglo-Saxons and Others*, ed. J. A. Giles, Caxton Society, 26 (1854).

Walsingham, Thomas, *Gesta Abatum Monasterii S. Albani a Thoma Walsingham*, ed. H. T. Riley, RS, 3 vols. (London, 1867–69).

William of Jumièges, *Gesta Normannorum Ducum*, ed. J. Marx, Société de l'Histoire de Normandie (Rouen, 1914).

William of Malmesbury, *De Antiquitate Glastonie Ecclesie*, ed. and trans. J. Scott (Woodbridge, Suffolk, 1981).

De Gestis Regum Anglorum, ed. W. Stubbs, RS, 2 vols. (London, 1887–89).

Vita Wulfstani, ed. R. R. Darlington, Camden Third Series, 40 (London, 1928).

Willelmi Malmesbiriensis de Gestis Pontificum Anglorum Libri Quinque, ed. N. E. S. A. Hamilton, RS (London, 1870).

William of Poitiers, *Histoire de Guillaume le Conquérant*, ed. and trans. R. Foreville, Les Classiques de l'Histoire de France au Moyen Age (Paris, 1952).

Wulfstan, *The Homilies of Wulfstan*, ed. D. Bethurum (Oxford, 1957).

Die 'Institutes of Polity, Civil and Ecclesiastical', ein Werk Erzbischof Wulfstans von York, ed. K. Jost, Swiss Studies in English, 47 (Bern, 1959).

Sermo Lupi ad Anglos, ed. D. Whitelock, 2nd edn (Exeter, 1976).

The York Gospels: A Facsimile with Introductory Essays, ed. N. Barker (London, 1986).

(B) LAWS, CHARTERS AND COLLECTIONS OF DOCUMENTS

Anglo-Saxon Charters, ed. and trans. A. J. Robertson (Cambridge, 1939).

Anglo-Saxon Charters: An Annotated List and Bibliography, ed. P. Sawyer, Royal Historical Society (London, 1968).

Anglo-Saxon Wills, ed. and trans. D. Whitelock (Cambridge, 1930).

Anglo-Saxon Writs, ed. and trans. F. E. Harmer (Manchester, 1952).

Calendar of Documents Preserved in France, ed. J. H. Round (London, 1899).

Bibliography

Die Canones Theodori Cantuariensis und ihre Überlieferungsformen. Untersuchungen zu den Bussüchern des 7., 8., und 9. Jahrhunderts, ed. P. Finsterwalder, vol. 1 (Weimar, 1929).

Cartularium Monasterii Sancti Johannis Baptiste de Colecestria, ed. S. A. Moore, 2 vols. (London, 1897).

Cartularium Saxonicum, ed. W. de G. Birch, 3 vols. and index (London, 1885–93, rpt. New York, 1964).

Charters of Burton Abbey, ed. P. H. Sawyer (London, 1979).

Charters of the Honour of Mowbray 1107–1191, ed. D. E. Greenway, British Academy, Records of Social and Economic History, n.s. 1 (1972).

The Charters of Rochester, ed. A. Campbell (London, 1973).

Chartes de l'Abbaye de Jumièges (v. 825–1204) conservées aux archives de la Seinte-Inferieure, ed. J. J. Vernier (Rouen and Paris, 1916).

The Chartulary of St John of Pontefract, ed. R. Holmes, 2 vols., Yorkshire Archaeological Society, 30 (1902).

Codex Diplomaticus Aevi Saxonici, ed. J. M. Kemble, 6 vols. (London, 1839–48).

Coucher Book of Selby, ed. J. T. Fowler, 2 vols. (Durham, 1881–93).

Councils and Synods with other Documents Relating to the English Church, vol. 1, ed. D. Whitelock, M. Brett, and C. N. L. Brooke (Oxford, 1981).

The Crawford Collection of Early Charters and Documents, ed. A. S. Napier and W. H. Stevenson (Oxford, 1895).

Diplomatarium Anglicum Ævi Saxonici, ed. and trans. B. Thorpe (London, 1865).

Documents Illustrating the Social and Economic History of the Danelaw, ed. F. M. Stenton, British Academy, Records of Social and Economic History, 5 (1920).

Domesday Book, seu Liber Censualis Willelmi Primi Regis Angliae, ed. A. Farley, 2 vols. (London, 1783); ed. H. Ellis, vols. 3, 4 (London, 1816).

Domesday Book, or the Great Survey of England of William the Conqueror, A.D. 1086, Zincograph Facsimiles, Ordnance Survey (Southampton, 1861–63).

Domesday Book, Facsimile Edition, ed. A. Williams *et al.* (London, 1986–).

Domesday Book, ed. J. Morris, 35 vols. (Chichester, 1974–86).

Domesday Book, trans. with commentaries in *The Victoria County Histories* (London, 1900–).

The Domesday Monachorum of Christ Church, Canterbury, ed. D. C. Douglas, Royal Historical Society (London, 1944).

Dugdale, W., *Monasticon Anglicanum*, rev. ed. J. Caley, H. Ellis and B. Bandinel, 6 vols. (1817–30).

An Eleventh Century Inquisition of St Augustine's Canterbury, ed. A. Ballard, Records in Social and Economic History of England and Wales (Oxford, 1920).

English Historical Documents, vol. 1, ed. and trans. D. Whitelock, 2nd edn (London, 1979).

English Historical Documents, vol. 2, ed. D. C. Douglas and G. W. Greenaway (London, 1953).

The Early Charters of Eastern England, ed. C. R. Hart (Leicester, 1966).

The Early Charters of Northern England and the North Midlands, ed. C. R. Hart (Leicester, 1975).

Bibliography

The Early Charters of the Thames Valley, ed. M. Gelling (Leicester, 1979).

The Early Charters of Wessex, ed. H. P. R. Finberg (Leicester, 1964).

The Early Charters of the West Midlands, ed. H. P. R. Finberg, 2nd edn (Leicester, 1972).

Early Yorkshire Charters, ed. W. Farrer, vols. 1–3, ed. C. T. Clay, vols. 4–12, Yorkshire Archaeological Society (1914–65).

Facsimiles of Anglo-Saxon Manuscripts, ed. W. B. Sanders, 3 vols., Ordnance Survey (Southampton, 1878–84).

Facsimiles of Early Charters in Oxford Muniment Rooms, ed. H. E. Salter (Oxford, 1929).

Facsimiles of English Royal Writs to A.D. 1100, ed. T. A. M. Bishop and P. Chaplais (Oxford, 1957).

Feudal Documents from the Abbey of Bury St Edmunds, ed. D. C. Douglas, British Academy, Records of Social and Economic History, 8 (London, 1932).

Formulare Anglicanum, ed. T. Madox (London, 1702).

Die Gesetze der Angelsachsen, ed. F. Liebermann, 3 vols. (Halle, 1903–16).

Gesta Abbatum Monasterii Sancti Albani, ed. H. T. Riley, RS, 3 vols. (London, 1867–69).

A Hand-Book to the Land-Charters and Other Saxonic Documents, ed. J. Earle (Oxford, 1888).

Inquisitio Comitatus Cantabrigiensis: Subjicitur Inquisitio Eliensis, ed. N. E. S. A. Hamilton (London, 1876).

The Laws of the Kings of England from Edmund to Henry I, ed. and trans. A. J. Robertson (Cambridge, 1925).

Leges Henrici Primi, ed. L. J. Downer (Oxford, 1972).

The Lincolnshire Domesday and the Lindsey Survey, ed. C. W. Foster and T. Longley, introd. F. M. Stenton, Lincolnshire Record Society, 19 (1924).

Placita Anglo-Normannica, ed. M. M. Bigelow (London, 1879).

Recueil des Actes des Ducs de Normandie de 911 à 1066, ed. M. Faroux, Mémoires de la Société des Antiquaires de Normandie, 36 (Caen, 1961).

Regesta Regum Anglo-Normannorum, vol. 1, ed. H. W. C. Davis (Oxford, 1913).

Registrum Antiquissimum of the Cathedral Church of Lincoln, ed. C. W. Foster and K. Major (Horncastle, 1931).

Royal Writs in England from the Conquest to Glanvill, ed. R. C. van Caenegem, Selden Society, 77 (1959).

Scriptores Rerum Gestarum Willelmi Conquestoris, ed. J. A. Giles, Caxton Society, 3 (London, 1845, rpt New York, 1967).

Select English Historical Documents of the Ninth and Tenth Centuries ed. and trans. F. E. Harmer (Cambridge, 1914).

The Will of Æthelgifu, ed. and trans. D. Whitelock (Oxford, 1968).

Winchester in the Early Middle Ages: An Edition and Discussion of the Winton Domesday, F. Barlow, M. Biddle, O. von Feilitzen and D. J. Keene, Winchester Studies, 1 (Oxford, 1976).

Bibliography

II SECONDARY WORKS

Abels, R. P., *Lordship and Military Obligation in Anglo-Saxon England* (Berkeley, 1988).

Anderson, O. S., *The English Hundred-Names* (Lund, 1934).

The English Hundred-Names: The South-Western Counties (Lund, 1939).

The English Hundred-Names: The South-Eastern Counties (Lund, 1939).

Aston, T. H., 'The origins of the manor in England', *TRHS*, 5th series, 8 (1958), pp. 59–83.

Bailey, W. F. and I. F. Straw, 'Nottingham', in *Atlas of Historic Towns*, ed. M. D. Lobel, 2 vols. (London, 1969–75).

Ballard, A., *The Domesday Inquest* (London, 1906).

Baring, F. H., *Domesday Tables for the Counties of Surrey, Berkshire, Middlesex, Hertford, Buckinghamshire, and Bedford, and for the New Forest* (London, 1909).

Barlow, F., *Edward the Confessor* (Berkely, 1970).

The English Church 1000–1066, 2nd edn (London, 1979)

Barnes, P. M. and C. F. Slade, *A Medieval Miscellany for Doris Mary Stenton*, Pipe Roll Society, n.s. 36 (1962).

Bates, D. R., *A Bibliography of Domesday Book* (Woodbridge, Suffolk, 1986).

'The character and career of Odo, Bishop of Bayeux', *Speculum*, 50 (1975), pp. 1–20.

'The land pleas of William I's reign: Penenden Heath revisited', *Bulletin of the Institute of Historical Research*, 51 (1978), pp. 1–19.

Normandy Before 1066 (London, 1982).

'*Notes sur l'aristocratie Normande*', *Annales de Normandie*, 23 (1973), pp. 7–38.

Baulant, M., 'The scattered family: another aspect of seventeenth century demography', in *Family and Society: Selections from the Annales*, ed. R. Forster and O. Ranum (Baltimore, 1976).

Bethurum, D., 'Six anonymous Old English codes', *Journal of English and Germanic Philology*, 49 (1950), pp. 449–63.

Biddle, M., 'Early Norman Winchester', in *Domesday Studies*, ed. J. C. Holt (Woodbridge, Suffolk, 1987), pp. 311–31.

ed., *Winchester Studies* (Oxford, 1976–).

Birch, W. de G., *Domesday Book: A Popular Account of the Exchequer Manuscript* (London, 1887).

Bishop, T. A. M., 'The Norman settlement of Yorkshire', in *Studies in Medieval History Presented to Frederick Maurice Powicke*, ed. R. W. Hunt, W. A. Pantin and R. W. Southern (Oxford, 1948), pp. 1–14.

Bosworth, J. and T. N. Toller, *An Anglo-Saxon Dictionary* (Oxford, 1898, rpt Oxford, 1972). Toller alone, *An Anglo-Saxon Dictionary: Supplement* (Oxford, 1921, rpt Oxford, 1972).

Bourdieu, P., *Outline of a Theory of Practice*, trans. R. Nice (Cambridge, 1977).

Boussard, J., 'Le Comte de Mortain au xie siecle', *Moyen Age*, 58 (1952).

Brooke, C. N. L. and G. Ker, *London 800–1216: The Shaping of a City* (London, 1975).

Bibliography

Brooks, N. P., 'Anglo-Saxon charters: the work of the last twenty years', *ASE*, 3 (1974). pp. 211–31.

The Early History of the Church of Canterbury (Leicester, 1984).

'England in the ninth century: the crucible of defeat', *TRHS*, 29 (1979), pp. 1–20.

Brown, R. A., *The Normans and the Norman Conquest*, 2nd edn (Woodbridge, Suffolk, 1985).

The Origins of English Feudalism (New York, 1973).

Browning, A. G., 'The early history of Battersea', *Surrey Archaeological Society*, 10 (1891), pp. 205–43.

Bullough, D. A., 'Early medieval social groupings: the terminology of kinship', *Past and Present*, 45 (1969), pp. 3–18.

Cam, H., 'The evolution of the medieval English franchise', *Speculum*, 32 (1957), pp. 427–42.

'*Manerium cum hundredo*: The hundred and the hundredal manor', *EHR*, 47 (1932), pp. 353–76.

Campbell, J., 'The church in Anglo-Saxon towns', in *Studies in Church History*, 16 (1979), pp. 119–35.

'Norwich', in *The Atlas of Historic Towns*, ed. M. D. Lobel, 2 vols. (London, 1969–75).

'Observations on English government from the tenth to the twelfth century', *TRHS*, 5th ser., 25 (1975), pp. 39–54.

'Some agents and agencies of the late Anglo-Saxon state', *Domesday Studies*, ed. J. C. Holt (Woodbridge, Suffolk, 1987), pp. 201–18.

E. John and P. Wormald, *The Anglo-Saxons* (Ithaca, 1982).

Campbell, J. K., *Honour, Family and Patronage* (Oxford, 1964).

Chadwick, H. M., *The Origin of the English Nation* (Cambridge, 1907).

Studies on Anglo-Saxon Institutions (Cambridge, 1905).

Chaplais, P., 'The authenticity of the royal Anglo-Saxon Diplomas of Exeter', *Bulletin of the Institute of Historical Research*, 39 (1966), pp. 1–34.

'Une charte originale de Guillaume le Conquérant pour l'Abbay de Fécamp: la donation de Steyning et de Bury (1085)', *L'Abbaye Bénédictine de Fécamp*, 2 vols. (Fécamp, 1959–60), pp. 93–104, 355–7; rpt in P. Chaplais, *Essays in Medieval Diplomacy and Administration* (London, 1981).

'The original charters of Herbert and Gervase, abbots of Westminster (1121–1157)', in *A Medieval Miscellany for Doris Mary Stenton*, ed. P. M. Barnes and C. F. Slade, Pipe Roll Society, n.s. 36 (London, 1962), pp. 89–110.

Charles-Edwards, T. M., 'The distinction between land and moveable wealth in Anglo-Saxon England', in *Medieval Settlement*, ed. P. H. Sawyer (London, 1976), pp. 180–7.

'Kinship, status, and the origins of the hide', *Past and Present*, 56 (1972), pp. 3–33.

Chibnall, M., *Anglo-Norman England 1066–1166* (Oxford, 1986).

Clark, Cecily, 'British Library Additional Ms. 40,000 ff lv–12r', *Anglo-Norman Studies*, 7 (1985), pp. 50–65.

Clay, C. T. with D. E. Greenway, *Early Yorkshire Families*, Yorkshire

Archaeological Society, record ser., 135 (Wakefield, West Yorkshire, 1973).

Clemoes, P., ed., *The Anglo-Saxons: Studies in some Aspects of their History and Culture presented to Bruce Dickins* (London, 1959).

'The chronology of Ælfric's works', in *The Anglo-Saxons: Studies in some Aspects of their History and Culture presented to Bruce Dickins*, ed. P. Clemoes (London, 1959), pp. 212–47.

and K. Hughes, eds., *England Before the Conquest* (Cambridge, 1971).

Cokayne, G. E., *The Complete Peerage* (London, 1887–98).

Cooper, J. M., *The Last Four Anglo-Saxon Archbishops of York* (York, 1970).

Corbett, W. J., 'The development of the duchy of Normandy and the Norman Conquest of England', *The Cambridge Medieval History*, vol. 5, ed. J. R. Tanner, C. W. Previte-Orton and Z. N. Brooke (Cambridge, 1926, rpt Cambridge, 1957), pp. 481–520.

Cox, D. C., 'The Vale estates of the Church of Evesham c. 700–1086', *Vale of Evesham Historical Society Research Papers*, 5 (1975), pp. 25–50.

Craster, E., 'The patrimony of St. Cuthbert', *EHR*, 69 (1954), pp. 177–99.

Crouch, D., *The Beaumont Twins: The Roots and Branches of Power in the Twelfth Century* (Cambridge, 1986).

Cunliffe, B. W., *Iron Age Communities in Britain*, 2nd edn (London, 1978).

Cutler, K. E., 'Edith, Queen of England, 1045–1066', *Medieval Studies*, 35 (1973), pp. 222–31.

Darby, H. C., *Domesday England* (Cambridge, 1977).

ed., *Domesday Geography of Eastern England*, 3rd edn (Cambridge, 1977).

and E. M. J. Campbell, eds., *Domesday Geography of South-East England* (Cambridge, 1962).

and R. W. Finn, eds., *Domesday Geography of South-West England* (Cambridge, 1967).

and I. S. Maxwell, eds., *Domesday Geography of Northern England* (Cambridge, 1962).

and I. B. Terrett, eds., *Domesday Geography of Midland England*, 2nd edn (Cambridge, 1971).

and G. R. Versey, *The Domesday Gazetteer* (Cambridge, 1975).

Darlington, R. R., 'Æthelwig, Abbot of Evesham', *EHR*, 48, (1933), pp. 1–22, 177–98.

ed., 'Introduction', *Cartulary of Worcester Cathedral Priory* (Oxford, 1968).

Davis, W. and P. Fouracre, eds., *The Settlement of Disputes in Early Medieval Europe* (Cambridge, 1986).

Davis, R. H. C., 'Alfred and Guthrum's frontier', *EHR*, 97 (1982), pp. 803–10.

King Stephen (Berkeley, 1967).

Dodwell, B., 'East Anglian commendation', *EHR*, 63 (1948), pp. 289–306.

Douglas, D. C., 'Edward the Confessor, Duke William of Normandy, and the English succession', *EHR*, 68 (1953), pp. 526–45.

'Les Evêques de Normandie (1035–1066)', *Annales de Normandie*, 8 (1958), pp. 87–102.

'The Norman Conquest and English Feudalism', *EHR*, 54 (1939), pp. 128–43.

'Odo, Lanfranc, and the Domesday survey', *Essays in Honour of James Tait,* ed. J. G. Edwards, V. H. Galbraith and E. F. Jacob (Manchester, 1933), pp. 47–57.

The Social Structure of Medieval East Anglia, Oxford Studies in Social and Legal History, 9 (Oxford, 1927).

William the Conqueror (Berkeley, 1964).

Du Boulay, F. R. H., *The Lordship of Canterbury: An Essay on Medieval Society* (London, 1966).

Dumville, D. N., 'The Anglian collection of royal genealogies and regnal lists', *ASE*, 5 (1976), pp. 23–50.

'The ætheling: a study in Anglo-Saxon constitutional history', *ASE*, 8 (1979), pp. 1–33.

'Kingship. genealogies, and regnal lists', in *Early Medieval Kingship*, ed. P. H. Sawyer and I. N. Wood (Leeds, 1977), pp. 72–104.

Dugdale, W., *The History of St Paul's Cathedral in London* (London, 1658).

Dyson, T., 'London and Southwark in the seventh century and later: a neglected reference', *London and Middlesex Archaeological Society*, 31 (1980), pp. 83–95.

Ekwall, E., *The Concise Oxford Dictionary of English Place-Names*, 4th edn (Oxford, 1960).

Ellis, H., *A General Introduction to Domesday Book*, 2 vols. (London, 1833).

English, B., *The Lords of Holderness 1086–1200: A Study in Feudal Society* (Oxford, 1979).

Eyton, R. W., *A Key to Domesday: The Dorset Survey* (London, 1878).

Farrer, W., *Feudal Cambridgeshire* (Cambridge, 1920).

'Introduction to the Yorkshire Domesday', in *VCH, Yorks*, 2 (London, 1912), pp. 133–89.

Finberg, H. P. R., 'Anglo-Saxon England to 1042', in *The Agrarian History of England and Wales*, ed. H. P. R. Finberg, vol 1., book 2 (Cambridge, 1972).

'The house of Ordgar and the foundation of Tavistock Abbey', *EHR*, 58 (1943), pp. 190–201.

'Sherborne, Glastonbury and the expansion of Wessex', *TRHS*, 5th ser., 3 (1953), pp. 101–24.

Tavistock Abbey (Cambridge, 1951).

Finn, R. W., 'The immediate sources of the Exchequer Domesday', *Bulletin of the John Rylands Library*, 41 (1959), pp. 360–87.

An Introduction to Domesday Book (London, 1963).

The Norman Conquest and its Effects on the Economy (London, 1970).

'Some early Gloucestershire estates', *Gloucestershire Studies* (Leicester, 1957).

Fisher, D. J. V., 'The anti-monastic reaction in the reign of Edward the Martyr', *Cambridge Historical Journal*, 10 (1952), pp. 254–270.

Fleming, R., 'Domesday estates of the king and the Godwinesons: a study in late Saxon politics', *Speculum*, 58 (1983), pp. 987–1007.

'Monastic lands and England's defence in the Viking Age', *EHR*, 100 (1985), pp. 247–65.

'The tenurial revolution of 1066', *Anglo-Norman Studies*, 9 (1987), pp. 87–102.

Foote, P. G. and D. M. Wilson, *The Viking Achievement* (London, 1970).

Bibliography

Ford-Johnston, J., *Hillforts of the Iron Age in England and Wales. A Survey of the Surface Evidence* (London, 1976).

Fowler, G. H., *Bedfordshire in 1086: An Analysis and Synthesis of Domesday Book*, Quarto Memoirs of the Bedfordshire Historical Society, 1 (Aspley Guise, 1922).

Fox, Sir Cyril, *Offa's Dyke* (London, 1955).

Freeman, E., *The History of the Norman Conquest of England*, 6 vols. (Oxford, 1867–79).

Galbraith, V. H., 'An episcopal land-grant of 1085', *English Historical Review*, 44 (1929), pp. 353–72.

Domesday Book: Its Place in Administrative History (Oxford, 1974).

The Making of Domesday Book (Oxford, 1961).

Garnett, G., 'Coronation and propaganda: some implications of the Norman claim to the throne of England in 1066', *TRHS*, 5th ser., 36 (1986), pp. 91–116.

Gelling, M., *The Place-Names of Berkshire*, 3 vols., English Placename Society, 49–51 (Cambridge, 1973–76).

Goody, J., *The Development of the Family and Marriage in Europe* (Cambridge, 1983).

ed., *The Character of Kinship* (Cambridge, 1973).

Gransden, A., 'Baldwin, abbot of Bury St Edmunds, 1065–1097', *Anglo-Norman Studies*, 4 (1982), pp. 56–76.

Green, J., 'The sheriffs of William the Conqueror', *Anglo-Norman Studies*, 5 (1983), pp. 129–45.

Grierson, P., 'The relation between England and Flanders before the Norman Conquest', *TRHS*, 4th ser., 23 (1941), pp. 71–112.

Hallam, E. M., *Domesday Book through Nine Centuries* (London, 1986).

Hart, C. R., 'Æthelstan "Half-King" and his family', *ASE*, 2 (1973), pp. 115–44.

'The ealdordom of Essex', in *An Essex Tribute: Essays Presented to Frederick G. Emmison as a Tribute to his Life and Work for Essex History and Archives*, ed. K. Neale (Colchester, 1987), pp. 57–81.

The Hidation of Cambridgeshire (Leicester, 1974).

Harvey, J. H., 'Bishophill and the Church of York', *YAJ*, 41 (1965), pp. 377–93.

Harvey, S. P. J., 'Domesday Book and Anglo-Norman governance', *TRHS*, 5th ser., 25(1975), pp. 175–93.

'Domesday Book and its predecessors', *EHR*, 86 (1971), pp. 753–73.

'The knight and the knight's fee in England', *Past and Present*, 49 (1970), pp. 3–43.

'Recent Domesday studies', *EHR*, 95 (1980), pp. 121–33.

'Taxation and the ploughland in Domesday Book', in *Domesday Book: A Reassessment*, ed. P. Sawyer (London, 1985), pp. 86–103.

Haskins, C. H., *Norman Institutions* (Cambridge, Mass, 1925).

Hazeltine, H. D., 'On Anglo-Saxon documents', in *Anglo-Saxon Charters*, ed. A. J. Robertson (Cambridge, 1956).

Hill, D., ed., *Ethelred the Unready*, British Archaeological Reports, British ser., 59 (1978).

Bibliography

Hill, J. W. F., *Medieval Lincoln* (Cambridge, 1948).

Hockey, S. F., 'William fitz Osbern and the endowment of his abbey of Lyre', *Anglo-Norman Studies*, 3 (1980), pp. 96–103.

Hollings, M., 'The survival of the five-hide unit in the Western Midlands', *EHR*, 63 (1948), pp. 453–87.

Hollister, C. W., *Anglo-Saxon Military Institutions on the Eve of the Norman Conquest* (Oxford, 1962).

'The greater Domesday tenants-in-chief', in *Domesday Studies*, ed. J. C. Holt (Woodbridge, Suffolk, 1987), pp. 219–48.

The Military Organization of Norman England (Oxford, 1965).

Holt, J. C., ed., *Domesday Studies* (Woodbridge, Suffolk, 1987).

'Feudal society and the family in early medieval England: 1. The revolution of 1066', *TRHS*, 5th ser., 32 (1982), pp. 193–212.

'1086', in *Domesday Studies*, ed. idem (Woodbridge, Suffolk, 1987), pp. 41–64.

Hooper, N., 'The housecarls in England in the eleventh century', *Anglo-Norman Studies*, 7 (1985), pp. 161–76.

Hoyt, R. S., 'The nature and origins of the ancient demesne', EHR, 65 (1950), pp. 145–74.

The Royal Demesne in English Constitutional History 1066–1272 (Ithaca, 1950).

Hudson, B., 'The family of Harold Godwinesson and the Irish Sea Province', *Royal Society of Antiquaries of Ireland*, 109 (1979), pp. 92–100.

Hunt, R. W., Pantin, W. A. and R. W. Southern, eds., *Studies in Medieval History Presented to Frederick Maurice Powicke* (Oxford, 1948).

Hyams, P., '"No register of title": the Domesday Inquest and land adjudication', *Anglo-Norman Studies*, 9 (1987), pp. 127–41.

'Warranty and good lordship in twelfth century England', *Law and History Review*, 5 (1987), pp. 437–503.

John, E., 'Edward the Confessor and the Norman succession', *EHR*, 94 (1979), pp. 241–67.

Land Tenure in Early England (Leicester, 1960).

Orbis Britanniae (Leicester, 1966).

'War and society in the tenth century: the Maldon campaign', *TRHS*, 5th ser., 27 (1977), pp. 173–95.

Jolliffe, J. E. A., *The Constitutional History of Medieval England*, 3rd edn (London, 1954).

Kapelle, W. E., *The Norman Conquest of the North: The Region and its Transformation 1000–1135* (Chapel Hill, 1979).

Kennedy, A. G., 'Cnut's law code of 1018', *ASE*, 11 (1982), pp. 57–81.

Ker, N. R., 'Hemming's cartulary', in *Studies in Medieval History Presented to Frederick Maurice Powicke*, ed. R. W. Hunt, W. A. Patin and R. W. Southern (Oxford, 1948), pp. 49–75.

Keynes, S. D., 'The Additions in Old English', *The York Gospels*, ed. N. Barker (London, 1986), pp. 81–99.

The Diplomas of King Æthelred 'The Unready' 978–1016 (Cambridge, 1980).

'The lost Abbotsbury cartulary', *ASE*, 18 (1989), pp. 207–43.

'Regenbald the Chancellor [*sic*]', *Anglo-Norman Studies*, 10 (1988), pp. 185–222.

Bibliography

'A tale of two kings: Alfred the Great and Æthelred the Unready', *TRHS*, 5th ser., 36 (1986), pp. 195–217.

and M. Lapidge, *Alfred the Great. Asser's Life of King Alfred and Other Contemporary Sources* (Harmondsworth, 1983).

King, P., 'The return of the fee of Robert de Brus in Domesday', *YAJ*, 60 (1988), pp. 25–9.

Knowles, D., *The Monastic Order in England*, 2nd edn (Cambridge, 1962).

and C. N. L. Brooke, *Heads of Religious Houses in England: England and Wales, 940–1216* (Cambridge, 1972).

and R. N. Hadcock, *Medieval Religious Houses: England and Wales* (London, 1971).

Laborde, E. D., *Bryhtnoth and Maldon* (London, 1936).

Lancaster, L., 'Kinship and Anglo-Saxon society', *British Journal of Sociology*, 9 (1958), pp. 230–50, 359–77.

Larson, L. M., *Canute the Great 995–1035* (New York, 1912).

The King's Household in England before the Norman Conquest (Madison, Wisc., 1904).

'The political policies of Cnut as king of England', *American Historical Review*, 15 (1910), pp. 720–43.

Lawson, M. K., 'The collection of danegeld and heregeld in the reigns of Æthelred II and Cnut', *EHR*, 99 (1984), pp. 721–38.

Lemarignier, J. F., *Recherches sur L'hommage en Marche et les Frontières Féodales* (Lille, 1945).

Le Patourel, J., *Feudal Empires, Norman and Plantagenet* (London, 1984).

'Geoffrey of Montbray, bishop of Coutances, 1049–1093', *EHR*, 59 (1944), pp. 129–61.

The Norman Empire (Oxford, 1976).

'The Norman colonization of Britain', *I Normanni e la loro espansione in Europa nell'alto medioevo*, Centro Italiano di Studi sull'Alto Medioevo, Settimana 16 (Spoleto, 1969), pp. 409–38.

Norman Barons (rpt London, 1971).

'The reports of the trial on Penenden Heath', in *Studies in Medieval History presented to F. M. Powicke*, ed. R. W. Hunt *et al.* (Oxford, 1948), pp. 15–26.

Lewin, J., *British Rivers* (London, 1981).

Lewis, C., 'The Norman settlement of Herefordshire under William I', *Anglo-Norman Studies*, 7 (1985), pp. 195–213.

Leyser, K., 'Maternal kin in early medieval Germany', *Past and Present*, 49 (1970), pp. 126–34.

Rule and Conflict in Early Medieval Society: Ottonian Saxony (Bloomington, Ind., 1979).

Lobel, M. D., ed., *Atlas of Historic Towns*, 2 vols. (London, 1969–75).

Loyd, L. C., 'The Origin of the Family of Warenne', *YAJ*, 31 (1934), pp. 97–113.

The Origins of some Anglo-Norman Families, ed. C. T. Clay and D. C. Douglas, Harleian Society, 103 (Leeds, 1951).

Loyn, H. R., *Anglo-Saxon England and the Norman Conquest* (London, 1962).

The Governance of Anglo-Saxon England 500–1087 (Stanford, Cal., 1984).

'The hundred in the tenth and early eleventh centuries', *British Government and Administration*, ed. H. R. Loyn and H. Hearder (Cardiff, 1974), pp. 1–15.

'Kinship in Anglo-Saxon England', *ASE*, 3 (1973), pp. 197–209.

Lynch, J. H., *Godparents and Kinship in Early Medieval Europe* (Princeton, N. J., 1986).

Mack, K., 'Changing thegns: Cnut's conquest and the English aristocracy', *Albion*, 16 (1984), pp. 375–87.

'Kings and thegns: aristocratic participation in the governance of Anglo-Saxon England, (unpublished research paper, University of California, Santa Barbara, 1982).

'The staller: administrative innovation in the reign of Edward the Confessor', *Journal of Medieval History*, 12 (1986), pp. 123–34.

Maitland, F. W., *Domesday Book and Beyond* (Cambridge, 1897, rpt Cambridge, 1987).

Margary, I. D., *Roman Roads in Britain*, 3rd edn (London, 1973).

Mason, E., 'Change and continuity in eleventh-century Mercia: the experience of St Wulfstan of Worcester, *Anglo-Norman Studies*, 8 (1985), pp. 154–76.

Mason, J. F. A., 'The "Honour of Richmond" in 1086', *EHR*, 78 (1963), pp. 703–4.

'Roger de Montgomery and his sons (1067–1102)', *TRHS*, 5th ser., 13 (1963), pp. 1–28.

William the First and the Sussex Rapes, Historical Association (Hastings, 1966).

Matthew, D. J. A., *The Norman Monasteries and their English Possessions* (Oxford, 1962).

McDonald, J. and G. D. Snooks, *Domesday Economy: A New Approach to Anglo-Norman History* (Oxford, 1986).

McGovern, J., 'The hide and related land-tenure concepts in Anglo-Saxon England, A.D. 700–1100', *Tradition*, 28 (1972), pp. 101–18.

Miller, E., *The Abbey and Bishopric of Ely* (Cambridge, 1951).

'The Ely land pleas in the reign of William I', *EHR*, 62 (1947), pp. 438–56.

Monkhouse, F. J., *Landscape from the Air: A Physical Geography in Oblique Air Photographs*, 2nd edn (Cambridge, 1971).

Morris, A., *The Medieval English Sheriff to 1300* (Manchester, 1927).

Mortimer, R., 'The beginnings of the honour of Clare', *Anglo-Norman Studies*, 3 (1981), pp. 119–41.

Murray, A. C., *Germanic Kinship Structure: Studies in Law and Society in Antiquity and the Early Middle Ages* (Toronto, 1983).

Neale, K., ed., *An Essex Tribute. Essays Presented to Frederick G. Emmison as a Tribute to his Life and Work for Essex History and Archives* (Colchester, 1987).

Nelson, L. H., *The Normans in South Wales 1070–1171* (Austin, Texas, 1966).

Nightingale, P., The origin of the Court of Hustings and Danish influence on London's development into a capital city', *EHR*, 102 (1987), pp. 559–78.

'Some London moneyers in the eleventh and twelfth centuries', *The Numismatic Chronicle*, 142 (1982), pp. 34–50.

Oleson, T. J., *The Witenagemot in the Reign of Edward the Confessor* (Toronto, 1955).

Palliser, D. M., 'York's west bank: medieval suburb or urban nucleus?', in *Archaeological Papers from York Presented to M. W. Bailey*, Yorkshire Archaeological Trust (York, 1984).

Parsons, D., ed., *Tenth-Century Studies: Essays in Commemoration of the Millenium of the Council of Winchester and Regularis Concordia* (London, 1975).

Petersson, H. and A. Bertil, *Anglo-Saxon Currency* (Lund, 1969).

Poole, R. L., *Studies in Chronology and History* (Oxford, 1934).

Radford, C. A. R., 'The later pre-Conquest boroughs and their defenses', *Medieval Archaeology*, 14 (1970), pp. 83–103.

Radley, J., 'Excavations in the defences of the city of York: an early medieval stone tower and successive earth ramparts', *YAJ*, 44 (1972), pp. 38–64.

Reuter, T., ed. *The Medieval Nobility*, Europe in the Middle Ages: Selected Studies, 14 (Amsterdam, 1978).

Richardson, H. G. and G. O. Sayles, *The Governance of Medieval England from the Conquest to Magna Carta* (Edinburgh, 1963).

Ridyard, S. J., *The Royal Saints of Anglo-Saxon England* (Cambridge, 1988).

Robinson, J. A., *Gilbert Crispin, Abbot of Westminster* (Cambridge, 1911).

St Oswald and the Church of Worcester, British Academy, Supplemental Papers, 5 (1919).

The Times of Saint Dunstan (Oxford, 1923).

Round, J. H., 'The death of William Malet', *The Academy*, 625 (1884).

'Domesday hidation of Essex', *EHR*, 6, 7 (1891, 1892).

Feudal England (London, 1895).

Geoffrey de Mandeville: A Study of the Anarchy (London, 1892).

'Introduction to the Bedfordshire Domesday', in *VCH, Beds.*, 1 (London, 1904), pp. 191–218.

'Introduction to the Buckinghamshire Domesday', in *VCH, Bucks.*, 1 (London, 1905), pp. 230–77.

'Introduction to the Essex Domesday', in *VCH, Essex*, 1 (Westminster, 1903), pp. 333–426.

'Introduction to the Hertfordshire Domesday', in *VCH, Herts.*, 1 (London, 1902), 263–99.

'Introduction to the Northamptonshire Domesday', in *VCH, Northants.*, 1 (Westminster, 1902), pp. 257–98.

Saltzman, L. F., 'Introduction to the Cambridgeshire Domesday', in *VCH, Cambs.*, 1 (Oxford, 1938), pp. 335–57.

Sanders, I. J., *English Baronies: A Study of their Origin and Descent, 1086–1327* (Oxford, 1960).

Sawyer, P. H., 'Charters of the reform movement: the Worcester archives', *Tenth Century Studies*, ed. David Parsons (London, 1975), pp. 84–93.

ed., *Domesday Book: A Reassessment* (London, 1985).

'Domesday Book: a tenurial revolution?', in *Domesday Book: A Reassessment*, ed. P. H. Sawyer (London, 1985), pp. 71–85.

'The royal tun in pre-Conquest England', *Ideal and Reality in Frankish and Anglo-Saxon Society*, ed. P. Wormald with D. Bullough and R. Collins (Oxford, 1983).

and A. T. Thacker, 'Introduction to the Cheshire Domesday', in *VCH, Chester*, 1 (London, 1987), pp. 293–339.

Schmid, K., 'The structure of the nobility in the earlier Middle Ages', in *The Medieval Nobility*, ed. T. Reuter (Amsterdam, 1978), pp. 37–59.

'Zur Problematik von Familie, Sippe und Geschlecht, Haus und Dynastie beim Mittelalterlichen Adel', *Zeitschrift für die Geschichte des Oberrheins*, 105 (1957), pp. 1–62.

Scholz, B. W., 'Two forged charters from the Abbey of Westminster and their relationship with St. Denis', *EHR*, 76 (1961), pp. 466–78.

Searle, E., 'The Abbey of the Conqueror: defensive enfeoffment and economic development in Anglo-Norman England', *Anglo-Norman Studies*, 2 (1979), pp. 154–64.

Predatory Kinship and the Creation of Norman Power 840–1066 (Berkeley, 1988).

'Women and the legitimization of succession at the Conquest', *Anglo-Norman Studies*, 3 (1981), pp. 159–70.

Sims-Williams, P., 'Cuthswith, seventh-century abbess of Inkberrow, near Worcester, and the Wurzburg manuscript of Jerome on Ecclesiasties', *ASE*, 5 (1979), pp. 1–21.

Sisam, K., 'Anglo-Saxon royal genealogies', *Proceedings of the British Academy*, 39 (1953), pp. 287–346.

Stafford, P., 'The reign of Æthelred II, a study in the limitations on royal policy and action', in *Ethelred the Unready: papers from the Millenary Conference*, ed. D. Hill, British Archaeological Reports, British Series, 59 (1978), pp. 15–46.

'The laws of Cnut and the history of Anglo-Saxon royal promises', *ASE*, 10 (1982), pp. 173–90.

Stenton, F. M., *Anglo-Saxon England*, 3rd edn (Oxford, 1971).

The Bayeux Tapestry, 2nd edn (London, 1965).

The Early History of the Abbey of Abingdon (Reading, 1913).

'English families and the Norman Conquest', *TRHS*, 4th ser., 26 (1944), pp. 1–12.

The First Century of English Feudalism 1066–1166, 2nd edn (Oxford, 1961).

'Introduction to the Derbyshire Domesday', in *VCH, Derbys.*, 1 (London, 1905), pp. 293–326.

'Introduction to the Nottingham Domesday', in *VCH, Notts.*, 1 (London, 1906), pp. 207–46.

The Latin Charters of the Anglo-Saxon Period (Oxford, 1955).

'Medeshamstede and its colonies', *Historical Essays in Honour of James Tait*, rpt in *Preparatory to Anglo-Saxon England*, ed. Doris Mary Stenton (Oxford, 1970).

Preparatory to Anglo-Saxon England, ed. D. M. Stenton (Oxford, 1970).

Stephenson, C., 'Commendation and related problems in Domesday', *EHR*, 59 (1944), pp. 289–310.

'The "firma noctis" and the customs of the hundred', *EHR*, 39 (1924), pp. 161–74.

Stevenson, W. H., 'An Old English charter of William the Conqueror in favour of St Martin's-Le-Grand, London, A.D. 1068', *EHR*, 11 (1896), pp. 731–44.

Bibliography

'Yorkshire surveys and other eleventh century documents in the York Gospels', *EHR*, 27 (1912), pp. 1–25.

Tait, J., 'Introduction to the Shropshire Domesday', in *VCH, Salops.*, 1 (London, 1908), pp. 279–308.

Tabuteau, E. Z., *Transfers of Property in Eleventy-Century Norman Law* (Chapel Hill, 1988).

Taylor, C., *Roads and Tracks of Britain* (London, 1979).

Tengvik, G., *Old English Bynames* (Uppsala, 1938).

Thompson, A. H., 'The monastic settlement at Hackness and its relation to the Abbey of Whitby, *YAJ*, 27 (1924), pp. 388–405.

Urry, W., 'The Normans in Canterbury', *Annales de Normandie*, 8 (1958), pp. 119–38.

van Houts, E. M. C., 'The ship list of William the Conqueror', *Anglo-Norman Studies*, 10 (1988), pp. 159–84.

Varley, W. J., 'The hill-forts and the Welsh marches', *Archaeological Journal*, 105 (1948), pp. 41–66.

Vinogradoff, P., *English Society in the Eleventh Century* (Oxford, 1908).

The Growth of the Manor, 2nd edn (London, 1911).

von Feilitzen, O., *The Pre-Conquest Personal Names of Domesday Book* (Uppsala, 1937).

Wallace-Hadrill, J. M., 'War and peace in the earlier middle ages', *TRHS*, 5th ser., 25 (1975), pp. 157–74.

Ward, J. C., 'The place of the honour in twelfth-century society: the honour of Clare 1066–1217', *Proceedings of the Suffolk Institute of Archaeology and Natural History*, 35 (1983), pp. 191–202.

Welby, A. E. C., 'Ulf of Lincolnshire, before and after the Conquest', *Lincolnshire Notes and Queries*, 14 (1917), pp. 196–200.

Wheeler, G. H., 'The genealogy of the early West Saxon kings', *EHR*, 36 (1921), pp. 157–74.

White, S. D., *Custom, Kinship, and Gifts to the Saints: The Laudatio Parentum in Western France, 1050–1150* (Chapel Hill, 1988).

'Feuding and peace-making in the Touraine around the year 1100', *Traditio*, 42 (1986), pp. 195–263.

Whitelock, D., 'The dealings of the kings of England with Northumbria in the tenth and eleventh centuries', *The Anglo-Saxons*, ed. Peter Clemoes (London, 1959), pp. 70–88.

'Forward', in *Liber Eliensis*, ed. E. O. Blake, Camden Third Series, 72 (London, 1962), pp. ix–xviii.

'Scandinavian personal names in the *Liber Vitae* of Thorney Abbey, *Saga Book of the Viking Society*, 12, pt 2 (1937–45), pp. 127–53.

'Wulfstan and the laws of Cnut', *EHR*, 63 (1948), pp. 433–52.

'Wulfstan *Cantor* and Anglo-Saxon Law', in *Nordica et Anglica. Studies in Honor of Stefán Einarsson*, ed. A. H. Orrick (The Hague, 1968).

'Wulfstan's authorship of Cnut's laws', *EHR*, 70 (1970), pp. 72–85.

Wightman, W. E., *The Lacy Family in England and Normandy, 1066–1194* (Oxford, 1966).

Bibliography

'The palatine earldom of William fitz Osbern in Gloucestershire and Worcestershire (1066–1071)', *EHR*, 77 (1962), pp. 6–17.

Williams, A., 'Introduction to the Dorset Domesday', *VCH, Dorset*, 3 (Oxford, 1968), pp. 1–60.

'Land and power in the eleventh century: the estates of Harold Godwineson', *Anglo-Norman Studies*, 3 (1981), pp. 171–87.

'*Princeps Merciorum Gentis*: the family, career, and connections of Ælfhere, Ealdorman of Mercia 956–83', *ASE*, 10 (1982), pp. 143–72.

Wilson, D. M., ed., *The Bayeux Tapestry* (New York, 1985).

Winters, W., *The History of the Ancient Parish of Waltham Abbey or Holy Cross* (Waltham Abbey, Essex, 1888).

Woolf, R., 'The ideal of men dying with their lords in the "Germania" and the "Battle of Maldon"', *ASE*, 5 (1976), pp. 69–81.

Wormald, P., 'Æthelred the lawmaker', in *Ethelred the Unready*, ed. David Hill, British Archaeological Reports, British Series, 59 (1978), pp. 47–80.

'A handlist of Anglo-Saxon lawsuits', *ASE*, 17 (1988), pp. 247–81.

'*Lex scripta* and *verbum regis*. Legislation and germanic kingship from Euric to Cnut', in *Early Medieval Kingship*, ed. P. H. Sawyer and I. N. Wood (Leeds, 1977), pp. 105–38.

ed., with D. Bullough and R. Collins, *Ideal and Reality in Frankish and Anglo-Saxon Society* (Oxford, 1983).

Wright, C. E., *The Cultivation of Saga in Anglo-Saxon England*(London, 1939).

Wright, T., *Anglo-Saxon and Old English Vocabularies*, 2nd edn, ed. and collated by R. P. Wülcker, 2 vols. (London, 1884).

INDEX

Abbess Roding, Ex, 128
Abbotsbury Abbey, 42
Abingdon Abbey, 12, 27, 43, 83,
  84n, 86, 88n, 127, 181n, 185,
  192, 202n
  Edwin, abbot, 33
  Siward, abbot, 80
Abington Pigotts, Ca, 117, 120, 122
Adelaid, wife of Hugh de
  Grandmesnil, 120n, 136
Æfflaed, wife of ealdorman
  Bryhtnoth, 23n, 26, 46
Ælfgar, ealdorman, 23, 45, 48, 97
Ælfgar, earl
  addressee on writs, 57n
  attestations, 104
  earldoms, 56
  holdings, 44, 47, 89, 216
  men of, 117–18, 120–3, 127, 193n
  revolts, 52
Ælfgifu Emma, 42
Ælfgifu, daughter of King Æthelred, 47
Ælfgifu, sister of Æthelweard the
  Chronicler, 27–8, 30n, 44
Ælfheah, earldorman,
  activities as ealdorman, 38, 40
  benefactions, 25n, 26n, 28
  family connections, 24–7, 32, 37
  holdings, 45, 48, 90
Æfhelm, ealdorman, 30, 37, 40, 44–5
Ælfhelm Polga, 46
Ælfhere, ealdorman
  activities as ealdorman, 38–40
  alliances, 32
  attestations, 32n, 36–7
  benefactions, 27–8
  family connections, 24, 28–30,
    31, 37, 51, 69
  holdings, 44–5, 48, 65

Ælfric Cild, ealdorman, 23, 28, 37,
  40–1
Ælfric of Doddington, 137
Ælfric of Hampshire, ealdorman, 37
Ælfric the Homilist, xv, 50
Ælfric Kemp, 116, 204
Ælfstan, ealdorman, brother of
  Æthelstan Half-King, 25
Ælfswith, wife of ealdorman
  Ælfheah, 29, 30n
Ælfthryth, queen, 25, 31, 39
Ælfwine, nephew of ealdorman
  Ælfhere, 23, 26
Ælfwynn, wife of Æthelstan Half-
  King, 31
Æthelflæd of Damerham, 28
Æthelflæd, wife of Æthelstan 'Rota',
  23n, 46, 97
Æthelmær the Fat, ealdorman
  activities as ealdorman, 37, 43,
    46
  family connections, 23–5, 26, 30,
    34, 36–7, 48
Æthelmær of Hampshire, ealdorman,
  28, 44n
Æthelnoth Cilt of Kent, 71n, 73–4,
  95, 189
Æthelred I, King, 30
Æthelred the Unready, King
  family connections, 25, 29–32, 34,
    49, 91
  reign, 19, 36–44, 46n, 48, 50–1,
    55, 93, 97
Æthelric, 43
Æthelric of Burgh, 131, 193n
Æthelric, brother of bishop
  Beorhtheah of Worcester, 172
Æthelric of Mærgeat, 111
Æthelsige, ealdorman, 38

249

Index

Æthelstan, Ætheling, 44, 84n, 88n, 91, 93n
Æthelstan Half-King, ealdorman
  activities as ealdorman, 31, 39
  benefactions, 27–8
  family connections, 25, 29–31
  holdings, 65
Æthelstan, King, 19, 29n, 31, 87
Æthelstan 'Rota', ealdorman, 28, 38, 97
Æthelweard, son of Æthelmaer the Fat, 43
Æthelweard the Chronicler
  activities as ealdorman, 36–9
  family connections, 25, 27–8, 30, 32
  holdings, 43, 45, 48, 90
Æthelweard, ealderman, son-in-law of Æthelmaer the Fat, 25, 40
Æthelweard, son of Æthelmaer the Fat, 34, 35n
Æthelweard, son of Æthelwine 'Friend of God', 27, 40
Æthelwig/Æthelwine of Thetford, 131–2
Æthelwine 'Friend of God', ealdorman, 4, 25, 27–9, 30n, 37, 51
Æthelwold I, ealdorman, 25, 26n, 28, 38, 93n
Æthelwold II, ealdorman, 25, 26n
Æthelwold, Saint, 41, 93n
Aitard de Vaux, 132
Aki, 134
Alan of Richmond, count, 113, 114n, 115, 125, 129, 149, 152, 153, 158, 167n, 177, 217–26, 228–30
Aldbourne, Wi, 45, 90, 102
Aldermaston, Br, 90
Alfred, King, xv, 19, 30, 35, 87, 91
Alric son of Goding, 115
Alvred d'Epaignes, 111, 164n
Alvred of Lincoln, 135
Alweald of Stevington, 73
Alwig/Alwine Bannesune, 111, 164n
Alwine Doddason, 115
Alwine Horne, 73
Amesbury Abbey, 85

Angmering, Sx, 91, 93–4
Ansgar the Staller, 44, 63, 71n, 73, 75n, 110n, 113–14, 122, 171, 193
Angsot of Rochester, 191
Arnketil of Northumbria, 166–7
Assandun, Battle of, 28, 40
Athelney Abbey, 18
Aubrey, earl, 111
Aubrey de Vere, 129, 130, 199n
Aûmale, countess of, 115, 142
Azur dispensator, 203–4
Azur the housecarl, 113
Azur of Sussex, 73, 95, 175

Baldwin, count of Flanders, 29n, 79n
Baldwin the Fleming, 136
Baldwin the Sheriff, 217–26, 228–30
Banwell, So, 85
Bardi, 149
Barking Abbey, 87n, 128
Barrington, Ca, 122, 127
Bath Abbey, 18, 43
  Ælfwig, abbot, 82
Battersea, Sr, 87–8, 170, 190
Battle Abbey, 168n, 170
Bec Abbey, 176
Bedfordshire, Norman settlement of, 118, 120, 124n, 126
Belvoir Priory, 173
Beorhtric, 111
Beorhtric Algarson, 175
Beorhtric Cilt, 74n
Beorhtweald, 37
Beorn, earl, 57n
Berenger de Tosny, 156–7, 167, 169
Beverstone, Gl, 79
Bincombe, Do, 88, 171
Blæchmann the priest, 86
Bolton Percy, Yk, 161
Bondi the Staller, 175
Bramber Castle, 94
Bramley, Sr, 189–90
Brightlingsea, Ex, 91, 97
Broadwater, Sx, 199
Brompton Regis, So, 89, 102
Bryhtferth, ealdorman, 38
Bryhtnoth, ealdorman
  activities as ealdorman, 37–40
  benefactions, 28, 89n

Index

Index

Printed in the United Kingdom
by Lightning Source UK Ltd.
120637UK00001B/290